The Jews of Georgian England, 1714-1830

TODD M. ENDELMAN

The Jewish Publication Society of America

Philadelphia 5739-1979

THE JEWS OF GEORGIAN ENGLAND

1714-1830

Tradition and Change in a Liberal Society

Copyright © 1979
by The Jewish Publication Society of America
First edition All rights reserved
ISBN 0–8276–119–0
Library of Congress catalog card number 78–78390
Manufactured in the United States of America

Designed by Adrianne Onderdonk Dudden

For Judy

Contents

Preface

The history of the Jews in England in the modern period has attracted few professional Jewish historians. Historiographically, as well as geographically, Anglo-Jewry has remained on the periphery of the European Jewish experience. As a consequence, Jewish historians, with one or two exceptions, have viewed modern Anglo-Jewish history as an extension of the history of the Jews in France and Germany—as a variation on a central theme being played out more clearly and more dramatically elsewhere in Europe. The historiographical assumption underlying this approach has been that the major themes in modern Jewish history transcend geographical borders. This is an assumption I accept, but with one important reservation: although the histories of the Jewries of the West display remarkable similarities, they also exhibit profound differences. These differences directly reflect the dissimilarities in the historical development of the states in which Jews have settled. No European Jewry lived in total isolation from the majority society; even those who remained cut off from non-Jewish currents until the end of the nineteenth century were not immune earlier in the century to the political fortunes of the states in which they lived. The political culture and social structure of England in the eighteenth and early nineteenth centuries bore little resemblance to those prevailing in France and the German states. Thus, the history of Anglo-Jewry cannot be subsumed under the general category of Western European Jewish history. This study is, then, an attempt to correct the Continental bias of modern Jewish historiography; it seeks to view Anglo-Jewish history within the context of English history—without, however, losing sight of the experiences common to Western European Jewry as a whole.

I have not written a narrative history of English Jewry in the eighteenth and early nineteenth centuries. There already are adequate narratives of various aspects of Anglo-Jewish history by Cecil Roth, Lucien Wolf, Albert M. Hyamson, and others. In addition, there are literally scores of specialized studies by members of the Jewish Historical Society of England, historians by avocation rather than by profession. Over the past seventy-five years, their painstaking and often exhaustive work has added immeasurably to our knowledge of Anglo-Jewish history. Building on their research—and adding to it in large areas they neglected—I have written an analytical history, arranged topically, of the processes by which the Jews who migrated to England became participants in modern English life. This work is a study of their acculturation to the values and customs of the English people, of their integration into spheres of activity that had formerly been closed to them, and of the forces and elements within English society that promoted these processes. To a limited extent, such an arrangement presupposes some familiarity with Anglo-Jewish history. Since I cannot always assume such knowledge on the part of readers but do not wish to repeat a story that has been told elsewhere, I have provided only as much of the narrative as is absolutely essential to my analysis and have indicated in the notes where further details may be found.

Having made this disclaimer, I must also note at the same time that the narrative aspects of Anglo-Jewish history in the Georgian period are limited. The history of the Jews in England in this period is overwhelmingly social rather than primarily political or intellectual. There were no great political milestones in Anglo-Jewish history between the Resettlement of the mid-seventeenth century and the struggle for political emancipation in the mid-nineteenth century. The clamor over the Jew Bill of 1753, an event of minor importance in English political history, had no long-term consequences for the Jews of England. Likewise, there were no seminal intellectual figures—lay or rabbinic—who contributed to the development of modern Jewish thought or continued the traditional scholarship of rabbinic Judaism.

A casual glance at the Table of Contents might suggest I have devoted a disproportionate amount of space to topics that have not played a prominent role in the narrative accounts of others, and that I might have thus provided a skewed view of the past. For example, it might appear I have written far too much about Jewish pickpockets or prizefighters or "philo-Semitic" missionaries than their "representativeness" would warrant. I am well aware that my emphases are different from those of earlier Anglo-Jewish historians. This is, in part, due to the fact that I could turn to a sizable body of secondary literature on some points and quickly summarize research and conclusions that had already been well established, but that on other points I had to do the basic groundwork myself and felt an obligation to present the data out of which I have built my generalizations. For example, because the readmission of the Jews to England and the political background to the Jew Bill clamor are well-researched topics, there was no need to dwell at length on them. On the other hand, the role of conversionist "philo-Semitism" in the relief of Jewish disabilities in 1753 and in the 1820s had never been adequately explored; thus, I have gone into some detail in evaluating the contribution of this religious tradition to the toleration of the Jews.

Some of the "imbalance" in this work is due to a shortage of primary materials for reconstructing adequately the historical experiences of the lower middle class, among whom were found the strongest supporters of traditional Jewish life. Jewish artisans and shopkeepers did not attract the attention of journalists, communal magnates, police magistrates, travelers, and others in the way the Jewish poor did. This was due, in part, to their numerical insignificance in comparison with the masses of poor Jews and, in part, to the more respectable nature of the ways in which they earned their living.

Much of the "imbalance," however, is only apparent. If one approaches Jewish history with preconceptions of what Jews were like in the eighteenth century, then my presentation will seem unbalanced. My purpose, however, is to do just the opposite: to restore some balance to Anglo-Jewish history by also focusing on those elements—the Jewish lower classes—that were numerically dominant and that hitherto have been seen as passive bystanders. For far too long it has been assumed or implied that the adaptation of the Jews to the customs and values of the states in which they have settled was a problem for the Jewish bourgeoisie exclusively. Yet even the most cursory examination of primary documents touching on the lives of the Jewish lower classes in England will reveal that the processes of integration and acculturation engaged them as dramatically as they did the well-to-do. Not only were the poor not the guardians of traditional Jewish life, but the non-Jewish values and customs they came to embrace were different from those adopted by the Anglo-Jewish elite. Thus, when I use the phrase, "English patterns of life and thought," I do not mean to imply that there was *one* standard of behavior to which all Jews aspired. Upwardly mobile merchant bankers and diamond traders sought to acquire the trappings of upper-class gentility, while street hawkers and petty shopkeepers assimilated some of the behavior patterns of the English class to which they belonged. This distinction has not been stressed by Jewish historians who have written on the period.

The choice of the term "Georgian" was to a large extent arbitrary, and was determined solely by the necessity of finding a convenient term with which to label the period I am discussing. The years marking the beginning and the end of the reigns of the first four Georges (1714–1830) have no specific significance for Anglo-Jewish history, nor did any of the Georges personally affect the fate of the Jews in England; I have not bound myself strictly by these dates. There is good reason, however, to consider the eighteenth century and the first three decades of the nineteenth century as a unified historical period. Before 1700, there were only a handful of Jews in London; their history is important insofar as they created precedents and patterns for later Jewish settlement, but as a community they do not pose much interest for the historian of integration and acculturation. By 1830, the tempo of Jewish immigration from the Continent had slowed down. Patterns of integration and acculturation were well established. The lay leaders of the community were just beginning to fight for the full removal of civil disabilities, and as this struggle was predicated on a new perception of the rights of Jews as English citizens, 1830 seemed an appropriate terminus ad quem.

As the overwhelming majority of English Jews at any point in the Georgian period lived in London, the sources I have drawn on naturally reflect conditions in the metropolis. I have turned to provincial sources only when they were readily available. It is possible that the processes of acculturation and integration were substantially different for provincial Jewry, but only an exhaustive study of local materials would definitively establish this.* Given the numerical preponderance of London Jews in the Georgian period and the constant movement of Jews back and forth between the capital and the provinces, I feel justified in believing that my sources, as London-oriented as they are, represent Anglo-Jewry as a whole.

A number of individuals in England and the United States facilitated my work on this subject by guiding me to primary sources and allowing me access to archives and collections in their care. I wish to acknowledge gratefully the assistance of Rabbi J. Sunshine, Archivist of the United Synagogue, London; Dr. Richard D. Barnett, Honorary Archivist of the Spanish and Portuguese Synagogue, London; Miss E. Broekema, formerly Librarian of Jews' College, London; A. I. Brown, Director of Education of the London Board of Jewish Religious Education; C. R. Fincken, formerly Assistant Librarian of the Mocatta Library, University College, London; Dr. Menahem Schmelzer, Chief Librarian of the Jewish Theological Seminary, New York; Dr. Vivian D. Lipman, London; Edgar R. Samuel, London; J. M. Shaftesley, London; Salmond S. Levin, London; Michael Anthony Shepherd, Center for the Study of Social History, University of Warwick; and Barbara Greenspahn, formerly of the Harvard Law School Library.

I am particularly grateful to Charles Tucker of London. His enthusiasm, kindness, and intimate knowledge of England's public records were a great aid to me.

This volume originated as a doctoral dissertation at Harvard University under the supervision of Professors Yosef Yerushalmi and David Landes. The high standards they set and the critical evaluation to which they subjected my work encouraged me to

---

*Bill Williams's recently published study of the Manchester community, *The Making of Manchester Jewry, 1740–1875*, is the only thorough study of a provincial Jewish community in the Georgian period. His findings, which I refer to at various points, agree substantially with my own.

avoid easy answers and simple explanations. I also profited greatly during my years at Harvard from the monthly meetings of the Modern Jewish History Study Group of Boston. The perceptions of many of its members have found their way into this work. I am grateful as well to a number of friends and colleagues —Alexander Bloom, Stephen M. Poppel, Lloyd P. Gartner, and Steven Bayme—who read an earlier version of this volume and offered me many valuable suggestions and corrections. In particular, I want to acknowledge the encouragement I have received over the years from Sheldon Rothblatt. He was responsible, over a decade ago at Berkeley, for initiating the train of events that led me to Anglo-Jewish history. His thoughtful and perceptive reading of my work has been immensely helpful. My wife, Judy, offered help and support at every stage of the way: to her I dedicate this book.

The Center for European Studies and the Department of History of Harvard University kindly provided funds for summer research in London.

The Jews of Georgian England, 1714-1830

Introduction

The central theme of Jewish history in Western Europe since 1700 is the migration of the Jewish people from the self-sufficient world of rabbinic tradition and corporate autonomy to the desacralized world of the modern European state. The acquisition of the rights of citizenship, the abandonment of medieval forms of ritual and belief, the adoption of non-Jewish values and modes of behavior, and the entry of Jews into new spheres of activity within state and society were the hallmarks of this journey. It is the history of this transformation as it was experienced by the Jews of England in the years 1714 to 1830 that is the subject of this work.

Over the course of the eighteenth and nineteenth centuries, the Jews of Western Europe abandoned the autonomous corporate structure of traditional Jewish society and chose to participate as individuals in the various spheres of modern life. They did so partly out of necessity (the state everywhere was encroaching on the privileges of corporate bodies) but also in the belief that the new society was religiously neutral and would at least tolerate, if not welcome, such participation. They were willing, often eager, to exchange some or many of the values and institutions of traditional Jewish life for the dominant mores of the states in which they lived, either because they believed that such values were necessary for survival or success in the modern world, or because they were convinced that these mores represented a genuinely superior cultural system.

Of course, not all Jews eagerly embraced the non-Jewish world once it became available to them. Many rejected the supposed advantages of social integration and condemned any form of ritual laxity so that, in the end, traditional Judaism, or Orthodoxy as it came to be called in the nineteenth century, survived. But it persisted only as one form of Judaism, not as an all-embracing, self-sufficient sociopolitical order. No group of Jews, it should be noted, emerged from the seventeenth century entirely unchanged in its faith, practices, and social organization. Even the ultra-Orthodox Hasidic enclaves of present-day London and New York have had to make certain accommodations to modern life.

For most Jews, integration into previously closed arenas of activity and acculturation to previously rejected or ignored values and modes of behavior resulted in a reordering of personal priorities rather than in a total rejection of Judaism. In the majority of cases, Jews ceased to define themselves in exclusively Jewish terms and began to expand the parameters of their social and cultural world to include much that was not Jewish. Jewishness became only a part of their sense of self. They remained Jews, but at the same time they also became Englishmen, Frenchmen, or Germans; Londoners, Parisians, or Berliners. In a world that was becoming increasingly despiritualized and compartmentalized, in which religion and ethnic identity occupied only one segment of life, Judaism ceased to be a civilization, a culture, a social order, and became instead a religion in the contemporary sense of the term. This redefinition of Jewishness applied as equally to those who remained attached to a highly ritualistic form of Judaism as it did to those who vehemently shed this ritualism as a medieval anachronism—with the one exception that the world had become less desacralized for those who remained attached to Orthodoxy. Some Jews did embrace the majority culture to such an extent that they ceased to be Jews altogether and formally embraced Christianity; although this was by no means the rule, it certainly occurred frequently enough to merit attention.

The transformation of Western European Jewry was a complex historical movement, and like most historical changes of any scope, there were enormous variations in the experiences of those who lived through it. Similar changes swept all of the European Jewish communities of Western Europe between 1700 and 1900, but the changes they experienced did not come about in a uniform way. For example, in the case of equality of legal status, by the end of the nineteenth century all the Jewries of Western Europe were fully emancipated, but the way in which emancipation was achieved varied enormously from country to country, depending in every instance on the specific political tradition and history of the country concerned. In France, the Revolution of 1789 brought emancipation in its immediate wake, and equality of status was bestowed on thousands of traditional Jews who had never expressed any desire to acquire the rights (and burdens) of citizenship. In Prussia, on the other hand, full emancipation only came in 1871, after the Bismarckian unification of Germany and after almost a century of anguish on the part of middle-class Jews over the humiliations of second-class status. In Great Britain and the United States, where more liberal political values flourished, equality of citizenship was never a major public issue and, thus, not a major source of anxiety to acculturated Jews unsure of their social acceptability. Because the nations of the West did not experience political modernization in the same fashion, the political fortunes of their Jewish minorities showed strong dissimilarities.

The ways in which European Jews adapted their own views and their own behavior to the modern world also depended on their socioeconomic status and on the cultural heritage of the group within Jewry to which they belonged. City-dwelling, secularly educated, well-to-do German Jews developed new religious ideologies (i.e., Haskalah and Reform) and new educational programs to assist their entry into European society and to justify their departure from tradition. The Yiddish-speaking Jewish poor of Central and Northern Europe, who comprised the great bulk of the communities in which they lived, responded to new conditions in a more immediate manner, without benefit of an articulated intellectual creed.

To complicate this schema even further, not all groups within European Jewry, when confronting modernity, started from the same religious and cultural point. The "orthodoxy" of European Jewry at the beginning of the eighteenth century was not monolithic. Just as Catholicism was not the same religion wherever it was practiced in the early modern period and just as it did not have any kind of uniform meaning for all its communicants, so too early modern Judaism was not homogeneous. The Judaism of the many Sephardim in London, Hamburg, Amsterdam, and Bordeaux who were refugees from the Iberian peninsula was fragmentary and unsettled, owing to the difficult conditions in which they had previously practiced their crypto-Judaism. In addition, prior to the modern period, they had adopted many, if not all, of the external marks of European culture as a consequence of having lived, ostensibly as Catholics, outside the corporate Jewish community. The Judaism of the Ashkenazi masses living in the small towns and villages of rural Germany and northeastern France was a Judaism far more securely rooted in the way of life of its adherents. It was not a sophisticated, intellectually rich Judaism, but rather an integral aspect of the fabric of daily behavior. The Judaism of the court Jews who served the German princes in the age of absolutism as bankers, minters, and army contractors was also a traditional Judaism, but the great fortunes they amassed and their exposure to aristocratic manners and tastes at court led them to embrace a luxury-filled style of living that set them apart from the bulk of Ashkenazi Jewry and eventually pushed them closer to the non-Jewish world.

The existence of varieties of early modern Judaism—to which we must now add the normative Judaism of the rabbinate and lay leadership—suggests that no single overarching historical model can be employed to discuss the modernization of all segments of Western European Jewry. For to employ a single analytical framework would be to distort and reduce the richness of the historical past. There was no uniform road to immersion in modern culture and the secular state, no single path from tradition to modernity.

Most accounts of the origins of modern Jewish history employ a combination of two historiographical perspectives to describe the critical changes European Jewry experienced in the eighteenth and nineteenth centuries. They focus on the revolution in Jewish self-consciousness that was initiated by Moses Mendelssohn (1728–86) and his disciples, the *maskilim* (that is, adherents of the Enlightenment), and on the gradual extension of political and civil equality to the Jews that began with the Edict of Toleration of the Habsburg emperor Joseph II in 1781 and 1782 and the emancipation of French Jewry in 1790 and 1791. The former highlights the internal intellectual transformation of European Jewry; the latter, the external revolution in their legal status. Both perspectives are crucial for understanding aspects of the modernization process in Western Europe, but even in tandem they are not sufficient to encompass the experiences of all European Jews, especially those who settled in England in this period.

In the intellectual history of Judaism, the Mendelssohnian Enlightenment marked a decisive break with previous patterns of thought. Mendelssohn's resolution of the conflict between the exclusive nature of the Sinaitic revelation and the universal claims of a religion of reason, his return to the Hebrew Bible as a source of religious wisdom and as a common ground of inspiration for Christians and Jews, his vision of a revitalized Jewry, fit to take its place in a more enlightened age, that is, a German-speaking Jewry, versed in the secular literature of Europe and the classics of antiquity, liberated from religious bigotry—all of these constituted important landmarks in the passage from tradition to modernity. Many of those in the next generation who counted themselves among the disciples of Mendelssohn went even further in promoting Judaism as a religion of reason and toleration and in doing so did away with much of the authority of Jewish law. They self-consciously proposed a new definition of Judaism—one that seemed to them less parochial and more universal—and set out to bring German Jewry into line with this definition, to revitalize it through educational reforms such as the introduction of secular subjects into the curriculum of the Jewish school, the reduction of the amount of time devoted to Hebrew instruction, the provision of artisanal training for the poor, and the catechizing of children in the abstract principles of the Jewish religion.

The revolution in fundamental attitudes that characterized the Haskalah was a self-conscious, systematic, intellectual response to the challenge of modernity. It was a response, however, that was thoroughly untypical of either European Jewry as a whole or German Jewry in particular. It was the response of the German Jewish haute bourgeoisie in Berlin, Königsberg, Hamburg, Copenhagen, and a few other cities and of an equally small group of secularly educated Jews who were employed by the well-to-do as clerks, private tutors, and teachers. The vast majority of European Jews, as they came to alter their customary habits, did not construct an intellectual system to justify the changes they were making or to promote those changes among others more traditional than themselves. Indeed, a full generation before the intellectual revolution inaugurated by Mendelssohn, many German Jews—rich and poor—were beginning to depart from traditional patterns of Jewish life. Ritual laxity, religious indifference, positive evaluations of secular learning, the imitating of non-Jewish fashions and manners, a preference for German over Yiddish, recourse to state courts rather than Jewish religious courts, a decline in the intensity of traditional Jewish learning, and outright apostasy were found among German Jews as early as the first decades of the eighteenth century. To be sure, those who were abandoning the ways of their fathers at this early date did not justify their deviations on the basis of a new world view. They did not challenge the basic assumptions of traditional Judaism with an articulate set of concepts. Their revolution was private rather than public.

This pattern of accommodation to modernity was more typical of European Jewry than that of the *maskilim,* for like most of their contemporaries, few Jews had clear ideological concerns. The great task confronting most European Jews before 1830 was that of earning enough to feed, house, and clothe themselves. The bulk of European Jewry before 1830 was impoverished; faced with the threat of hunger, many slipped into new patterns of behavior without much thought or serious pangs of guilt. To focus too exclusively on conscious perceptions of shifting values is to ignore these mundane adjustments in human behavior that constitute the stuff of social reality. Decisions that may appear to later historians as the outcome of careful reflection often were made in a casual, almost unconscious manner. Apathy and carelessness promoted the acculturation of European Jews as much as did the Haskalah.

This indifference to religious tradition reflected the increasingly secular nature of the western world in the eighteenth century. In England, France, and to a lesser extent, Germany, the hold of religion over the minds of men was beginning to slacken. It lost much of its relevance to many areas of activity in day-to-day living. The voice of God did not speak with the authority it once had. Many Jews, especially those in large cities, felt that organized religion of any kind was no longer essential to their well-being. They did not mount an assault on rabbinic Judaism so much as slip away from ritual and belief altogether. Once they had given up the traditions of Judaism, they did not feel the need to replace them with anything similar. Thus, they neither created a reformed Judaism nor flocked to Christianity, but remained instead merely indifferent, or lapsed, Jews.

In Georgian England, there was no Haskalah in the sense there was in Germany. Yet the acculturation and integration of Anglo-Jewry advanced at a pace unmatched by any other Jewish community in the West at such an early period, with the exception of the tiny communities in the West Indies and North America. The transformation of Anglo-Jewry at all levels of the social ladder took place largely in terms of new patterns of behavior rather than new lines of thought. Old practices were given up and new ones acquired without an accompanying active intellectual response. This was in part due to the character of the Jews immigrating to England in these years from Holland, Germany, Poland, and the Levant, most of whom landed with very limited educational and material resources. But it is even more attributable to the high degree of toleration prevailing in England—the result of political and social conditions that contrasted dramatically with those on the Continent. In Prussia, for example, the road to full citizenship was more obstacle-ridden than elsewhere in the West, and as a consequence, spokesmen for Prussian Jewry felt they had to demonstrate publicly that German Jews could be made loyal, productive citizens and that Judaism was in harmony with the demands of the modern state. Their ideological response reflected the autocratic, quasi-medieval political and social conditions of Prussia at the time. The increasingly liberal character of English society during the Georgian period presented a very different background for the transformation of Jewish life. The uniqueness of this liberal setting will constitute one of our major focuses as we examine the integration of the Jews into English society in the Georgian period and follow their acculturation to English patterns of life and thought.

If a concern with the conscious redefinition of Jewishness and Judaism is an inappropriate perspective with which to view the modernization of Anglo-Jewry, so too is the other historiographical component in standard accounts of modern Jewish history—the struggle for legal equality. The attainment of full civil and political rights, of course, concerned all European Jewries to a greater or lesser degree. The recognition of Jews as equal citizens was a landmark in intellectual as well as political history, for a mental revolution had to occur first in the image of Jews held by statesmen before any concrete administrative or legislative relief could be obtained. In France, the emancipation of the Jews in 1790 and 1791 by the National Assembly is the great watershed between the premodern and modern periods, just as the Revolution itself stands out as the epoch-making event in the decline of the old regime. The Jews of France became the first Jews in Europe to enjoy all the rights of full citizenship, including the right to serve in the legislature, something that was still denied to English Jews. Almost overnight the corporate identity of French Jewry disappeared, and the Jews of France became free to participate as individuals in the life of the nation. After a short period of regression under Napoleon, this grant of equality paved the way for the entry of hundreds of Jews into the highest positions of prestige in nineteenth century France—the government, the army, and the universities.

In Georgian England, no single legislative action had so great an impact on the Jewish population. In the eighteenth century, aside from the Jewish Naturalization Bill of 1753, which would not have affected the status of nine-tenths of Anglo-Jewry, there were neither attempts to emancipate the Jews nor any public debates, aside from the short-lived one of 1753, on the ability of Jews to assume the rights and obligations of citizenship. The reason for this is clear: the position in which Jews found themselves was not onerous enough to warrant a campaign for their emancipation. Jews born in England or her colonies were considered citizens of the state; those born abroad enjoyed almost as many rights. Granted, they suffered from some political and civil disabilities, but their legal position was not much worse than that of other non-Anglican minorities such as Quakers, Roman Catholics, and Baptists. The emancipation campaign in the middle decades of the nineteenth century was designed to remove the small number of remaining disabilities that blocked the political and social advancement of ambitious members of the Anglo-Jewish elite. In short, the emancipation movement in Anglo-Jewish history was of a very different complexion from those across the Channel.

Almost a century before the full legal emancipation of Anglo-Jewry in 1871 (the passage of the Universities Tests Act, which allowed Jews to take degrees at Oxford and Cambridge) large segments of the community had already shed much of Jewish tradition and were on their way to becoming Englishmen in social and cultural terms. In matters of dress, manners, speech, living habits, and cultural aspirations, they were ceasing to be identifiably Jewish. The acculturation of these Jews to non-Jewish patterns of life and thought was a process largely determined by the Jews themselves—by their social aspirations and their evaluation, articulate and otherwise, of the respective merits of Jewish tradition and English culture. It was not dependent on their acceptance as full members of the body politic. Nor was it dependent on their integration into English social circles, voluntary associations, and civic groups—a process that, unlike acculturation, depended on the goodwill of the host population and not on the efforts of the Jews. Indeed, thoroughly acculturated Jews were often refused entry to non-Jewish circles whose members did not want to mix with Jews regardless of their refinement, wealth, and manners. Thus, Jewish integration depended ultimately not on Jewish achievements, but on the attitudes of those with whom the Jews wanted to mix. They may have believed that their acculturation would lead directly to their integration, but as often as not this was a dream that remained unrealized. In England, as well as in Germany, acculturation preceded social integration and political emancipation. The three processes were all aspects of the movement from tradition to modernity, but they were not coterminous, operating on the same timetable everywhere in the West.

These distinctions will allow us to indicate with some precision the elements and forces within English society and within Anglo-Jewry that encouraged or retarded the different components of Jewish modernity in Georgian England.

1

The Secular Basis for Jewish Toleration

The remarkable degree of toleration Anglo-Jewry enjoyed during the Georgian period cannot be traced back over the centuries to a long-standing policy of goodwill toward the Jews. It was the result of political and religious developments that had their origin in the seventeenth century. Medieval England was as rabidly anti-Semitic as Germany or France or Spain; Church and Crown showed remarkable zeal in enforcing most of the anti-Jewish restrictions set forth by Rome. Indeed, official Church policy toward the Jews may have been more rigidly implemented in England than in any other country of Europe. The mob was no less active in expressing its dislike for the Jews. Popular outbreaks of violence, spurred on by accusations of ritual murder and often culminating in bloody massacres, were an integral part of medieval Anglo-Jewish history.

For the Crown, the Jews, who were largely restricted to various forms of moneylending, were an important and convenient source of revenue. The profits they extracted from loans to the king's subjects were in turn squeezed out of them by the Exchequer. At the end of the twelfth century, taxes and occasional exactions on the Jews amounted to about £3,000 annually, or approximately one-seventh of the total revenue. But in the thirteenth century, a combination of fiscal ineptitude and religious zeal resulted in increasingly severe restrictions on the scope of Jewish moneylending, so that toward the end of that century the average annual contribution of the Jews amounted only to some £700, or little more than 1 percent of the total revenue. Particularly heavy exactions in the 1270s and 1280s impoverished the community even more. Theologically despised and fiscally unproductive, the Jews were banished from England by Edward I in 1290.[1]

From 1290 to the mid-1650s, Jews were barred by royal edict from visiting or settling in England; in practice, this was not the case. In the three and a half centuries before the ascendancy of Oliver Cromwell, individual Jews as well as small groups of New Christian merchants managed to live in England for sporadic periods. A few impoverished charlatan-adventurers trickled in, attracted by the rewards offered to Jewish converts by the well-endowed Domus Conversorum in London. A smaller number of celebrated Jewish physicians from France and Italy were brought over to treat a few very wealthy patients. But only in the sixteenth century, following the expulsion of the Jews from Spain in 1492 and the forced conversion of the Portuguese Jewish community in 1497, did small colonies of Iberian Jews—or, more accurately, New Christians who might potentially return to Judaism—begin clandestinely to renew the Jewish settlement in England. In the first half of the sixteenth century, there were tiny communities of Portuguese New Christians in Bristol and London, numbering forty families at the most at any one time. Some of these conversos were practicing Jews posing as Protestant refugees in order to escape detection, while others were no doubt sincere adherents to their new faith. In either case, they were attracted to London and Bristol by their desire to benefit from the expansion of trade in northern Europe and to avoid the grasp of the Inquisition, which was not overly scrupulous in distinguishing between Judaizing and sincere New Christians. When the Catholic Queen Mary came to the throne in 1553, the community probably dispersed.

Under Elizabeth, there again assembled a Marrano merchant community numbering a hundred or more persons, but it declined toward the end of the sixteenth century owing to three disparate factors: the increasing attractiveness of Amsterdam as a commercial center; the involvement of one of its prominent members, Dr. Roderigo Lopez, in a court intrigue to remove Elizabeth from the throne (he was hanged at Tyburn in 1594);

and an internal quarrel in 1609 that ended in one of the disaffected parties denouncing to the authorities his opponents as secret Jews. Following this, all Portuguese merchants suspected of Judaizing were expelled.

In the 1630s, a circle of Marrano merchants again appeared in London. This time there was no attempt on the part of the government to expel them, although it was well known to both the merchant community and important political figures that they were Jewish refugees. The government took no steps to rescind officially the edict of expulsion or to encourage further Jewish resettlement. This tiny band of merchants was tolerated out of inertia on the one hand, and a total preoccupation with the more pressing issues arising from the Civil War of the 1640s on the other. When an officially tolerated and avowedly Jewish community appeared in the mid-1650s, some of its members could trace their settlement in England back to the "underground" days of the pre-Cromwellian period, but in general there was little continuity between the Sephardim who pioneered the Jewish resettlement under Cromwellian aegis and the temporary settlers in the earlier period.

The story of the resettlement of the Jews in England has already been told in detail elsewhere:[2] a few aspects of that story nevertheless should be noted so that we can better understand why large-scale Jewish immigration to England only became possible from the mid-1650s on.

The initial impulse for the return of the Jews to England came from the Sephardi community of Amsterdam. The Navigation Act of 1651, which was aimed at boosting English overseas trade at the expense of the Dutch, required merchandise imported into England to be carried in English ships or in ships belonging to the country where the goods originated (i.e., merchandise was not to come to England via the Dutch entrepôt). If the Jewish shippers of Amsterdam could establish themselves or their relations in London, then the crippling intentions of the Navigation Act could be bypassed. Manasseh ben Israel, the Amsterdam rabbi who conducted most of the negotiations with Cromwell on behalf of the Amsterdam community, was also driven by the messianic expectation that the return of the Jews to England would complete their scattering to the four ends of the earth, a necessary prelude to the redemption of Israel. It is doubtful, however, that the men who sponsored his diplomacy shared his faith in the immediate messianic potential of the resettlement.

The second element that needs to be stressed in the resettlement story is that no public document was ever issued either rescinding Edward I's edict of expulsion or extending legal recognition to those few Jews already living in London when Manasseh ben Israel and Cromwell began conferring in 1655. The Whitehall Conference of December 1655, which Cromwell and the Council of State had convened to investigate the possibility of admitting the Jews, ended without making any recommendation; the Council was probably not as enthusiastic about readmission as Cromwell and saw the Conference as a maneuver to gain time or to evade direct responsibility for any positive decision. Cromwell probably had sensed that opinion in the Conference was running against him and had dissolved the Conference at its fifth session after a vigorous speech in favor of readmission. Cecil Roth speculated, on the basis of the removal of some pages from the Order Book of the Council of State for 25 June 1656, that a decision authorizing Jewish worship in England was taken on that day; if this is true, it is surprising that there are no contemporary references to this action.[3] In any case, it can be safely inferred that Cromwell must have given some guarantees to the Jews residing in London, because in the winter of 1656–57 the little Marrano community acquired a cemetery and a house for public worship and began expanding through a flow of immigrants from Holland. No formal declaration, however, seems ever to have been issued, and the legal status of the Jews in England, down to the middle of the nineteenth century, remained ill defined; whatever precision it attained was largely due to a series of ad hoc judicial rulings.

The crucial question raised both by Cromwell's decision to permit Jewish settlement and the absence of widespread protests against this policy of informal toleration is that of causality: why did a new Jewish settlement become a possibility in England in the mid-1650s? The standard accounts of the resettlement have offered two complementary hypotheses. One traces the positive attitude to Jewish resettlement to a missionary or conversionist impulse in English Puritanism, to a belief that the millennium could not be achieved without the national conversion of the Jews and that the visible saints in England had a key role to play in effecting that conversion. If the Jews could experience firsthand the purified faith of Englishmen in an atmosphere free of coercion and restraint, then they would renounce their errors and embrace Christianity. (This rationale for readmission is often described as philo-Semitic, in that its short-term objectives favored the settlement of Jews in England; ultimately, of course, philo-Semitism was hostile to the Jews in that it sought to destroy their existence as Jews.) The other hypothesis stresses the growing influence of economic considerations in the formulation of government policy. It holds that Cromwell and his party, in their concern for encouraging English commerce, were willing to subordinate purely religious considerations to the attractions of Jewish capital and enterprise.

These hypotheses about the readmission—the philo-Semitic conversionist rationale and the economic utility rationale—have an importance that transcends their ability to explain the specific events associated with Oliver Cromwell and Manasseh ben Israel. They suggest the major modes of explaining the toleration accorded the Jews through all of the Georgian period. Cromwell's economic realism points to a growing concern in England for the maximization of material growth and to the liberal individualist assumptions that developed alongside this concern. The Puritan party's sympathetic attitude to the Jews as the descendants of the biblical Israelites looks to an activist philo-Semitism that sought, particularly in the early nineteenth century, to remove Jewish disabilities in the belief that this would promote their integration and, ultimately, their conversion. This chapter will explore the manner in which the increasingly liberal social and economic structure of English life advanced Jewish toleration; the following chapter will evaluate the nature of philo-Semitic religious sentiment in England and the impact it had on the status of the Jews.

Cromwell's interest in the readmission of the Jews was of a practical nature, untinged by doctrinaire or visionary concerns of any kind. Their resettlement was for him a minor element in a more general policy of expanding overseas trade: permitting Jewish merchants to settle in London strengthened England in her commercial rivalry with Holland. At the same time, it allowed Cromwell to repay the Marrano community in London for the assistance that several of its members had given him. These Marrano merchants with agents abroad had provided him with intelligence reports, while the most prominent member of the group, Antonio Fernandez Carvajal, was a major army contractor. Cromwell certainly did not expect that the commercial activities of one or two hundred Jewish families would change the complexion of English economic life. Nor did he ever indicate that he saw any potential gain for Anglo-Christianity in the resettlement of the Jews. Their readmission was an incidental consequence of a more general economic policy and never a matter of intense governmental concern. England had no major branch of economic life that was neglected and to which the tiny band of Marranos could have been considered essential.*

*Cromwell's motives, as well as the unsystematic character of the resettlement in general, set off the Anglo-Jewish experience from other resettlements in which economic motives were dominant. In the German states, wealthy Jews were invited by the princes to settle in their territories because there were specific tasks that needed to be performed. These principalities lacked adequate credit facilities; their taxation systems and trading contacts with the larger world were poorly developed. The Jews who functioned as army contractors, mint masters, jewelers, bankers, importers, and tax collectors for them played a key role in the campaign of the princes to weaken and control the power of the estates. In Italy in the sixteenth century, new Jewish communities were founded or old ones secured in their privileges because governments thought that Jewish economic activity was essential to their economies and treasuries. In 1509, the Venetian government granted permanent residence to Jewish moneylenders because it was financially hard pressed and because Jewish moneylenders offered advantages to the money-borrowing public that the charitable *monti di pieta* did not. In 1541, the Levantine Jewish merchants were allowed to settle and trade in Venice under more generous terms than before because the government wished to improve its trade with the former European territories of the Ottoman Empire. And in 1589, the government issued a charter securing the status of the Levantine and Ponentine Jews because it wished to bolster trade with the Ottoman Empire and because it was ready to establish a major commercial center at the Venetian town of Spalato in Dalmatia, where the Jews were prominent in trade. In the Duchy of Savoy, Emmanuel Philibert, who hoped to turn Nice into a major port for trade with the East, issued privileges in 1572 to encourage Marrano merchants and artisans to settle in Piedmont. The project failed because the Pope and Philip II of Spain eventually pressured Emmanuel Philibert to expel the Jews who came (many of them were refugees who arrived directly from Spain). In Livorno, however, a similar invitation by the Duke of Tuscany in 1593 resulted in the establishment of a Jewish community that soon became a thriving center of the Sephardi diaspora. In all these instances, privileges were extended to the Jews because they were active in areas of commerce and finance essential to the strength of the state, but in which there was little interest or aptitude on the part of the native population. Selma Stern, *The Court Jew: A Contribution to the History of the Period of Absolutism in Central Europe*, trans. Ralph Weiman (Philadelphia, 1950); Benjamin Ravid, "The Legal Status of the Jewish Merchants of Venice, 1541–1638" (Ph.D. diss., Harvard University, 1974) [a summary of the dissertation can be found in *The Journal of Economic History* 35 (March 1975): 274–79]; Brian Pullan, *Rich and Poor in Renaissance Venice: The Social Institutions of a Catholic State to 1620* (Cambridge, Mass., 1971), pt. 3; Haim Beinart, "Hityashvut ha-Yehudim be-Dukasut Savoyah be-ikvot ha-privilegyah shel shenat 1572" [The Settlement of the Jews in the

Although Cromwell never justified his decision to readmit the Jews by making a general argument for toleration on the basis of economic utility, supporters of Jewish resettlement outside the government, who were primarily interested in the religious benefits of recalling the Jews, did do so. But since they were not well versed in commercial affairs and presented their economic arguments largely as a concession to the times, they did not develop a systematic or convincing case. For example: the Jews were prominent as bullion brokers because of their trading contacts with the Iberian peninsula. As mercantilist economic thought stressed the importance of building up a nation's stock of gold, it would have been natural for the readmissionists to emphasize this aspect of Jewish economic activity, but they rarely did so. In general they tended to elaborate on the role of the Jews in importing luxury goods; only occasionally did they mention how they would increase exports, then as now a primary goal of economic policy.[4] The government's reluctance to defend favors to the Jewish merchants of London in more general terms and the eagerness of pro-Jewish polemicists outside the government to do just that were paradigmatic of Anglo-Jewish history through the early nineteenth century.

Charles II and James II, like Cromwell before them, continued to protect the tiny community of Sephardi merchants (about thirty-five families in 1660, about ninety families in 1684)[5] without definitively altering their status or encouraging further Jewish immigration. Charles had no particular conscientious objections to Jews settling in his kingdom and was willing to protect them out of a concern for England's overseas commerce. In addition, while still in exile, he had approached the Amsterdam community for financial aid. When the mission of Manasseh ben Israel appeared to have ended in failure, the Amsterdam leaders responded to Charles's initiative and began seeking guarantees of toleration from his agents if (or when) Charles returned to the throne. General Middleton, on behalf of the king, promised the right of settlement and the abolition of discriminatory laws in return for help in financing the reconquest. The loan eventually

Duchy of Savoy in the Aftermath of the Privileges of 1572], in *Scritti in memoria di Leone Carpi*, ed. Daniel Carpi, Attilio Milano, and Alexander Rofe (Jerusalem, 1967), pp. 72–85.

fell through, but Charles and his advisers remained convinced that the Jews would be useful subjects, and a number of Jewish families followed the king to London.

When the Lord Mayor and the Corporation of the City of London petitioned the king, soon after his return, to enforce all the medieval regulations concerning the Jews, Charles refused to take any action. He acted in a similar fashion four years later when the Conventicle Act of 1664 came into force, prohibiting religious services not in conformity with the Church of England. Although designed to repress Christian nonconformity, the Act was used by a Mr. Rycaut and the Earl of Berkshire to blackmail the Jewish community into paying for protection in order to avoid prosecution. The Jews turned to the king for protection, and the Privy Council wrote them on 22 August 1664 that no orders had been given to disturb them and that they might continue to live and trade as before, so long as they did so peaceably, without scandal to the government and in due obedience to the laws.[6]

In March 1673, the cancellation of Charles's Declaration of Indulgence, which had conferred the right of public worship on Roman Catholics and Dissenters, provided another opportunity to the enemies (and commercial rivals) of the Jews to bring legal action against them. At the Guildhall Quarter Sessions during the winter of 1673–74, the leaders of the Jewish community were indicted for riotous assembly on the grounds that they had gathered together for the exercise of their religion. They again petitioned the king, who in February 1674 issued an Order in Council to the Attorney General to halt all legal proceedings against them.

In the fall of 1685, with Charles dead since February, another attempt was made to prosecute the Jews under legislation originally aimed at Catholics. Thirty-seven Jewish merchants were arrested while at the Royal Exchange for recusancy—failure to attend the Church of England—under an act of Elizabeth, which imposed a fine of £20 a month for nonattendance. The suit was brought by Carlton and Thomas Beaumont, relatives and dependents of Alderman Sir Robert Clayton, a former Lord Mayor. As it was in James's interest as defender of the Catholic cause to protect non-Anglicans of any kind, he issued an Order in Council to the Attorney General to suspend all proceedings.[7]

From this brief sketch of the political fortunes of Anglo-Jewry during the Commonwealth and the Restoration, it is already possible to identify some of the forces that were to promote, and to hinder, the entry of the Jews into English life. The most powerful ally of the Jewish community in these early decades and through most of the eighteenth century was the Crown and its ministers. Not having a narrow constituency whose demands they had to satisfy, Cromwell, Charles II, James II, and those who succeeded them could afford to follow the dictates of raison d'état and to extend their protection to the Jews. As monarchs and ministers have often done, they simply ignored theology when it ran counter to the necessities of statecraft. Their willingness to do so reflected the increasing concern of England's rulers with the expansion of overseas trade. The merchant community of London, on the other hand, saw no further than its own immediate economic interests: every privilege extended to the Jews was perceived as a threat to its own economic security. The attitudes of laissez-faire capitalism were as foreign to their outlook as they were to most men in the seventeenth century. From Cromwell to George IV, the City, both corporately and individually, steadfastly fought every move of the Jewish community to improve its position and, prior to 1700, actively worked to revoke the entire basis for resettlement.

At the time of the original debate over readmission, during the stormy fifth session of the Whitehall Conference on 18 December 1655, the great City merchants vigorously protested the readmission of the Jews, arguing that they would enrich themselves at the expense of the native population. To gain the support of the City, the Baptist minister Henry Jessey proposed a compromise: the Jews would only be allowed to settle in ancient, stagnating ports and would pay double customs rates. But the commercial jealousy of the City was too great to be overcome, and this, along with expressions of theological anti-Semitism, forced Cromwell to dissolve the Conference at the end of the day. Soon after Oliver Cromwell's death in September 1658, a group of London merchants petitioned Richard Cromwell to expel the thirty or so Jewish families then in London and confiscate their property.[8]

During the Restoration, the City merchants continued to work at undoing the Cromwellian resettlement. Although all these efforts ended in failure, they were successful in limiting the scope of Jewish economic activity. When the Corporation reorganized the admission of sworn brokers (agents for the sale and purchase of commodities) to the Royal Exchange in 1697, it limited the number of Jewish brokers to 12 out of a total of 124, which included 12 non-Jewish alien brokers as well. In 1723, 1730, and 1739, Jewish delegations petitioned the Court of Aldermen for an increase in the number of Jewish brokers, but each time the Court decided against them, although in 1739 the vote was eight to seven. A petition to the Lord Mayor and Court of Aldermen from the early decades of the century argued against increasing the number of Jewish brokers on the grounds that Jews were not necessary to English commerce. The petitioner maintained that not more than half the Jewish brokers were helpful to merchants in any branch of trade. He thought there already were too many Jews engaged in drawing and remitting money overseas by bills of exchange. As a result, he concluded, almost half the Jewish brokers had turned to buying and selling stocks, which had brought about numerous irregularities.[9]

Because of the opposition of the great London merchants, the number of licensed Jewish brokers continued to be limited to twelve until 1830. Whenever one of the twelve Jewish brokers died or resigned, there was intense competition to obtain the vacated position. This allowed the Lord Mayor, who had the right to name a successor, to exact a substantial fee from whomever he nominated.* In 1815, for example, Moses Montefiore's uncles paid £1,200 to obtain a broker's medal for him. Seven years later *The Times* reported that it cost £2,000 to obtain a broker's medal. And in 1829, at a meeting of the committee appointed by the Court of Common Council to consider Jewish disabilities, it was stated that sums of £1,300, £1,400, and £1,500 had been paid to the Lord Mayor by newly appointed Jewish brokers. In addition, Apsley Pellatt (1791–1863), a nonconformist glass manufacturer who championed Jewish emancipation, revealed that same year that the customary fee for transferring a broker's medal to a son or business partner, for example, had risen from £100 to £500.[10]

*The colorful advocate of political liberties John Wilkes, when elected Lord Mayor in 1774, was said to be counting on a vacancy among the Jewish sworn brokers to increase his income. When one of the brokers appeared to be dying, he asked so frequently about the man's condition that the broker's son accused him of wishing his father dead. To this charge, Wilkes replied, "My dear young man, you wrong me. I would rather see all the Jew brokers dead than your father." Charles Duguid, *A History of the Stock Exchange* (London, 1902), p. 47.

At a meeting of the Court of Common Council in May 1830, Pellatt suggested that the Court increase the Lord Mayor's allowance by £100 annually to compensate him for the loss of income that would result from abolishing the restriction on the number of Jewish brokers. Interestingly, he mentioned that he had discovered a precedent for such an increase. In 1782, the Lord Mayor had been granted an additional £50 a year for abandoning his right to an annual gift from the Spanish and Portuguese Jews' Synagogue. The practice to which Pellatt was referring is further confirmation of the extent to which the Sephardi elite perceived the great City merchants as potential adversaries who needed to be appeased. The records of the Sephardi congregation reveal that, from very early on, the Jewish community made an annual gift to the Lord Mayor. In 1671, it was a pipe of wine, costing £48; some years later it became the practice to present him with a purse containing fifty guineas; ultimately the monetary gift was replaced by a specially designed silver salver. (In 1679, the salver contained sweetmeats; in 1716, fifty to sixty pounds of chocolate.) Offering bribes to powerful and arbitrary officials was, of course, the practice in every Jewish community in the premodern world. The Dutch and French Protestant communities in London also presented the Lord Mayor with an annual tribute—a pair of silver flagons—but they gave up this practice in 1739, when they considered it unnecessary. The Jews, on the other hand, continued to make an annual offering for another forty years.[11]

The City merchants were also successful in limiting the expansion of Jewish influence in domestic and overseas trade. The requirement that tradesmen take a Christian oath prior to taking up the freedom of the City (i.e., acquiring all the privileges of a freeman of the City) guaranteed that no Jews would operate retail businesses there. And to prevent religiously indifferent Jews from converting in order to gain the privilege, in 1785 the Court of Aldermen made a standing order that baptized Jews could not be admitted. In this particular instance, economic rather than religious exclusiveness was clearly the principle; this is not to say, however, that City men were free of religious prejudice. Some of the monopoly trading companies followed the same policy. When Anthony da Costa, who was born in England, applied to the Russia Company in 1727, he was told that no Jew had ever been admitted and that the directors would have to take the

Attorney General's opinion. The Attorney General gave a decision favorable to da Costa, but the Company refused to admit him and later defied a writ of mandamus issued by the Court of King's Bench ordering his admission. The directors finally obtained from Parliament a revision of their charter that provided for exclusion on the grounds of religion. When a bill came before Parliament in 1744 for the reorganization of the Levant Company, which would have permitted the admission of Jews, the merchants who traded with Turkey strongly objected. Unlike the Russian trade, London Jews had a considerable interest in trade with the Levant, but because they had been barred from the Levant Company they were forced to trade indirectly with Turkey, via Livorno for example, or to employ other subterfuges. As most of the wholesale brokers in Turkey were Jews on whom European merchants were totally dependent, English merchants feared that the entire Turkey trade would fall into Jewish hands. The Turkish Jews, a broadside argued, would give preference to their brethren because they all formed one nation. As their "unmixableness" was an indelible character trait, the English Jews who established warehouses in Turkey would live among their coreligionists there, who were also refugees from Italy and Spain. The outcry was so great that the bill was rejected. When a reorganization scheme was passed in 1753 that effectively terminated the Company's monopoly by making its freedom easy to obtain, a clause was inserted stating that Anglo-Jewish merchants could not employ Jewish factors in the Levant.[12]

The restrictionist economic views of the City again worked against improving the status of the Jews in 1753 in the clamor over the so-called Jew Bill. This was a measure introduced by the government, at the request of Joseph Salvador (1716–86) and other wealthy Sephardi merchants and brokers, to free foreign-born Jews from discriminatory regulations in the conduct of foreign commerce. Legislation such as this was necessary because the legal status of Anglo-Jewry had remained undefined since Cromwell's abortive attempts to gain public acceptance of Jewish resettlement. The well-to-do members of the community who were born in England or the colonies enjoyed most of the commercial privileges of native-born Englishmen and did not suffer grievously from an ill-defined second-class citizenship. Jews who had been born abroad, however, had the same commercial privileges and disabilities as other aliens. They could not hold land or other real property, own or hold a share in a British sailing vessel, or engage in the colonial trade. In addition, they were required to pay alien duties, such as discriminatory customs rates and special port fees. They could not become naturalized citizens by the expensive means of a private act of Parliament because a statute of 1609 required every petitioner to receive the sacrament before his bill was introduced. The only alternative for a foreign-born Jew was to be made a free denizen by the purchase of royal letters patent, which was a costly measure and one that did not confer all the benefits of naturalization. It gave the right to engage in the colonial trade, but did not grant exemption from alien duties.

In 1753, the ministry of Henry Pelham and his brother, the Duke of Newcastle, agreed to introduce legislation into Parliament exempting Jews from taking the sacrament before the passage of private acts of naturalization. This bill was not an act of general naturalization, designed to promote the emigration of Jews to England, but a favor to Salvador and others who had been active in supporting the financial policies of the ministry and who had now solicited a favor from the government. It did not alter or fix the legal status of Jews who were born in England, and among the foreign-born, its benefits were available only to those who could afford the considerable expense of getting a private bill through Parliament. The ministry's only intention was to free foreign-born Jewish magnates from commercial discrimination.[13]

Long before the matter of the Jew Bill came to the attention of the general public, the City moved to defeat it. On 7 May, following the second reading in the Commons, Sir John Barnard, the idol of the lesser merchants of the City and a prominent critic of loan contracting, stockjobbing, and other aspects of aggressive finance capitalism, rose to denounce the bill as injurious to the interests of English commerce. Several days later, the merchants who traded with Portugal met to draft a petition to Parliament against the bill. The pseudonymous pamphleteer Philo-Patriae wrote that they were motivated by "narrow principles" and a "view to their own private interests" and were "disgusted at seeing the Jews trade in the same countries with them, and think their trade would be more profitable by there being fewer traders." On 21 May, the day before the bill was to be debated for the final time, the City delivered a vehement official protest against Jewish naturalization that represented the full spectrum of City interests—the Lord Mayor (the suspected Jacobite Edward Ironside), the Aldermen (men of wealth who normally tended to be Whig and Latitudinarian), and the Common Councilmen (retail shopkeepers and artisans who tended to be Tory and High Church). The ministry and the Jews were able to muster two merchants' petitions, which alleged that the bill would increase the nation's trade, but it is clear by the official action of the City government that the prominiterial merchants were not a representative or powerful bloc within the City.[14]

The objections of City merchants to Jews were not exclusively economic and went far beyond anything that was specifically provided for in the bill. The City petition not only warned of the disastrous economic consequences of the bill, but also expressed the fear that it would dishonor the Christian religion and endanger the Constitution. These religious protestations, which will be discussed more fully in a later chapter, should not be discounted as a mere smokescreen for concrete economic interests. Authentic religious bigotry and economic self-interest are often complementary. Nevertheless, in the light of the above evidence, it does seem likely that the initial motive for City opposition to the Jew Bill was economic. The City was not a hotbed of liberal economic sentiment. One would look in vain among the powerful merchants and bankers for precursors to Adam Smith. As a group, they were orthodox restrictionists who wanted to protect the monopolies and privileges they enjoyed. Their view of the national economy was a static one; the amount of wealth in the world was finite, and increasing the number of persons who were allowed to scramble for it could only result in smaller shares for those who were already in the field. Until the late 1820s, a clearcut majority of the Corporation held to this position.

Liberal capitalist thought, on the other hand, did have the potential for improving the condition of the Jews insofar as it looked with disfavor on all monopolistic impediments to unrestrained economic growth. This outlook had its adherents in the eighteenth century, but they were not generally found at the center of commercial and financial life. One of its earliest exponents was the moderate deist John Toland, a hack writer in the pay of various political figures. Toland had campaigned for passage of a Whig measure in 1709 to permit the naturalization of foreign Protestants. The bill had passed, but the Tories had repealed it after their smashing electoral victory in 1710. In 1714, Toland published his *Reasons for Naturalizing the Jews in Great Britain and Ireland,* in which he expressed regret that the Jews had not been included in the bill of 1709. Toland believed that "numbers of people are the true riches and power of any country" and that the Jews "increase the number of hands for labor and defense, of bellies and backs for consumption of food and raiment, and of brains for invention and contrivance, no less than any other nation." Persons who were opposed to Jewish immigration because they feared competition, Toland felt, did not realize that Jewish immigration meant that there would be more merchants to export English goods, rather than more shoemakers or tailors "taking the bread out of their mouths." Evidence for the truth of this assertion could be found in the cases of Spain and Portugal, which had become "prodigiously weak and poor" since the expulsion of the Jews, while Livorno, previously "a paltry fishertown," had been transformed into a thriving port by an influx of Jewish merchants beginning in 1593.[15]

The voice of liberal political economy was heard even more strongly in an anonymous pamphlet that appeared in 1751 when another proposal to naturalize foreign Protestants was before Parliament. The author of *The Expediency of a General Naturalization of Foreign Protestants and Others* began with the same premise as Toland: "That the increase of people is the means of advancing the wealth and strength of a nation." But he also stressed the advantages to be derived from increased competition: manufacturers would be forced to turn out higher quality goods at lower prices, which would give England a competitive edge over her foreign competitors and boost her exports. As for the charge that the Jews would work for less and thus take the bread out of the mouths of the poor, he specifically disclaimed that the state had any responsibility for those who could not compete with the more industrious:

> Surely the lazy and idle manufacturer, who, by the present high price of labour, riots in idleness two or more days out of six, and is thereby the cause of our being underworked, and conse-

quently undersold by foreigners in many branches of our exports, deserves no other regard or attention from the legislature, than the endeavouring to bring him back to a reasonable frugality and temperate way of living.[16]

It is important to remember that views such as these were not part of the shared outlook of the political nation at midcentury. The liberal critique of restrictionist policies was the property of an avant-garde and made very little impact on the commercial classes who controlled the City of London or on the landed families who dominated the Parliament. When the Pelham ministry acceded to the wishes of the Sephardim in 1753 for a naturalization bill, they did not agree to sponsor a broadly conceived measure to attract hordes of industrious Jews from the Continent; they were merely repaying a debt to a small band of financiers who had proven helpful in the past.

This expression of gratitude was the kind of nonideological political opportunism that the Pelham brothers were known for and that antiministerial writers of the time constantly denounced. A parody of the Jewish financier Samson Gideon (1699–1762) by the actor and author Arthur Murphy—a short dramatic sketch entitled "The Temple of Laverna," first published in 1752— attacked this mutually beneficial relationship between government ministers and Jewish financiers. Because the central figure in the piece was Caiphas, a powerful Jewish broker with close government ties,* it was twice reprinted in 1753 during the Jew Bill controversy. Caiphas is described as "the very Atlas of the state—our ministers have recourse to him in all their distresses, and are never able to carry any point, I mean in the money way, but when he co-operates with them." When Caiphas is absent from Change Alley one morning, one Jewish broker explains to the rest that "he has been all this morning closeted with the Great Man [Henry Pelham? the Duke of Newcastle?]. There is a grand council held this day upon affairs of the greatest importance to our nation. We shall soon be upon a footing with the best of them —but mum for that. Caiphas brings all this about: they dare not refuse him any thing." When Caiphas appears, the Jewish brokers ask him why he has not offered himself as M.P. for Middlesex, since "everybody is surprised that a gentleman of your fortune

---

*Joseph Caiaphas was high priest in Jerusalem at the time of Jesus' execution.

does not go into Parliament." Caiphas's answer is that his own ambitions do not lie in that direction, but that he hopes his son will make his way in English society and someday be made a duke.[17]

The subject of this attack, Samson Gideon, was the most prominent stockjobber and loan contractor of the period. His connection with the government went back to 1742, when during the War of the Austrian Succession, he organized for the first time a consortium of Jewish subscribers for an important Treasury loan. As the war went on, his "list" of Jewish subscribers became increasingly important in taking up government loans, and he became increasingly prominent as an adviser to the ministry on floating loans and placing them on the market. In 1745, when the early successes of "Bonnie Prince Charlie," the Stuart pretender to the throne who had landed in Scotland that summer, caused a panic in the London financial world and there was a real danger of a run on the Bank of England, Gideon was one of four prominent City men who helped to restore credit. He continued to act as one of the government's chief financial advisers until his death in 1762.

Gideon's ties to the government allowed him to amass an enormous fortune. After twenty years of close cooperation with the Pelham administration in financing England's war effort, he was worth £350,000. The extraordinary profits Gideon and, on a lesser scale, other Jewish magnates were able to accumulate from the 1690s on were part of the spoils that great financiers and well-placed politicians were reaping from the far-reaching changes in Britain's system of public borrowing in the first half of the eighteenth century, changes known collectively as the financial revolution. Between 1688 and 1756, England was at war for twenty-eight years, mostly with France, in a bitter struggle for influence in Europe and for control of colonial markets. These wars, fought on a scale hitherto unknown in Britain, required the expenditure of unprecedented sums of money. To raise the necessary funds, successive governments resorted to long-term borrowing on an increasingly greater scale. Jews, among others, were able to benefit from the government's need for larger and larger loans each year and from the creation of a market in securities, which allowed the purchase and sale of claims on the state debt.

Those who profited from the financial revolution were a minority: a few Jewish, Dutch, and Huguenot financiers, government ministers and their friends, the monied interest in the City of London. Public reaction on the whole was hostile. The national debt, to which some antiministerial writers attributed all of England's ills, increased the tax burden of the landowners while it brought to prominence a clique of parvenu financiers and corrupt politicians. The rapid rise of Samson Gideon shocked the sensibilities of the country squires and the more orthodox merchants of the City of London. As Peter Dickson, the historian of the financial revolution, remarks, "Good Protestants regarded him [Gideon] as a symbol of the corruption of English society by wealth and power." Loan contracting and stockjobbing aroused the distrust of Englishmen unaccustomed to sophisticated forms of financial speculation. There was something unseemly, it seemed, about making a fortune out of the buying and selling of slips of paper. Sir John Barnard, who led the City's opposition to the Jew Bill, was an inveterate opponent of stock market speculation, and in 1734 he succeeded in having Parliament pass a bill to curb option contracts and buying on margin. (The act, incidentally, was never effectively enforced.) The desire to curb stockjobbing and to limit the privileges of Jewish stockjobbers went hand in hand among most City merchants and country squires. Only among the very powerful and the very wealthy was there a willingness to accommodate the wishes of the Jewish elite for an improvement in their legal status.

The fortune that Gideon accumulated fired his social ambition and caused him to look beyond the confines of the Sephardi community. In 1758, after helping to raise a loan for George III in his capacity as Elector of Hanover, Gideon proposed to the Duke of Devonshire that he be rewarded for his services with a baronetcy. The king would not risk the public furor that would have been created by making a Jewish broker a baronet, but in 1759 he was persuaded to bestow a baronetcy on Gideon's thirteen-year-old, recently baptized son, then at Eton. Ironically, Gideon himself, having been born in England, strongly objected to the efforts of the Sephardi congregation to obtain a naturalization bill for foreign-born Jews, particularly since he, the most prominent Jew in England, became the object of public vituperation. He wrote at the time that he was opposed to any innovation, "but contrary to my wishes and opinion it was solicited in folly and want of knowledge, granted in levity and good nature as a matter of no consequence, and now prosecuted with malice to serve a political purpose."[18]

Whatever status Gideon and his family enjoyed in English society and whatever favors he could obtain from the government derived from the size of his fortune and the shrewdness of his advice. In this respect, his son's baronetcy (and his daughter's noble husband, Lord Gage) resembled Salvador's Jew Bill: they were "bought" rather than freely dispensed by the march of liberal ideas or the growth of capitalism. Similarly, when the Board of Jewish Deputies decided in 1829 to seek political emancipation, it was the wealth and government connections of Nathan Mayer Rothschild (1777–1836) and Isaac Lyon Goldsmid (1778–1859) that gave them entrée to the ministry in the first place. In this very specific sense, one can argue that material developments directly promoted the integration of Jews into English society.

The number of Jews who benefited in this way from their economic utility was a tiny percentage of the total Jewish population at any time. The great bulk of Anglo-Jewry in the Georgian period were desperately poor. For reasons that will be explored at length in a later chapter, England became a magnet for the Jewish poor of Holland, Germany, and even the Levant. At the time of the Jew Bill controversy, when there were between 7,000 and 8,000 Jews in England (mostly in London), Philo-Patriae, who was sympathetic to the Jewish cause, put the number of Jewish merchants who could raise £5,000 on credit at something more than one hundred. But Jonas Hanway, who was as familiar with the commercial world as Philo-Patriae, challenged that assertion. He thought that the number of "opulent" families was not more than twenty, that there were barely another forty brokers, and that the rest, aside from a few physicians, were "a train of hawkers, peddlers, and traffickers in every imaginable commodity." William Romaine, another opponent of Jewish naturalization, estimated that there were not more than ten Jewish houses in London that carried on any large foreign trade and not more than ten Jews, regardless of the source of their income, who possessed great fortunes. Hanway exaggerated the absence of a substantial Jewish shopkeeper class, but evidence from *Kent's*

London Directory for 1753 supports his and Romaine's rather than Philo-Patriae's view: only 108 Jews, out of some 3,800 names in all, carried on a business substantial enough to merit an entry. Half a century later, when there were about 15,000 Jews in England, the situation was only marginally different. Joshua Van Oven (1766–1838), a surgeon who was active in communal affairs, thought "the bulk of the nation" were poor and the opulent families "few." Levy Alexander (1754–1853), a Hebrew printer who emerged as spokesman for the Jewish petite bourgeoisie in the course of a protracted dispute with the Chief Rabbi in the early nineteenth century, put the number of rich congregants in the Great Synagogue at twenty-five, in the Hambro Synagogue at twenty, and in the New Synagogue at four, and thought that some of these had no more than £5,000 to £6,000 in capital.[19]

It would be a mistake, moreover, to assume that because the majority of wealthy Jews in England before 1800 were Sephardim that poverty was an exclusively Ashkenazi problem. The Salvadors, Gideons, Mocattas, and Montefiores were almost as much a minority among the Sephardim as the Goldsmids, Rothschilds, and Franks were among the Ashkenazim. In 1726, when there were between 1,050 and 1,700 Sephardim in England, the Sephardi synagogue in Bevis Marks spent £2,786 on poor relief—the equivalent of £40,000 in the 1960s. In 1795, the Secretary of the Congregation put the number of Sephardi poor at 1,100, or a little more than one-half of the entire group.[20] This was not as depressing a picture as that painted by reformers and critics of Ashkenazi Jewry, but it hardly suggests that the economic utility of the group as a whole was effective in promoting their acceptance into English society. On the contrary, as a later chapter will show, the ways and means that the bulk of Anglo-Jewry chose to keep from starving actually exacerbated public feeling and worked against their social and political integration. Without entering further into the matter at this point, it might be safe to say that the removal of Jewish disabilities was accomplished *despite* the occupational make-up of the community.

The limited scope of the Jew Bill and the economic inutility of the Jewish community as a whole did not prevent antimonopolists and other friends of the Jews from arguing their case in the broadest possible terms. Andrew Henderson, a London bookseller and the author of popular histories and biographies, and

Josiah Tucker, Rector of St. Stephen's in Bristol and later Dean of Gloucester, proceeded on the assumption that the strength of the nation depended on the number of its inhabitants. As the Jews were exporters and importers rather than manufacturers, one anonymous pamphleteer reasoned, "the wares and merchandize they traffick in must be the manufactures of the people with whom they trade." Hence, "the more merchants there are, the greater quantity of goods will be exported, and consequently a greater number of hands will be required to work up manufactures to supply the augmented demands." Philo-Patriae provided a detailed survey of the activity of Jewish traders in Italy, France, England, Germany, and Holland, but the most sophisticated treatment of the question in economic terms came from Josiah Tucker, who anticipated Adam Smith's arguments against monopoly. Unlike other writers, he began by accurately defining the narrow scope of the Jew Bill, reminding his readers that its purpose was to exempt wealthy, foreign-born Jews from paying Alien Duties. These duties, he argued, had been artfully but mistakenly presented as a tax on foreigners. In reality, they were a tax on the English themselves— "a tax upon raw materials imported for the employment of our poor; a tax upon the exportation of our own produce, labour, and manufactures to be sold and consumed in foreign parts; an impediment to the circulation of industry and labour; and a general burden upon the landed interest." Tucker denounced wily monopolists who sought to dupe country gentlemen into thinking that England would be invaded by swarms of destitute Jews who would force up the poor rates. He tried to convince them that the true interest of the gentry lay in an open economy: "In a word, no impediments should lie in the way of commerce but every thing be calculated to promote and extend it." Tucker's views, it must be remembered, were far in advance of their time. Symbolic of this is the fact that a mob celebrating the defeat of Nugent's naturalization bill of 1751 had burned Tucker in effigy.[21] One cannot begin to speak of a consensus among the propertied classes regarding the evils of monopolies and the virtues of free trade until the mid-nineteenth century at the very earliest.

There are, however, more subtle and indirect ways in which long-term shifts in the economic patterns of English life may have worked to improve the position of Anglo-Jewry. In the century and a half after the Glorious Revolution (1688), the forces that gave birth to the Industrial Revolution profoundly transformed the social outlook of the propertied classes in England. The paternalistic and aristocratic values of a predominately agricultural society slowly gave way to the more rationalistic commercial values of an industrializing, increasingly urban society. The traditional rulers of England, the aristocracy and the gentry, were not displaced by a new elite, but retained much of their control over English life by making room for industrial and commercial wealth in the governing class and, perhaps unwittingly, by absorbing much of the economic morality of capitalism before the first decades of the nineteenth century. On this last point, both Marxist and non-Marxist historians of the industrial and agricultural revolutions are in agreement. G. E. Mingay has written that "even by contrast with the more developed European countries, English landowners displayed an extraordinary breadth of interests, an exceptional degree of energy and enterprise, a liberal outlook on economic matters and occasionally some real entrepreneurial ability." "The eighteenth century gentry," in the words of Edward Thompson, "made up a superbly successful and self-confident capitalist class. They combined, in their style of living, features of an agrarian and urban culture." He reminds us that *"laissez faire* emerged not as the ideology of some manufacturing lobby, not as the intellectual yarn turned out by the cotton mills, but in the great agricultural corn-belt. Smith's argument [in *The Wealth of Nations*] is derived, very largely, from agriculture." English society as a whole, writes David Landes, demonstrated "an exceptional sensitivity and responsiveness to pecuniary opportunity.This was a people fascinated by wealth and commerce, collectively and individually." Nowhere in Europe was the countryside so closely integrated into the commercial world of the city. Nowhere, with the possible exception of Holland, "was society so sophisticated commercially. Nowhere was the response to profits and loss so rapid; nowhere did entrepreneurial decisions less reflect nonrational considerations of prestige and habit."[22]

The commercialization of the traditional ruling class over the course of the Georgian period indirectly promoted the cause of Jewish integration and emancipation. Insofar as it encouraged a rational orientation to life, it helped to break down the application of arbitrary criteria (e.g., religious beliefs) to spheres of life (e.g., politics and business) in which such criteria were, from the standpoint of performance alone, inappropriate. That is, by accustoming landowners and merchants to think in objective terms about how their resources might be employed most profitably, the ethos of capitalism led them to devalue (although not abandon) purely emotional criteria in evaluating men and measures in other spheres. Learning to think in a hardheaded way about profits helped to relax the hold of older irrational feelings as guiding principles in public policy.

This fascination with the accumulation of wealth also lessened much of the sting of older prejudices that derived from the historical association of Jews with commerce and finance. As moneymaking in England did not carry the stigma that was associated with it elsewhere, it was not plausible for entrepreneurially inclined aristocrats to despise Jews for their associations with business. In Central and Eastern Europe, on the other hand, where capitalism had made fewer inroads and where commercial concerns had hardly percolated into the ruling strata, landed and professional groups looked with disdain on commerce and on the Jews for being rooted in it. Marx's unflattering equation of Judaism with "practical need," "self-interest," "huckstering," and "money" in his 1844 essay on Jewish emancipation drew on long-standing, deeply rooted sentiments in the German-speaking world. In the first half of the eighteenth century in England, during the decades of the financial revolution, such prejudices were not uncommon, as mentioned, but by the end of the century and even more so by 1830, these sentiments were far less entrenched than previously, especially among the politically powerful.

The commercialization of English society was paralleled by the development of a liberal noninterventionist theory of government that was equally important in creating favorable conditions for Jewish settlement. Assertions of the royal prerogative by the Stuart kings in the seventeenth century had made Georgian aristocrats and squires distrustful of strong central government, and throughout the eighteenth century, they fought to restrict the power of the Crown. Large areas of social and economic activity, which on the Continent were subject to centralized bureaucratic regulation, were either ignored by the government in London or left to the control of local squires and magistrates. The provision

of most social services was left to the initiative of voluntary associations and charities. The state took little responsibility for
improving the minds, the morals, or the health of its citizens. The
central executive numbered barely two thousand men at the end
of the eighteenth century, including sinecure holders but excluding military officers and tax officials. In Georgian England, the
"state" meant not central administration but, in Geoffrey Best's
words, "the higgledy-piggledy mosaic of local authorities, most
of them parishes, boroughs, and counties, self-governing within
the large limits of statute law."[23] In the overcrowded quarters of
London where most of Britain's Jews lived, the state intervened
relatively infrequently in the lives of its citizens. This was due in
part to its administrative inability to do so and in part to a strong
conviction that the state should not regulate and supervise the
beliefs and activities of its citizens.

The extent to which this quasi-laissez-faire theory of government, as well as the ethos of commercial gain, helped to create
a setting in which Jews could be regarded as acceptable members
of society can be gauged by the increasing frequency with which
liberal conceptions of toleration were invoked in public debates
on the Jews. In the Jew Bill controversy of 1753, the argument
most frequently used by defenders of the Bill was that which John
Locke first propounded in 1689 in his "Letter Concerning Toleration": the state had no legitimate interest in examining the
religious beliefs of its citizens as long as they adhered to the civil
laws. Every man, wrote an anonymous pamphleteer, had a right
"to exercise his faculties and employ his talents in such a manner
as he supposes will turn most to his advantage." All men were
members of "the great commonwealth, the world," linked together by the universal tie of commerce. Religion and trade were
two very different things, although, complained this author, "we
often see too near a connection between them." To start disturbing the religion of the Jews would be dangerous, wrote another
anonymous author, for it would be merely a pretext on the part
of the state to begin interfering in matters with which it had no
concern: "For were it once admitted that it is proper for the
public to examine people's private right on account of their religion, none can answer where that would end." Reason and Nature dictated that persons not be barred from settling and trading
in England on account of their religious beliefs. Andrew Hender-

son laid it down "as a maxim, that in the nature of things, no difference of nation, religion, interest, or any other thing, ought to preponderate with a person who is guided and directed by reason strictly and properly so called." Asked another anonymous tract: "What law in Nature can there be against any person's enjoying the common privileges of a society or nation into which they are born and to which they were joined by their own consent and loyal obedience to the rules of that polity." The English translator of the Abbé Grégoire's *Essay on the Physical, Moral, and Political Reformation of the Jews* (1791) thought it necessary that a well-regulated society have some differences in status and rank in order to impress the minds of the people with a higher idea of the dignity of government, but he saw no reason for "excluding particular bodies of men, merely because they worship God after their own manner, from the enjoyment of those natural rights which no power on earth can annihilate."[24] It was appropriate for the state to discriminate against men on the basis of property, but not on the basis of religion.

The most sustained argument from a liberal perspective came from Josiah Tucker. He explained that under "the ancient Gothic constitution" of England (i.e., feudalism) the Jews had not belonged to any of the estates but had been dependents of the Crown. They and their property belonged to the king because there was no other place in the interlocking hierarchy of society into which they could fit. The Glorious Revolution, however, had finally put an end to the tyrannies and oppressions of the medieval order and had inaugurated "a new system of civil and commercial government," in which "the slavery of the Jews" along with "other kinds of slavery and a thousand articles of a similar nature" (i.e., the various arbitrary powers of the Crown) had been swept away. In the new system, all men of property enjoyed a kind of rough equality. Why then, asked Tucker, must we be guided "in these modern times by obsolete precedents and examples drawn from a constitution which no more relates to us in this affair than the constitution of Turkey or Morocco?" The "Patriots" and "the Country Interest" who held that the king had an inherent right over the lives and fortunes of the Jews by virtue of the royal prerogative as it stood in the thirteenth century really wanted to revive the obsolete claims of the prerogative and subject "life, liberty, and property to the absolute will and pleasure

of the Crown without judge or jury."[25] For Tucker, then, the Jew
Bill was a necessary consequence of the Glorious Revolution.

A basic tenet of this liberal rationalist outlook was that Jews
were essentially men like other men, rather than misanthropic
creatures of the Devil, a popular view in earlier centuries. "A
Clergyman in the Country" found that despite the charge of
deicide he could not help from looking on the Jews as men. Their
bodies were of the same shape and form as other men's; their
mental processes likewise similar. He was not even ashamed to
say he felt "something of a fellow-tenderness" towards them as
beings who occupied the same place in the scheme of creation
with himself. Of course, the Jews labored under "most unhappy
prejudices," but for these they were answerable to God and not
to him. The anonymous author of *A Looking-Glass for the Jews* took
notice of the remarkable similarity between Jews and other men.
However different they might be in terms of religion or national-
ity, he believed they were derived from one common stock with
the rest of mankind. These conclusions hardly appear remarkable
today, but to concede the common humanity of the Jews in the
eighteenth century was a revolutionary declaration. It followed,
moreover, that if the Jews were not in league with the Devil or
in a state of perpetual hostility to Christianity, then they could be
expected to obey the civil laws. The author of *The Crisis* pointed
out that Judaism taught that government was divine and that the
system of government instituted by Moses resembled the English
constitution. Unlike Catholicism, several writers pointed out,
there was no antagonism between the tenets of Judaism and the
English form of government. The Jews had no "bloody and fiery
laws" against heretics and recusants. Indeed, remarked one pamphleteer, in this regard the Jews were more Christian than the
Papists, and Judaism was infinitely nearer to Protestantism.[26]

These lofty declarations of toleration that pro–Jew Bill pamphleteers made did not imply any denial of the Christian nature
of the English constitution. Their argument was only that non-
Christians could be good citizens in a Christian state and that
economic life was a sphere of activity in which religious considerations were irrelevant. No one chose to argue in 1753, as they
would eighty years later, that the Jews should be admitted to
equal political rights. Andrew Henderson clearly indicated that
while the Jews "ought to be received with open arms, to be

admitted into the circle of our friendship," it would be inadvisable to bring them "into the center." They had best "stay hard-by the circumference" until they had proven by their zeal for the public good that they had become sufficiently patriotic.[27] Given Henderson's imprecise metaphor, it is impossible to know how much in terms of concrete privileges he was willing to allow the Jews. His language nevertheless conveys the limited way in which liberal notions were applied at midcentury.

It would not, however, be altogether accurate to speak of liberal laissez-faire theory as the ideology of the Georgian aristocracy and gentry. In the sense that ideology implies a coherent definition of social goals and a program for achieving them, there were few landowners who could be said to have had explicit ideological concerns. Between Walpole and Pitt certainly, principles and policies were not a prominent feature of English political life. If, however, liberal noninterventionism is taken to mean a loosely held group of assumptions, often unarticulated, about how society should operate and what the state should and should not do, then it would be correct to say that this term closely approximates the outlook of a prominent part of the gentry and the aristocracy. This was not the outlook, it should be noted, of all the landed class, but only of the sector that was most important in the exercise of political power at the national level. For there was by no means any kind of consensus within the landed class on matters of public policy. In general, the great landholders who were allied to successive ministries in London were more likely than not to take a nonrestrictionist position on religious and economic affairs, while the smaller landowners, the so-called squirearchy, were more likely to be High Church Tory paternalists. With the passage of time, the country squires came increasingly to adopt a more liberal economic perspective without, however, abandoning their High Church sympathies. As Chapter 3 will make clear, Toryism as a general orientation to life, as an inchoate social theory, rather than as a factional political party, was not a spent force in Georgian England.

That the more liberal segment of the landed class governed England through most of the eighteenth century proved indirectly advantageous to Anglo-Jewry. The aristocrats who filled the major ministerial posts were not liberal ideologues or activist reformers, although they might engage such men to do their pamphleteering. On their own account they did not initiate or propose thoroughgoing reforms of Jewish status, as did the men of the left in the French National Assembly, or the Prussian bureaucrat Christian Wilhelm Dohm, or even the "enlightened" monarch Joseph II of Austria. Nevertheless, when approached by the leaders of the Jewish community to remove specific disabilities, their response was generally friendly. In this sense, the political supremacy of the great landed families contributed directly to the secure position of Anglo-Jewry. From another perspective, however, it may have been more decisive that the groups who most desired to obstruct Jewish integration were effectively barred from power. Unlike Germany, those members of the ruling class who fervently believed in an organic Christian state never had the opportunity to set government policy toward the Jews. Their views about the Jews may have had wide popular support, but they could never effectively translate them into public policy. In fortuitous circumstances, such as in 1753 or in the early 1830s, they could force a government to retreat temporarily, but they could not seriously retard the entry of the Jews into new spheres of English life.

By the early 1830s, when the question of Jewish emancipation was before Parliament for several years running, the liberal argument for toleration had come to replace almost entirely the philo-Semitic conversionist rationale and the economic utility rationale. Lord John Russell summarized the liberal position by telling the Commons on 17 May 1830, "It has been decided over and over again, by majorities of this House, that no man is objectionable on the ground of his religion but that loyalty to the King and fidelity to the State are the only qualifications now necessary."[28] If Roman Catholics and Dissenters were recognized as full members of the political nation, then it only followed that Jews should be so recognized as well. Even Evangelicals who were motivated in large part to pursue Jewish emancipation for their own religious ends now chose to emphasize the secular argument for toleration. Whereas in 1753, liberal pamphleteers like Josiah Tucker, Philo-Patriae, Andrew Henderson, and Edward Weston (son of the Bishop of Exeter) had defended the Jew Bill by invoking both conversionist and secular arguments, a major Evangelical spokesman like Robert Grant now chose to plead the case on secular grounds alone.

An important consequence of the liberal belief that standing could be acquired through merit was a reevaluation of the causes of Jewish "degradation" (the term used to describe the lower-class, un-English characteristics of the bulk of Anglo-Jewry). If it was recognized that the Jews were men like other men and not the bearers of some ineradicable hereditary curse, then it became possible to account for "unattractive" Jewish characteristics by referring to the historical circumstances under which they had lived. Almost without exception, liberals came to attribute Jewish "degeneracy" to the oppression they had suffered through the centuries. One author explained that because the Jews had been driven from place to place they had contracted the habits of peddlers, who had nothing to lose from making exorbitant profits on each sale since they rarely saw the same customer twice. "Schools, synagogues, etc., were so unwillingly allotted them, and their appearance in Christian schools so shamefully resisted, that they were sunk into a degree of ignorance, which increased to themselves and others the difficulty of bettering their condition." The degeneracy of the Jews, wrote William Hamilton Reid, was "produced by the crimes of our ancestors, whose descendents must be considered as their accomplices" as long as the Jews remained unemancipated. Given "the force of birth and the prejudice of education," wrote the barrister William Jackson, even the sincerest Christian had no assurance that he would not have remained a Jew if he had been born of Jewish parents and raised and educated as a Jew.[29]

When, after 1770 or so, the highly visible presence of Jews in criminal activity periodically attracted public comment, friends of the Jews (as well as Jewish leaders themselves) explained that Jewish criminality was "the natural result of the treatment they receive." Apsley Pellatt admitted that among the lower classes of the Jewish community there was much crime and immorality, but insisted that this was not due to hereditary and therefore incurable factors. Vice was the effect of oppression; disabilities had a necessarily degrading tendency. In a similar fashion, the much-remarked Jewish penchant for the pursuit of wealth was explained by saying that the same defect was found to an equal degree among the English, only in the latter case there was a tendency to gloss over it. The premise was that the Jews as a group were no better or no worse than the English. They had no innate national characteristics of their own, but came to adopt the standards and patterns of the countries in which they settled. As early as 1714, John Toland denied that the economic skills of the Jews were due to a certain natural genius or bent of mind. They derived solely from accident, he thought, that is, from different methods of education and government. Portuguese Jews were as different from German Jews as Portuguese Christians from German Christians. A dictionary of slang from 1823, under the heading "Hebrews," explained that although Jews were treated as a distinct nation it was clear that a Jew could be an Irishman or an Englishman.[30]

The relative absence of anti-Jewish agitation at the national level was also due to the worldly character of much of the Church of England, especially its hierarchy, from the middle decades of the eighteenth century on.[31] The heated religious controversies of the previous century and, in particular, the social consequences of sectarian enthusiasm had exhausted Churchmen and left them wary of religious fanaticism in general. Moderate Churchmen wanted to make the Established Church as inclusive and truly national a body as possible; thus, they played down divisive points of doctrine. Sermons and tracts emphasized the moral duties that religion imposed on men in this world; they urged sobriety, moderation, and good works, rather than excessive displays of piety. In the eighteenth century, a minority found in Anglicanism little more than a well-balanced religion of reason, a moral code for living the virtuous life. Most educated persons, however, strongly repudiated Deism and staunchly defended Revelation. Aristocrats, squires, lawyers, physicians, and merchants read and discussed theological works. They revered, moreover, the Church of England as a national institution with practical advantages in the social and political spheres. But for most of them religion had ceased to be "a normal ingredient in vivid personal experience," in G. R. Cragg's phrase. Outside the Methodist and Evangelical camps, it was not a vital force in daily living. The Church did not seek to whip up religious enthusiasm, to enlist the faithful in any great spiritual campaign, to intensify the religious emotions of its adherents. The Evangelical revival that began at the end of the eighteenth century was a protest against the nominal character of Georgian Christianity and a plea for greater religious intensity and earnestness on a personal level. The calm of Georgian Anglicanism was not conducive to sustained Jew-baiting; the rapidity with which the Jew Bill clamor died down is evidence of this. Once the political aims of the country party had been served, High Church vicars who had been most vocal in denouncing the Jews and Judaism showed no further interest in doing so.

The moderate character of the Church of England in this period can be explained in part by the fact that after 1750 the men who guided it were of the same outlook, and often of the same social class, as those who dominated the Parliament. For reasons that are not yet clear, the Anglican clergy became a suitable occupation for younger sons of the gentry around midcentury. The second half of the eighteenth century saw a rise in clerical status and an improvement in the financial position of the lesser clergy, so that by the end of the Georgian period there was little social gap between the squire and the parson. Clergymen of undistinguished birth adopted the ideals and the conduct of country gentlemen if they could, while those of high birth brought into the Church the social and political outlook of the manor house and the House of Commons, of which their older relations were often members.

Thus, the Church did not constitute an independent corporate body with traditions and interests distinct from those of the secular elite (as was the case, for example, in prepartition Poland, where the *szlachta* and the Church were constantly at odds over the privileges of the Jews). In the words of Geoffrey Best,

> In an age when respectable clergy danced attendance at court, farmed their glebes with science and zeal, and took their place on the bench of magistrates; and when noble names were as common on the bench and in the close as county names were in the close and in all the richer livings of the land—then there could no longer be any danger of clerical ascendency, merely because the concept of a separate, independent clerical estate had evaporated from popular thinking.

Advancement within the Church depended less on the religious qualifications of candidates than on their relationship to some noble family. As Dr. Johnson remarked in 1775, "No man can now be made a bishop for his learning and piety; his only chance for promotion is his being connected with somebody who has parliamentary interest." Men of lesser rank could enter the Church and rise through its ranks, but since most wealthy livings and episcopal appointments were in the gift of powerful aristocrats and ministers of state, these men could hardly hope to get very far if they pursued a policy of bold independence. In light of the social and political character of the Church hierarchy, it is hardly surprising then that in 1753 the bishops in the House of Lords chose not to oppose the Jew Bill, although a few of them had reservations about it.[32]

Equally important in determining the position of the Jews in Georgian England was the fact that they were only one of several religious minorities, although the only non-Christian one. The religious diversity spawned by the Reformation and nourished by the breakdown of social and judicial restraints during the Civil War was irreversible. The traditional rulers of England had to recognize that the Established Church no longer enjoyed a religious monopoly and that there was little that could be done about it, since the consequences of imposing uniformity by force were politically dangerous. The Toleration Act of 1661 gave legal recognition to this state of religious diversity by legitimizing the public worship of Protestant Dissenters who remained within the bounds of Trinitarianism. Church and political leaders still believed, however, that the links between the Established Church and the State were indissoluble. Consequently, they continued to bar non-Anglicans of all kinds from full participation in the political life of the State until the end of the Georgian period. The Corporation Act of 1661 barred from membership in municipal and commercial corporations those persons who refused to take Holy Communion according to the ritual of the Church of England; the Test Act of 1673 disqualified such persons from political and civil service offices. But little could be done to suppress the worship of non-Anglicans or to hinder their commercial activity. Englishmen were learning to be religiously tolerant because they had no other choice, and although the toleration of fellow Christians was of a different order than the toleration of Jews, it is not inconceivable that the former made the latter easier to accept. For example, the proposition advanced by pro–Jew Bill pamphleteers that the State had no legitimate interest in the religious beliefs of obedient citizens was certainly derived from earlier arguments in defense of the rights of Dissenters.

The political status of the Jews in England was thus influenced by the fate of other religious minorities. During the Civil War, several petitions and resolutions calling for the toleration of all religious sects included the Jews. John Toland was prompted to write his 1714 plea for the naturalization of the Jews by the failure of a naturalization bill a few years before to include Jews within its scope. The application of the Sephardim to the Pelham ministry in January 1753 came not long after Robert Nugent's General Naturalization Bill of 1751. Nugent had been asked by the Sephardim to include a clause in their favor, but although personally sympathetic, he had refused, knowing that his bill would have a difficult enough time without including the Jews. The first proposal in Parliament to remove the political and civil disabilities of the Jews was made in 1820 by John Cam Hobhouse during the course of a debate on the situation of the Catholics and the Dissenters. Hobhouse announced on 14 July 1820 that, as the Commons had just heard on the previous night of the position of the Catholics and the Dissenters, he would bring before the House in the next session the disabilities under which the Jews labored (which, apparently, he never did).[33]

The connection that Hobhouse drew between the positions of the various non-Anglican groups was not exclusively a humanitarian one based on their moral status as religious outcasts. Dissenters, Jews, and Catholics were frequently victims of the same Parliamentary legislation. Jews were not the objects of special laws, as they were elsewhere; they were barred from political life and the universities, like Dissenters and Roman Catholics, because they were not Anglicans, not because they were Jews per se. There was no parallel to this situation elsewhere in Europe, largely because no other European state had the religious diversity England had. Of course, because the "dissent" of the Jews from the Established Church was so different from that of non-Anglican Christians and because Anglo-Jewry had no political clout, many members of Parliament who had been willing (or were pressured) to relieve the disabilities of Dissenters and Catholics would not immediately consider doing the same for Jews. When the Test Act was repealed in 1828, the Tories insisted on replacing the sacramental test, which had ostensibly kept all non-Anglicans out of public office, with a declaration of loyalty that included the phrase "upon the faith of a Christian." It is uncertain whether the clause was directed explicitly against the Jews. It may have been intended primarily for Deists and Benthamites, although its supporters were well aware that it left the Jews worse off than before.[34] When, two years later, the first Jewish Emancipation Bill came before Parliament, Lord John Russell reminded the House of Commons that if they were going to relieve Dissenters and Catholics, then the same principles required them to act in favor of the Jews. Eighteen years later, a majority in Parliament finally came to see the question of Jewish emancipation in that light.

The presence of other religious minorities also made life less hazardous for Anglo-Jewry in that it offered the majority alternative targets on which to vent their pent-up hostility and resentment. At various times throughout the eighteenth and early nineteenth centuries, Methodists, Unitarians, Baptists, and, in particular, Roman Catholics became the objects of popular prejudice and mob action. In the High Church riots in London in 1709 and 1715–1716, a dozen dissenting chapels and meeting houses were destroyed. John Wesley and George Whitefield, in their early years as field preachers, were frequent targets of mob hostility, especially when local magistrates fed the fires of religious zeal by supplying the mob with free liquor. While speaking at Moorfields Fair on Whit Monday 1742, Whitefield was pelted with stones, rotten eggs, and dead cats. The same year, while Wesley was preaching near Whitechapel, a thrown rock struck him between the eyes, and a herd of cattle was driven into the crowd. In the Gordon Riots of 1780, when patriotic Church and King mobs shouting "No Popery" and similar slogans rioted for seven days, fifty buildings, mostly belonging to wealthy Catholics, were destroyed or seriously damaged, and over 275 persons killed by the military, who had to be called in to restore order. Twenty-five persons were hanged for their participation in the riots, and another twelve were imprisoned. In the Priestley riots in Birmingham eleven years later, Church and King mobs sacked one Baptist and two Unitarian meeting houses and burned and looted the houses and shops of a score of well-to-do Dissenters.[35]

With this tradition of active hostility to religious minorities, it might seem that the Jews would have been as appropriate a target as any other group. In London, from 1750 or 1760 on, the Jewish community was highly visible by reason of its geographical density, its occupational makeup, and its peculiar social and religious customs. It was also none too respectable in terms of the trades its members followed. Yet there are no known instances of any large-scale mob activity against the Jews, with the exception of one minor incident in 1763 (to be discussed in Chapter 3). There were many more instances of small-scale anti-Jewish hooliganism than have previously been recognized, but it is impossible to find any political content in these beatings and pranks. When the traditional anti-Jewish bias of Christianity was employed for factional political aims in 1753, there was no underlying element of social discontent to give the clamor the fury that was present, for example, in the Gordon Riots of 1780. In part, this may explain why whatever hostility was expressed toward the Jews did not end in the sacking of Duke's Place, the heart of the Jewish quarter.*

The most critical element in this deflection of violent hostility away from the Jewish community undoubtedly was the long-standing hatred of Englishmen for Catholics and Catholicism, a hatred that in its intensity and in its structure closely resembled anti-Semitism. The Reformation had taught Englishmen to regard Catholicism, the Pope, and papal institutions as the very embodiment of Antichrist, the personification of evil. This identification was reinforced by the series of lengthy wars England fought with the Catholic powers of Europe in the sixteenth, seventeenth, and eighteenth centuries, and by the political threat posed to the Hanoverian succession by the Stuart pretenders and their French and Irish supporters from 1688 to 1745. Popery came to be seen as more than a disagreeable religious system; it was associated with the arbitrary exercise of power and other allegedly un-English customs. Long after there was any real possibility of England's coming under popish tyranny, politicians continued to use emotional language about the Catholic threat to English freedoms and institutions. The intensity of the sentiment may even have increased with the passage of time.[36]

Even the liberal pamphleteers who championed the cause of

---

*Duke's Place was the site of the Ashkenazi Great Synagogue and the center of the Jewish settlement within the City of London. Contemporaries used the term to refer to the Jewish community in general, in the same way in which we use the term "the White House" to refer to the President and his staff or "Madison Avenue" to refer to the advertising industry. Bevis Marks, the location of the Sephardi synagogue, was used in a similar fashion.

the Jews in 1753 branded Catholics in general as incapable of becoming good citizens. The anonymous author of the above-cited pamphlet *The Crisis* thought there was "a dangerous repugnancy" between the tenets of Catholicism and the English constitution. The clamor about the threat of a Jewish preponderance was, he believed, groundless, senseless, and iniquitous; it was raised and supported chiefly by the avowed enemies of Church and State, the backers of the popish Stuart Pretender. They posed the real danger to the established order: "Are there not ten thousand insulting Jacobites and favourers of a foreign interest in our land to one insulted Jew?" The author of *A Looking-Glass for the Jews* also believed that the real danger to Church and State came not from the Jews but from the Papists. In his opinion, the Jews were more Christian than the Papists and their religion far closer to Protestantism. At the same time, pro–Jew Bill writers were careful to remind their readers that the Jews had come to the defense of England when the Young Pretender had invaded Scotland and England in 1745. Philo-Patriae told how the lower-class Jews had enrolled in the City militia, even though it meant they would have to transgress some of their religious customs, and how the wealthy Jews, in order to maintain confidence in the financial institutions of the government, bought up bank notes at par, imported specie, and subscribed to a new government loan.[37]

After the last Jacobite invasion, anti-Catholic feeling became an increasingly unfocused and wildly all-embracing kind of hatred. It did not focus on flesh and blood Catholics, such as the growing colonies of Irish poor in London, Manchester, and Liverpool, but treated Popery in the abstract as a serious danger. In G. F. A. Best's words, anti-Catholicism became "indistinguishably mixed up with the common cant of manly freedom-loving patriotism."[38] For many Englishmen, it functioned in the same way that anti-Communism did for conservative Americans in the Cold War years and anti-Semitism for Germans in the Third Reich. It was a catch-all sentiment into which all kinds of fantasies and fears could be poured, but one that did not accurately reflect any serious threat to English freedoms or security. By its all-embracing nature, anti-Catholicism was thus able to deflect a good part of the hostility that might have been directed at Anglo-Jewry.

Antipathy to Jews, however—whether in the guise of traditional religious doctrine, or of social snobbery, or of a romantic
revolt against modernity—had not disappeared from Georgian
England. It should already be clear that there was strong opposition in certain sectors of English society to the entry of Jews into
the political and economic life of the nation. But it should be even
more clear by now that there were strong countervailing forces
that prevented these anti-Jewish sentiments from finding permanent expression in either the laws of the country or in an ongoing
clerical crusade. Having explored the secular foundations of Jewish toleration, we now look to a specifically religious tradition,
"philo-Semitism," which operated alongside secular phenomena
in promoting Jewish integration.

2

Philo-Semitism in Anglo-Christianity

The first Englishmen to promote the readmission of the Jews were radical Puritans who believed that the Millennium would be realized in the not too distant future and that Protestant England had an active role to play in its realization. The idea that moved them to call for the return of the Jews—the belief that the national conversion of the Jews (and, in some versions, their return to the Holy Land) had to precede any final scheme of redemption —was not unique to English Puritanism nor to the seventeenth century. It had its roots in the apocalyptic millenarianism of the early Church Fathers and was widely diffused in apocalyptically inclined circles throughout northern Europe in the seventeenth and eighteenth centuries. In France, for example, the Jansenists rejected the orthodox Catholic position that the biblical prophecies regarding Israel's future blessedness referred to Christians, believing rather that God had assigned the Jews an important role in the final days. The Abbé Grégoire, the great clerical champion of Jewish emancipation at the time of the Revolution, was much influenced by these Jansenist views. The Swiss theologian Johann Caspar Lavater's well-known attempt to convert Moses Mendelssohn in 1769 was rooted in the belief that the conversion of the Jews was tied up with the thousand-year reign of Jesus and the Saints at the end of time. The conversion of the chief representative of enlightened Jewry was to set an example to other

Jews and speed up the process of the general conversion of the Jewish people.[1]

In England, religious sentiments such as these acquired an influence and a power they lacked elsewhere, largely because they were associated with the revolutionary demands for a new religious and social order that arose during the Civil War years. They partook of the tremendous release of popular energy that followed the breakdown of social and judicial restraints in the 1640s and continued to influence attitudes toward Anglo-Jewry up through the early nineteenth century (although with the passage of time the impact of these sentiments tended to decline, as, indeed, did the impact of most religious beliefs).

The early Church Fathers Justin Martyr, Irenaeus, Tertullian, and Lactantius had preached an apocalyptic millenarianism in which the return of Jesus and his victory over Antichrist led to the Millennium (a thousand-year kingdom of peace), the general resurrection of the dead, and the Last Judgment. This potentially revolutionary promise of a reordered terrestrial paradise was not, however, suitable to a bureaucratically organized Church, which by the fourth century was enjoying a position of supremacy in the Mediterranean world and was recognized as the official religion of the Roman Empire. "The Catholic Church," Norman Cohn has written, "was now a powerful and prosperous institution, functioning according to a well-established routine, and the men responsible for governing it had no wish to see Christians clinging to out-dated and inappropriate dreams of a new earthly Paradise."[2] In the early fifth century, Augustine propounded the doctrine that the Church itself embodied the millennial kingdom of God. This became orthodox doctrine; millenarian ideas ceased to be at the center of Church theology and were forced underground or to the fringes of Church activity. Whenever the older disruptive tradition surfaced during the next twelve centuries—usually in conjunction with popular movements of social discontent—the Church sought to suppress it.

When this popular millenarian tradition broke through the restraints of institutional Catholicism in the medieval world, its attitude toward the Jews was one of unrelenting hostility. They were associated with the hosts of Antichrist whom the saintly armies of the dispossessed were seeking to overthrow—the Church authorities, well-to-do burghers, and higher nobility who tried to protect the Jews from popular violence because they valued their economic utility and because they were more aware of the ambivalent attitude of the Church to the continued existence of the Jews. Revolutionary millenarianism in pre-Reformation Europe held that Antichrist "would be born at Babylon; he would grow up in Palestine and would love the Jews above all peoples; he would rebuild the Temple for them and gather them together from their dispersion. The Jews for their part would be the most faithful followers of Antichrist, accepting him as the Messiah who was to restore the nation."[3]

Protestant chiliasm tended to take a less harsh attitude toward the continued existence of the Jews. In England, instead of inciting the poor to loot and slaughter the Jews, the belief that great events were at hand worked to encourage Jewish resettlement and, at a later date, to ease the legal disabilities from which they suffered. This kind of "philo-Semitic" tradition was ultimately not pro-Jewish, insofar as toleration was intended solely to promote the conversion of the Jews. But the short-term objectives that English "philo-Semites" pursued in their campaign to convert the Jews were to the temporal advantage of Anglo-Jewry.[4]

Englishmen first began to discuss publicly the national conversion of the Jews in the last decades of Elizabeth's reign. In repudiating the authority of Rome, the English Reformation had accustomed men to turn to the Bible for guidance and inspiration. As the Reformation in England was also a nationalist revolt against the claims of the Church to intervene in English affairs, and as England was the only major Protestant power, Englishmen came to see themselves as an elect nation with a divine role to play. Their attachment to the Bible encouraged them to identify themselves—metaphorically and, in some instances, in a very vividly real sense—with the Children of Israel. By 1600 or so, Luther's belief that the Pope was Antichrist was widespread and respectable, accepted by men of all religiopolitical outlooks. Calculations of the number of the Beast, the coming of Antichrist, and the End of Days were widely circulated. Anglo-Christianity, it was generally believed, had a God-chosen role to play in destroying Popery and inaugurating the Millennium; cleansed of pagan superstition and idolatry, it would accomplish great things. It would succeed where the Roman Church had failed.[5]

A number of works appeared in the first three decades of the seventeenth century that reflected an increasing concern with the place of the Jews in the Christian scheme of redemption. Thomas Brightman, Fellow of Queen's College, Cambridge, wrote an extensive commentary on the book of Daniel (*A Revelation of the Revelation*, published posthumously in 1615), in which he proved that the Pope was Antichrist and foredoomed to utter destruction. His overthrow was to be followed by the defeat of the Turks, the conversion of the Jews, and their return to the Holy Land. A more revolutionary statement of the impending universal upheaval was Sir Henry Finch's *The Worlds Great Restauration or the Calling of the Jews* (1621). Finch considered all the prophecies in the Old and New Testaments concerning the Jews and argued that they applied to the fleshly descendants of Abraham and were not allegorical references to the Church. On the basis of passages in Daniel, he calculated that the redemption of the Jews would come in 1650 and provided an elaborate description of their journey back to the Promised Land, including their battles with the Turkish army. Finch was not a religious lunatic, but a respected lawyer and Member of Parliament whose work on the common law was only superseded in the mid-eighteenth century.[6] As outlandish as his hopes may seem, it would be wrong to impose current standards of reasonableness on them and thus confine them to the disreputable fringes of seventeenth-century religious thought. For Englishmen sympathetic to Puritanism, the defeat of Antichrist and the national conversion of the Jews were vivid and meaningful possibilities, as real as the Fall of Man or the Crucifixion of Jesus.

The outbreak of the Civil War saw the removal of all restraints on the religious imagination, and millennial expectations became more widely diffused than ever before, penetrating even the most orthodox religious groups. Before the 1640s, episcopal courts, censorship, and ecclesiastical control of education had held back the flow of unorthodox religious doctrines that often resulted from bibliolatry and the doctrine of the priesthood of all believers. When censorship and church courts broke down and the social authority of the gentry ceased to be effective, previously unorthodox ideas received a far wider hearing, particularly among those who supported the Parliamentary cause. In the intoxicating atmosphere of the new freedom, Christopher Hill has remarked, no holds were barred. Scholars, politicians, and ordinary people alike expected the Millennium in the near future. B. S. Capp's statistical survey of works by ministers supporting Parliament in the period 1640–53 found that just under 70 percent of his sample could be identified as millenarians, only 3.5 percent as antimillenarians. By midcentury, a consensus seemed to have been reached: the mid-1650s would see the fall of Antichrist, perhaps the Second Coming, and the Kingdom of Heaven on earth.[7]

The conversion of the Jews and their restoration to Zion were an integral element in the millenarianism of the 1640s and 1650s. The Fifth Monarchist John Archer, lecturer at All Hallows, Lombard Street, expected the conversion of the Jews in 1650 or 1656, and the fall of the papacy in 1666. He expressed great respect for the Jews, who were the first chosen people, in *The Personal Reigne of Christ upon Earth* (1641 and many subsequent editions), asserting that after their conversion the Jews would have the greatest glory in the Millennium. The royalist mathematician William Oughtred thought Jesus would return in 1656 to convert the Jews. This date for the conversion and restoration of the Jews was also the most popular among Fifth Monarchists. In a sermon of July 1644, Stanley Gower assured the House of Commons that the Jews would be converted in 1650. In 1647, the influential Baptist Hugh Peter, chaplain to the New Model Army, called for a return of the Jews to England as part of a solution to the economic problems brought on by the war, but he added that he expected their conversion as well. By the Whitehall Conference of 1655, however, Peter had changed his mind. He now doubted that the Jews could be converted and feared the harm they would do with their own missionary efforts among the Christian population. In January 1649, Johanna Cartwright and her son Ebenezer, Baptists who had fled to Amsterdam during the Marian persecutions, petitioned the Army Council to repeal the expulsion edict of 1290. They believed that repeal of the ban would appease God's anger over the innocent blood being shed in England. They also believed that redemption was at hand and that England and Holland were to supply ships to transport the Jews back to the Holy Land.[8]

The sympathetic identification of the Puritan party with the Israelites of the Old Testament led in some instances to the adoption of Jewish practices and in a few cases to attempts to restore the Jews to Zion by "paramilitary" adventures. Some sectarians reverted to the practice of circumcision and to the observance of Saturday as the Sabbath. John Traske, who kept the dietary laws and other rituals of Judaism, was prosecuted in Star Chamber in 1618 for maintaining that the Jewish Sabbath should be observed and no work done on that day. He had followers in London, a few of whom eventually settled in Amsterdam and formally converted to Judaism, and confessed to trying to make converts. In a debate in the House of Lords in May 1621, the Archbishop of Canterbury critically declared that "many were inclined to Judaism and dream that the Jews shall have regiment and kings must lay down their crowns to their feet." Hence, he wished Sunday to be styled the Lord's Day, rather than the Sabbath with its Jewish connotations. Mary Chester of London was prosecuted in 1635 by the government for holding Judaical tenets such as the Jewish Sabbath and the distinction between clean and unclean meats. In the early 1650s, Fifth Monarchy men called for the abolition of all existing laws and courts and the introduction of the Mosaic code—not just the Ten Commandments, but all the judicial laws and penalties included in the Pentateuch. With the restoration of monarch and prelacy, the Fifth Monarchists Thomas Tillam and Christopher Pooley established a Judaizing community of English émigrés in the Palatinate. The settlement practiced Jewish rites, including circumcision, and wished to rebuild the Temple. Several motions were made in the Barebones Parliament (July–December 1653) for the return of the Jews, with Samuel Hering telling the members to recall the Jews, "for their time is near at hand." But the most active steps for Jewish redemption were taken by two messiahlike figures who flourished in the early 1650s. John Robins, a farmer, was proclaimed King of Israel in 1650 by the Ranter Joshua Garment. Robins announced that before the coming of Michaelmas he would split the sea like Moses and lead the Children of Israel back to the Holy Land. He began assembling a projected army of 144,000 men to reconquer the Land from the Turk. They trained on dry bread, vegetables, and water (ale being the drink of the Beast). The London silversmith Thomas Tany, who may have been associated with Robins, discovered about the same time that he was a Jew descended from the tribe of Reuben, and that he had been called to return the Jews to the Land of Israel and reerect the Israelite state and Temple, with himself as High Priest. He had himself circumcised, learned Hebrew in preparation for the return to Zion, and some years later built a small boat to carry him to Jerusalem. He set out for Holland "to call the Jews there," and either drowned on the way or disappeared after reaching Amsterdam.[9]

The previous examples of seventeenth-century conversionist "philo-Semitism" must not be seen as unqualified expressions of love for flesh-and-blood Jews. In almost every instance of pro-Jewish sentiment cited so far, "the Jews" were little more than the personification of some abstract religious idea or feeling, like the negatively charged symbols of the Beast and the Antichrist. Englishmen had almost no personal contact with real Jews at this early date; there had not been any Jewish community in England for three and a half centuries; hence, images of "the Jews" were unaffected by the realities that influenced Jewish-Christian relations on the Continent. Given these reservations, it would hardly be prudent to take every favorable reference and benevolent proposal at face value.

These "pro-Jewish" sentiments were, moreover, largely confined to the Puritan-Parliamentary camp, which in the crucial decades of the 40s and 50s was the ascendant force in English political life. Royalists and High Churchmen generally did not share these philo-Semitic sentiments. They might be willing to tolerate the presence of Jews in England, as proved to be the case, but they did not do so out of any desire to convert them. Millenarian speculation, they well knew, was subversive of the established order in Church and State. Even when no explicit call was sounded to turn the world upside down, a vision of God's kingdom on earth carried with it an implicit condemnation of the status quo. After the publication of Finch's *Great Restauration,* Laud preached a sermon at court against the "error of the Jews" (i.e., the radical Puritans) that "Christ's kingdom should be temporal."[10]

What these examples of extravagant philo-Semitism illustrate, along with the other evidence cited so far, is the extraordinarily positive position the Jews occupied in one major strain of English religious thought. And, if it is impossible to state with any precision how this philo-Semitism made life easier for the Jews in the early years of resettlement, it is also equally hard to believe it was without impact. In negative terms, it meant there was a large body of religious thought that did not identify the Jews with the forces of evil. This is no small thing when we consider how potent was the identification of the Jew with the Devil in most Continental anti-Semitism before the nineteenth century.[11] At the time of the Jewish Naturalization Bill of 1753 and of the campaign for Jewish emancipation from 1828 onward, the influence of this philo-Semitic strain in Anglo-Christianity is more immediately apparent: some of the most active supporters of Jewish rights were those who desired their conversion.

Although millenarian dreams were sharply checked by the restoration of the monarchy in 1660, conversionist philo-Semitism did not disappear. It had found a place in the religious culture of England and continued to exert a hold over many persons for the next two centuries, even though the revolutionary setting that had first fostered it had disappeared. Broad groups of Englishmen also continued to acknowledge, even if only in a formal sense, the possibility of a millennial redemption within their own lifetimes, but they did so without the intensity or urgency of the Civil War years. Still, it is of some importance that millenarian aspirations, no matter how faint, were not restricted to small circles of intense chiliasts. The excitement created by the Sabbatean movement in 1665 and 1666, for example, revived a widespread interest in England in the restoration of the Jews that was in no way limited to the sectarian fringe. At least eight separate tracts on this messianic movement were published in England in the two years of Sabbatai Zevi's active messiahship (1665–66).[12] When Samuel Pepys visited his bookseller in St. Paul's Churchyard on 19 February 1666, he noted,

> [I was] told for certain, what I heard once or twice already, of a Jew in town, that in the name of the rest do offer to give any man £10 to be paid £100, if a certain person now at Smyrna [Sabbatai Zevi] be within these two years owned by all the Princes of the East, and particularly the grand Signor as the King of the world, in the same manner we do the King of England here, and that this man is the true Messiah. One named a friend of his that had received ten pieces in gold upon this score, and says that the Jew hath disposed of £1,100 in this manner, which is very strange; and certainly this year of 1666 will be a year of great action; but what the consequences of it will be, God knows![13]

Henry Oldenburg, the German-born secretary of the Royal Society from 1662 to 1677, wrote to Spinoza on 8 December 1665:

> Here everyone spreads a rumor that the Jews having been dispersed for more than two thousand years are to return to their country. Few in this place believe it, but many wish for it. You will tell your friend what you hear and judge of this matter. For myself, so long as this news is not conveyed from Constantinople by trustworthy men, I cannot believe it, since that city is most of all concerned in it. I should like to know what the Amsterdam Jews have heard of this and how they are affected by such important news which, if it were true, would seem to bring some catastrophe on the whole world.[14]

Through his extensive correspondence with men of letters and science abroad, Oldenburg kept informed of the latest news concerning Sabbatai Zevi and passed it on to friends in England. His interest in the restoration and conversion of the Jews was a long-standing one. Eight years earlier, while traveling in France as tutor to Richard Jones (Lord Ranelagh), he had written to Manasseh ben Israel, whom he had met during the latter's mission in London, about an unpublished work on the restoration of the Jews that he had just come across:

> I for my part, most honoured Sir, am convinced that those prophecies which were made to you in the books of Moses and of the Prophets concerning your return to the land of Judah and your perennial happiness therein were by no means fulfilled on your return from the Babylonian captivity. Indeed, although the Holy Land was recovered at that time, nevertheless you never enjoyed then that liberty and that flourishing state which the prophecies announced. . . . Here you may see how those splendid promises regarding your future have remained unfulfilled. It is hence to be concluded that they will come to pass in the future.[15]

Oldenburg's interest in the restoration of the Jews to Zion well illustrates the ease with which the intellectual elite of the period could pioneer an experimental, rationalist approach to the material world while still clinging comfortably to traditional notions of Divine Redemption. John Locke and Isaac Newton, for example, were firm believers in the national conversion and physical restoration of the Jews. Locke, in his commentary on the Epistles of Paul, expressed his belief that God would assemble the Jews in one body "and set them in flourishing condition in their own Land." Newton, who like many of his contemporaries believed in the possibility of a scientific approach to biblical prophecy, offered a more detailed interpretation. In his commentary on Daniel and the Apocalypse of St. John (published posthumously in 1733), Newton hypothesized that the initiative to return to Zion might not come from within the Jews themselves, but perhaps from some world power that was friendly to them (England?). He never explained how this intervention might come about, but concluded guardedly, "The manner I know not. Let time be the interpreter."[16]

The first half of the eighteenth century witnessed a decline in the intensity of conversionist philo-Semitism, in large part due to the decline in religious intensity in general. But such beliefs, embedded as they were in millenarian hopes and speculation, still enjoyed informal acceptance by a wide audience. As Franz Kobler, Meir Vereté, and Clarke Garrett have adequately demonstrated, pamphlets, tracts, sermons, and treatises on millenarian themes circulated widely throughout the eighteenth century.[17] What remains to be done is to examine the relationship between this millenarian yearning and specific measures to improve the legal position of English Jews.

The first attempt on the part of the government to better the status of Anglo-Jewry came in 1753, when the ministry of Henry Pelham and his brother the Duke of Newcastle agreed to introduce legislation into Parliament exempting Jews from taking the sacrament before the passage of private acts of naturalization. The Jewish Naturalization Bill, or Jew Bill, as contemporaries called it, was not an act of general naturalization, designed to promote the emigration of Jews to England, but a favor to some of the Sephardi mercantile elite who had been active in supporting the financial policies of the ministry and who had now solicited a favor from the government.[18]

The limited scope of the Jew Bill, however, was almost totally ignored in the outburst of both the pro- and anti-Jewish passions it provoked. Prominent among the arguments advanced by the pro–Jew Bill ministerial party was the "philo-Semitic" belief that naturalization would lead to conversion. Although the standard account of the affair has dismissed this clamor as a smokescreen for the clash of competing political interests,* it is difficult to see the real outpouring of conversionist sentiment that was part of the pro-Jew Bill propaganda as merely epiphenomenal. The genuine desire to effect the conversion of the Jews was complementary—and not merely subordinate—to whatever political or ideological gains were to be made from passage of the Bill.

The conversionist proponents of Jewish naturalization argued fundamentally the same case as their sectarian predecessors in the previous century, but they did so now with a greater awareness of Jews as real creatures, rather than as spiritual abstractions. By 1753, there had been an openly tolerated Jewish community in London for almost a century, and the belief that the integration of Jews into Christian social circles would lead eventually to their conversion had some foundation. The pseudonymous author Philo-Patriae noticed that converts had already been made from many prominent Jewish families and concluded that it was easier to convert the Jews by allowing them to enter England so they might mix with Christians than by driving them

---

*The standard account of this episode by Thomas W. Perry in *Public Opinion, Propaganda, and Politics in Eighteenth-Century England: A Study of the Jew Bill of 1753* (Cambridge, Mass., 1962) admirably places the clamor within the context of British political history, but in doing so reduces the entire affair to nothing more than a purely political event, minimizing, in the process, its nastier anti-Semitic aspects (to be discussed in Chapter 3) and ignoring altogether the issue under discussion here—the vitality with which philo-Semitic conversionist arguments were employed by the pro–Jew Bill party.

Perry's thesis is an attempt to refute Sir Lewis Namier's views about the nonideological character of mid-eighteenth century politics. Perry argues that the controversy was basically a renewal of a long-standing conflict over immigration and naturalization policy that, when seized upon by the antiministerial country party (with High Church support) for election purposes, "became in effect a doctrinal issue in the old Whig and Tory tradition . . . the arguments employed by both sides, too, were the standard, familiar ones, with *incidental* pro- and anti-Jewish variations" [emphasis added] (p. 178). There is no question that Perry is correct in arguing that the initial motive for attacking the recently passed Jew Bill was to promote the factional aims of the country squires and High Church parsons who disliked the corrupt politics and latitudinarian church policy of the Pelham brothers. Where he errs is in subsuming every tract, sermon, editorial, and speech under the categories of that conflict. A host of nonpolitical emotions and issues were released by this controversy that deserve to be treated on their own terms. Evidence for this may be found in the fact that propagandists on both sides rarely debated the merits of either this particular bill or of naturalization policy in general. In regard to the anti-Jewish aspect of the debate, Jacob Katz has remarked that "the easy success of the propaganda and the nature of the arguments used during the campaign are telling testimonies to the image of the Jew prevailing in the public mind." "The term 'Jewish Emancipation': Its Origin and Historical Impact," in *Emancipation and Assimilation: Studies in Modern Jewish History* (Westmead, Farnsborough, Hants., 1972), pp. 29–30.

away.[19] In a sermon to a fashionable London congregation, the Rev. Thomas Winstanley predicted that extending the privileges of Englishmen to the Jews would incline them "to cultivate a friendship and familiarity with us; which, of course, must bring them, in due season, to a conformity of manners, and an imitation of our ways and customs." By mixing with the English, the Jews would imbibe those generous sentiments that arise in a society where pure Christianity prevails, and would come to entertain more favorable feelings concerning other men, and "these more favourable sentiments concerning us may be improved, e'er long, into a more favourable opinion of our religion [and would ultimately lead to conversion]."[20] On the basis of the same evidence adduced by Philo-Patriae, however, William Romaine, a central High Calvinist figure in the early Evangelical revival, argued that naturalization would not lead to conversion. He reminded his audience that in Cromwell's time the Jews had been resettled under the pretense that it would be the means of their conversion, but that no such thing had happened. "We have had experience of them near one hundred years and how many converts have been made in all that time? So few, that for our own honour we had better conceal their number."[21]

Pro–Jew Bill polemicists continued to emphasize how uniquely qualified England was to effect the conversion of the Jews. Andrew Henderson, a London bookseller and the author of a number of popular histories and biographies, thought that the Jews never had a better opportunity for being converted than at the present. They would be unworthy of the favor God had bestowed on them "if they did not at times go to hear the shining lights of the Church of England, whose institution is the best antidote against nonsense, and whose members adorn the doctrine of God their Saviour by a modest and peaceable behaviour." In the spirit of the easygoing latitudinarianism that characterized the established church at midcentury, Henderson and others repudiated the use of force in propagating the Gospel to the Jews. For Henderson, the glory of the Christian religion was that it was spread by cool representations and would prevail by dispassionate argument. Philo-Patriae did not expect the Jews to be converted with one swift motion, but gradually, without compulsion, when they were at ease, "when the mind can more coolly reflect and submit itself to the dictates of reason and truth."[22]

According to conversionist philo-Semites, the obstinacy of the
Jews down through the centuries could be attributed to the persecuting spirit of the Roman Catholic Church. The inhumanity
they had experienced in England and on the Continent "during
the times of Popish darkness and ignorance," wrote Edward Weston, son of the Bishop of Exeter, had been an obstacle to their
conversion. Philo-Patriae found proof of this assumption in the
differences between Jews who lived in Protestant countries and
those who lived in Catholic ones. The former were influenced by
the "free way of thinking" that prevailed in Protestant states and
had begun to question the authority of their rabbinical writings.[23]

A conversionist strategy based on showing compassion to the
Jews was linked with a reevaluation of the older doctrine that God
had damned the Jews for all eternity. Andrew Henderson thought
that the Jews had not been so totally rejected by God as everyone
was prepared at first to imagine. He wondered whether the Jews
living in his own time were not the descendants of those Jews
already living outside the Land of Israel at the time of Jesus'
crucifixion, and hence not responsible for his death. He also
suggested that those Jews in Jerusalem who had conspired to do
away with Jesus had been slaughtered by the Romans and thus
could not have been the progenitors of European Jewry. In a
similar vein, one anonymous author argued that the Jews of his
own age were no more responsible for the crucifixion than the
descendants of the Englishmen who had lived in the reign of
Charles I were for his murder.[24]

A more common conversionist tack in defending Jewish naturalization was to deny that it was God's Providence that the Jews
be harshly stigmatized for all time. Edward Weston asked those
who opposed the Jew Bill on traditional religious grounds where
in Scripture God had forbidden them to harbor and befriend the
Jews. God's punishment of the Jews, he maintained, consisted
only in the destruction of the Temple and their separation from
their national land. If Scripture said nothing about not admitting
the Jews as citizens or not allowing them to acquire homes in the
Diaspora, then the Jew Bill in no way contradicted the decrees of
God. The pseudonymous author By-stander quoted New Testament texts against Christians who believed that there was an
eternal curse on the Jewish people and, hence, that it would be
impious to attempt to better their condition before God's ap-

pointed time. Did not Jesus plead, "Father, forgive them, for they know not what they do"? Should Christians "go on to the last to reproach them with their infidelity and at such a distance of time from the Crucifixion of our Saviour; when St. Paul, immediately after their committing that cruel act, treated them with all the tenderness and compassion?" One anonymous pamphleteer even went so far as to argue that the Jews could not be eternally stigmatized for an act that God had providentially decreed as atonement for the sins of all mankind. Furthermore, he reasoned, if the Jew Bill ran counter to the ends of Providence, then it would not have been possible for the bill to pass in the first place.[25] The public clamor arose, it should be remembered, only after the bill had been passed.

The firm belief of some Jew Bill apologists that naturalization would promote conversion was not matched by any equally strong faith that this conversion would herald the Millennium. Unlike their sectarian predecessors of the 1640s and 1650s, for whom the possibility of a millenarian redemption was an immediate reality, advocates of Jewish naturalization in 1753 expressed only the most generalized hopes that great events would follow the passage of the bill. They did not deny the central role of the Jews in the drama of the Millennium, but when they spoke of the fulfillment of prophecy they did not do so with the certitude and fervor of earlier conversionists. Josiah Tucker reasoned that since the general conversion of the Jewish nation had to begin somewhere, it made no sense to prevent its beginning in England: "Why should the members of the Church of England, the glory of the Reformation, be the last to bring back the ancient people of God?" As Christians were commanded to pray for the conversion of the Jews, "they are certainly obliged to use some benevolent means towards promoting that good end and not content themselves with offering unto God a little, cheap, unavailing lip labour." The same vagueness about the timing of the Millennium appears in the anonymous tract *A Looking-Glass for the Jews.* The author urged his countrymen to preserve and cherish the Jewish people so that they might promote and not obstruct the completion of the prophecies. "Unless you can see into future events," he asked, "and are acquainted with the precise time of their call, how do you know but their naturalization here is the first step to their conversion and that England is the happy country where this great revolution in the affairs of the world is to commence?"[26] Churchmen, then, were still eager to pronounce the English branch of Christianity the most godly in Christendom, but they no longer cherished any dreams that this would soon result in the Millennium. The consensus, rather, seemed to be: as long as there was to be a Second Coming, it did no harm to promote England as its initial site.

For most Englishmen, the religious urgency of the Civil War years had given way to a low-key faith that abjured freakishness and enthusiasm. The revolutionary impulse that had led wide bodies of men in the mid-seventeenth century to expect the Millennium within their own lifetimes had been replaced a century later by the less ideological politics and moderate religion of mid-Georgian stability. The actual impact of the conversionist argument on the outcome of the controversy was probably negligible. The ministry's original decision to introduce the bill had been made on unideological grounds, although their decision to seek repeal of the act a few months later was made to avoid losing any seats in the coming general election.[27] The presence of the conversionist argument for toleration in the public debate is not, however, irrelevant. It indicates that some part of the political nation did wish to bind the Jews more tightly to the English people—and ultimately to convert them—by way of extending greater privileges to them. These men had little political clout in the 1750s, but in the late 1820s, they were able to influence the political process to relieve specific Jewish disabilities. In a roundabout way, the persistence of conversionist philo-Semitism among the politically conscious at midcentury meant there were that many fewer persons of influence willing to tolerate or encourage new discriminatory measures or popular outbreaks of hostility. This kind of negative reasoning is of necessity imprecise, but it would be foolish to disregard altogether the simple proposition that every philo-Semite meant one less potential anti-Semite.

After the general election of 1754, the evidence for the persistence of conversionist philo-Semitism became sporadic until the revival of millenarianism at the time of the French Revolution and the concurrent emergence of a strong Evangelical movement. The fulfillment of God's promises to the Jewish people remained, however, a topic of interest for religious writers, but they did not urge Englishmen to take any particular action to hasten the process, largely because there were no political moves to stimulate this kind of exhortation. In 1759, a letter from G. appeared in *The Gentleman's Magazine* expressing horror over the prospective conversion to Catholicism of thousands of Polish Jews. G. had read in the newspapers about the messianic movement led by Jacob Frank, the self-proclaimed heir of Sabbatai Zevi, which ended in the voluntary conversion of large numbers of Jews to Catholicism. G. was greatly agitated that the Jews were abandoning the Law of Moses to embrace the idolatry of Popery. "Hold out then for God's sake a little longer," he urged them, "and bow not down to idols, nor pay any reverence to images of wood and stone, who can neither hear your addresses, nor see your worship, nor have power to relieve you in your distresses." If the Jews believed that the Christian religion was true, they should turn to Protestantism, "that true Christianity . . . without the false traditions and wicked inventions and additions of the Popes, who have entirely perverted the truth and corrupted primitive Christianity." G. calculated that in 1816 the order would go out to return to Zion and rebuild the Land, and that in 1865 Jesus would return to earth to initiate the Millennium.[28]

The restoration of Israel continued to be a subject for learned religious works in the 1770s and 1780s. These included Joseph Eyre's *Observations upon the Prophecies relating to the Restoration of the Jews* (1771), E. W. Whitaker's *A Dissertation on the Prophecies relating to the Final Restoration of the Jews* (1784), and Richard Beere's *An Epistle to the Chief Priest and Elders of the Jews.* All three authors were Church of England ministers with strong millenarian beliefs. References to the restoration of the Jews also appeared frequently in sermons, religious tracts, and studies on prophecy and scriptural exegesis, as well as in the polemical literature of the controversy over Deism. As Clarke Garrett explains, "The *assumptions* on which seventeenth century millenarianism had rested were not repudiated in the more placid times that followed."[29]

The French Revolution and the Napoleonic wars, with their overthrow of the old order in France, Germany, Holland, and Italy, reawakened and stimulated millenarian speculation and thereby focused public attention once again on the restoration of the Jews. Not since the highly charged days of the Civil War had so many Englishmen acutely felt that the world was in the midst of some great upheaval. For those who were inclined to look to the Bible for guidance, it was not difficult to find scriptural texts that had long ago prophesied the shattering of established authority. Richard Beere, who believed that the final restoration of the Jews to the Holy Land would begin in 1791, wrote to William Pitt on 10 November 1790 to encourage him to keep the British fleet at full strength so that England might bring about the great event. Beere, interestingly, assured Pitt that his was "not an Utopian or visionary scheme, or the effects of a fruitful imagination; but founded in Revelation, Historical facts, and sound argument with the most accurate calculations." James Bicheno, a well-to-do Baptist minister who had participated in the David Levi–Joseph Priestley controversy in the late 1780s over the christological interpretation of prophecy, offered a systematic millenarian interpretation of the events in France in *The Signs of the Times.* Bicheno reasoned that as there was great purpose in God's works, there must have been some great meaning in the fall of one of the pillars of the Papist system. The key to understanding the meaning of those events was to be found in the prophecies of Daniel and Revelation, as well as in the prophets of ancient Israel. Bicheno claimed not only to understand what had happened in France, but also to be able to predict what lay ahead— the overthrow of the Pope and the ingathering of the Jews in preparation for their conversion. Four editions of Part 1 of Bicheno's *The Signs of the Times* appeared between 1792 and 1794. Part 2 appeared in early 1794, and by the end of the year three additional editions combining both parts had also come out. The following year saw the publication of three editions of another work by Bicheno, *A Word in Season,* which essentially repeated the same themes as his earlier effort.[30]

The most extravagant millenarian prophet of the period was Richard Brothers, a retired naval captain on half pay, who claimed that the French Revolution was the calamity foretold by Scripture, and that the restoration of the Hebrews (the Jewish people and the descendants of the Ten Tribes, i.e., the English) was at hand. Brothers began prophesying in 1794 that he had been sent by God to redeem England and lead the Jews back to the Holy Land, where he would rule over them until the Second Coming. His and his followers' pamphlets sold in the thousands. His *Revealed Knowledge of the Prophecies and Times* was discussed in all the literary reviews. He even managed to attract the support of an otherwise unknown Sephardi, Moses Gomez Pereira, who publicly accepted Brothers as the deliverer of the Jewish people in a tract published in 1795. The Privy Council considered Brothers a serious enough threat to law and order to arrest him in March 1795, have him declared insane, and confine him in a private madhouse in Islington until 1806.[31]

The single greatest boost to millenarian hopes in this period came from Napoleon's adventures in the Near East: his lightning conquest of Egypt in the summer of 1798, his capture of Jaffa and siege of Acre in the late winter and early spring of 1799, and his solemn appeal to the Jews of Africa and Asia to join him in marching against Syria and restoring the kingdom of Jerusalem.* The revolutionary force that had toppled the French episcopal hierarchy and humbled the Pope in his own territory was now doing battle with the Turk in the Holy Land itself, in preparation, it seemed, to restoring the Jews to their own territory. For the antiquarian Edward King, the French conquest of Egypt foreshadowed the return of the Jews to their homeland in boats provided by the French. The Unitarian minister Joseph Priestley, writing in the fall of 1798 from Pennsylvania, where he had been forced to flee because of his revolutionary political views, told friends in England that great prophecies were about to be fulfilled: the great work of restoring the Jews to their own country was "in agitation." "No period since that of our Saviour has been of so much importance as the present; and it is evident that the state of things is in a rapid motion. What is now done is only the commencement of something greater." Napoleon's appeal to the Jews convinced him that the French were intent on effecting the return of the Jews.[32]

When Napoleon summoned the Assembly of Jewish Notables in Paris in 1806 to endorse his program for the integration of Franco-Jewry and when in 1807 he convoked the Great Sanhedrin to give the decisions of the former body greater religious

---

*Interestingly, Napoleon's appeal to the Jews aroused little interest among the Jews themselves. In Eastern Europe, where the traditional faith in the return to Zion remained unshaken, little confidence was placed in the proclamation, while in Western Europe the desire to win political rights had gained precedence over the longing to return to Zion. Baruch Mevorach, ed., *Napoleon u-tekufato* [Napoleon and His Age] (Jerusalem, 1968), p. 15.

sanction, some Englishmen again looked to France to realize God's promises to the Jews. The reestablishment of the Jewish "legislature" after a hiatus of 1700 years suggested to religiously excitable persons that Divine Providence was at work, even in atheistic France. The first annual report of the London Society for Promoting Christianity among the Jews (hereafter referred to as the London Society) noted that, although Napoleon's aims may have been narrowly political, the proceedings of the Parisian Sanhedrin were "by no means void of incidents which lead the reflecting mind to anticipate the completion of God's promise." The Unitarian *Monthly Repository* commented:

> The events in relation to the Jews that have lately occurred in France cannot fail of exciting the attention of all such, of whatever religious profession, as are "waiting for the consolation of Israel;" though we are aware that the mere man of the world will smile at them, and the mere politician deem them beneath his notice. The Almighty sometimes mocks human expectations by bringing about the greatest results from operations that are almost imperceptible. The world has witnessed, with total unconcern, the annihilation, within these few years, of the papal dominion, and the judgments of Heaven upon those countries which had "given their power to the beast," and "become drunk with the blood of the saints."[33]

Among the books the London Society recommended to its members was F. D. Kirwan's translation of the transactions of the Sanhedrin, published in London in 1807. On the surface, Kirwan's own motives in making the proceedings available in English seem prosaic; he explained that he sought to gratify the great curiosity aroused by "the novelty of a Jewish assembly deliberating on the national interests of a people which had so long ceased to be numbered among nations." But he also appeared angered and disappointed by the Sanhedrin's decisions encouraging acculturation. In the introduction, he criticized French Jewry for bending the Jewish law to fit Napoleon's demands: "They have manifested a culpable readiness to accede to or even anticipate whatever might suit the views of their government, without much regard to the precepts of their law." If it had not been for the resistance of the rabbis in the Sanhedrin, they would have gone so far as to endorse mixed marriages. The impiety of the French, Kirwan sadly noted, was strongly contagious and had crept in among the Jews. At one solemn gathering, "the cyphers of Napoleon and of Josephine were profanely blended with the unutterable name of Jehovah, and the Imperial Eagle was placed over the Sacred Ark." Kirwan's regret over the reformist outlook of the Sanhedrin is in itself evidence that his interest in the Jewish assembly was more than that of a disinterested journalist. As a good patriot, he could have been expected to lambaste anything French, but why should he have been so vexed over the compliance of the Franco-Jewish leadership unless he expected something higher of them?[34]

The decisions of the Sanhedrin to which Kirwan had reacted so negatively were also interpreted in a positive manner by men of equally strong conversionist beliefs. An anonymous reviewer of Robert Atkins's *A Compendious History of the Israelites* in *The Gentleman's Magazine* in 1810 spoke encouragingly of the progressive improvement in the Jews of France made by recent events. Bonaparte's object—"to assimilate the customs and ceremonies of the Jews to those of the Christians"—was a laudable one. The moral degeneracy of the Jews was diminishing, and in Atkins's words (as quoted by the reviewer), "a new era in the history of this remarkable race of people has recently commenced which will probably produce a complete regeneration in their modes of thinking and acting."[35] Although the reviewer never explicitly stated that he viewed the change in the manners and morals of the Jews as a prelude to their conversion, it is difficult to believe that this hope was far from his thoughts for, as we have seen, a basic assumption of English conversionism was that the more thoroughly English the Jews became, the nearer they would come to embracing Christianity.

On the other hand, the fascination of Englishmen with emancipation and its aftermath in France was not in every instance the manifestation of conversionist philo-Semitism. The two articles on the Parisian Sanhedrin by Isaac D'Israeli (father of the Tory Prime Minister), in the *Monthly Magazine* in 1807,[36] were not written to cater to any particular religious outlook, but to satisfy a genuine curiosity of an educated public that was familiar with the broad contours of ancient Jewish history and to whom the reappearance of the Sanhedrin, however altered, would in itself be a startling event. One major obstacle to seeing the hand of God in Napoleon's Jewish assemblies was the intensely conservative outlook that the educated classes of England had adopted after their initial enthusiasm for the French Revolution had turned sour. In 1799, Samuel Horsley, Bishop of Rochester, attacked Edward King's interpretation of the happenings in France and the Near East as a fulfillment of prophecy and urged a moderate, reasonable interpretation of Scriptural texts. Horsley believed that interpretations that referred prophecy to purely secular events were fanciful and mischievous and ultimately dangerous to the established political and social order. He thought it highly improbable that the "atheistical democracy" of France would be instrumental in the conversion of the Jews; on the contrary, "the French democracy, from its infancy to the present moment, has been a conspicuous and principal branch at least of the Western Antichrist."[37]

Millenarian ideas, moreover, were unpatriotic insofar as they attributed any special mission to the French, with whom Britain was at war almost continuously from 1793 to 1815, and dangerous to the established order insofar as they projected a new, radically different world. The desire for stability and the urge to reject any idea or program too closely associated with the upheavals in France made it unlikely that the propertied classes would seriously entertain any notion of reforming the status of the Jews so as to bring about their conversion. The Evangelical party, which included both Anglicans and Dissenters—the party within Anglo-Christianity most eager to convert the Jews—was also one of the pillars of the reaction. Their political conservatism prevented them from advocating any change in the political status of the Jews until years after Waterloo. The net impact, then, of the millenarianism stimulated by the Revolution on the condition of the Jews was probably as negative as it was positive. It appealed too much to sectarian sensibilities and was too closely associated with the radical discontent of the poor to influence the traditional rulers of England.

The divorce between conversionism and emancipation in the three decades after the outbreak of the French Revolution did not mean that there was any waning of interest on the part of respectable Englishmen in converting the Jews. On the contrary, the growth of Evangelicalism at the end of the eighteenth century and the beginning of the nineteenth created a broad base of support for the first organized effort to convert the Jews by direct missionary activity. With its great emphasis on practical piety and its repudiation of an excessive concern with abstruse doctrinal issues, Evangelicalism sought to engage both Churchmen and Dissenters in a campaign to make England a religious nation. The humbling of Papal power made the Evangelicals feel that the denominational divisions of the past were intolerable and that great conquests could be made by acting in unison.[38] This non-denominational concern for practical activity manifested itself in the creation of a number of voluntary societies that, in the words of one historian, "provided a romantic cause which could enlist idealism and harness vague feelings of benevolence to religious ends."[39] The major institutional creations of Evangelicalism included the London Missionary Society (1795), the Religious Tract Society (1799), the British and Foreign Bible Society (1804), the London Society for Promoting Christianity among the Jews (1809), and the Society for Promoting the Observance of the Sabbath (1809).

The London Society for Promoting Christianity among the Jews, then, was not an isolated effort of a handful of fanatics, but a small part of a wide-scale undertaking to revitalize religious life in England. As an institution, it grew out of a special committee that the London Missionary Society had created in 1806 or early 1807 to work exclusively among the Jews of the metropolis. The central figure in the committee and later in the early years of the London Society was Joseph Frey, an erratic and ambitious convert from Judaism who eventually proved to be a great embarrassment to his respectable Christian supporters. Born in Franconia in 1771, Frey had received a traditional Jewish education and in his early years had earned a living as a private tutor, *shohet*, and *hazan*. Under unknown circumstances, he was baptized in 1798 and went to study at a seminary in Berlin. In July 1801, having completed his studies, he sailed for London to join the London Missionary Society, intending to travel with a group bound for South Africa to do missionary work there. The Missionary Society decided that Frey would be more effective among the Jews of London than among the unconverted natives of Africa, so he was sent to study at a seminary at Gosport until May 1805, when he commenced "his regular labours" among the Jews of London.[40]

Frey's missionary activities included composing Hebrew tracts, preaching the Gospel in the Jewish areas of London (the eastern fringe of the City, Houndsditch, Spitalfields, Whitechapel, and Goodman's Fields), and directing a school for the children of the Jewish poor, which the Society opened in January 1807. As the London Missionary Society's chief object was the conversion of the heathen in Africa and the Indies, it did not lavish much money or attention on the conversion of the Jews in England. Frey, on the other hand, was bursting with ambition and energy. He wanted a boarding school for Jewish children to remove them from their home environment and extensive financial aid for potential converts, but his plans were repulsive to most evangelical sensibilities at the time. He grew increasingly restless at his inability to expand his activities within the framework of the London Missionary Society. How, he asked the committee, "can you be satisfied with 12 children in the school whilst at least 50 or 100 might share the same unspeakable blessings? God forbid!" In the summer of 1808, he and some of the members of the Jewish Committee broke away from the parent body and formed the London Society for Promoting Christianity among the Jews.[41]

The Society grew rapidly from its inception, both in the scope of its activities and in the amount of financial support it enjoyed. In 1809, it took a long lease on a former Huguenot chapel in Brick Lane, Spitalfields,* in order to have a permanent center for its missionary work in the Jewish quarter. The Society continued to provide lectures to the Jews, expanded its free school, and established various workshops (a basket manufactory, a printing shop, a candlewick manufactory) to provide jobs for converts, who were without exception destitute and cut off from all future employment within the Jewish community by virtue of their conversion. For those Jews who turned to the Society, its most powerful attraction may well have been the Temporary Relief Fund, which offered financial aid to prospective and recent converts. The Society financed its programs through nationwide fund-raising tours and annual membership dues. In 1829, there were

*The building, which is still standing, has an interesting history. It was erected in 1743 by Huguenot refugees, leased to the London Society in 1809, and then converted to a Wesleyan Chapel, which it remained for most of the nineteenth century. In 1898, it was occupied by an ultraorthodox Jewish group, *Mahzikei Ha-Dat,* and known as the Spitalfields Great Synagogue. It has recently been purchased from the *Mahzikei Ha-Dat* by Pakistani Moslems who intend to convert it to a mosque.

thirty-six provincial auxiliaries, many in rural areas where there were very few real Jews to be converted. H. H. Norris, a key figure in the High Church party, stated in 1825 that since its founding the London Society had disbursed £135,000. Melvin Scult has calculated that the one hundred or so converts (half of whom were children) made under the auspices of the London Society between 1809 and 1816 cost about £500 each, and that the average annual income of the Society in the first ten years of its operations was £7,290. In the 1820s, the average annual income rose to £12,687. Not all this money was spent in London, since in 1818 the Society began operating small missions in Germany, Poland, and the Near East. But the amounts raised annually give a good indication of the extensive support the Society enjoyed.[42]

The day-to-day work of the Society was carried on by Frey and several little-known clergymen, but the officers were drawn from the front ranks of the Evangelical party. William Wilberforce was vice-president from its inception. When the Society became a Church of England institution in 1815, Sir Thomas Baring, of the famous banking firm of the same name, assumed the presidency and held that office until his death in 1848. Other prominent Evangelicals who were active in the London Society included Charles Simeon, Fellow of King's College, Cambridge; Robert Grant, younger son of Charles Grant, an energetic member of the Clapham Sect; Henry Thornton, Wilberforce's next door neighbor on Clapham Common; Legh Richmond, the author of many popular tales of simple piety; and Thomas Babington, his son Thomas, Jr., and Zachary Macaulay—the uncle, first cousin, and father, respectively, of Thomas Babington Macaulay. As a young woman of intense Evangelical faith, Anne Gladstone, the older sister of the future Prime Minister, was greatly interested in the work of the Society.[43] The Duke of Kent, younger brother of the Prince Regent (later George IV), served as Patron of the Society until 1816, adding the proper note of royal approbation to the enterprise.

Despite almost universal agreement about the desirability of converting the Jews, the London Society was not without its critics. Many thoughtful Christians who were in full agreement with the aims of the London Society looked askance at the methods Frey used, questioning not only their ethicality but also their efficacy. Detractors of the Society felt that the material relief the

Society offered to the Jewish poor was little more than a bribe to comply with the outward forms of Christianity. As destitution was so prevalent in the Jewish community, it was felt that many of the Jews converted by the Society were rogues and opportunists, who were willing to undergo conversion for any kind of short-term material gain. M. Sailman's contemporary exposé of the Society, *The Mystery Unfolded,* claimed to describe in detail how Frey and his associates would go about gaining converts. Sailman charged that they would purchase some small article for a few pennies from the Jewish boys who hawked things in the streets and then would leave five or seven shillings for it. The same benevolent deed would be repeated again and again. Once the confidence of the lad had been gained, he would be told that if he came to hear Frey on the following Sunday he would receive a fine suit of clothing. The anonymous Jewish author of a *Letter to Mr. Frey* reported the case of a young man who was bribed with £2 to attend Frey's lectures and told by Frey, "Never mind your father, come to hear me, bring with you as many Jewish boys as you can procure, and I'll make a man of you." As one critic poetically summed the matter up:

> 'Tis true 'tis strange, and strange 'tis true,
> Cash *buys* but cannot *keep* a Jew.
> The meanest, trembling, bribed to lie,
> Back to the "God of Israel" fly,
> When poverty has ceased to scare,
> And hope is buoyant o'er despair.
>
> . . . .
>
> All faiths are equal to a wretch in need.
> Not one from choice has joined their train,
> Or can from principle remain;
> Aware of this, they compromise,
> And wear a sort of thin disguise.
> So Cohen can both faiths unite,
> Still Jew, and yet a Christian quite;
> Receives the rites and pay of both,
> And serves two masters nothing loth.[44]

In the nature of things, the specific accusations hurled at Frey and his associates cannot be confirmed or denied. At the same time, however, there is no question that his detractors were correct in denouncing conversion by purchase. The 246 Jews converted in London under the Society's auspices between 1809 and 1838 were a ragged and none too respectable lot. Middle-class Jews who embraced Christianity or married Christians during these years did so without any push from the London Society, whose missionary work reached only the very poorest element in the Jewish community. The Society itself admitted that "persons of superior station amongst the Jews . . . prefer private baptism." The author of a *Letter to Mr. Frey* challenged him to produce "one respectable Jew, one honest man" among the converts he had made. A notorious case frequently cited by critics of the London Society was that of the convert Jacob Josephson, who while serving as clerk to the Rev. Lewis Way, a zealous and generous supporter of the London Society, was caught stealing the plate from Way's country estate, as well as forging a check on Way's banker for £600. Prior to his apprehension, his name had figured in another scandal of equally embarrassing dimensions. It was discovered in 1816 that Frey was carrying on an affair with Josephson's wife, a "reformed" whore who had already produced several illegitimate children by a recruiting sergeant. The London Society hushed up the matter as best it could and packed Frey off to New York, where he carried on his missionary work under the banner of the American Society for Meliorating the Condition of the Jews. After the scandal broke, critics of the Society also charged Frey with being a frequent visitor to houses of ill repute. There were numerous other instances in which the Society's converts embarrassed their supporters. Judah Catarevus, a Jerusalem-born "rabbi," reputedly of great learning, who was baptized with much ceremony and employed by the Society to do missionary work in London, was found visiting a whorehouse in Houndsditch and dismissed from his post. In January 1812, the Secretary of the Society wrote to the Spanish and Portuguese Jews' Synagogue about rumors that certain books that had come into the possession of the Society, presumably through recent converts, had been stolen from the synagogue. A home for female converts set up in 1813 had to be shut down in 1816 because the women were too rowdy and dissolute—"the general habits of the lower classes of Jewish females" were "an obstacle to its successful management."[45]

In 1816, another of Frey's converts, William Leigh (born Benjamin Levy), stood trial in the Court of King's Bench for his participation in a scheme to defraud a group of merchants of goods worth more than £50,000. Leigh had married a non-Jewish woman in the Church of England and changed his name at the time. The following excerpt from the court proceedings confirms the charge of the London Society's critics about the hollowness of the conversions made under its auspices:

Q: Is your father a Gentile too?
A: You had better inquire, I never asked him.
Q: You became a Gentile, and, of course, became a Christian?
A: I was taken to a Jewish chapel at Hackney, and had some water thrown upon me.
Q: You still swear by the old testament?
A: Yes.
Q: You are a Jew still?
A: Yes.[46]

The Liverpool *maskil* Moses Samuel chided the London Society in 1827 for treating the conversion of a solitary Polish Jew as a magnificent triumph and glorious addition to the strength of Christianity. He reminded them of "the men whom you blazoned forth as champions of conversion a few years back" who had "dropped off one after the other, some through treachery, others through repentance, leaving you nothing behind but the narrations of their wonderful conversion."[47]

Even the children who were enrolled in the London Society's free school were not above suspicion. It was charged that they were the illegitimate offspring of Jewish men by Christian women, especially servant girls working in Jewish homes. The records of the London Society confirm at least some of the charge. For example, in March of 1810, Daniel William Hipkins, about ten years old, the illegitimate son of a Jew by a Christian woman, was proposed for admission into the school. A year later the Committee decided that no illegitimate children should be received into the school, a tacit admission that this had been the practice previously. At the time the scandal erupted over Frey's affair with Mrs. Josephson, however, it was said that some of her illegitimate children were enrolled in the school.[48]

The remarkable thing about the tawdry triumphs of the London Society's day-to-day activity is that it did not shake the faith of the officers and membership. As the previous evidence indicates and as the Society's detractors were well aware, the gap between the lofty, spiritualized rhetoric of the Society and the dismal, almost pathetic results of its efforts was enormous. It is astonishing that men of character and intelligence like Wilberforce and Grant could believe that the conversion of a few dozen down-and-out Jews, many of questionable morals, was a magnificent triumph for Christianity. One explanation may be suggested by the concept of cognitive dissonance, a notion used by social psychologists to describe the phenomenon of continuing to uphold one's deepest beliefs in the face of empirical evidence contradicting these beliefs. The commitment of the Evangelicals to the desirability and possibility of the conversion of the Jews was so strong that it was able to overcome any rational evaluation of the London Society's results.

A less neurotic reaction to the actual results of the London Society's efforts over the years would have been one of futility and disgust. But the Society's official reaction remained just the opposite: the Jews were God's special people; they had preserved the truth Christians now enjoyed and were to have the honor of introducing the Millennium. For all this, Christendom owed the Jews a debt of gratitude. How, then, were the English to show their gratitude to the Jews and at the same time also compensate them for the wrongs inflicted in the past? A political reform of the status of the Jews was never a real possibility in the minds of conversionists in the first few decades of the new century, for offering the Jews greater civil liberties would have meant tampering with the established order in Church and State. As the Rev. Joseph Woolf, a convert whom the Society employed as a missionary in the Near East, wrote to the *Morning Chronicle* in 1827, "I should be very sorry to see a Jew or Papist in Parliament. A Protestant government ought never to be mixed with Talmudists or Papists." The arch-Tory Sir Robert Inglis, a member of the Committee of the London Society from the very beginning, was a vociferous opponent of the Jewish Emancipation Bills introduced in the Commons from 1830 on. The Society's policy was to show the Jews kindness and civility "whenever the business of life, or the accident of meeting bring you near to a Jew," and through this attitude of care and compassion to bring the Jews closer to Christianity, the ultimate act of loving-kindness. In the words of one anonymous pamphleteer:

I am inclined to believe this soft and silent mode of universal conciliation in outward behaviour alone would be a powerful engine towards the conversion of the Jews. It would be like the water thrown upon the stone while the mason is cutting it. It would soften their hearts . . .; it would dispose them to attend to the arguments offered to their consideration by the learned, and to accept the larger, but not less real offers of service made to them by the rich of employment for themselves and education for their children.[49]

In the mid-1820s, a change in the British political climate encouraged a new approach to the Jews among some liberal conversionists. Fears for the stability of the established order that had been generated by the French Revolution and the working-class agitation between 1815 and 1820 had receded. It became possible to reexamine certain traditional principles of political life. Bills to emancipate Roman Catholics, for example, were passed in the House of Commons in 1821 and 1825, although they were defeated in the Lords. In this less repressive political atmosphere, a number of conversionists came to believe that perhaps the most appropriate way of bestowing kindness on the Jews, and of eventually converting them, was to grant them greater civil rights. Conversionists of this school broke away from the London Society in 1826 to form an organization that would reflect their more tolerant perspective—the Philo-Judaean Society; some retained membership in the parent organization as well. They were joined by Evangelicals from outside the Church of England, who had been shut out of the London Society in 1815 and who were naturally eager to deprive the Anglican Church of its privileged position within the state.

In its day-to-day work, the Philo-Judaean Society resembled the London Society: it distributed tracts, sponsored lectures, operated a free school, and provided relief to the Jewish poor. But in all its efforts, the Philo-Judaean Society was much less aggressive in winning over individual converts. In its literature, it never explicitly declared that its immediate goal was the conversion of individual Jews, although the ultimate conversion of the entire Jewish people was the implicit aim of all its work. Like the London Society, it stressed the indebtedness of Christianity to Judaism, and like the London Society, it maintained that the restoration of the Jews to their own land would bring a great measure of blessedness upon all the nations of the world. But this restoration had to be preceded by some visible changes among the Jews, and on this point, the Philo-Judaean Society parted company with the London Society. It declared that however many individuals among the Jews were converted, redemption could come only from God. As a nation, the Jews would remain unconverted until God chose to do something about them.[50]

The major role of the Philo-Judaean Society, then, was to prepare the way for divine intervention in the fate of the Jews. As one speaker at the first annual meeting put it, "The time was coming, judging from appearances, rapidly too, when God would again lead his chosen people out of captivity. Though it may not be in our power to erect the building, yet we may collect the materials, like David, to whom was said, 'It is well for thee that it was in thy heart to build a temple for the great God.' " The Jews had sunk into "a lamentable state of intellectual debasement" through their isolation from the intellectual and moral advancement of the modern world, an isolation constantly reinforced by Christian hostility and ill-treatment. The Philo-Judaeans sought to remedy this in part through their educational and charitable work—a kind of softening-up operation prior to heavenly intervention— although they were quick to deny that the material aid they offered was a bribe to profess Christianity.[51]

The major difference between the two groups was, of course, the commitment of the Philo-Judaeans to promoting the integration of the Jews into English life through the removal of discriminatory statutes at the national and local level. In the words of the journal of the London Society, the Philo-Judaeans embraced "the temporal as well as the spiritual interests of the Jewish nation." On 29 June 1827, a petition of several members of the Philo-Judaean Society was read in the House of Commons urging the repeal of the "oppressive" laws under which the Jews labored. The petition was ordered to be laid on the table and nothing more was heard of it; a second petition was presented some time later. Interestingly, this effort at Jewish emancipation antedated by a full year any public activity on the part of the Jews themselves. The first move by a Jew was the petition of Moses Levy of Great Alie Street. It was read in the Commons on 19 June 1828 and suffered the same fate as the petitions of the Philo-Judaean Society.[52] Both of these early moves to obtain legislative relief preceded the well-chronicled efforts of the financiers Isaac Lyon Goldsmid and Nathan Rothschild, which only came after the successful repeal of the Test and Corporation Acts in 1828 and the passage of the Catholic Emancipation Act in 1829.

The liberal Evangelicals who supported the Philo-Judaean Society were more successful in improving the status of the Jews within the City of London than they were at the national level. The first case to engage their attention was that of the brothers Abraham and Saul Saul.[53] Their father, David Saul, a butcher with a shop in Old Gravel Lane (which was in the East End, outside the jurisdiction of the City of London), was born in England and raised as a Jew. Some time before the birth of his eldest son, Abraham, in 1779, he openly repudiated Judaism without, however, undergoing baptism. He carried on business on the Jewish Sabbath, observed none of the festivals or fasts, belonged to no congregation, and sold pork in his shop. At his wife's insistence, though, he did agree to have his sons circumcised, but she died soon after the birth of the younger son, Saul, and he raised the boys as Christians. He sent them to Christian schools and apprenticed them to Christian butchers. In November 1802, Abraham Saul married Elizabeth Phillpot in Hackney parish church and in September of the following year was baptized in that same church. Saul Saul married Frances Adams in February 1804 in Dagenham parish church, Essex, and he, too, was later baptized there. Both brothers raised their children as Christians.

The Saul brothers, who were, strictly speaking, no longer Jews, encountered head-on the anti-Jewish hostility of the City of London's merchant rulers when they moved their residences and their business to Aldgate High Street, within the borders of the City, in the fall of 1815. The statutes of the City required persons who wished to operate retail businesses there to take up the freedom of the City—a course not open to believing Jews, since it required taking an oath upon the faith of a Christian. The Saul brothers did not consider themselves Jews, however, so they applied accordingly to the Chamberlain's Office to purchase the freedom of the City, Abraham in November 1815 and Saul in June 1816. In both instances, they were required to petition the Court of Aldermen for permission to be admitted as freemen, since a standing order of the Court of Aldermen from 3 May 1785 barred baptized Jews from purchasing their freedom. (This standing order was motivated, clearly, by commercial rivalry: it was intended to keep Jews who had converted for temporal gain from setting up retail shops within the City. The Saul brothers claimed that their conversions did not fall within the spirit of the order, since they had occurred thirteen years prior to their taking up residence within the City.) The Court of Aldermen never responded to their petitions, so the brothers continued to carry on their retail business in Aldgate High Street.

Late in 1819, probably at the instigation of rival butchers, the Chamberlain prosecuted the brothers in the Lord Mayor's Court for being in violation of the City's statutes. They again petitioned the Lord Mayor and the Court of Aldermen, but to no avail, so in Easter term 1820, they applied to the Court of King's Bench for a writ of mandamus compelling the Court of Aldermen to complete their application for the freedom of the City. The Court refused to act, however, claiming that such a matter was not within its jurisdiction. In December of that year, commercial rivals of the brothers commenced twenty-four separate penal actions against them in one day. The legal expenses alone were ruinous, amounting to between £300 and £400, so the brothers agreed in January 1821 to move their shop out of the City if all the proceedings against them were dropped. But first they tried one more move and applied to the Court of Common Council, a more liberal body, whose Committee for General Purposes recommended to the Court of Aldermen, in July 1821, their admission to the freedom of the City. The Court of Aldermen ignored the recommendation and the status quo remained. On 13 May 1826, four fresh actions were entered against them in the Lord Mayor's Court. A year earlier, however, the Saul family had determined a new course of action to head off legal proceedings such as these. In July 1825, David Gill Saul, age twenty-two, the eldest son of Abraham Saul, also a butcher and a Christian from birth, applied to the Court of Common Council to be admitted a freeman of the City. After a year of petitions and counterpetitions, of committee recommendations and reconsiderations, the Court of Common Council and the Chamberlain had agreed to admit him. Faced with a new wave of persecutory suits, which may have been promoted by the successful application of young David Gill Saul, Abraham and Saul Saul again petitioned the Court of Aldermen in July and December of 1826 to dismiss the charges pending against them and to admit them as freemen. Once again they received no satisfaction, and once again they turned to the Court of Common Council. The latter body recommended once more that the Court of Aldermen accede to their petition; once more the Aldermen refused.[54]

At this point—the spring or summer of 1827—the Philo-Judaeans took up the Saul brothers' cause. They began a campaign to repeal the standing order of 1785. They publicly attacked the narrow-mindedness of the Court of Aldermen: it made a mockery out of the supposed advantages, spiritual and material, that conversion was supposed to bring. John A. Q. Brown, an active member of the Society with strong millenarian views, wrote to the religious weekly *The World* in July 1827 to denounce the persecutory attitude of the Aldermen: "If this be the wisdom of the present day then I deplore the barbarism of England and believe that the spirit of persecution and intolerance is as much now ready to rear its . . . bestial heads as ever it was . . . during the dominance of popery or Mahomedanism." The Philo-Judaean Society petitioned the Court of Aldermen to rescind its standing order, and the nonconformist glass manufacturer Apsley Pellatt, a member of the Committee of the Philo-Judaean Society and later a leading member of the Protestant Dissenting Deputies, used his influence as a member of the Court of Common Council to gain passage of a resolution in favor of the Saul brothers. On 4 March 1828, the Court of Aldermen unanimously rescinded the standing order of 1785.[55]

The gain to the Jewish community in this particular case was negligible, but Pellatt and the Philo-Judaeans persisted in their efforts and set out to gain the same privileges for professing Jews. In 1829, Pellatt published a carefully reasoned plea for removing the barrier to admitting Jews to the freedom of the City. That same year, at Pellatt's urging, the Court of Common Council set up a special committee, of which Pellatt was a member, to consider this matter as well as the statute limiting the number of licensed Jewish brokers on the Royal Exchange to twelve. In December 1830, in accordance with the recommendation of the Committee, the Court of Common Council ruled that any person who was admitted a freeman could take the requisite oath in a manner conforming to his religious beliefs.[56]

Liberal Evangelicals were also active in the Parliamentary campaigns for the removal of Jewish disabilities, particularly in the early years of the struggle. Although the Philo-Judaean Society had petitioned Parliament as early as 1827, there was no concerted effort on the part of the Jewish community to obtain legislative relief until the debate over Catholic emancipation encouraged a few Jewish leaders to press for their own emancipation bill. Within Parliament, they found support among three groups —liberal Whigs, Utilitarian radicals, and conversionist Evangelicals—but particularly among the last two. The first Jewish Disabilities Bills (in 1830, 1833, 1834, and 1836) were introduced in the Commons by Robert Grant, a Philo-Judaean, and in the Lords by Lord Bexley (Nicholas Vansittart, Chancellor of the Exchequer, 1812–23), one of the founders of the Philo-Judaean Society. In the debate on the first Jewish Disabilities Bill, in April and May of 1830, the conversionist argument for emancipation did not figure prominently, even in the opening speech by Robert Grant. He mentioned the origins of Christianity in Judaism and hinted at the involvement of Christians in the fate of the Jews, but at the same time he indicated that he would not raise the question of prophecy. In all likelihood, he felt that this kind of argument would carry little weight with his colleagues—a testimony to the decline of millenarian-conversionist ideas—and so he argued his case on secular, liberal grounds.[57] In the course of the debate, Thomas Babington Macaulay made his maiden speech, a defense of religious toleration along thoroughly secular lines. Although the young Macaulay had abandoned the evangelical faith of his father and uncle, both active members of the London Society, it is likely that some of their abstract compassion for the Jewish people had rubbed off on him. That the philo-Semitic concerns of other Evangelical fathers also may have encouraged the pro-emancipation views of their liberal sons is an intriguing possibility, but one that could never be satisfactorily confirmed.

Perhaps the most startling example of the commitment of some Evangelicals to improving the temporal lot of the Jews was their participation in a series of protest meetings over anti-Jewish decrees in Russia. On 2 December 1827, the Czar signed two ukases designed to restrict further the territory allotted to Jewish settlement. One decreed the transfer of the Jews from all villages in the Grodno region into the towns; the other ordered the banishment of all Jewish residents from the city of Kiev. The London daily papers carried stories about the expulsions, and early in December, at a meeting of a group of Christians and Jews who met regularly to discuss theological issues, the plight of Russian Jewry was discussed. Moses E. Levy, a wealthy lumber merchant, army contractor, and sugar planter in Cuba and Florida, then resident in London,[58] proposed that London Jews meet to protest the Russian decrees. Largely through his initiative, meetings were held on 5 and 19 December at the London Tavern, Bishopsgate, from which the communal notables were conspicuously absent. Levy thought the reason was that "those who had money" were too "engaged in the improvement of their fortunes or in fashionable amusements" or too "in dread of exciting any hostile feelings in persons possessed of power," but an equally powerful motive for their absence may have been their suspicion of Levy. His schemes to redeem Jewry by founding Jewish colonies in Florida and his participation in public meetings on religious topics no doubt made them uncomfortable. According to one account, the meetings were not "numerously attended," but there were a number of Christians present.[59]

A few weeks later, on 1 January 1828, the liberal Christians who were participating in the previously mentioned religious discussions staged a sympathy meeting at the King's Head Tavern in the Poultry to protest the Russian persecutions. Apsley Pellatt served as chairman of the meeting and delivered a long plea for religious toleration. It was not fitting, he said, that on account of their religion men should be deprived of advantages that belonged to them as members of civil society. Every man had a right to his own religious beliefs, for which he was answerable only to God. His discussion of the expulsions in Russia quickly broadened into a wide-ranging discussion of anti-Jewish persecution through the ages, in England and elsewhere. Speakers touched on and deplored the expulsion of the Jews from England in 1290, the exclusion of the Jews from the freedom of the City, and the abysmal position of the Jews in the Papal States. In closing, the meeting passed a number of resolutions condemning the decrees and affirming its desire to assist the Jews in any effort they made to obtain their rights in England and on the Continent.[60]

Public protests in London had no impact, of course, on Russia's Jewish policy. The importance of this display of concern, however, lies not in what it actually accomplished, but in what it reveals about the priorities and sensibilities of an important group within Anglo-Christianity. To be a religiously tolerant man is one thing; to champion publicly the cause of oppressed Jews living more than a thousand miles away is something altogether different. There were no parallel expressions of concern on the part of Protestants elsewhere in Europe; this kind of activist philo-Semitism was a uniquely English phenomenon. And if liberal Evangelicals were powerless to influence events overseas, they were not so weak at home. In the struggle to extend the full scope of civil rights to the Jewish population, prominent Evangelicals appeared again and again in the front ranks of those whom the Jews relied on to promote their cause.

Philo-Semitic Evangelicals were only one element within the Church of England. There was, however, also a vocal High Church party, which, with its anti-liberal belief in an organic Christian state, preached a brand of anti-Semitism unchanged since the medieval period. Although the High Church party never came to dominate church affairs or to influence political life decisively at any time in the Georgian period, the Evangelicals were energetic and activist and knew how to flex their political muscle to achieve their ends. As for the long-term impact of conversionist philo-Semitism, it would appear that England possessed a religious tradition largely absent elsewhere, one that wished to appease rather than persecute the Jews. In the final analysis, however, other social and intellectual developments— the multiplication of religious sects, the spread of religious indifference, and the triumph of a noninterventionist view of the state —were more instrumental than conversionist philo-Semitism in creating an atmosphere of tolerance for Anglo-Jewish life.

3

Anti-Jewish Sentiment—Religious and Secular

Anti-Jewish sentiment in England during the eighteenth and early nineteenth centuries is a tribute to the persistent character of religious bigotry. Prior to the expulsion of 1290, anti-Jewish beliefs in their classical religious form—the Jew as Christ-killer, as the servant of Satan, as the eternally damned outcast—were as widely diffused in England as they were on the Continent. The absence of a Jewish community in England from 1290 to 1655, while reducing the intensity of this hostility, did not result in its complete disappearance. Religious plays and pageants kept alive the physical caricature of the grotesque, misanthropic Jew, and sermons, which became an important means of spreading Christian doctrine in the thirteenth century, explored his theological odium.[1] The gradual desacralization of English life in the eighteenth century and the spread of philo-Semitic conversionist hopes begun in the previous century robbed these medieval beliefs about the depravity of the Jew of much of their force and confined them to increasingly smaller circles of High Church enthusiasts. At no time during the Georgian period, however, did these beliefs ever fade away completely. They may not have been able decisively to influence official state policy toward the Jews, but this does not mean that they were absent from the debates over what that policy should be. Much of the ardor that had been invested in theological anti-Semitism, moreover, was rechanneled in the eighteenth century into secular versions of anti-

Jewish hostility. The Jews still functioned as objects of hatred and contempt for individuals displacing and projecting their own feelings, but this hatred was now expressed in a form more appropriate to an increasingly secular society. Fortunately for Anglo-Jewry, the secularization of religious bigotry was only one small aspect of a much larger transformation that also gave rise to beliefs and forces deeply opposed to the perpetuation of virulent anti-Semitism.

To discover the survival of medieval beliefs about the Jews well into the eighteenth century comes at first as something of a shock. The Georgian period, with its calm veneer of political stability and its apparent high regard for rationality, would seem to be an incongruous setting for the blood libel, the charge of deicide, and other medieval superstitions. Educated Englishmen, with their disdain for religious enthusiasm and their worship of reason, would not seem to be the ideal purveyors of intolerant theological doctrines from the early centuries of Christianity. Yet, more than a few otherwise sensible men, most of whom were adherents of the High Church party, continued to hold beliefs about the Jews that were in no significant way different from those held several centuries before. It was believed by many persons that the Jews continually blasphemed Jesus in their prayers and writings; that they considered it meritorious to plunder Christians; that they murdered Christian children in order to obtain their blood; that they were children of the Devil, the incarnation of Evil, the synagogue of Satan, and Antichrist; that they had one eye smaller than the other; that they were distinguished by a peculiar smell; that their skin was impregnated with an inordinate amount of filth; and that they had a mark of blood on one shoulder and a "malignant blackness" underneath their eyes that bespoke their guilt as murderers.[2]

The assumption underlying this catalogue of Jewish characteristics was a theological one: the Jews, having murdered Jesus, had placed themselves outside humanity; spiritually and physically, they were marked as perpetual aliens. Through the centuries they had remained obstinate and incorrigible in refusing to acknowledge the truth of Christianity. As outcasts and outlaws, as allies of Antichrist, they sought to overthrow Christendom. In the words of an anonymous pamphleteer in 1753, they prayed "in all their public and private devotions . . . for the sudden, universal, total and final subversion, extirpation, and perishing of the king-dom of Christ, of his gospel, and of all his members." The hostil-ity of the Jews to Christianity was so great, according to the Rev. William Romaine, a central figure in the early Evangelical revival, that they would crucify Jesus again if they had it in their power. "Are not the Jews open and professed enemies to our holy reli-gion?" Romaine asked. "Are they not bound in conscience to destroy it? Do not they still justify the horrid act of crucifying our blessed Saviour? Do they not deny his laws and government?"[3]

These traditional religious objections to treating the Jews in a humane way served as the primary argument against Jewish natu-ralization in 1753. The essence of Judaism, editorialized the *West-minster Journal,* was "an avowed contempt of Christ, an implacable hatred to Christians, and an impious detestation to Christianity." The opposition of the Jews to Christianity was as implacable as the opposition of the Devil, wrote one anonymous pamphleteer. "For they are his subjects, not Christ's, and as subjects to the Devil, they are in perpetual hostility with Christ, so that there can be no peace between them and Christians." The antinaturaliza-tion propagandists reasoned that, given the unrelenting hostility of the Jews to Christianity, it was foolhardy and dangerous to try to incorporate them into the English nation. The English consti-tution in church and state was Christian, founded upon the prin-ciples of Christianity, and, wrote one anonymous pamphleteer, "whatever openly and avowedly opposes these principles must endanger the constitution so far as its opposition has power." As the Jews prayed daily for "the total extirpation of Christianity and of all Christians," how, asked Romaine, "can it ever be thought that any Christian state should allow such professed enemies to be admitted into its privileges, much less to be on the same footing with its own natural-born subjects?" Archaicus admon-ished the public: "All intercommunity, by naturalizations, incor-porations, etc. with them [is] to be avoided as the future cause and forerunner of destruction to all that shall set so light by the word and decrees of the Omnipotent as to introduce any such monstrous and unnatural unions and connexions with them." Indeed, to naturalize the Jews or to act in any way to improve their temporal condition would be to challenge the will of Provi-dence. God had cast the Jews out of their native land and dis-persed them throughout the world. He had declared that they were to find no ease in their dispersion, but were to be preserved as a separate people, as a living monument to the truth of Christianity. If God had decreed all these arrangements, how could England take the Jews in and naturalize them? To do so would be to fly in the face of Scripture and to defy the decrees of the Almighty. Naturalization, wrote Jonas Hanway, by weakening the distinctive alienness of the Jews, must "wound" Christianity.[4]

The extent to which the vocabulary of traditional religious polemics dominated the antinaturalization propaganda is revealed by a content analysis of the Jew Bill literature. The label most frequently applied to the Jews in the antinaturalization literature was "crucifiers"; the next most commonly used epithet was "professed enemies of Christianity." Both labels frequently appeared in company with other religiously derived terms of disparagement, such as "infidels," "Antichrist," "children of the Devil," and "synagogue of Satan."[5]

Quantitatively, then, the enmity of the Jews toward Christianity was the primary characteristic used by the antinaturalization writers to stigmatize the Jews. This approach to understanding the nature of the anti-Jewish argument leaves unanswered, however, the question as to how this evidence is to be evaluated. The contexts in which these labels appeared may be more revealing than the actual labels themselves. It is not inconceivable, for example, that anti-Jewish pamphleteers used the vocabulary of a previous age, although they themselves no longer were moved by the religious concerns of that age. The labels, in other words, might have degenerated into general terms of abuse bereft of their original religious significance. Religiously indifferent propagandists may have employed these old labels as a matter of form, as a bow to the customary way of attacking Jews. Thomas Perry has argued in this vein that most of the violent anti-Jewish language of the 1753 clamor was inspired by the partisan nature of the political struggle underlying the controversy and should not be taken at face value. Clearly, this is an important caveat to bear in mind in evaluating the persistence of medieval attitudes toward the Jews. Supporters of the Jew Bill themselves recognized that much of the zeal for Christianity manifested by the opposition was politically inspired and manufactured for the occasion. Philo-Patriae explained that the agitation was got up by "those discontented with the administration" who needed an issue with which to challenge the ministry in the coming election. The opposition to the Jew Bill, he wrote, "proceeded mostly from party, envy, selfish views, and gross misrepresentations, as likewise *with a view to the future elections and not from Christianity, as the pretence is.*" The anonymous author of *The Crisis* thought that the word *Judaism* had become a cant word in the verbal arsenal of the opposition—"a mere Babel of ideas according to the character of the man that uses it."

> In the mouth of a Jacobite, Judaism is another name for the revolution of 1688, a limited monarchy, the Hanover legacy, and the royal family. . . . In the mouth of a pretended patriot and flaming bigot, Judaism is a Whiggish administration and House of Commons, a Protestant Bench of Bishops, liberty of conscience and an equitable toleration.

One anonymous pamphleteer sarcastically remarked how amazed he was by the lively spirit of Christianity that had so suddenly and remarkably started up. He had thought Christianity was not far from giving up the ghost, and then, lo and behold, the Jew Bill was passed and religion recovered. Now "we have convinced the world that we are a nation of Christians and not Jews."[6]

What then can be concluded about the anti-Jewish clamor of 1753? Was it primarily the resuscitation and manipulation of outdated religious attitudes for partisan ends, or was it the expression of a genuine religious antipathy to the Jews that was a carry-over from earlier periods? The answer, not unexpectedly, is a synthesis of both positions. Without doubt, much of the opposition to the Jew Bill derived from purely partisan objectives. The extravagance and foolishness of much of the propaganda against the Bill, such as doggerel about roast pork and foreskins or fraudulent advertisements signed with absurd Jewish names, are good evidence of this. The existence of this material, however, does not negate the clearly sincere and authentic religious sentiments of such anti-Jewish pamphleteers as the Rev. William Romaine. The clamor may have been precipitated for short-term political gains, but the feelings it allowed to surface and on which it played were hardly contrived for the occasion. Negatively charged images of the Jew, engendered originally by medieval anti-Semitism, had become part of England's cultural heritage. The very fact that the opposition saw there were political advantages to be gained by exploiting the latent religious anti-Semitism of the population is a testimony to the real existence of those feelings. One pro–Jew Bill pamphleteer pointed out that the leaders of the clamor, knowing "that the monosyllable *Jew* has some ideas attending it not very favorable to that people," saw "that they could with ease work up that inbred prejudice to a frenzy and make those believe, who will not be at pains to think for themselves . . . that St. Peter's Westminster and St. Paul's London are in danger of being turned into synagogues."[7]

Religious opposition to the Jew Bill was spearheaded by High Churchmen and country squires, but the main source of their political strength came from the lower-class support upon which they were able to draw. Whig observers, in attempting to understand the sudden upsurge of opposition to the Bill, concluded that the prejudices of the uneducated masses were responsible for the uproar. The Earl of Chesterfield, in a letter to his son on 26 November 1753, denounced the timidity of the Duke of Newcastle in giving in to "the absurd and groundless clamours of the mob." Horace Walpole thought that "the holy spirit" engendered by the agitation "seized none but the populace and the very lowest of the clergy." The hostility of the lower classes to the Jews in 1753 at times overflowed the boundaries of rhetorical excess and erupted in acts of violence. "Poor travelling Jews, who seek their daily bread by hawking and selling small wares in the country," were molested, insulted, and abused. In some instances, innkeepers refused to serve them food or to rent them rooms.[8]

It becomes increasingly difficult to trace after 1753 the presence and influence of traditional Christian beliefs about the Jews. In the absence of legislative moves around which such views might have been articulated, information about the older forms of animosity remains sporadic. That they continued to exist into the first decades of the nineteenth century, though, is attested to. A German visitor to England in 1782, while traveling in a coach from Dunstable to London, heard a tenant farmer remark that the Jews were eternally damned, "as cold-blooded and certain of himself as if he already saw them burning." When a deadly fever broke out on Gibraltar in the fall of 1804, a writer to the *St. James*

Chronicle suggested that the filth of the Jews was a probable cause of the pestilence, and in doing so, made reference to a number of ancient canards: "From the beginning of time they were a dirty race. They were driven out of Egypt on account of a contagious distemper, which, by means of their filthiness, was always among them, and the Romans would not allow them to dwell in Rome." The anonymous author of this letter believed that anyone who visited the Jewish districts of London would find that "the followers of Moses are the most nasty and filthy people under the canopy of heaven." In addition, he thought that if they did not reform themselves they should be shut up in a ghetto, as in Rome or Venice, and made to wear a badge when they came into the city. Robert Southey, in 1807, told of a public school where the boys rushed out of chapel on Easter Sunday singing

> He is risen, he is risen
> All the Jews must go to prison.

Southey also related the story of how one day some of these boys cut the straps of a Jewish hawker's box, causing all his ginger-bread nuts to fall into the street. When the master of the school demanded an explanation from the boys, one of them stepped forward and said, "Why, sir, did not they crucify our Lord?" As late as 1825, a popular collection of anecdotal material, *The Laughing Philosopher,* reprinted the following list, originally dating from the seventeenth century, of ailments suffered by the twelve tribes of Israel for their role in the crucifixion:

> The tribe of Judah treacherously delivered up our Lord, and thirty of them die by treason every year.
> The tribe of Reuben seized our Lord in the garden, and therefore the curse of barrenness is on all they sow or plant, and no green thing can flourish over their graves.
> The tribe of Gad put on the crown of thorns, and on every March 25th their bodies are covered with blood from deep and painful wounds.
> Those of Asher buffeted Jesus, and their right hand is always nearly a palm shorter than the left.
> Those of Naphtali jested with Christ about a herd of swine, since when they are all born with tusks, like wild boars.
> The tribe of Manasseh cried out, "His blood be on us and our children," and at every new moon they are tormented by bloody sores.

The tribe of Simeon nailed our Lord to the cross, and on the 25th of March, four deep and dreadful wounds are inflicted on their hands and feet.

Those of Levi spat on the Saviour, and the wind always blows back their saliva in their faces, so that they are habitually covered with filth.

The tribe of Issachar scourged Christ, and on the 25th of March blood streams forth from their shoulders.

The tribe of Zebulon cast lots for the garments, and on the same day the roof of their mouth is tortured by deep wounds.

The tribe of Joseph made the nails for crucifying Jesus, and blunted them to increase his sufferings; and therefore their hands and feet are covered with gashes and blood.

Those of Benjamin gave vinegar to Jesus; they all squint and are palsied, and have their mouths filled with little nauseous worms, which, in truth, (adds our author) is the case with all Jewish women after the age of twenty-five, because it was a woman who entreated the tribe of Joseph not to sharpen the nails used for the crucifixion of our Lord.[9]

Although medieval views of the Jews had not disappeared from English life by the beginning of the Victorian period, there is strong reason to believe they did not have the appeal—even for Tories—that they possessed in the mid-eighteenth century. During the early years of the parliamentary campaign for Jewish emancipation, conservative M.P.'s voiced their objections in largely secular terms. They did not stress, as their predecessors had, that the Jews were blasphemers and deicides, but emphasized that they were a distinct people and thus could not be considered part of the English nation. They still insisted on the inseparableness of religious and secular concerns, declaring that the constitution was Protestant and that Christian principles underlay the law of the land. But they did not argue from a theological viewpoint that it was Jewish enmity to Christianity that prevented their incorporation. What they did was to translate what had been formerly viewed as a theological characteristic of Jews —their status as outcasts and aliens—into more secular terms. In the minds of conservatives, it was still the status of the Jews as outsiders that prevented their integration, but this quality now had a much larger political and social dimension. "You cannot call them English," said the Tory Viscount Belgrave in the Commons on 17 May 1830, "even though they are born among us. They are no more Englishmen (in the sense, at least, of civil identification) than they are Romans, Poles, or Prussians, among whom we also find them." The arch-Tory Sir Robert Inglis told the Commons three years later, "A Jew could never be made an Englishman, even though he be born here. So long as he looks forward to another Kingdom, his sympathies would be given more to a Jew in Paris or Warsaw, than to a person residing in the same, or the next county to him."[10]

The above outlook characterized the thinking of most conservatives, but it should be noted that there still remained a fanatic fringe that couched its objections to Jewish emancipation in medieval religious terms. A Mr. Trant reminded the Commons on 17 May 1830 that those who were soliciting admission to the political nation were the descendants of those who had crucified Jesus. Although he had no wish to persecute them, he also saw no reason to bestow privileges on "those who were the enemies of Christ—who persecuted and opposed him, and trampled the cross under foot, and who would do so again if they had the opportunity."[11]

The belief in the Christian nature of the English state was a serious obstacle to admitting Jews to a full share in the political life of the nation. In the 1830s and 1840s, there were still enough men of influence who accepted this as a fundamental political principle to prevent the passage of a Jewish emancipation bill. This refusal to grant political equality was, however, a very different matter from the objections to Jews qua Jews raised in 1753. The intolerance expressed in that earlier debate was bitterly uncompromising and persecutory. By reviving charges about the fundamental inhumanity of the Jews and their murderous wishes toward Christians, the anti–Jew Bill agitators had appealed to the darker side of men's nature, awakening deep and troublesome fears. Eighty years later, this kind of appeal, pandering to the worst instincts of the population, had almost completely disappeared. The emancipation controversy was, by any standard, a polite and dignified affair, with no known instances of anti-Jewish hooliganism.

The gradual decline in the appeal and the credibility of the older anti-Semitism was largely a function of the secularization of English life. To believe that the Jews were allies of Antichrist and sought the overthrow of Christendom, men had to accept the demonological tenets of orthodox Christianity. The worldly character of Georgian religion, with its distaste for enthusiasm, did not provide a fertile setting for the cultivation of such views. From the end of the seventeenth century, Englishmen were becoming increasingly less likely to blame their misfortunes on the operation of demonic forces; they were beginning to conceive of an orderly and regular universe they could understand by rational means and of social and physical environments they could control and improve.[12] This kind of orientation to the natural world was in the long run hostile to the preservation of medieval modes of thinking about the Jews.

The demise of demonological anti-Semitism between the 1750s and the 1830s was not due entirely to the increasingly secular nature of English life and thought. Some consideration must also be given to the fact that the initial strength of this theologically derived anti-Semitism was not as great at the beginning of the eighteenth century as it was elsewhere in Europe. The relative weakness of this tradition, and the corresponding strength of conversionist philo-Semitism, can be traced to the absence of a visible Jewish presence during the three and a half centuries preceding the Cromwellian resettlement and to the concomitant lack of an ongoing tradition of concrete hostility on the part of Christians. This is not to imply that the presence of flesh-and-blood Jews created and sustained anti-Semitism, since it is the psychological needs of Christians—and not the actual character of Jewish life—that give anti-Semitism its power and appeal. In the absence of an organized Jewish community in the period 1290–1655, demonological stereotypes of Jews still managed to survive. What was lacking for over 350 years, however, were concrete issues on which anti-Jewish feelings could be focused. There were no protracted struggles, as in Germany, Poland, and Italy, over economic privileges or rights of settlement. Englishmen did not have the opportunities to exercise their anti-Semitic beliefs in the way other Europeans did; for three and a half centuries, they had no practice in hating real Jews, and so they were not particularly well prepared to hate Jews when a Jewish community was reestablished at the start of the modern period.

Although medieval forms of anti-Jewish sentiment tended to disappear over the course of the eighteenth century, there was no parallel movement—at least to the point of almost complete disappearance—in the level of anti-Jewish feeling itself. What appears to have happened is that much anti-Semitism that had been expressed in an exclusively religious framework underwent transformation and reappeared in a variety of secular forms. The fundamental assumptions of anti-Semitism remained constant: the Jews still appeared as the great enemies of civilization, only now it was not so much Christendom they threatened as it was the social basis of English life. They were believed to embody values that would undermine the established order in Church and State. Thus, in a functional sense, there was no shift in the role the Jews played in the fantasy life of Christians; the latent content of the fantasy remained the same—only the manifest content had changed its shape.

The earliest instances of the secularization of anti-Jewish sentiment are to be found in the work of the Deists of the first half of the eighteenth century.[13] As the opponents of revealed religion, it was natural that the Deists denounced Judaism, both as a revealed religion in its own right and as the progenitor of Christianity. Their contempt for Judaism and hatred of the Jews, however, went far beyond what a rationalist critique of Judaism required. On the one hand, they denied that the Jews had contributed anything unique to religious life. They claimed that the eternal verities of natural religion had existed long before any special revelation on Sinai and that the Jews had borrowed their customs and beliefs, such as the Sabbath, circumcision, and the prohibition on images, from other Near Eastern peoples. While denying the achievements of Judaism, they also, somewhat contradictorily, singled out Judaism—the religion from which Christianity had developed—as the source of all the world's woes. The errors that had tainted Christianity for centuries were due to the Jews; the Jews were responsible for introducing various superstitions and barbaric practices into the world. Matthew Tindal, for example, ridiculed the Temple sacrifices, declaring them a fraud perpetrated on the people by the priesthood in order to obtain for themselves the best cuts of meat! For Tindal, all the crimes and bloodbaths of history were inspired by the brutal ferocity of biblical precedents. Thus, the massacre of millions of Indians by the Spanish conquistadores was copied from the religiously motivated massacre of the Canaanites.

The theocratic nature of the ancient Jewish state rendered Judaism particularly odious in the eyes of the anticlerical Deists.

They found abundant illustrations of the evils of priestcraft in the history of ancient Israel: the prophets were intolerant fanatics, the warrior-judges ruthless barbarians. Some of their animus against Judaism derived from their antagonism to Christianity, but the zeal with which they attacked Judaism and the Jews, without regard to any historical periodization, suggests that it was not just Judaism that was under seige as the progenitor of Christianity. Further evidence for this interpretation can be found in the fact that they did not hesitate to use anti-Semitic material from the New Testament and the Church Fathers. Shaftesbury, for example, wrote in 1711 that "hanging was the only remedy they could prescribe for anything that looked like setting up a new revelation. The sovereign argument was, Crucify, Crucify."

Aggressive Deism in England was too much the preserve of an ineffectual intellectual coterie to play an important role in shaping popular attitudes toward the Jews. Unlike their counterparts in France, the English Deists were not a distinguished intellectual circle. They were, in Leslie Stephen's words, "but a ragged regiment, whose whole ammunition of learning was a trifle when compared with the abundant stores of a single light of orthodoxy; whilst in speculative ability most of them were children by the side of their ablest antagonists." They never formed a political faction or influenced in any way public issues. Their aggressive antireligious posture was not to the liking of most Englishmen. *The Gentleman's Magazine,* for example, ran a series of articles between September 1770 and November 1773 attacking the hostile views of Voltaire and the English Deists on Judaism, divine revelation, and contemporary Jewry. By 1750, Deist agitation had come to an end. Neither in the Jew Bill clamor of 1753 or in the parliamentary debates on emancipation in the early 1830s was there a hint of Deism's anti-Christian anti-Semitism. As Edmund Burke asked in his *Reflections on the Revolution in France* (1790), "Who, born within the last forty years, has read one word of Collins, and Toland, and Tindal, and Chubb, and Morgan, and that whole race who called themselves Freethinkers? Who now reads Bolingbroke? Who ever read him through?"

A far more pervasive way of stereotyping Jews in secular terms was to see them as the embodiment of unrestrained economic individualism—to focus on, in the words of one critic writing in

1810, "their unremitting diligence and constant attention to the main object of all their undertakings, their unquenchable thirst for wealth." This striving for gain was more than a normal desire to earn a decent living. The character of the Jews was such that they were never satisfied. "A little money accompanied with industry gets more, and so on *ad infinitum;* but whilst the generality of Englishmen know where to stop and repose themselves in the bosom of affluence, unannoyed by the cares of trade, the Jew studies the arithmetic of infinites incessantly and never delays his progress one instant, till the hand of death impedes his course and calls him to the silent retreat of his fathers." Their ceaseless pursuit of wealth was a consequence of their dehumanized nature; unlike Shakespeare's Shylock, they did not have "hands, organs, dimensions, senses, affections, passions," nor did they bleed when pricked, laugh when tickled, die when poisoned, or seek revenge when wronged. They were reduced to one emotion only: a lust for money, even when circumstances demanded a different emotional response. This is the underlying animus, for example, in the following two anecdotes published in 1804:

> When a Jew, who was condemned to be hanged, was brought to the gallows, and just on the point of being turned off, a reprieve arrived; when Moses was informed of this, it was expected he would have instantly quitted the cart, but he staid to see his two fellow travellers hanged, and when asked why he did not get about his business, said, "He waited to see if he could bargain with maister Ketch [the hangman] for the two gentlemen's clothes."

> On one of the nights when Mrs. Siddons first performed at Drury Lane, a Jew boy, in his eagerness to get to the first row in the shilling gallery, fell over into the pit, and was dangerously hurt. The managers of the theatre ordered the lad to be conveyed to a lodging, and he was attended by their own physician; but, notwithstanding all their attention, he died, and was decently buried at the expence of the theatre. The mother came to the playhouse to thank the managers, and they gave her his clothes and five guineas, for which she returned a curtsey, but with some hesitation added, they had forgot to return her the shilling which Abraham had paid for coming in.[14]

The one-sided character of the Jews, it was believed, led them to take advantage of those with whom they traded. The record of history, said a figure in an imaginary dialogue from 1804, proved that the Jews were a "knavish people, who will over-reach and cheat you if they can; a hard-dealing, hard-hearted people, taking all manner of advantage of the necessities of others." An anonymous pamphlet reprinted several times during the course of the eighteenth century described the Jews as "the subtlest and most artful people in the world," as "so dextrous in bargaining that it is impossible for Christians to expect any advantage in their dealings with them." Even among the Sephardim, who appeared to be more decorous in their dealings, "the love of gain has obtained such an absolute empire in their souls that there is not the least remains, the least umbrage of candor or virtue." The Jewish peddler of a popular song published in the early 1830s bragged about being a cheat and a rogue, recounting his triumphs in the marketplace with "good gold rings of copper gilt" and "sealing wax of brick-dust and pencils without lead." In Charles Stuart's play of 1787, *The Distressed Baronet,* a Jew who had offered to arrange a contrived state of bankruptcy to help a baronet out of his financial distress told him, "You will never be worth a groat until you follow our maxim, and think that honesty is the best policy—that is, *to be honest only to yourself.* Ha, ha, ha!" Here was economic individualism stripped of any rationalizing adornment and exposed as rampant self-interest.[15]

The stereotyping of Jews as dehumanized money-makers was the dark underside of the "pro-Jewish" myth about the economic utility of the Jews. If it was believed that the Jews possessed a particular talent for performing certain economic tasks to the benefit of the state, it could also be maintained that those skills, whether inherent in the race or the product of history, could also be employed to benefit the Jews at the expense of the Christian population. The economic utility argument was, then, a double-edged sword, for the question was, *"Whose* utility?" An anonymous tract appearing in 1809, *The Commercial Habits of the Jews,* attacked those who justified the economic aggressiveness of the Jews—on the grounds of liberal political economy—as a contribution to national prosperity. To encourage these capitalists was to identify falsely their interests with those of the country, to make economic growth paramount to morality and public virtue, to sacrifice the weak at the altars of the strong. Every merchant, of course, pursued his own interest in preference to those of others: this was a principle that characterized human nature.

"But although this admission may go far towards acquitting the Jews of the charge of particular criminality, it will not render their peculiar ability of exercising this selfish trait less to be lamented."[16]

The great wealth of the Jews, conservatives claimed, posed a threat to the established order in church and state. A recurrent fantasy in the anti–Jew Bill literature of 1753 was that the Jews would use their fortunes to gain control of the kingdom. With the wealth they would bring with them to England and with what they would gain through dominating trade, they would buy up the estates of the nobility and the gentry. A Jewish landed interest would arise, which, with the money at its disposal, would be able to sway its tenants and carry any election, in much the same way the established rulers of England had already done. "Would not a Christian be overawed frequently by a Jew Justice of the Peace?" asked one pamphleteer. Dominion would follow property. Once in Parliament, wrote Archaicus, their money would "bring all government under their own influence and management"; they would have places in the government from which they would be able to oppose and destroy Christians. As jurors, they would automatically condemn any Christian who appeared before them, whether he were guilty or innocent. Their wealth would also release corrupt ministers from their dependence on the House of Commons for raising money. The prime minister, wrote Old England to the *London Evening Post,* "with the riches of the Jews always at hand for occasional services," could "either buy a majority in the house, or send them to their own homes, and order Jewish sentinels to keep watch over them."[17]

This anxiety about a Jewish take-over was not prompted by any evidence that Jews desired to enter Parliament, although many wealthy Jews had already set themselves up as country gentlemen by this date. In the absence of any concrete precedents out of which to construct a scenario for the future take-over, antinaturalization writers concocted elaborate burlesques on what life would be like in England a century later when the Jews were in control. The *London Magazine,* for example, reprinted the reports of an imaginary "Hebrew Journal" from 1853:

We are . . . informed, that the statue of Sir John Barnard, formerly father of this City, and a strenuous asserter of Christianity, is ordered to be taken down, and that of Pontius Pilate is to be put up in his room.

Last night the Bill for naturalizing Christians was thrown out of the Sanhedrim by a very great majority.[18]

The whimsical character of these accounts has misled some historians into thinking they are bereft of any meaning other than the desire to poke fun at the Whigs for supporting Jewish naturalization. When seen, however, in the larger context of Christian fantasies about the almost unlimited power and hostility of the Jews, these lighthearted spoofs take on a different character. For in a psychodynamic sense, the belief that Jews want to turn St. Paul's into a synagogue is the same as the belief that they want to destroy Christendom.

The power of Jewish money to corrupt the English way of life again became a popular theme at the end of the eighteenth century. The entry of the Goldsmid brothers, Benjamin (1755–1808) and Abraham (1756–1810), into the field of government loan contracting in 1795 and the spectacular financial career of Nathan Mayer Rothschild in the second and third decades of the new century helped to revive popular fears about the power of the Jews. Moreover, radical opposition to the system of public finance initiated by Pitt—indeed to the whole arrangement by which the propertied classes exploited the government apparatus for their own benefit—intensified the suspicion that Jewish stockjobbers and loan-mongers were working against the national interest. The anonymous author of *The Commercial Habits of the Jews* denounced Pitt's transactions with the Jews and the control he thought they exercised over the stock market. Their insensitivity to the interests of the many derived, he felt, from their lack of "all local attachments," from their separation from "the universal mass," and, correspondingly, from the "community of principles, of sentiments, of antipathies, and of pursuits" that they shared only with other Jews. Indeed, it was this community of interests that allowed them to cooperate with their brethren in the great capitals of Europe in controlling the stock market. "Under the influence of this common feeling between distant correspondents, the market becomes the vehicle of forwarding the designs only of a few interested individuals, who pay no respect to the ineffectual struggles and imbecile attempts of the many."[19]

The assault on the Jews as the carriers of finance capitalism reached its fullest development in the writings of the radical populist William Cobbett, who revived the anticapitalist doctrines of opponents of the financial revolution from the first half of the eighteenth century. The hatred Cobbett felt for Jews was an amalgam of medieval anti-Semitism and antimodern radicalism. For thirty years, he waged war on the financial institutions of urban England, believing them to be the chief cause of rural distress and discontent. Among those responsible for the breakdown of the old England, he always included the Jews. Denunciations of "loan-jobbers, stock-jobbers, and Jews," of "Jews, loan-jobbers, stock-jobbers, placemen, pensioners, sinecure people, and people of the 'dead weight' [the annual burden on the taxes represented by pensions and officers' half-pay]," of "Jews, jobbers, and tax-eaters" regularly appeared in everything he wrote from 1805 to his death in 1835. Cobbett's dislike of Jews, however, was not confined to the role that a few families out of several thousand played in the world of high finance. It was a far more comprehensive kind of hatred, one that drew on several varieties of anti-Jewish sentiment.

> My dislike of the Jews is that which our forefathers had of them: I dislike them as insolent ruffians, who mock at the religion and morality of Christians; I dislike them as *people that never work,* and a form of wretches who live by trick; I dislike them as usurers, and the great agents of those systems of usury by which so many nations have so severely suffered. . . . There is something hateful in the very nature of those ceremonies which they have the infamy to call religious. . . . their whole lives are spent in getting at money somehow or other; they are the great props of gaming houses; as soon as prize fighting became a sort of base gambling, they took possession of that blackguard concern. This system [the political-financial establishment] is their element. . . . They are everywhere the friends of political corruption; and as naturally the enemies of political freedom.[20]

The list of charges is a dizzying one. It is difficult to find among his contemporaries, either radical or conservative, individuals who combined such an assortment of abuse. But it is not at all hard to hear fragments of what Cobbett was saying among other critics of the emerging capitalist order. His physiocratic bias, for example, his belief that the Jews never created anything by their labor but merely shifted from hand to hand what others created, was shared by Tories and Radicals alike. Lord Malmesbury thought that the Jews did not have in them "the principle of bodily industry. They were never seen wielding the flail, or mounting the ladder with the hod." The author of *The Commercial Habits of the Jews* believed that the Jewish character was inimical to the hard labor required by farming and was lacking the large amount of ingenuity required by manufacturing. "Orator" Hunt denounced "Jews and stockbrokers, and contractors, and government agents . . . those who live upon, and have been living upon the taxes drawn from the pockets of the industrious people."[21]

Cobbett and other enemies of modernity also revived the fear that Jewish money would corrupt, or further corrupt, the English constitution. In 1830, during the debate in the House of Commons over the first Jewish emancipation bill, Harrison Batley contended that if such a measure were passed, twenty-five Jews would be able to buy themselves seats and "a few of the leading men amongst them would soon obtain as much influence there as they already possessed over the 3-per-cent consols." Cobbett was particularly disturbed by changes in the "natural" hierarchy of rural England and imagined that the Jews posed a threat to the paternalist rule of his idealized squirearchy through their purchase of country estates. In describing Lord Egremont's country seat in Sussex, for example, he remarked:

> It is, upon the whole, a most magnificent seat, and the Jews will not be able to get it from the *present* owner; though if he live many years, they will give even him a *twist.* If I had time, I would make an actual survey of one whole county, and find out *how many of the old gentry have lost their estates,* and have been supplanted by the Jews, since PITT began his reign. I am sure I should prove that, in number, they are one-half extinguished. . . . As the rents fall off, *sales* must take place, unless in case of *entails;* and, if this thing go on, we shall see acts passed to *cut off entails,* in order that the Jews may be put into full possession.[22]

The characterization of the Jews as a people motivated solely by commercial impulses predates the Georgian era by several

centuries. Grasping Jewish usurers were an important component in the stereotyping of Jews in the late medieval and early
modern world. From the middle of the eighteenth century, however, this kind of grotesque characterization gained in popularity
—in part because it could be detached from the theological un-
derpinnings that had helped to create it, but largely because it
was psychologically satisfying to groups caught up in the throes
of modernization. The commercial values of urban England were
beginning to disrupt the traditional social relations of rural England. Landowners began treating their estates solely as invest-
ments to be carefully and dispassionately managed; their relationships with their tenants began taking on a contractual rather
than a paternalist character. Small farmers and master craftsmen
all over England were increasingly drawn into a national and
international market economy that threatened their independence and economic well-being. The WEN, as Cobbett called
London, was invading the countryside and the small market
towns of the provinces. Money rather than birth seemed to count
for more than it had previously. Given the commercial and urban
character of Anglo-Jewry and given the negative and stereotyped
ways in which most people already thought about Jews, it is not
surprising that the Jews would be cast among the chief villains of
the piece. It is no coincidence that those persons who were most
consistently hostile to the Jews, with the exception of those who
fought the Jews as economic rivals, came from those groups
fighting a rearguard action against the new order—Tory paternalists, romantic Radicals, High Church country parsons.

   In England, the enemies of modernity never possessed the
social and political power they possessed in Central and Eastern
Europe, and thus the power and the appeal of antimodern anti-
Semitism were sharply reduced. Englishmen of status and power
were more heartily engaged in "getting and spending" than their
counterparts elsewhere. It would have been incongruous for the
landowners who ran the nation to condemn the Jews as capitalists
when they themselves devoted a good amount of their own energy to the pursuit of wealth, including speculating in the stock
market. Cobbett himself pointed out that the landowners, "in
order to save themselves from being 'swallowed up quick,' " were
willing to marry the daughters and widows of "paper-money
people," including Jews. A capitalistic orientation to life had

made such rapid strides in England among the educated and the
property-owning classes that antimodern anti-Semitism never really had a chance to establish itself solidly. As "the sentimental
Jew" of a popular song of that title said,

> De vorld's for money, I own, so are ve;
> Tis the only point in vich ve all agree;
> Drop a purse,—vould a Christian there
> long let it be?

Or, as Sheridan explained through a dialogue between a Jewish
peddler and his son:

Shadrac: Don't all Christians play us some tricks too?

Moses: O yes, great many, dey are as willing to sheat us, as
we are to sheat dem, a great many of them have all
dese instrouctions by heart, and when dey put dem in
practice, dey are worse den any Jew in de world, for
when a Christian turns rogue, he will cheat his vader,
his mother, and what is worse, the devil himself.[23]

In addition to the secular and religious varieties of anti-Jewish
sentiment already mentioned, there were other stereotypical
ways of thinking about Jews that, although not necessarily hate-
ful, were far from flattering, at least to the Anglo-Jewish elite.
This kind of stereotyping, which was not confined to any identifi-
able social groups but diffused throughout society, picked up
certain social and physical characteristics of some of the Anglo-
Jewish community and blew them up into qualities inherent in the
Jewish people as a whole. At times, it was nothing more than the
expression of social snobbery on the part of the well-to-do, but
at other times it was the expression of a deeply rooted fear that
the Jews were frighteningly inhuman and alien.

The most common mode of physically stereotyping Jews, at
least after the late 1750s, was to treat them as ragged peddlers
and dirty old-clothes men.* When Jews appeared in cartoons and

---

*In the cartoons supporting the antiministerial party in the Jew Bill furor,
Jews were almost always portrayed as wealthy Sephardim with improbable and
extravagant biblical names. The only exception I have come across is "The
Circumcised Gentiles, or a Journey to Jerusalem," in which the Jew is a poor
Ashkenazi, with a prominent nose, a short beard, and a large slouch hat. See
Herbert M. Atherton, *Political Prints in the Age of Hogarth: A Study of the Ideographic*

popular songs, for example, they were inevitably portrayed as street traders with foreign accents. In *The Universal Songster,* a three-volume collection of songs published in 1834, there are fifty songs about Jews collected under the heading "Jews' Songs"; the protagonists of all of them are peddlers, old-clothes men, and low-class shopkeepers. And while the songs are not viciously anti-Semitic—they never refer to Jews as deicides or as tools of the Devil, nor do they ever mock the Jewish religion— they are decidedly malicious. This kind of social stereotyping must have been particularly galling to Jews who wished to escape the stigma attached to lower-class, un-Anglicized Jews. It is easy to imagine, for example, the chagrin that upwardly mobile, acculturated Jews must have felt when they read in the *Morning Chronicle* on 15 September 1801 that two persons had come to the masquerade celebrating the jubilee of the town of Preston dressed as a Jewish peddler and a Jewish quack doctor. The latter figure—in real life, a Dr. Barnsley of Manchester—was "one of the principal entertainments" of the evening, frequently haranguing the company in heavily accented English "in the best Quack Doctor style." The dramatist Richard Cumberland captured the social stigma attached to Jews in general by their concentration in the street trades in an imaginary letter from one Abraham Abrahams that appeared in *The Observor,* in which Abrahams complained of his inability to take his wife to the theatre without being annoyed:

> I no sooner put my head into an obscure corner of the gallery, than some fellow roars out to his comrades, "Smoke the Jew! Smoke the cunning little Isaac!" "Throw him over," says another, "hand over the smoutch!" "Out with Shylock," cries a third, "out with the pound of man's flesh." "Buckles and buttons! Spectacles!" bawls out a fourth—and so on through the whole gallery, till I am forced to retire out of the theatre, amongst hootings and hissings, with a shower of rotten apples and chewed oranges vollied at my head, when all the offense

---

Representation of Politics (Oxford, 1974), p. 165. Soon after 1753, Sephardi magnates disappeared from English prints and were replaced by Jewish peddlers— an obvious reflection of the changing composition of Anglo-Jewry. (Interestingly, poor Ashkenazim were already the numerically preponderant group in 1753, and had been since 1720 at the latest. Popular images, it would seem, lagged behind the social reality.) The earliest picture of a Jewish old-clothes man is from 1789. See Alfred Rubens, "Portrait of Anglo-Jewry, 1656–1836," *TJHSE* 19 (1955–59): 13–52.

I have given is an humble offer to be a peaceable spectator, jointly with them, of the same common amusement.[24]

Behind the stereotyping of Jews as peddlers and old-clothes men lay the social reality that most Jews earned their living in low-status street trades. But this reality did not justify either the tone of the stereotyping or the addition of extraneous negative characteristics to the stereotype. To portray London Jewry as "the most nasty and filthy people under the canopy of heaven," as did one writer to the *St. James Chronicle* in 1804, to point out that "their skin [was] so impregnated with filth as to defy the powers of fuller's soap," as did William Kidd in a London guide-book from the mid-1830s, was to distort grossly the fact that the poor could not afford to be as fastidious about cleanliness as the rich. Yet, the stink and filth of Jewish street traders, and by extension all Jews, served still as a popular motif in anecdotal accounts of Jews. Coleridge, who was friendly with the Polish-born *maskil* Hyman Hurwitz and certainly no raving anti-Semite, nevertheless recorded the following story of his encounter with a foul-smelling Jew:

> Once I sat in a coach opposite a Jew—a symbol of old clothes' bag—an Isaiah of Holywell Street. He would close the window; I opened it. He closed it again; upon which, in a very solemn tone, I said to him: "Son of Abraham! thou smellest; son of Isaac! thou art offensive; son of Jacob! thou stinkest foully. See the man in the moon! He is holding his nose at thee in the distance; dost thou think that I, sitting here, can endure it any longer?" My Jew was astounded, opened the window forthwith himself, and said he was sorry, he did not know before I was so great a gentleman.[25]

This kind of apolitical and a-religious anti-Semitism was further inflamed by a widely diffused dislike for things and persons of foreign origin. From the 1690's onward, substantial colonies of foreigners settled in the Soho area of London. Their alien presence and the growth of an exuberant nationalism from the middle decades of the eighteenth century, partly in reaction to the extended wars England was fighting with various Continental powers, reinforced an older, widely diffused heritage of xenophobia. Foreigners of all religious persuasions became the objects of prejudicial stereotyping. In the political prints of the

middle decades of the eighteenth century, for example, Frenchmen were portrayed, often in the form of apes or monkeys, as
vain, overcivilized dandies and as pretentious, fawning rascals;
the Scots as coarse, wretched, bony, backwoods bumpkins with
sharp features, such as a protruding chin and nose, and tattered
clothes.[26] England's isolation during the Revolutionary and
Napoleonic wars, as well as the association of atheistic, revolutionary ideas with the Continent, strengthened popular prejudices about foreigners in general. Since the Anglo-Jewish community was doubly foreign—that is, in terms of its origins and in
terms of its religion—this generalized dislike of the alien bore
down particularly hard on it.

Even upper-class Englishmen who mixed socially with
thoroughly anglicized Jews retained doubts about the assimilability of these Jews. It seemed to them that in some undefined way
Jews always carried with them a touch of alienism; they might
dress and talk like well-to-do Englishmen, but there was some
lingering quality of foreignness that still set them apart. Thomas
Babington Macaulay, the great parliamentary spokesman for Jewish emancipation, wrote to his sister Hannah in 1831 that a costume ball given by the financier Isaac Lyon Goldsmid, a nephew
of Benjamin and Abraham, had "a little too much of St. Mary Axe
[a Jewish neighborhood in the City] about it,—Jewesses by doz-
ens, and Jews by scores." He explained to her that after the ball
he could not fall asleep right away, as "the sound of fiddles was
in mine ears, and gaudy dresses, and black hair, and Jewish noses
were fluctuating up and down before mine eyes." Horace Walpole, who supported the Jew Bill, at times wrote condescendingly
of his Jewish acquaintances, treating them as slightly exotic creatures. In a letter to George Montagu in 1763, he said, "I have
given my assembly, to show my gallery, and it was glorious; but
happening to pitch upon the Feast of Tabernacles, none of my
Jews could come, though Mrs. Clive proposed to them to change
their religion; so I am forced to exhibit once more." Then he
added in a postscript, "My next assembly will be entertaining;
there will be five countesses, two bishops, fourteen Jews, five
papists, a doctor of physic, and an actress; not to mention Scotch,
Irish, East and West Indians." Charles Lamb found this social
integration deeply disturbing because it tended to blur the essen-

tial distinctiveness of Jews and to paper over the deep disharmony of earlier ages:

> I boldly confess that I do not relish the approximation of Jew
> and Christian which has become so fashionable. The reciprocal
> endearments have, to me, something hypocritical and unnatu-
> ral in them. I do not like to see the Church and Synagogue
> kissing and congeeing in awkward postures of an affected
> civility. If *they* are converted, why do they not come over to us
> altogether? Why keep up a form of separation when the life of
> it is fled? If they cannot sit with us at table, why do they keck
> at our cookery? I do not understand these half-convertites.
> Jews christianising—Christians judaising—puzzle me. I like
> fish or flesh. A moderate Jew is a more confounding piece of
> anomaly than a wet Quaker. The spirit of the Synagogue is
> essentially *separative.* [27]

One indication of the reservations that many educated persons
had about the true assimilability of anglicized Jews was the common practice of referring to Jewish converts to the Church of
England as Jews long after their conversion. The memoirist Sir
Nathaniel Wraxall, in commenting on the generosity of Sir Sampson Gideon (the baptized son of the famous financier of the same
name), wrote that he might have furnished the prototype of the
virtuous Jew in an essay of Richard Cumberland. The *Annual
Register* of 1806 referred to Sir Manasseh Lopes (1755–1831),
who had converted around 1802 so that he might sit in the House
of Commons, as "a Jew baronet." When the distinguished lawyer
John Adolphus (1768–1845), whose mother was a Christian and
who had been raised a Christian, defended the Life Guard officers accused of murdering two men in a riot at the funeral of
Queen Caroline, a caricaturist depicted him with a brief inscribed
"Jew v. Jury."[28] Jewishness obviously could not be obliterated by
a splash of water from the baptismal font.

Interestingly, the social prejudices of the great landowning
families toward Jews seem rarely to have influenced their outlook
on the removal of Jewish disabilities. Whatever reservations they
had about the social character of English Jews were confined to
the sphere of their clubs and country homes. Their political com-
mitments and their snobbish predilections were compartmentalized to the extent that the latter were unable to overwhelm the
former. Or, to put the same matter in a slightly different perspec-

tive, the political culture they shared with utilitarians and radicals imposed standards of consistency in the political sphere that operated as a countervailing force to personal prejudices. To a certain extent, this dichotomy between public and private life may be taken as paradigmatic of the relationship between Jews and non-Jews in Georgian England as a whole. For although England imposed fewer restrictions on the Jews who settled there than did any other European country, the level of personal hostility to Jews may not have been much different than that elsewhere. A German traveler in England in 1782, noticing how his companions on a stagecoach objected to a Jew joining them inside the coach—"as they said, he was nothing but a Jew!"—remarked that anti-Semitism was stronger in England than among the Germans.[29] Perhaps this was an exaggeration; still, the hostility that this visitor from abroad saw must have been fairly pervasive to prompt this observation in the first place.

The failure to translate English anti-Semitism into legal restrictions is evident in the absence of anti-Jewish agitation after the repeal of the Jew Bill. Given the tone of the controversy, one might have expected strong demands for political measures to restrict the wide freedoms Jews enjoyed. Yet, once the ministry had obtained the repeal of the act, public anti-Jewish activity disappeared. Once the status quo had been restored—a status quo that was not, by the standards prevailing elsewhere in Europe, oppressive—"the Jews" ceased to be a topic of public debate. Parliament never considered legislation to impose restrictions or taxes on the Jewish community, although, interestingly, there were numerous proposals from outside Parliament to do so. For example, in 1723, one Tacitus proposed in the *Whitehall Journal* that Anglo-Jewry as a body pay an annual tax of £150,000, since it was "mighty proper that we should, in our turns, enjoy these Jews a little, who have enjoy'd us so much." Tacitus believed that a Jew who obtained his wealth by defrauding Christians was "honoured and almost worshipped for his meritorious advances in the methods of winding and turning his own money, and screwing other people's, by legerdemain, out of their pockets." Vox Populi wrote to *The Gentleman's Magazine* in 1747 to propose that the Jews contribute £400,000 toward the funds needed to carry on the War of Austrian Succession. He justified this assessment on the ground that the chief economic activity of the Jews—which was, according to him, importing precious stones—impoverished rather than enriched the English. He also reasoned that the Jews would not leave England to escape the tax because they still would not be able to find a place of settlement where they would enjoy such advantages as they did there. In 1775, at a time when Jews were becoming particularly notorious as receivers of stolen goods, A True Englishman proposed to Lord North an annual poll tax of two guineas a year on the Jews. "I am not for exterminating of them," he wrote, "but surely, My Lord, it will be equitable and just to make them pay something for such extraordinary favours." (At the same time, he also proposed a tax on dogs of five or ten shillings each, dogs being "very detrimental, both to man and beast.") An anonymous tract published several times in the eighteenth century, *Reasons for Preventing the Growth of Judaism,* called for legislation that would force Anglo-Jewry as a whole to make good any losses Christians unfairly suffered in business dealings with Jews—a reversion to the medieval notion of collective responsibility.[30] Significantly, there is no indication that Parliament, nor, indeed, any political faction, ever showed any interest in implementing these proposals.

This parliamentary reluctance to institute anti-Jewish measures should not be interpreted as enthusiasm for relieving Jewish disabilities. As indicated previously, the question of the legal status of the Jews only came before Parliament when the Jews themselves pressed the issue (i.e., in 1753 and the early 1830s), and in both instances the conservative elements in the political nation were strong enough to defeat pro-Jewish measures. In short, the ruling class as a body did not feel it was important to do anything at all about the Jews.

The lack of initiative on the part of England's rulers in removing Jewish disabilities, which contrasts strongly with the active role played by modernizing bureaucrats in the German states, meant that many decisions regarding precisely what Jews could and could not do legally were made by the High Court of Chancery. And, insofar as it is possible to generalize, its attitude over the course of the Georgian period was a conservative but not a persecutory one. In the absence of any clear-cut guidelines, it preferred to adhere to the notion that England was a Christian state, but interpreted this notion in a relaxed and moderate way.

In 1754, for example, the court ruled in the case of Da Costa v. De Pas that the bequest of £1,200 that Elias de Pas had set aside to maintain a *yeshivah* was illegal because it promoted a religion contrary to the established one; the court awarded £1,000 of the sum to the Foundling Hospital. This ruling, however, did not forbid other charitable bequests to Jewish institutions or interfere with Jewish worship in any way. Indeed, the matter would never have come to the attention of the state if there had not been litigation among de Pas's heirs. In 1786, in a similar case, that of Isaac v. Gompertz, the court ruled that the annuity of £40 that Benjamin Isaac had left to the Hambro Synagogue for support and maintenance was illegal, but the court allowed, at the same time, other charitable bequests to the synagogue (annuities totalling £140) for educating Jewish children and for relieving the Jewish poor.[31]

As a rule, this kind of interference arose only when privately sponsored litigation made the state take an active part in determining the precise status of the Jews. Another notable example of this is the Bedford Charity case of the late 1810s. The Bedford Charity maintained a free school in the town of Bedford, paid the apprentice fees for a number of the children of the town chosen by lottery, granted marriage portions to poor girls, and offered rewards to young people who completed their apprenticeships. Joseph Lyon and Michael Joseph had lived in Bedford for twenty-one years and thirty-one years respectively; the latter was the first Jew to settle there. The children of both men had enjoyed all the benefits of the Charity prior to 1816, and the fathers had voted in the annual election of trustees of the Charity. In that year, the trustees had refused to permit fourteen-year-old Sheba Lyon to draw a lot for the apprentice fee to be paid to girls because they found that the number of Jews in Bedford had been increasing. With the backing of a number of wealthy London Jews, including Isaac Lyon Goldsmid, Lyon and Joseph took the matter to court. Lord Chancellor Eldon, in ruling against them, wrote: "I apprehend that it is the duty of every judge presiding in an *English* Court of Justice, when he is told that there is no difference between worshipping the Supreme Being in chapel, church, or synagogue, to recollect that Christianity is part of the law of England."[32]

Thus, when pressed to be explicit about the status of Jews in

England, Parliament and the High Court of Chancery tended to deny Jews the full rights of English citizenship. For their part, most English Jews probably concluded that the wisest policy was to avoid having the state make any decisions about their precise status. For the absence of a well-developed bureaucracy and police meant that there was no concerted effort on the part of the state to enforce the law in all its severity. Through the apathy of public officials or by means of rather obvious subterfuges, Jews enjoyed many privileges that were not necessarily theirs to enjoy. Those who wanted to operate retail shops in the City of London styled themselves wholesale merchants, called their establishments "warehouses," but sold on a retail basis to anyone who walked in off the street. Foreign-born Sephardi merchants who were not naturalized and needed to circumvent the Navigation Acts purchased ships in the names of their English-born clerks. Anglicized Ashkenazim who wanted to set themselves up as country gentlemen but were concerned about the possibility that Jews could not legally purchase landed estates (preexpulsion statutes that had never been repealed prohibited Jewish landholding) registered their purchases in the names of Christian employees. Benjamin Goldsmid's real property, for example, was held by a Mr. Hamerton, his steward and tutor to his children. By the end of the eighteenth century, at the very latest, liberal election officials were permitting Jews to vote in parliamentary elections, although they were, strictly speaking, incapable of taking the oath of abjuration, which contained the words "upon the true faith of a Christian." A James Gillray etching from 1788 attacking corrupt election practices in Westminster shows among the crowd a Jew holding a bill "for perjury and procuring Jew voters." When the radical Horne Tooke was High Bailiff of Westminster, he permitted Jews who voted to omit the words "upon the true faith of a Christian" when repeating the oath. During the House of Commons debate on the first Jewish emancipation bill in 1830, Sir Robert Wilson stated that Jews in Southwark voted in parliamentary elections, although they were not legally permitted to do so, and that if an individual chose, he could require them to take the oath of abjuration and thus effectively exclude them.[33]

Anti-Jewish sentiment among the propertied classes was largely confined, then, to verbal abuse, social exclusivity, and the political determination to preserve what little remained of the

Christian character of the state. The lower classes were far less successful, however, in channeling their hostility into socially acceptable forms—acceptable, that is, by the standards of gentle-folk. The hatred and the anger of the untamed strata of English society frequently spilled over into acts of violence and petty hooliganism. As previously shown, the Jew Bill agitation of 1753 whipped up popular hostility and temporarily made life hazardous for itinerant Jewish peddlers. According to Henry Mayhew, who was writing a century after the event and hence may not be thoroughly reliable, it became unsafe for "a Hebrew old clothes man, however harmless a man, and however long and well known on his beat, to ply his street-calling openly, for he was often beaten and maltreated." It may not be mere coincidence that in November of 1753, at the height of the clamor, Jonas Levi, a Jewish peddler, was found murdered between Abergavenny and Crickbowel in Monmouthshire. That robbery was the motive there is little doubt—his box had been plundered of most of its goods—but the manner in which he had been slain suggests a fury unrelated to the mere act of robbery: he had first been strangled, and then his skull had been smashed and battered with such force that several pieces were found lying beside him.[34]

The harassment of Jewish street traders and itinerant peddlers was a frequent occurrence even without the additional provocation of political events. Israel Hart, a pencil-maker who sold his wares directly to shops and carpenters, testified at the Old Bailey in 1757 that "it was a common thing with them when Jews came to offer pencils to sell, to take them away and throw them out at the window." In 1769, at Monmouth Assizes, a man was convicted for forcibly sitting a Jewish peddler before a large fire with his hands tied behind him and then stuffing hot bacon down his throat. In a similar incident in 1776, a woman who kept a public house was found guilty at Westminster Quarter Sessions for assaulting a Jew and greasing his chin with pork. Even respectable Jews could become the victims of this kind of hooliganism. On the first day of Passover in 1824, Leah Meldola, the daughter of Haham Meldola, chief rabbi of the Sephardim in England, was attacked by Joseph Jones, a donkey driver, while she was walking in the Tenter Ground with a friend. Jones grabbed her by the arms and threatened to drag her into a nearby house and force her to eat pork and bread. She was rescued by a young Jewish man before Jones could carry through his threat. The Haham then took out a warrant against Jones and the woman who owned the house. When they appeared at the Lambeth Street Police Office, the presiding magistrate, the Rev. Mathias, dismissed the charge against them and reprimanded the Meldolas for taking up his time. "You Jews," he told them, are "a quarrelling people" who are "continually bringing forward frivolous cases."[35]

On rarer occasions, popular hostility took the form of mob action, and in these instances the damage to property and person was not inconsiderable. In 1763, on the King's birthday, an incident occurred that prompted a mob assault on a number of Jewish houses in Duke's Place. As a crowd of persons was pushing through the postern on Tower Hill to see the fireworks, the rails surrounding a spring suddenly gave way and many people tumbled into the spring. During the ensuing confusion, a sailor had his pocket picked by a Jew. The sailor's companions caught hold of the Jew and began to give him a good dunking. Pretending that he had broken his leg, the Jew begged for his release and was carried off by some of his friends. But the sailors, discovering that they had been tricked, pursued them to Duke's Place, where at first they were beaten off by the Jews. They soon returned, however, with fresh reinforcements, mounted a new attack, and succeeded in breaking into three houses, throwing outside all their contents, including three children sick with smallpox, breaking all the windows, and tearing up the beds. Thirteen years later, a mob, with no apparent provocation, "insulted and otherwise ill-used" a group of Jews attending a funeral at the Jewish burial ground near Bear Street. The wall of the burial ground fell in from the pressure of people climbing on it, and one of the Jews was seriously injured. In the 1790s, when England's xenophobic tradition was further inflamed by the wars with France, the Jews of Ipswich, wrote a historian in 1830, "were frequently insulted and maltreated in their progress to and from their place of worship, and they at this time applied to the magistrates for constables to protect them from the illiberal and disgraceful behaviour of the rabble."[36]

As tragic as these attacks were for their victims, they did not constitute a serious threat to the physical security of the Anglo-Jewish community. They were not part of any concerted anti-Jewish movement, but were, rather, typical of the pervasive violence that characterized English life in the pre-Victorian period. By the standards of the age, incidents such as the above were hardly extraordinary. Indeed, by comparison with other minorities, the Jews were fortunate, for they suffered far less from the mob than did non-Anglican Christian groups. The most serious damage to Anglo-Jewry was inflicted neither by mob violence nor by legislative disabilities, but by the opprobrium popularly attached to the word "Jew." The very word, according to the Rev. Charles B. Tayler, Rector of St. Peter's, Chester, was "associated with what is vulgar and degraded and contemptible. . . . The Jewish name is commonly coupled with a reproach, with the idea of low cunning and sordid avarice."[37]

The cruel and humiliating manner in which Englishmen stereotyped Jews was a psychological blow to those Jews who sought to enter into English life. It was a harsh affront to those Jews who had internalized the values of non-Jewish society and now sought its approval and acceptance. Restrictive measures in the economic sphere could successfully be circumvented, but it was impossible to escape the unpleasant associations that clung to the group as a whole. There is no question that anglicized Jews were very sensitive to their group image. When Mary Nathan, who kept a shop in Petticoat Lane, prosecuted two men who had robbed her shop, she asked her Christian servant girl to swear in court against them, for, as the girl said, "She told me, as I was an Irish person and a Christian, a word from me would go farther than ten from her." When John Solomons took to the sea, he went by the name of John Smith because he thought "they would not take him on board of ships in the name of *Solomons,* knowing that he was a Jew." Moses Ricardo intended to write a biography of his brother David a few years after his death, but the rest of the family prevailed on him to give the matter up because, according to a contemporary, "they are now people of fortune and of some consequence, and landed gentry [and] they do not like that the public should be reminded of their Jewish and mercantile origin." As Lord Kames concluded,

> The Jews, while they suffered the severest persecution in all Christian countries, continued obstinate in their religion. In England, being now treated with humanity, they daily become converts to Christianity, not being able to bear with patience

the slight contempt their religion lies under, nor the unsociableness of their ceremonies, which oblige them to eat separately from others.[38]

Conversion was not, however, the only escape from the stigma of Jewishness. Anglicized Jews who desired acceptance, but not at the price of conversion, had another alternative: to dissociate themselves from popular stereotypes of "the Jews" by cultivating an image as English gentlemen.

4

Gentlemen Jews: The Acculturation of the Anglo-Jewish Middle Class

Over the course of the eighteenth and early nineteenth centuries, traditional Jewish life everywhere in Western and Central Europe began to weaken. Among the Jewish middle class, especially the Jewish haute bourgeoisie, many wanted to abandon the isolation of the legally autonomous, culturally self-sufficient Jewish community in order to participate in the life of the larger societies in which they lived. Their willingness to desert or refashion ancient patterns of life and thought was motivated in some cases by the conscious belief that Jewish traditions were outmoded and that the values and institutions of European culture were necessary for survival and success in the modern world. In other instances, the motive underlying the reordering of Jewish priorities was the unarticulated and more prosaic wish to conform to the way of life of the majority—the wish to reduce Jewish distinctiveness, to blend in with the dominant group in society, to escape the stigma of being different.

With the weakening of juridical and social restraints, the Jewish middle class began turning to the majority society for patterns of behavior and modes of thought they had found previously within the confines of Jewish life. This internalization of non-Jewish values was an admission—whether it was made explicit or not—that the traditional culture of Judaism was either insufficient or inappropriate for the modern world and, as such, marked a major turning point in Jewish history. Judaism was no longer an all-embracing, self-sufficient civilization; it was reduced to a system of religious observances and beliefs. Jews who embraced European modes of thought and behavior no longer defined their lives in exclusively Jewish terms. They rearranged their personal priorities in such a manner that their Jewishness came to occupy only a segment of their personal identity.

The path from tradition to modernity was not a rapid, direct, uninterrupted one. Those on the Continent who sought to modernize Jewish life, even those who made no attempt to change others but merely embarked on the path of self-modernization, encountered the hostility of traditionalists. The radicalism of the extreme reformers steeled the commitment of the confirmed traditionalists to the old ways. Institutions and patterns of behavior that were centuries old also served to slow down and moderate the break with the past, restraining the less adventurous and the less assertive. In England, and in North America as well, however, many of the inhibiting elements present on the Continent were absent or less strong, so that the framework for Anglo-Jewish acculturation was looser and more open; hence, the pace of this acculturation was more rapid and more thoroughgoing. The absence of an organized Jewish community during the later Middle Ages and the early modern period, as well as the subsequent failure to reestablish an all-embracing autonomous corporation after the Resettlement, meant there were no communal institutions to monitor effectively the social behavior of Jews who settled there. There was no legally recognized Jewish communal organization to which all Jews were required to belong, as was the case elsewhere in Europe. Voluntarism was the only organizing principle of Anglo-Jewish communal life. Those who uprooted themselves to migrate to England were coming to an underdeveloped Jewish community in a country that gave its inhabitants an extraordinary degree of personal freedom. Anglo-Jewish life, from the perspective of traditionalism, suffered from a lack of restraints. In comparison with the rest of the European diaspora, London was a frontier boom town, with all the freedom from authority that this term implies. Over the course of the eighteenth century, the Jewish population of the capital jumped from a little more than 750 persons to over 15,000 persons, while the communal institutions necessary to sustain a traditional Jewish culture for a population that size failed to keep pace.

The overwhelming majority of Jews, rich and poor, who settled in England during the eighteenth and early nineteenth centuries came from traditional Jewish communities in Poland, Germany, and Holland. Their arrival in England did not represent, however, their first contact with the modern world; they were not pious innocents newly emerged from the ghettos of Central Europe. The ancient Jewish communities of Germany were exposed to the seductions of European cultural and social life from the first half of the eighteenth century, and, in some cases, it may have been the corrosive appeal of the non-Jewish world that moved Jews to begin a new life across the Channel.

The extent to which Jewish immigrants to England were already europeanized depended on a number of variables—their socioeconomic background, the region or town from which they came, the relative lateness of their migration. Jews who came from Posen, Silesia, Bavaria, and Baden, which were strongholds of traditionalism, were more likely to be less europeanized than those who came from the more commercially developed cities of Amsterdam, Berlin, and the Rhineland. Jews who had been raised in upper-middle-class households were more likely to have been exposed to European learning and manners than those from poor families who had been put to work at an early age.

Among the various groups of immigrants that came to make up the Anglo-Jewish population, one in particular had absorbed more of European culture previous to settling in England than the others—the Sephardim. Many of them had lived in Spain or in Portugal or in southwestern France, ostensibly as Catholics, and had adopted all the external marks of European culture. They were, as Yosef Yerushalmi has written, the first considerable group of modern Jews, having had "their most extensive and direct personal experiences completely outside the organic Jewish community and the spiritual universe of normative Jewish tradition."[1] Even those Sephardim who had not lived the dual life of Marranos were immersed in the social and cultural life of the non-Jewish world, for the Sephardi centers in Europe preserved and passed on the cultural receptivity of the Iberian Jewish tradition to later generations of Sephardim. In matters of dress, speech, manners, and the like, bourgeois Sephardim were indistinguishable from their non-Jewish counterparts. They cultivated non-Jewish learning, composed poetry, plays, and philosophical treatises in European languages, and still attempted to preserve the learning and customs of traditional Judaism. For the Sephardim who settled in England, and for their children, the acquisition of English manners and attitudes did not represent as dramatic a break with the past, as it did for their Ashkenazi coreligionists.*

In England, those who abandoned the ways of their fathers rarely ever articulated their motives for doing so. Unlike their German and French counterparts, the Anglo-Jewish elite did not create an ideology (the Haskalah) to justify and to promote the modernization of Jewish life. For reasons that will be made clear further on, well-to-do Jews who embraced the English way of life felt no need to appeal to a set of ideas to justify their actions. They showed little interest in an intellectual reconciliation of English culture and Jewish tradition. The loan contractors, merchant bankers, bullion brokers, gem merchants, and stockbrokers who comprised the Anglo-Jewish elite, as well as the wholesale merchants and prosperous shopkeepers immediately below them on the economic ladder, were driven by the psychological need to feel at home in England. They wished to be as much like wealthy Christians as was possible without having to renounce their identity as Jews. Their unarticulated ideal was that of upper-class gentility; like other new men of unsure status, such as newly enriched City merchants and members of the lesser professions, they wanted to be English gentlemen.[2] They internalized—in some cases, slowly and hesitatingly, in others, with speed and abandon—the values of the English ruling class and then applied these values to refashioning their own lives and the life of the community.

This refashioning process eventually encompassed every aspect of Anglo-Jewish life—dress, language, manners, recreations, sexual behavior, diet, religious customs, education, literature. Some elements in the traditional culture of Ashkenazi Jewry were given up easily, without much discomfort, such as the use of Yiddish or the wearing of the long caftanlike coat. Other ele-

---

*As it would be awkward, if not impossible, to treat the acculturation of Ashkenazim and Sephardim in England as two distinct experiences, I have not done so. Nevertheless, their radically different backgrounds should be kept in mind throughout the following discussion. It will be clear which points refer only to Ashkenazim and which to both groups.

ments, such as the traditional worship service and Hebrew education, were too central to Jewish identity to be thrown out altogether, so they were modified and adapted to English conditions.

The first elements in traditional Jewish life to be abandoned by
the Anglo-Jewish middle class were those that set them apart
visibly from non-Jews—the long beard and the distinctive dress
of Central Europe. Wealthy Jewish men in Georgian England
were clean shaven and fashionably dressed. As an anonymous
writer in the *Whitehall Journal* in 1723 remarked, "They are distinguished in nothing from our greatest merchants and gentlemen."
If one saw a Jew wearing a beard, noted a Huguenot diplomat in
London in 1729, one could be certain he was either a rabbi or a
very recent immigrant. For traditionalists among the Ashkenazim, a beard was not just a matter of fashion, but an integral
aspect of religious life. There was a specific prohibition against
shaving, derived from the biblical injunction not to "destroy the
side-growth of your beard" in the fashion of the pagans (Lev.
19:27). Chief Rabbi Hirschel Levin* told his congregants in the
late 1750s that they had transgressed against one of the fundamental tenets of Judaism by shaving their beards. A traditionalist
opponent of anglicization, writing in 1789 under the nom de
plume Lord George Gordon (the erratic Protestant zealot who
converted to Judaism in 1787), attacked Jews of all ranks for
being "greatly ashamed of appearing with beards." Wealthy
Jews, he wrote, were "ashamed of appearing with beards before
the Christian merchants at the Exchange and the nobility at the
playhouses" because this "outward and visible sign, given unto
them by God himself" publicly distinguished them from the nobility and the gentry of the land. Poor Jews, recently arrived from
abroad, were pressured into shaving their beards, he claimed, by
not being employed as teachers in the homes of the well-to-do
as long as they remained unshaven. An anonymous Hebrew tract
published that same year, *Olam hadash olam hafukh* (A New World,
A World Turned Upside Down) also took anglicized Jews to task
for following English fashions in dress and grooming. The author

*The title of Chief Rabbi was, during the Georgian period, assumed by the
rabbis of the Great Synagogue in London, the wealthiest and largest congregation in the metropolis. Their authority was not recognized by the state, and their
power within the Jewish community extended only to congregations and individuals who voluntarily looked to them for guidance in matters of Jewish law.

complained that whereas Jews in former times had let their hair grow during the period of mourning, they now cultivated long hair for reasons of personal vanity. As a pious Jew, he bemoaned the fact that it had become impossible to tell a Jew from a non-Jew. By the 1820s, Anglo-Jewry as a whole had become so lax about the ban on shaving that Reb Mordechai, the *hazan* of the New Synagogue, imagined that he could shave his beard without giving offense. This kind of behavior in a religious functionary was not acceptable, however, even to the highly acculturated lay leadership of the synagogue. By a vote of twelve to four, the *parnasim* (wardens) decided to suspend him from his job for two weeks.[3] The mildness with which they treated this deviation from tradition may mean that they did not consider it a very serious offense.

The wives of these Jewish gentlemen were no less eager to be fashionably attired and suitably coiffed. They ignored the traditional regulation that married women must not appear in public with their own hair visible and that they must dress in a modest and circumspect way. In the late 1750s, Chief Rabbi Hirschel Levin attacked those women who wore low-cut dresses that exposed their flesh to public view. Their aim, he thundered, was "not to appear like daughters of Israel." An amusing caricature by James Gillray of Polly de Symons, the wife of the diamond broker Lyon de Symons and the sister of Abraham and Benjamin Goldsmid, depicts a stout woman with ample breasts spilling out of a dangerously low-cut gown. Even outside the fashionable whirl of London, prosperous Jewish women abandoned the custom of wearing wigs. None of the more than twenty known portraits of Jewish women in Devon from the eighteenth and nineteenth centuries depicts them wearing wigs.[4]

Yiddish suffered the same fate as the other external marks of Jewish distinctiveness. In previous centuries, when German Jews had migrated to Poland, Hungary, Bohemia, and other countries, they had continued to speak the German-Jewish dialect of their country of origin and, unlike the Sephardim, often never learned the vernacular of the countries in which they settled. By the eighteenth century, Yiddish was so closely associated with the traditional religious culture of Ashkenazi Jewry that it had acquired a quasi-sacred status; its abandonment, like that of the beard, represented a sharp break with the past. For economic reasons, most Jews who settled in England eventually had to learn some English. The Jewish lower classes, however, seem to have continued to speak Yiddish among themselves even after they had picked up English. The almanacs published for itinerant Jewish peddlers after 1772 were written in Yiddish, with a liberal sprinkling of English words spelled out in Hebrew characters. Middle-class Jews, on the other hand, were eager to abandon this distinctive linguistic mark of Jewishness. It had become a badge of "shame" to them, claimed the author of *Olam hadash olam hafukh.* They insisted that their children learn English and that they address them in English as mama and papa. By 1815, the three major London synagogues, the leadership of which was upper-middle-class and anglicized, had switched from keeping their records in a combination of Hebrew and Yiddish to keeping them entirely in English. Yiddish had such negative associations that in May 1826 the *parnasim* of the Great Synagogue determined that all anouncements made during services or posted on the outer doors of the synagogue should be in English and Hebrew, instead of Yiddish, despite the fact that many Jews understood only Yiddish. Chief Rabbi Solomon Hirschell (1762–1842) objected to the decision, since "the bulk of the labouring class," who comprised the majority of worshipers, did not understand Hebrew well, let alone English. He reminded them that, when the time of the commencement of the Sabbath was announced in Hebrew for the first time, there had been great confusion and much noise among the congregation, as people tried to find out what was being said. The *parnasim* realized the situation was absurd and reversed their decision.[5]

One sign of how far the external acculturation of the Anglo-Jewish middle class—indeed, of Anglo-Jewry as a whole—had gone was that writers who were hostile to the Jews began to emphasize from the 1750s on their physiognomical distinctiveness. Realizing that the Jews had abandoned the outward signs of dress and speech that had set them apart previously from other men, essayists and journalists rediscovered the alleged distinctiveness of the Jews in the physical structure and coloring of their faces—something Jews were then incapable of changing. How can one know a Jew at first sight? asked the Rev. William Romaine in 1753. What are his distinguishing features?

It is not his dirty skin, for there are other people as nasty; neither is it the make of his body, for the Dutch are every whit as odd, awkward figures as the Jews. But look at his eyes. Don't you see a malignant blackness underneath them, which gives them such a cast as bespeaks guilt and murder? You can never mistake a Jew by this mark; it throws such a dead livid aspect over all his features that he carries enough evidence in his face to convict him of being a Crucifier.

The dark cast of Jewish facial features was a frequent motif in anti-Semitic passages. Robert Southey noted that although the law did not require Jews to wear any distinctive mark, it was still possible to tell them apart from Christians by "a cast of complexion and features," "a Portuguese look." *Kidd's London Directory* told visitors to London in the mid-1830s that on the faces of Jews was "legibly written 'outcast,' and 'perdition,' engraved in every wrinkle." Macaulay, it will be remembered, had difficulty falling asleep after Isaac Lyon Goldsmid's costume ball because "gaudy dresses, and black hair, and Jewish noses were fluctuating up and down before mine eyes." It was so widely believed that the Jews were distinguished by "a national countenance" that Isaac D'Israeli, felt it necessary to explain in his novel *Vaurien* (1797) that what contemporaries thought was the "Jewish visage" was really Spanish. The dark complexion, full black eyes, and aquiline nose of the Jews had been acquired in the Iberian peninsula. The Ashkenazim, he told his readers, had fair complexions, grey eyes, and red hair, like the peoples of Central Europe among whom they had dwelled previously.[6]

The life-style of the Anglo-Jewish elite was not noticeably different from that of other wealthy Englishmen. They attended the theater and the opera, gossiped and played cards in the coffee houses of the City, had their portraits painted by the best artists of the period, lost money at the faro tables in St. James Square, threw lavish parties and entertainments, took the waters at Bath, and rested by the seashore at Brighton. In 1761, Dr. Ralph Schomberg (1714–92), who was married to a Christian, wrote from Bath to Emanuel Mendes da Costa (1717–91), the eminent naturalist and antiquary, that there were "a good many *b'nai yisrael* [Jews] here." Brighton was especially popular as a resort with London Jews because of its closeness to the capital. An observer in the 1820s noted that "the heads of the houses of

Israel run down on a Saturday, after the Stock Exchange closes, and often do as much business here [in Brighton] on the Sabbath, in gambling speculations for the account day, as they have done all the week before in London." Asher Goldsmid (Isaac Lyon's father and Benjamin and Abraham's brother) apparently retired there at the close of his active business career. In June 1822, he wrote his son, who was hard at work in the City, that he had heard from his "stock friends" who had come down to Brighton that "you fatigue yourself too much in the stock and other businesses. If you think of your family, you ought not to do it." An upper-class visitor there in 1819 wrote disdainfully:

> What a multitude of people we have here, Jews, haberdashers, and money-lenders without number, a sort of Marine Cheapside, Mr. Solomons, Mrs. Levis, and all the Miss Abrahams; in short, Hook Noses, Mosaical Whiskers, and the whole tribe of Benjamin occupy every shop, every donkey-cart, and every seat in Box, Pit, and Gallery.[7]

As the ideal of gentility derived from the life-style of the landed class, the acquisition of a country house was a prerequisite for men who had grown rich in trade and wanted to stake a claim to gentlemanly status. As long as well-to-do Jews remained active in the City, they had to live in London and could not set themselves up as country gentlemen in the depths of some distant shire. But they did, as early as the 1720s, purchase small estates to the west and northwest of London, where they could sample the country life for short periods and where their wives and children could live on a more regular basis. In 1720, Moses Hart (1675–1756), the dominant figure in the Great Synagogue in the first half of the eighteenth century, purchased a house along the Thames at Isleworth. In its many rooms hung paintings by Van Dyck, Rubens, Brueghel, Poussin, Hals, and Holbein; rather surprisingly, the subject matter of the paintings included explicitly Christian themes, such as St. Francis, the martyrdom of St. Lawrence, the inside of the Jesuit Church at Antwerp, Jesus driving the money changers from the Temple, and Jesus bearing his cross. That Hart was able to view these paintings from a largely aesthetic perspective and disregard their religious content is an index of how thoroughly acculturated many Anglo-Jewish magnates were becoming. In the nearby villages of Teddington, Twickenham, and Richmond, the Franks (to whom Hart had married two of his daughters), the Salvadors, the Prados, and the Nunezes also purchased homes. When the Palestinian rabbi Haim Yosef David Azulai visited London in the spring of 1755 to collect funds for the Hebron yeshivah, he found that all the wealthy Jews had left the city for their country estates. At the end of the century, both Benjamin and Abraham Goldsmid maintained splendid country homes to the west of London. In 1792, Benjamin acquired a sixty-acre freehold at Roehampton and erected a thirty-bedroom mansion. It was an extravagant, marble-laden place, with numerous drawing rooms, music rooms, a ballroom, and a dining room that was sixty feet by forty feet. The walls were hung with fine paintings, the cellars stocked with the best wines. His brother Abraham had a place at Morden that was described by the Rev. Edmund Nelson, after he was entertained there in 1805, as a "fine house" with gaudy, tasteless furnishings. A few years later, Abraham acquired the country home of Lady Hamilton (Admiral Nelson's mistress) Merton, Place.[8]

That these men of wealth desired to live in a conspicuously elegant manner, surrounded by fine and costly furnishings, was not a new phenomenon in Jewish history. Their luxurious lifestyle in itself was not a radical break with the past. What was new was that the life of a country gentleman, even if only lived for a part of the year, meant a physical separation from the mass of the Jewish community. Those who chose to live along the banks of the Thames in Richmond or Isleworth were declaring, in effect, that most of their neighbors were not to be Jews. Benjamin Disraeli recalled that his paternal grandparents, who had taken a large country house in the early 1770s at Enfield, north of the City, did not mix much with other Jews, but were friendly with some of their English neighbors.[9] Jews who moved to the country also cut themselves off from those institutions essential to the preservation of traditional Judaism—synagogues, Jewish schools, kosher butcher shops. Benjamin Goldsmid maintained a private synagogue in his home at Roehampton and reputedly served only kosher meals there, but this would appear to be an exception. In any case, these arrangements seem to have had little lasting influence on the rest of his family. Within a few years of his death in 1808, his wife and seven children had embraced Christianity.

The affluent members of the Jewish community who continued

to pursue active business careers in London and maintained residences there did not desert the primary area of Jewish settlement, the eastern end of the metropolis, with the same speed with which they purchased country homes. Until the end of the eighteenth century, most well-to-do Jews continued to live above thier counting houses in St. Mary Axe, Bishopsgate, and Broad Street, or in the elegant new dwellings in Devonshire Square, Billiter Square, Finsbury Square, and Wellclose Square, or in the streets of private mansions bordering Goodman's Fields. Toward 1800 or so, with the City being increasingly abandoned for the West End by well-to-do merchants and bankers, the wealthier Sephardim began moving to Kennington, Islington, Bloomsbury, Mayfair, Kensington, and Belgravia. Moses Montefiore (1784–1885) grew up in Kennington Terrace. When he married in 1812, he and his wife moved across the river to New Court in the City, next door to his brother-in-law, Nathan Rothschild, but thirteen years later they moved westward to Green Street and from there, after a short stay, to 99 Park Lane. In 1792, when David Ricardo (1772–1823) was twenty, his family moved from their home in Bury Street in the City to the village of Bow, a few miles to the east. There David met, fell in love with, and married the oldest daughter of a neighbor, an eminent Quaker physician —to the horror of both families. Wealthy Ashkenazim were slower, on the whole, to abandon the area of primary Jewish settlement. Nathan Rothschild moved from New Court to 107 Piccadilly only in the 1820s. The *Hebrew Intelligencer,* a short-lived Anglo-Jewish newspaper, reported in January 1823 that Edward Goldsmid was leaving Finsbury Square for Park Lane, where he had purchased an elegant mansion for £10,000, including furniture. "We also hear," the paper added, "that a well-known gentleman has expressed his determination of quitting the neighbourhood of Goodman's Fields, which, he declares, no longer sufficiently select for him."[10] The fashionable neighborhoods of the West End, like the gentle countryside to the west of London, were not conducive to the maintenance of traditional Jewish life. There, in spendid isolation from the bulk of the Jewish community, the Anglo-Jewish elite came to live, leaving behind them in the City the religious and educational institutions that sustained traditional Judaism.

The upper-class life-style that wealthy Jews came to embrace entailed more than the adoption of a luxurious, fashion-conscious way of living and dressing. It also entailed the acceptance of a code of sexual behavior radically freer than that permitted by Jewish law. English gentlemen, before the onslaught of Evangelical and Victorian morality, were remarkably indiscreet about their extramarital affairs, indulging themselves with open abandon in high-class brothels and with expensively maintained mistresses. Jewish brokers and bankers took to this style of open bawdiness with alacrity. The literature of the first half of the eighteenth century contains numerous references to the philanderings of rich Sephardim. Plate 2 of Hogarth's *Harlot's Progress,* which was painted in 1731, was usually entitled "The Quarrel with Her Jew Protector." It depicts a prostitute, said to be the notorious Kate Hackabout, living under the protection of a wealthy Jew, who has arrived unexpectedly for breakfast, causing her to overturn the tea table to cover the escape of another man with whom she has been dallying. Hogarth's set of engravings inspired Theophilus Cibber, in turn, to compose a pantomime with songs, also called *The Harlot's Progress,* in which Kitty, Beau Mordecai's mistress, is discovered making love to Harlequin. Before being turned out by Beau Mordecai, Kitty sings:

> Farewell, good Mr. Jew;
>   Now I hate your tawny face;
> I'll have no more to do
>   With you or any of your race.

The same year in which Cibber's pantomime was published (1733), an anti-Jewish pamphlet appeared that called for, among other things, the castration of Jews who were detected defrauding Christians or cohabiting with Christian women. Henry Fielding's *Miss Lucy in Town,* first performed in 1742, is set in a high-class brothel patronized by well-to-do Jews. Mrs. Midnight, the owner, declares: "If it was not for Mr. Zorobabel and some more of his persuasion, I must shut up my doors." The action begins with a country yokel and his lovely but naive wife coming to London for the first time and mistakenly applying for lodgings at the brothel. Mrs. Midnight decides to take advantage of this accident and schemes to offer the young woman to either Mr. Zorobabel or the dissolute Lord Bawble. When the former hears that Mrs. Midnight may offer the woman to Lord Bawble, he complains to her:

> Zor: How, Mrs. Midnight, promise her to a lord without offer-
> ing her to me first? Let me tell you, 'tis an affront not only
> to me, but to all my friends: and you deserve never to
> have any but Christians in your house again.

> Mid: Marry forbid! Don't utter such curses against me.

> Zor: Who is it supports you? Who is it can support you? Who
> have any money besides us?

> Mid: Pray your worship forgive me.[11]

Most of these references to Jewish sexuality were inspired by anti-Semitism. The hyperbole in dialogues such as the above derived from the then common prejudicial notion that Jews were exceptionally lustful and that their wealth, when put at the service of their sexual longings, was a threat to English womanhood. A guide to London published in 1744, for example, used the simile that undertakers wait as impatiently for the last gasp of persons of quality as do Jews for the opportunity to debauch their wives' maids. That anti-Semitism inspired such expressions, however, does not necessarily mean there was no element of truth in them. Behind the exaggeration and the prejudice lay a reality that even Jewish voices acknowledged. Dr. Meyer Schomberg wrote in 1746 in a Hebrew tract entitled *Emunat omen* (The True Faith) that the wealthy Jews of London loved whoredom and adultery:

> Not only do they lie with women, daughters of the gentiles, as
> if they were fulfilling a commandment, without shame, but they
> also live and dwell and lodge with them in intimate embrace
> and reject the *kasher* daughters of Israel who are our own flesh
> and blood.[12]

For the second half of the eighteenth century, there is much more explicit evidence that well-to-do Jews had adopted the sexual morality of the English upper class. Joseph Salvador, a *parnas* of Bevis Marks for a number of years and chief promoter of the Jew Bill, was openly linked with the fashionable courtesan Mrs. Margaret Caroline Rudd. According to one source, Salvador was the most faithful and the most generous of her patrons. He also became involved with a Belgian woman known as the Countess of Moriencourt, who bore him a natural son. In the last third of the century, Ephraim d'Aguilar (1739–1802) was notorious for bringing home ragged unfortunate girls whom he put to work as servants and then went on to seduce. He had several daughters out of wedlock. Samuel Vita Montefiore (1757–1802), an uncle of Sir Moses, acknowledged in his will four illegitimate children by two non-Jewish women. Toward the end of the century, a Mr. Salomon, a rich Jewish broker of Fenchurch Street, kept Sally Tucker, a former barmaid who took the more Sephardi-sounding name Diana Peynado. According to Levy Alexander, numerous Jewish brokers and bankers attended her levees. "It would not be an exaggeration to say that she had received as visitors all the heads of the nation and most particularly the gentlemen [the Goldsmids] who had any business with the premier [Pitt] when he advertised the loans." Even at the most humble levels of the Jewish middle class, among artisans and shopkeepers, extramarital relations were not unheard of. The rules of two Jewish friendly societies from the early 1830s—the United Israelites and the Guardians of Faith—explicitly banned from membership Jews who cohabited with non-Jews.[13]

What is significant about the extramarital sexual activity of these Anglo-Jewish magnates is not that they carried on as they did, but that they did so with such apparent disregard for the conventional morality of traditional Judaism. Individuals who committed sexual transgressions were not unknown in early modern Jewish history, but they hardly flaunted their immorality in the way the Anglo-Jewish elite did, attracting the attention of the non-Jewish world. Indeed, sexual misconduct in the traditional Jewish communities of Central Europe was more often to be found among the lower classes than among the leadership stratum. In eighteenth-century England, there was no well-established, traditionally inclined ruling elite to act as a countervailing force to the attractions of the fashionable life. London's rabbis, as will be explained at greater length shortly, were the servants of the lay leadership and unable to exert any independent social or moral restraint. There was, moreover, no tight-knit Jewish community, isolated from the non-Jewish world, that was capable of exerting social pressure on deviant members. Wealthy Jews could act in any manner they pleased, for there was no Jewish public opinion to fear. There were no penalties—juridical, social, or religious—for offending the morality of their ancestors.

The absence of intracommunal restraints, the desire to conform to English social patterns, and the increasingly secular character of eighteenth-century life in general combined to produce a degree of religious laxity among English Jews, rich and poor, that was without parallel in the Jewish world of the time, with the possible exception of the tiny communities in the New World. Some Jews ceased to practice the rites of Judaism altogether, without necessarily abandoning their identity as Jews—that is, without converting or intermarrying, and without developing an intellectual justification for their break with the past. Many others came to adopt an attitude toward the *mitzvot* that was casual and selective, continuing to observe some *mitzvot* and ignoring others. An individual might close his business on the Sabbath, but eat nonkosher food when visiting Christian friends. He might attend synagogue on one Sabbath and stay at home on the next. Overall, there was little consistency in how much was given up and how much retained. No doubt the vagaries of personality and the length of time spent in England were among the decisive factors in each case.

Among the upper levels of the Jewish middle class, religious laxity was widespread by the 1730s or the 1740s. The laws of *kashrut,* for example, were ignored or observed haphazardly. In 1733, Abigail Franks of New York (the sister-in-law of Aaron, Abraham, and Isaac Franks of London) wrote to her son Naphtali, then living in London, to warn him never to eat a meal "unless it be bread and butter" at the home of her brother, Asher Levy, "nor no where else where there is the least doubt of things not done after our strict Judaical method." In the late 1750s, Chief Rabbi Hirschel Levin complained that as a result of Jews feasting with non-Jews on Christian holidays "the Christmas pudding which the Christians prepare in memory of the Apostles is more favored than the *matzot."* According to another traditionalist, the anonymous author of *Olam hadash olam hafukh,* some Jews said that all that God desired was that men not do evil to each other and that they thus might eat or drink whatever they liked. When Hirschel Levin's son, Solomon Hirschell, arrived from Germany in the fall of 1802 to assume the position of Chief Rabbi (or "High Priest of the Jews," as *The Times* called it), he announced that he would not dispense with the observance of any of the rites of the Jewish religion and that he would punish with excommunication "all such Jews who indulge their appetites with wild fowl."[14]

Rabbi Hirschell was extraordinarily naive, or at least unfamiliar with English conditions, if he seriously believed he would be able to influence the eating habits of his wealthy congregants. Officially, of course, the institutions of Anglo-Jewry remained fully traditional. The directors of the Talmud Torah, for example, in preparing for the annual dinner at the New London Tavern in 1803, gave specific instructions to the Jewish cook whom they hired for the occasion not to use the dishes, cutlery, and kitchenware of the inn, but to provide his own. As private individuals, however, the magnates who dominated the Talmud Torah and the other institutions of Anglo-Jewry were more easygoing in their observance of the laws of *kashrut*. Moses Montefiore and his wife ate nonkosher meat at the seaside inns they visited on their honeymoon in 1812. At a meeting of representatives of the Hambro and the Great Synagogue that same year to discuss the division of the *shehitah* (ritual slaughter) profits, Daniel Eliason (a Goldsmid brother-in-law) said that "some of the Hamburger *shul* takes meat amongst *goyim.*" S. Samuel complained that the Sephardim were receiving too large a share of the *shehitah* profits because they purchased very little kosher meat, less even than the members of the Hambro. The most convincing evidence of the decline in the consumption of kosher meat throughout Anglo-Jewry is the fall in the number of *shohetim* (ritual slaughterers) and *shomerim* (inspectors) hired by the Board of Shehitah, which had responsibility for supervising ritual slaughter in London. In 1804, the Board appointed six *shohetim* and four *shomerim;* in the 1830s, the numbers were reduced to three each, despite the fact that the Jewish population of the metropolis was increasing.[15] It is possible that some Jews purchased kosher meat slaughtered by unlicensed *shohetim,* but this alone would not account for the decline, since there is no reason to believe that more Jews purchased from unlicensed sources in the fourth decade of the century than in the first.

Synagogue attendance also dropped radically over the course of the eighteenth century. By the end of the century, at least two of the three major London synagogues experienced difficulty in gathering a *minyan* (ten men, the requisite quorum for prayer) for daily services. After the 1790s, the New Synagogue appears to have been forced to hire men to make up a *minyan*. In 1807, the Hambro Synagogue hired two persons at sixpence a week for this purpose. At the same time, it also gave notice to those persons on the charity list of the synagogue that they would have sixpence a month deducted from their usual allowance unless they attended services regularly. In 1825, there again was "a deficiency of *minyan* to attend divine service in the synagogue," forcing the Hambro to hire two additional men. The problem apparently became worse, for in 1829 the *parnasim* devised a system to force the poor of the synagogue to attend services. A list was made of all men receiving charity from the congregation, including those who received coals during the winter and *matzot* during Passover, who were capable of attending morning and evening daily services. From this list of forty-three persons, five names were to be taken in rotation every week, and these persons were to be notified in writing to attend regularly. Those who did not attend and were unable to provide a satisfactory excuse were to be deprived of all charity. The largest synagogue in London, the Great Synagogue in Duke's Place, probably did not experience difficulty in finding a *minyan*, because many Jews who were too poor to pay the membership fees of any synagogue attended there. The Great Synagogue did have trouble, however, with members (i.e., middle-class Jews) who were obligated to attend the synagogue on certain festive occasions to be called to the Torah, as is, for example, a bridegroom on the Sabbath prior to his wedding. In 1816, the Committee of the Great Synagogue discussed "the serious evil and inconvenience arising from members returning their letters of *aliyot la-Torah*," and in 1821 it again turned to "the serious and growing evil of persons absenting themselves from the *shul* when they are *hiyyuvim* [obligated]." The revised bylaws of the Great Synagogue, which appeared in 1827, provided fines for those men who refused to be called to the Torah on various occasions: £5 to £10 for a bridegroom, £2 to £5 for the father of a *bar mitzvah*, £2 to £5 for the father of a newborn child.[16]

The casual way in which the Anglo-Jewish middle class observed the dietary laws and attended synagogue also characterized their observance of the laws of Sabbath rest. Jewish brokers, according to Dr. Meyer Schomberg, walked through Change Alley on the Sabbath to learn whether there had been a rise or a fall in the price of stocks. They discussed business matters with one another and even gave instructions regarding the purchase and sale of securities and bills of exchange. "Their day of rest," Schomberg added caustically, "is not a day of rest for them either in this world or the next, because they go to feed themselves at a nearby place, eating of the produce of the land that which it is forbidden to eat and drinking the wine and liquor that makes maids merry, in the company of strange [i.e., non-Jewish] women." Chief Rabbi Hirschel Levin was continually berating his congregants for desecrating the Sabbath. On one occasion, after having listed a number of their transgressions, including cooking on the Sabbath, he burst out: "God knows how tired I am of my life when I see all your doings. I am even afraid to hear what, I am told, is happening publicly, let alone of how you desecrate the Sabbath day in private." The anonymous author of *A Letter to the Parisian Sanhedrin* (1808) reported that there were wealthy Jews who attended synagogue on the Sabbath and the festivals, but immediately afterwards rushed off to the Exchange and the coffee houses. He found nothing "more offensive to decency and to the spirit of genuine piety than to see a set of men, who profess themselves to be members of the Jewish faith, openly and shamelessly transgressing one of its most sacred institutions by publicly and flagitiously transacting business on a day so solemnly set apart by the Divine Will."[17]

The decline in orthodoxy among the Anglo-Jewish elite was as much a compromise with the social and economic demands of English life as it was a rejection of the Jewish past. It would thus be a mistake to view their casualness in religious matters solely as an attempt to escape their Jewishness. Although many wealthy Jews personally strayed from the path of traditional Judaism, they still maintained strong institutional ties to Jewish life. They continued to serve as the lay leaders of nominally orthodox institutions (synagogues, charities, and schools) and to provide financial support for Hebrew scholarship. There were, moreover, even among the wealthiest stratum of Anglo-Jewry, a few individuals and families who preserved the customs of traditional Judaism despite their affluence and their acquisition of English manners. Judith Montefiore (1784–1862) recalled that in the home of her father, the wealthy merchant Levy Barent Cohen, they observed the Ninth of Av by sitting in mourning attire on low stools and reciting the Book of Lamentations. In the home of Mrs. Assur Keyser in Finsbury Square in the 1820s, the first night of Shavuot was observed in the traditional fashion with study and prayer. The diamond merchant Levy Salomons (1774–1843) was known for his piety and his strict adherence to orthodoxy, although he lived in a superbly furnished forty-eight room mansion in Bury Street and maintained a country home at Frants in Sussex. He attended synagogue daily, amassed a library of over four hundred volumes of rare Hebraica, and continued to study traditional religious texts until his death. When he died, he left over £7,750 in bequests to various synagogues and charities, including £2,000 for the Jewish poor of Safad, Tiberias, Hebron, and Jerusalem.[18]

Levy Barent Cohen and Levy Salomons were the exceptions, not the rule. Anglo-Jewry as a whole was not characterized by either its piety or its learning. The one stronghold of orthodoxy in the community was the lower middle class. There, among shopkeepers, artisans, and mildly prosperous street traders, traditional Judaism survived for two or three generations. These men of modest means, many of whom were recent immigrants, formed their own *hevrot* (study groups) and *minyanim* (private prayer meetings), in which they preserved the forms of learning and worship they or their fathers had known in Poland, Germany, and Holland; in fact, an anonymous contributor to *The Gentleman's Magazine* in 1811 claimed that there were many Jewish old-clothes men with a better knowledge of Hebrew than either Chief Rabbi Hirschell or Haham Meldola. One island of traditional piety and scholarship was the Hevrah Shaarei Zion, established around 1770, with Moses ben Judah of Minsk, who gave Talmud *shiurim* (lectures) to the *hevrah,* as its *darshan* (preacher). Some of the *derashot* (sermons) he delivered during his residence in London were published in 1772 as *Sefer even shoham* (The Book of Onyx). Toward the end of the century, a similar group formed around the Lithuanian-born Rabbi Pinchas ben Samuel, who delivered *shiurim* to the *hevrah* three times a week. His *Midrash Pinchas,* a commentary on Talmudic *aggadot* (legends and tales), was published in London in 1795. Among the subscribers to this work were small merchants from Margate, Exeter, and Woolwich.

There were other small groups about which, due to their modest character, even less is known. A *hevrah* called Mahzikei Torah (Upholders of the Law), which later evolved into the Rosemary Lane Synagogue, was established in 1748. In the early 1770s, there was a *hevrah* for *tikkun leil shavuot* (the custom of remaining awake all night on Shavuot in order to read selections from the Bible and rabbinic literature), and from the 1790s through the early 1820s there was a *minyan* for *maariv bizmanah* (for evening prayer at its proper time—a reference to the custom of anglicized Jews of ignoring the laws governing the time of evening prayer [due to the late hour at which the sun sets in England part of the year] and praying at night at an earlier hour). In the 1790s, two Polish *minyanim* were established in Houndsditch, one in Gun Square and the other in Cutler Square.[19]

The traditionalist orientation of the Jewish petite bourgeoisie also manifested itself in the friendly societies they created. The Rodfei Shalom (Pursuers of Peace) Friendly Society appointed a rabbi to deliver a *derashah* every Sabbath afternoon and to attend the *minyan* of the society on the first night of Shavuot and Hoshanah Rabbah and during the period of mourning. The Path of Rectitude Benefit Society provided a rabbi to teach *mishnah* during the period of mourning. The United Israelites barred from membership men who cohabited with non-Jewish women and who were not married according to Jewish law, while the Guardians of Faith, in addition to the above stipulations, barred persons who kept their shops open on Saturday morning and personally attended to business on that day.[20]

Representative of the traditional outlook of this small group of Jews was their willingness to submit voluntarily to the rulings of religious authorities. For example, at Sheerness, on the Kent coast, where a Jewish community grew up during the wars with France at the end of the eighteenth century, a group of Jewish shopkeepers who transgressed the laws of Sabbath rest in a particularly noticeable way in 1812 accepted the penalties imposed by the *bet din* (religious court) in London. This group boarded an English naval vessel on a Friday to collect money the crew owed them. They were apparently unable to complete their business before sundown, for one of them remained aboard the entire night, with the others returning the next day, before the close of the Sabbath. They then proceeded to sell merchandise, as well as write and erase in their account books. The *bet din* ordered those who went aboard the ship to make a public confession in the Sheerness synagogue and to fast on Mondays and Thursdays for forty days. In London, in 1819, David Davis voluntarily appeared before the *bet din* and repented for selling nonkosher cheese to Jews. He signed a document to the effect that he would no longer sell cheese of any kind and agreed to give charity to atone for his wrongdoing.[21] Those who accepted this kind of religious discipline were, it must be remembered, a small minority.

The decline in orthodoxy among the Anglo-Jewish elite was due both to a desire for social conformity and to a growing indifference to religion in general. Contemporaries, however, who despaired over this decline saw only the desire for status as a motive for acculturation. They viewed those who abandoned traditional Jewish practices as unprincipled opportunists eager to obtain the approbation of their gentile peers. "We want to be like them," Chief Rabbi Hirschel Levin complained, we "dress as they dress, talk as they talk, and want to make everybody forget that we are Jews." Another traditionalist, writing in 1789, described those Jews who neglected the *mitzvot* as

> covetous and aspiring persons, apprehensive that a strict adherence to the ways of religion would be utterly inconsistent with their views of rising in the world; who make haste to be rich and find religion would be an obstacle in their way—who, having formed a plan for making a fortune, or for obtaining preferment, resolve to mind nothing that would divert them from the prosecution of it.

That same year the author of *Olam hadash olam hafukh* made much the same argument: "They turn everything upside down. . . . their only purpose in doing all this is to gain honor for themselves and to gain a reputation among the gentiles."[22]

Unquestionably there was a strong component of opportunism in the decline of orthodoxy. Self-made men like the Goldsmids and the Franks were eager to win a place for themselves in upperclass circles; their splendid country homes, their lavish entertaining, and their contributions to non-Jewish charities were designed to advance their claims to gentile status. With such exalted social aspirations, they were unlikely to have allowed the rigorous demands of Halakhah to stand in their way. They could have won a far greater degree of acceptance if they had chosen apostasy, but this was generally too radical a break with the past for them to consider. Their children and their grandchildren, however, who were a full generation or more removed from traditional Judaism, frequently did accept baptism as the most effective means of gaining social acceptability. A Sephardi critic of such conversions, writing at the end of the eighteenth century, called them conversions of pride and vanity: "To the rational man of either religion it must appear a gross abuse of the sacred functions of divine worship."[23]

Still, the desire to moderate Jewish distinctiveness was not the only motive at work in the decline of orthodoxy. Equal consideration must also be given to the increasingly secular nature of English life in general. The intense concern with religious issues that characterized the middle decades of the seventeenth century had relaxed by the middle decades of the eighteenth. Religion ceased to be a matter of overriding interest for the majority of Englishmen, in part because the commercially expansive material culture of England was not conducive to the cultivation of purely spiritual concerns. Within the Church of England, there was a decline in the observance of holy days and of weekday public prayers. Frequently, the Sunday sermon was the major attraction at church services. Anglo-Jewry was not immune to the forces that were desacrilizing English life; however, because religion was so closely bound up with personal and social identity in the case of Jews, English Jews tended not to throw religion overboard altogether but to practice it in a haphazard and nonrigorous manner. The casualness with which many English Jews approached the rituals of Judaism led to glaring inconsistencies by traditional standards. Men with non-Jewish wives maintained their membership in synagogues, demanded that they be called to the Torah, had their children circumcised by unauthorized *mohelim,* and left instructions in their wills that they be buried in Jewish cemeteries. Samson Gideon, whose wife was not Jewish and whose children were raised as Christians, retained his membership in Bevis Marks until 1753, when he resigned over the unauthorized use of his name by the Jewish promoters of the Jew Bill. He continued, however, to contribute to the synagogue anonymously and, when he died, bequeathed a legacy of £1,000 to the congregation, requesting at the same time that he be

buried in the Sephardi cemetery and that his name be commemorated annually on Yom Kippur as one of the benefactors
of the synagogue. At first there was some question whether the
synagogue authorities would allow him to be buried in their
cemetery, "as he had so much deviated from them in his life
time," explained a contributor to *The Gentleman's Magazine* in
1795, "but a large legacy to charitable uses, which they must else
have lost, at last conquered their scruples."[24]

An even more idiosyncratic approach to Judaism was demon-
strated by John King (ca. 1750–1823), né Jacob Rey, a notorious
moneylender, political pamphleteer, and apologist for Judaism.
Educated at the Sephardi charity school in London, King made
his way in the commercial world of the City and married Sara
Lara, sister of the wealthy benefactor of Bevis Marks, Moses Lara.
He later divorced her and married the widowed Countess of
Lanesborough, without, however, converting or formally renouncing Judaism. In 1795, having been sworn in on the New
Testament as a witness in the Court of King's Bench, he was
asked whether he was a Jew or a Christian. He replied that although born a Jew he had been of the established religion since
he had been old enough to think for himself. But he also admitted, under further questioning, that his first wife had been Jewish,
that they had been married according to Jewish rites, and that he
had never been baptized. In 1812, he wrote a series of letters to
the Mahamad (executive committee) of Bevis Marks, proposing
a number of reforms to make the synagogue service more decorous. He explained that his absence from the synagogue for so
many years was due to the irreverent atmosphere there. When he
died in 1823, he left £20 to the synagogue, half to discharge part
of his debt there and half to entitle him to an annual memorial
prayer.[25]

The erratic religious career of John King was symptomatic of
the growing secularization of Anglo-Jewry. In prior centuries, it
would have been unthinkable that a Jew who married a Christian
would have desired to remain within the Jewish community or
that the community would have allowed him to do so, but by the
second half of the eighteenth century, large numbers of both
Christians and Jews were willing to tolerate this kind of behavior.
The religious ideals of the past had lost their old paramountcy.
Most English Jews, regardless of their socioeconomic status, no

longer saw the world through religiously tinted spectacles. They did not particularly care whether other Jews were scrupulous in observing the commandments, because Judaism as a religious system was no longer a crucial element in their own lives. In 1801, when Benjamin Wolfe offered to sell a mahogany dressing case to William Wakefield on a Saturday and Wakefield expressed surprise that Wolfe would do business on the Jewish Sabbath, Wolfe explained that he was "naturalized" (i.e., sufficiently anglicized to ignore Halakhah). Three years earlier, when Abraham Samuels was asked in a court of law whether Jews were not prohibited from using money on the Sabbath, he answered with a straightforward "no." On then being asked, "Are you not so taught [i.e., that it is forbidden] by your priests?" he snapped, "No, it is only a parcel of fools that say so; I will touch money at any time." Doctrines, rituals, customs, and laws—even the question of whether one was a Jew or a Christian—were handled with a casualness and an irreverence that would have been impossible in the previous century. In 1783, John Watson, a Jewish butcher, astonished an English judge by being sworn on a New Testament and then, when resworn on a Hebrew Bible, by not covering his head. The judge found his behavior incomprehensible, as the following exchange reveals:

Court: What do you mean by taking the oath as you did?

J. W.: I never took an oath in my life. . . .

Court: Pray, friend, do not you know when people of your profession take an oath they always put on their hats?

J. W.: I work among Englishmen and I was always among Christians.

Court: Do you mean to take the oath as a Jew or as a Christian?

J. W.: I can call myself a Christian because I am never among the Jews.

Court: What do you call yourself, are you Jew or Christian?

J. W.: I do not know, please your honour; what you please to call me.

Court: I wish you would understand that it is an exceeding indecent thing in you, or any man, to come here to trifle with any religion in the sort of way you do.

J. W.: I follow more the Christian ways than I do the Jews.

Court: You are a good-for-nothing fellow, I dare say, whatever you are. Stand down.[26]

The spread of a secular outlook among English Jews brought about a decline in the moral authority of the traditional rulers of the Jewish community—the rabbis and the *parnasim*. In the premodern world, the prestige attached to the rabbinate was due to the central role of Halakhah in Jewish life. The rabbi was the preeminent authority on ritual matters, the judge who administered the religious law, the head of the local *yeshivah,* and the spiritual shepherd of his flock. In a society in which religious and social concerns were inseparable, he was essential to the maintenance of that society. In England, where talmudic knowledge had little practical value for most Jews and Jewish self-government did not exist, the rabbi possessed little influence. Rabbinic learning was cultivated and valued by only a tiny minority. The Ashkenazi community never supported a *yeshivah,* for example, and in the late 1750s Chief Rabbi Hirschel Levin complained that he did not have even a colleague with whom to pursue his studies. His successor as Chief Rabbi, David Tevele Schiff, made the same complaint.[27]

In those states where the Jewish community enjoyed legal autonomy, the rabbi had to adjudicate complex civil proceedings. In England, from the very first years of the Resettlement, Jews had full access to state courts and only turned to their own religious courts to settle cases involving marriage, divorce, and *kashrut.* As the polemicist Solomon Bennett (1761–1838) wrote in 1818, it was not "necessary for a rabbi in this country to be overstocked with difficult learning," for in most civil matters, including inheritance, Jews went to the courts of the realm. "It is only over the ritual law and some ceremonial institutions peculiar to our nation that the rabbi has his sway, though with little effect, as his adherents pay very little obedience to those rites and observances, nor does the rabbi reprimand their trespasses." Even in marriage cases it was not unknown for well-to-do Jews to have recourse to non-Jewish courts. In two well-known cases of the 1790s (Goldsmid v. Bromer and Lindo v. Belisario)—in each a young man secretly married, according to Jewish ritual, the sixteen-year-old daughter of a wealthy Jewish merchant—the irate fathers sought to have the marriages annulled in the Consistory Court of London, a quasi-ecclesiastical court. In both cases, the fathers argued that the marriages were invalid according to Jewish law; the judge, in turn, decided the cases according to Jewish law as it was expounded to him by several expert witnesses.[28]

The authority of the rabbinate was also weakened by the widespread recognition that it had lost much of its independent moral authority and had become subservient to the great magnates who, as *parnasim* of the synagogues, dominated communal affairs. The *takkanot* (bylaws) of the Great Synagogue in effect from 1722 to 1791 imposed severe restrictions on the rabbi of the congregation: he was not allowed to place anyone in *herem* (excommunication), nor to officiate at a marriage or a divorce, nor to intervene in any private quarrel without the sanction of the *parnasim*. The *takkanot* adopted in 1826 required the rabbi to obtain the prior consent of the *parnasim* whenever he wanted to deliver a Sabbath afternoon sermon. In 1801, when the Ashkenazi synagogues of London were discussing the hiring of a new Chief Rabbi, the privileged members of the Hambro Synagogue decided, by a vote of 20 to 13, that it was unnecessary to have a Chief Rabbi at all. Solomon Bennett, a bitter critic of Chief Rabbi Hirschell, publicly denounced Hirschell for his subservience to the Anglo-Jewish elite. In a pamphlet he published in 1818, he charged that Hirschell obtained his position in London through the influence of wealthy merchants in Berlin who did business with the Goldsmids and the Keysers; Hirschell's father, Hirschel Levin, the former Chief Rabbi in London, was then Rabbi of Berlin. Being indebted to such powerful men, Bennett charged, Hirschell ignored their transgressions. Why, he asked, was Hirschell "so indifferent to [the sins of] the bulk of his synagogue, the followers of his standard?" He was certainly aware that the Royal Exchange, the Stock Exchange, and the adjoining coffee houses were filled with Jewish merchants transacting business on the Sabbath and the festivals. He was aware that most Jewish merchants worked in their warehouses and offices on the Sabbath, that most Jewish shopkeepers kept their stores open on the Sabbath, that picture dealers and secondhand clothing and furniture dealers attended public auctions on the Sabbath, "all without blushing before the Christian community." Why did he not rebuke his congregants? "Because it would not answer so well his purpose, or because his followers would look upon him with a frown." When Hirschell gave his official sanction to a mildly nonorthodox catechism for youth, *Shorshei emunah* (The Roots of Faith), by the German *maskil* Shalom Cohen, he did so, according to Bennett, at the request of "some of the grandees of the synagogue," although he knew full well that Cohen had little regard for rabbinic Judaism.[29]

Bennett was not an entirely disinterested critic. As a young man living in Berlin in the 1790s, he had clashed with the father Hirschel Levin, and in London, when he had been unable to pay the costs of a suit he had lost, he had been confined to Newgate Prison by two Jewish printers supported by the son Solomon Hirschell. Beneath the personal animosity that inflamed his judgment, however, there was an irrefutable kernel of truth: Hirschell, who was Chief Rabbi from 1802 to 1842, had little impact on Anglo-Jewish life. It is abundantly clear from the minutes of the London congregations and of the *bet din* over which he presided that his influence was limited to matters in which the Anglo-Jewish middle class had no personal interest. Only in a very few instances did they seek his opinion or follow his lead. In 1805, for example, the Hambro Synagogue asked him if there was any halakhic impediment to selling the building it then occupied to the East India Company. In 1826, as mentioned earlier, he convinced the *parnasim* of the Great Synagogue that it was foolish to make announcements in a language most of the worshipers could not understand. And in 1829, he ordered Barnard Van Oven, physician to the poor of the Great Synagogue, to abstain from writing prescriptions for the poor on the Sabbath, an order which was upheld by the *parnasim* after Van Oven appealed the matter to them.[30] Such minor judgments were typical of the limited power Hirschell exercised.

Contempt for the authority of the rabbinate manifested itself in a conscious evasion of rabbinical control over marriage, divorce, and conversion. As the state took no interest in regulating marriages between Jews, and as a Jewish marriage can be solemnized without the presence or the consent of an ordained rabbi,

English Jews openly contracted marriages prohibited by Jewish law. Indeed, among the Jewish poor, couples often lived together as husband and wife without benefit of any Jewish ritual whatsoever. In one particularly notorious case in 1825, Solomon Bennett performed a marriage that the Chief Rabbi had previously refused to sanction. Aaron Cohen wanted to marry Rachel, a convert to Judaism, the daughter of Jacob Harris, a Jew, and a Christian woman. Jewish law, however, does not permit a Cohen (a descendant, in theory, of the ancient priesthood) to marry a proselyte. In open defiance of the Chief Rabbi, Bennett and Jacob Michalki, a Sephardi, celebrated the marriage and then submitted a document (now unfortunately lost) defending themselves by a liberal reinterpretation of certain passages in Maimonides. Hirschell and Haham Meldola declared their reasoning to be a perversion of the law: "The words [of Maimonides] are decidedly contrary to the sense upon which the said marriage was allowed and celebrated." Announcements were made in the synagogues declaring the marriage invalid and prohibiting the bridegroom from enjoying any synagogal honors.[31] In actuality, though, there was nothing any of the communal leaders could do to separate the couple. The Jewish community was not an autonomous corporate body with legal authority of its own, but an array of voluntary associations. The rabbis and the *parnasim* of the various congregations had no real powers of coercion. Once the inner compulsion to obey the law and its interpreters, the rabbinate, had weakened, there was little to restrain individual Jews from doing as they pleased. They did not have to fear social ostracism, for the London Jewish community was too heterogeneous and open to the surrounding world to permit that kind of pressure. There were, moreover, enough like-minded nonconformists within Anglo-Jewry to provide a supportive peer group for those who defied the official leadership.

The Sephardi authorities also faced challenges to their rule, being plagued particularly with the problem of unauthorized conversions. The Mahamad refused to permit Christians to be converted to Judaism under its authority, because it believed that the original terms of the Resettlement prohibited them from proselytizing in England. Persons, generally women, who wished to marry Jewish partners were required to travel to Holland to undergo conversion. But as conversion, like marriage, does not require the presence of an ordained rabbi, and as many potential converts did not want the bother of traveling to Holland or could not afford to, conversions took place in defiance of the Mahamad. As early as 1751, Bevis Marks wrote to the Hambro and the Great synagogues about "the growing evil among us," that of admitting proselytes, and asked them to forbid their members from officiating at conversions. In 1824, when Joshua Sarfaty de Pinna requested permission from the Mahamad to marry a woman with whom he had been living for a number of years, the Mahamad refused because the woman had been converted in England. The following year, when the Haham and M. Lindo refused to permit the burial of a child of Joseph Martines and a Christian woman who lived with him as his wife, Martines distributed a handbill about Change Alley, where the stock brokers transacted business, in which he charged that the tempest created by their refusal would lead to "an exposure of how many Christian females have been made Jewesses in London contrary to Law" (i.e., the bylaws of the Sephardi congregation, not Jewish law). An even more flagrant disregard for communal authority and religious orthodoxy manifested itself in the conversion of Sarah Inness in 1816. In that year, Joseph Jonas, a Sephardi, married Sarah Inness in a Christian ceremony, but because this upset his father, Jonas decided that it would be best if she were converted and they were also married according to Jewish rites. The father made arrangements with Elimelech Mudahy, who was known to perform clandestine conversions for a fee, to have her converted at the Ashkenazi *mikveh* (ritual bath) in Heneage Lane. The witnesses were Ashkenazim, who were made to swear that they would not reveal any of the circumstances. The father then applied to the Mahamad for permission for his son to marry Sarah bat Israel.[32]

The synagogal authorities, lay and rabbinic, Ashkenazi and Sephardi, were slow in perceiving that they were no longer living under the same set of social and political circumstances their fathers had been accustomed to elsewhere in Europe, that the old forms of social control had broken down, that internal and external pressures for conformity had weakened. Repeatedly they acted in a high-handed and arrogant way toward recalcitrant individuals, expecting them to submit naturally to their authority. When members refused to pay fines for not accepting office or for not attending the synagogue when they were to be called to the Torah, they roared and thundered and slapped them with more fines. When these persons then threatened to withdraw, the authorities replied that they were not permitted to do so. They acted as if they were not fully aware of the voluntaristic character of Jewish communal life in England, as if their decisions carried the weight of law. But as Thomas Witherby explained in 1809,

> The Jews, as such, are under no control in this land, as to their religion; they stand, in this respect, upon the same ground as every other dissenter from the establishment, and you must well know that a dissenting minister has no power over the members of his congregation, further than that deference and respect extends which everyone should pay to his instructor.[33]

The inability or refusal of synagogal authorities to recognize the nature of Jewish life in a liberal state led to a number of stormy confrontations with members who would not defer to their rule. In 1772, for example, when the Haham and the Mahamad excommunicated a member of the Lara family for his part in the clandestine marriage of Sarah Ximenes and Joshua Lara, an anonymous writer ridiculed their efforts to coerce dissident members:

> You impose fines without having power to exact them; and you prohibit your refractory brethren from the ceremony of a reputable burial, as if you seriously believed it to be a matter of consequence whether the inanimate carcase of a man rots in your ground or in that of St. Paul's. Your anathemas may frighten old women and children, and very probably alarm the weak and bigotted of your society; but men of common understanding regard them with the most perfect indifference; and if, in compliance with the prejudice of their friends, they should desire to be restored to the customary rites of the Synagogue, in those moments when far removed, they are no longer subject to your censures. A legacy of £1000 conditionally bequeathed in their wills will soften the severity of your displeasure [a reference to Samson Gideon], and induce you to receive the repentant sinners to your bosoms, although they had violated one of the most sacred and established laws of your society, by marrying a follower of Jesus Christ.

When Samuel Cohen was notified in 1817 that he had been elected a *parnas* of the Hambro Synagogue, he wrote to the Committee that he had been abroad the past ten years, was now living in the country, was unfamiliar with the bylaws of the synagogue, and had no interest in learning them. The Secretary replied that the fine for refusing the office was thirty guineas, but that as Cohen had served in this office previously the fine would be only fifteen guineas. With this letter, the Secretary enclosed a copy of the bylaws. Cohen returned the booklet with the following note:

> S. Cohen thinks a Secretary of the H[ambro] Chambers ought to understand a plain English letter, so he returns their law book. His arbitrary government could hardly expect he would serve the office, so he'll abide by being pilfered—not to use a harsher word. And it will put them in the power of destroying more money then [than they] have already.

Isaac D'Israeli's formal withdrawal from the Sephardi community was prompted by precisely the same kind of shortsightedness on the part of the Elders of Bevis Marks. Although he was not an observant Jew, D'Israeli had always paid an annual assessment of £10, as well as a few guineas more for charity. In 1813, he was elected a *parnas;* he declined the office and was fined £40. In a lengthy reply to the Mahamad, in which he explained his absence from the synagogue—"your public worship . . . as now conducted . . . disturbs instead of exciting religious emotions"—he charged the Mahamad with weakening even further the bonds that held acculturated Sephardim together in a religious community:

> the government of a small sect can only be safely conducted by enlightened principles, and must accommodate itself with practical wisdom to existing circumstances, but above all with a tender regard to the injured feelings of its scattered members. Something like the domestic affections should knit us all together—a society existing on the voluntary aid of its members is naturally in a feeble state, and if it invests itself with arbitrary power, a blind precipitation in a weak body can only tend to self-destruction. Many of your members are already lost; many you are losing! Even those whose tempers and feelings would still cling to you, are gradually seceding.[34]

In North America, where the same liberal principle of voluntarism determined the organization of Jewish life, the problem of discipline also plagued synagogue authorities. In 1786, the wardens of Congregation Shearith Israel in New York City wrote several letters to Lion Jonas, who had transgressed the laws of Sabbath rest for a considerable time, demanding that he appear before them. He ignored their demands and appeared in the courtyard of the synagogue on the Ninth of Av to denounce them. In Philadelphia, in 1782, a Cohen married a widow who had been converted to Judaism before her first marriage, despite a specific prohibition from the authorities of Congregation Mikveh Israel not to do so. Three years later, this same congregation complained to the rabbis of Sephardi congregations in Amsterdam and The Hague about the difficulty of enforcing their will:

> In this country each man does as he sees fit . . . the local congregation has no power to force or to punish anyone, with the single exception of the small fine of withdrawing from such people the honors of the synagogue and not to reckon them among the quorum necessary for religious purposes, and despite this penalty these people still insist on attending services at the synagogue as this cannot be prevented owing to the laws of the country.[35]

Anglo-Jewry was not especially verbal about its break with the past. Unlike the German Jewish bourgeoisie, it did not create an ideology to justify the departure from tradition, nor did it undertake to reinterpret Judaism in the light of reason and modern culture.* Thus, it is difficult to know how most English Jews regarded their abandonment of orthodoxy. Some persons came to justify this break on the grounds that ethical behavior was more important in God's eyes than the observance of the ritual law. As early as the 1750s, there were Jews in London who claimed that they need observe only the seven ethical Noachide laws (derived from the early chapters of Genesis), since they were of the same stock as Christians, all of them being descendants of Noah's three sons. A traditionalist critic of religious laxity, writing in 1789, reported that there were Jews who saw no insult to

---

*There was no Haskalah in England in the sense there was in Germany—that is, there was no *movement* for the modernization of Judaism and Jewish life. There were a few individuals who shared some of the aspirations of the German *maskilim*, but they created no ideological movement. There were also a few learned Hebrew scholars who wrote in a modernized Hebrew style, at times on themes of general cultural interest. This, however, can hardly justify Cecil Roth's claim that there was a Haskalah in England. See his article, "The Haskalah in England," in *Essays Presented to Chief Rabbi Israel Brodie on the Occasion of his Seventieth Birthday*, ed. H. J. Zimmels et al., 2 vols. (London, 1967), 1:365–76.

God in mixing meat and milk or in eating forbidden foods because all that God desired was that they not do evil to other persons. As for customs and rituals, they retorted, "What is all this to God? What does it matter if we do or we do not do all these things?"[36]

Other individuals went much further and rejected revealed religion altogether. At the end of the eighteenth century, Jacob Mocatta urged the Elders of the Spanish and Portuguese Synagogue to institute reforms in order to prevent the defection of young persons who preferred "the promiscuous paths of Scepticism, Deism, and Christianity." A pamphlet published sometime early in the next century by the London Society for Promoting Christianity among the Jews reported that it was not uncommon "to meet with Israelites who are not ashamed to profess that they think as little of Moses as of Christ, and who on the uncertainties of Deism ground all their religious principles."[37]

By the 1830s, the number of Jewish Deists and skeptics had multiplied considerably. Robert Southey wrote to a friend in 1830 that rich Jews were "pretty generally of Mendelssohn's religion, or of Voltaire's, the difference between them is only in morals not in dogmas [*sic*]."[38] H. J. Marks, a convert to Christianity, divided the nonorthodox into a few Jews who rejected the authority of the oral law but considered themselves bound to the written law, and a numerous class who were "as regardless of the one as the other." Rabbi Tobias Goodman, in a polemical work published in 1834 "to rescue the sacred words of God from the attacks of the enemies of Holy Scripture and Revelation," listed two kinds of enemies to traditional religious beliefs: those who denied altogether the truth of the events described in the Bible, considering them to be fabulous tales, and those who acknowledged that the events occurred, but denied that Divine Providence was at work, attributing all the miracles to chance and nature.[39]

These opponents of traditional Judaism were not a vocal or well-organized group. Their militancy and their strength were no doubt exaggerated by both the orthodox Jews and the Christian missionaries who took notice of them for reasons of their own. They rarely ventured into print and never undertook any campaign to embarrass the orthodox camp. Their critique of traditional Judaism was more emotional than rational, more effusive than systematic. The anonymous author of *A Peep into the Synagogue,* one of a handful of printed works that attacked Jewish practices for conflicting with Reason and Nature, was as much motivated by a concern for social propriety and conformity as he was by the dictates of reason. His diatribe on circumcision conveys something of the emotional nature of his argument:

> In the extravagant catalogue of Jewish absurdities, there is not one more shameful and reprehensible than that of circumcision. It is a barbarous violation of the principles of humanity and an insult to the God of Nature. For what can be more unhuman than to punish an infant by a cruel operation on a part of its body, done by a bungling butcher of a rabbi: or what can be more insulting to the all wise Creator than for a stupid fool of a fellow to presume to correct His workmanship by finding one superfluous part and taking that away to reduce the subject to perfection.

In all likelihood, many of those who were branded as Deists by the traditional camp did not deserve the name. Many were merely religiously apathetic, having given up traditional worship and ritual from a desire for social conformity. When pressed to justify their defection, such persons appealed, not always coherently, to an amorphous body of enlightenment notions. The wealthy merchant Samuel Emden, testifying at the Old Bailey in 1810, gave such a confused defense of his "Deism" as to suggest that it was a hastily contrived rationale for something else:

Q: You were sworn at the [magistrate's] office upon the New Testament?

A: I was.

Q: You, being a Jew, do not like the New Testament?

A: That I deny.

Q: My question is whether you believe the New Testament.

A: I believe it so much; I believe that a great part of the New Testament is made out of the Old Testament, and that I am bound upon oath to the Supreme Being to speak the truth.

Q: Are you a Christian or a Jew?

A: I am of the Jewish persuasion.

Q: You think it the same thing to swear by the Holy Gospels as by the Old Testament?

A: I answer, I swear by the Supreme Being; if I swear by either, or both the books, my oath is binding to me.

Q: You know the nature of an oath. If you swear by the New Testament, you swear believing the contents of that book, and that Christ is God; now, as a Jew (if you are a Jew), that is inconsistent. You are not a Christian. A man that does not believe the Godhead of Christ is not a Christian.

A: If I have been in an error, I believe that in swearing, so help me God, I swear by the Supreme Being, my oath is binding to me.

Q: If you are a Jew, do you believe it to be the same thing to swear upon the five books of Moses, as upon the Evangelists?

A: I did answer that. I certainly do believe I am bound to speak the truth on one book as well as the other. I believe Jesus Christ to be a prophet.

Q: You believe Jesus Christ to be a prophet. Then you are a Mahometan? He believed in the New Testament; he did not believe Jesus Christ to be God.

A: I believe him to be a great man—a very great prophet.[40]

The most articulate critic of traditional Judaism, oddly enough, was Isaac D'Israeli. In his novel *Vaurien,* in an essay on Moses Mendelssohn (1798), and in *The Genius of Judaism* (1833), he developed a critique of traditional Jewish culture that closely resembled that of the radical *maskilim* in Germany. D'Israeli explicitly rejected the authority of the oral law. The rabbis of ancient Judaism, whom he called "dictators of the human intellect" and "a race of dreaming schoolmen," had tricked the Jews into accepting their decisions as divine law. They had "cast their people into a bondage of ridiculous customs." The Jews were immersed "in a mass of ritual ordinances, casuistical glosses, and arbitrary decisions." The Talmud, the bête noire of *maskilim* everywhere, was

a prodigious mass of contradictory opinions, an infinite number of casuistical cases, a logic of scholastic theology, some recondite wisdom, and much rambling dotage; many puerile tales and oriental fancies; ethics and sophisms, reasonings and unreasonings, subtle solutions, and maxims and riddles.

D'Israeli believed that even the Mosaic code had not been designed for perpetuity, that many laws had become obsolete because their objects were no longer relevant, and that laws should change or be abandoned with changing times. The traditional Jewish educational system, which was devoted exclusively to the cultivation of rabbinic learning, had made the Jews intellectually inferior to other Europeans. It was "inimical to the progress of the human mind" and "little favourable to form a taste for the productions of nature and art." This narrow preoccupation with talmudic knowledge, abetted by "the silken cord of commerce," had made the Jewish national character "monotonous," extinguishing "the bolder and prominent passions." "Everywhere the Jew degenerates: this degeneracy has passed from their mind to their form; diminuitive and timorous." Jewish students were sickly; they avoided athletic exercise and wasted their youth "in growing pale over this immense repository of human follies [the Talmud]."[41]

The regeneration of the Jews, D'Israeli argued, would be brought about through their own self-regeneration. They would have to cease to believe that the Torah contains all that is worth knowing and begin to educate their youth "as the youth of Europe and not of Palestine; let their Talmud be removed to an elevated shelf, to be consulted as a curiosity of antiquity, and not as a manual of education." D'Israeli praised the "modern literary Jews" of Berlin—and Mendelssohn in particular— for the great strides they had made in embracing European culture and those among "the higher classes of the Hebrews" in England who were educating their children in Christian schools. He called on the Jews to reject every "anti-social principle" in their culture, that is, almost everything that set them apart from non-Jews, so that they might fuse socially and politically with their fellow citizens: "let them only separate to hasten to the Church and to the Synagogue."[42]

D'Israeli's attack on traditional Judaism was in several respects typical of the radical opposition to orthodoxy. It was made by a person who was already alienated from religious life and whose ties to the organized community were tenuous and formal. It evoked little, if any, response within the community, probably because it was the product of an outsider, of a person who had no influence on the community as such. Above all, it was the opinion of only a handful of English Jews. Most Jews who gave up traditional Judaism did not go to the lengths D'Israeli did to intellectualize that break; they maintained a nominal allegiance to the ideas and the institutions of orthodoxy and simply ignored those elements that were an obstacle to their enjoyment of life in this world. They were, to use a paradoxical phrase, nonobservant orthodox Jews. Like the majority of property-owning Englishmen in the eighteenth and early nineteenth centuries, they were content to remain within the bosom of the established church (or synagogue) without giving much time or thought to the demands of their formal religious identity. How they felt about their ambiguous, somewhat paradoxical position—if they ever thought consciously about it at all—is impossible to know.

There was, however, from about 1800, a small group of very moderate reformers who did articulate a critique of traditional Judaism in the hope of reviving and modernizing Jewish life. Unlike their German counterparts, they did not set out to make sweeping changes in Jewish tradition, nor did they develop any systematic intellectual framework for their dissent from orthodoxy. Indeed, only in the area of education for the Jewish poor did they have any impact as an active force for modernization. But it is possible, despite their silence from a programmatic viewpoint, to gain some sense of their liberal approach to Jewish tradition from comments they made in other contexts. As a group, they were opposed to what can only be described as an unbending orthodoxy; still, they were never very specific about how rigid was too rigid. The anonymous author of *A Letter to the Parisian Sanhedrin* felt that some reforms were necessary "to restore our religion to its primitive purity and excellence." Over the centuries, a few errors and superstitions had become attached to the oral law. Many of the rabbis, quite innocently and out of a mistaken sense of piety, had put "laboured, forced, and unnatural constructions" on "the *plain* and manifest sense and meaning of several passages in our holy writ," with the result that they had "done more to weaken and impair, than to strengthen the religion they were so anxious to defend." The author of this tract, however, had no sympathy at all for the radical repudiation of

Jewish tradition undertaken by the Sanhedrin in Paris. He recognized quite clearly that the decisions Napoleon was pressuring the Sanhedrin to adopt, under the false pretense of introducing salutary reforms, were aimed at the "entire subversion" of the Mosaic law. The external forms of Judaism were necessary to preserve the Jewish religion. If the dietary laws or the prohibition on intermarriage were to be relaxed, "every vestige of our religion will quickly disappear; and at the hymeneal altars and convivial boards of those, whose religious worship differs from ours, every trace of Judaism would be speedily lost." When Chief Rabbi Hirschell admonished Asher Goldsmid for wearing leather boots, instead of cloth slippers, on Yom Kippur in 1808 and ordered him to come down from the reading desk after he had been called up to the Torah, the Hebrew printer Levy Alexander accused him of "bracing up the already too rigid precepts of our ceremonial law": "The exactness with which you acted in the Synagogue during the Service, on so pious a day, may gain you respect only among little minds more scrupulous than wise."[43]

These moderate reformers commented more frequently on the necessity of expanding the intellectual perspective of Anglo-Jewry than they did on the necessity of changing this or that particular custom. They rejected the belief that the study of rabbinical texts should be the foundation of Jewish education and all other learning should be peripheral to that. Levy Alexander regretted "the want of a due respect to learning among our people . . . the bulk of whom [were] without education" and noted admiringly, in his biography of Benjamin Goldsmid, how the German *maskilim* "had advanced themselves forward in the Republic of letters."

> Would that as much could be said of our people here in England! But Heaven forbids their union with learning in this country and leaves them abject slaves of prejudice and obstinacy like their forefathers were several centuries ago.

Solomon Bennett, a native of Polozk, Russia, having lived in Berlin from 1795 to 1799, remarked how the Jewry of the Prussian capital had managed to pursue a wide variety of intellectual activities despite their degraded political status, and how worthy they were of acceptance among the most refined classes of mankind. He hoped that the rabbis of his own time would study the secular arts and sciences (Hirschell, for example, could not read English) so that they could thereby enhance the Jewish religion in the way Judah Ha-Levi, Maimonides, Abraham Ibn Ezra, and Isaac Abravanel had done.[44]

Moses Mendelssohn was singled out by Bennett and the others as the great symbol of Jewish enlightenment and progress in the modern era. Moses Samuel, the most extreme of this group of Anglo-Jewish *maskilim,* thought Mendelssohn the most brilliant constellation seen on the Jewish horizon since the twelfth century, that is, since Maimonides. In 1825, he published a biography of Mendelssohn in which he praised in the most extravagant terms the Jewish philosopher's work to revive the Jewish people:

> *Moses* the son of *Amram* delivered his brethren from bodily slavery; the glorious task of emancipating their *minds* was reserved for *Moses* the son of *Mendel.* . . .

> Like his prototype and namesake *Moses, Mendelssohn* delivered his people from the bondage of their benighted task-masters; like him, he led them forty years through the desert of ignorance and superstition, during which he sustained them with the manna of his wisdom, bore meekly and patiently with their stubbornness and perversity, and defeated their adversaries.[45]

Interestingly, in celebrating Mendelssohn and his heirs as the embodiment of Jewish enlightenment, these English reformers rarely said anything specific about the content of their intellectual achievement. This would seem to suggest that they were more concerned with the social consequences of enlightenment (i.e., with proving to the non-Jewish world that Jews were capable of becoming Europeans) than they were with the intellectual reconciliation of Judaism and European culture. If true, this would also explain why they treated the German *maskilim* as a homogeneous coterie and ignored or remained ignorant of the profound differences between the radicals, the moderates, and Mendelssohn himself (who never departed from orthodox practice). Indeed, these Anglo-Jewish moderates would have found the ideas of the German radicals, such as David Friedländer or Lazarus Ben-david, totally unacceptable. That they treated them in this indiscriminate way may mean also that they did not know much of their work at first hand and relied largely on accounts of persons who had some personal contact with the German Haskalah, like Benjamin Goldsmid (who had traveled in Germany in the late 1770s), Solomon Bennett, and Michael Josephs (who had lived in Berlin, also in the late 1770s). The symbolic importance of enlightenment, in any case, appears to have been more important to them than the actual content of any ideological program.

Despite a lack of intellectual rigor and a general tendency toward vagueness, the Anglo-Jewish reformers were fairly explicit in their attitude toward the oral law and the study of rabbinic texts. Moses Samuel took the most extreme position of any: rabbinic learning consisted of "farfetched and distorted quotations, arbitrary and preposterous definitions, together with eccentric deductions." The youth of Germany and Poland, he wrote, were "taught to prattle mechanically the Mishna and Gemara concerning laws of betrothing, divorce, legal damages, sacerdotal functions, and other similar matters above their comprehension before they were able to read and understand a single text of Scripture correctly." Other writers downgraded the primacy of rabbinic learning in the Jewish tradition by simply ignoring it. In Joshua Van Oven's translation of Shalom Cohen's *Shorshei emunah* (1815), a guide to Judaism for young people, there was no mention at all of any source of Jewish authority other than the Bible. When the author raised the question whether there were any sacred books besides the Torah, the answer was, "Yes, the Prophets and the Writings," and then he added: "We must likewise *respect* the works of those latter sages who have elucidated these books" [emphasis added]. In his own *Manual of Judaism,* published twenty years later, Van Oven acknowledged the Mosaic origin of the written and the oral law and stated that Judaism required an exact observance of all the laws and statutes contained in the Torah. But, despite this formal acknowledgement, he devoted very little of the *Manual* to describing these laws and statutes. Instead he concentrated on explaining abstract religious concepts and ethical principles. His purpose was not to teach children the *mitzvot,* but to awaken their spiritual capacity "so that the vivid sensation of a divinity, inherent in the human soul, may be roused into a sacred feeling, and the pupil gradually impressed with a full and proper sense of devotion towards an Almighty and protecting God."[46]

Only one of the Anglo-Jewish reformers articulated a coherent and balanced view of the rabbinic tradition—the Polish-born autodidact, Hyman Hurwitz (1775/76–1844), the master of the first Jewish public school in England and later the first Professor of Hebrew at University College, London. In 1826, Hurwitz translated and published a collection of *aggadot* from the Talmud and the Midrash, to which he added a long introductory apology for rabbinic literature. Hurwitz argued that the Talmud had been treated unfairly by its detractors. They had ransacked it for every absurdity they could find, they had taken allegorical expressions and stories at face value, they had considered every witty saying, every jeu d'esprit, as a serious expression—all without any concern for the age in which the Talmud had been composed. What Hurwitz called for in evaluating the Talmud was a sense of history. The rabbis of that age, he explained, had expressed their thoughts in the language of metaphor and allegory, just as other oriental philosophers had. He was willing to admit that the Talmud contained many things an enlightened Jew might wish had never appeared there and that it included a host of contradictions, but he argued that these could be satisfactorily explained by a historical perspective. The objectionable passages came to be inserted because every utterance of the sages was accorded reverence by the Jews of earlier ages; the contradictions were to be expected in a work composed by "thousands of learned men, of various talents, living in a long series of ages, in different countries, and under the most diversified conditions."[47]

Like most of the German *maskilim*, Hurwitz was not willing to grant that the oral law was on the same level as the written law. His friend Coleridge cast him as "the Luther of Judaism, in recalling his brethren from the swamps of Talmudism to the terra firma of Holy Writ." The same historical perspective that allowed him to appreciate the fabulous elements in the *aggadah* also permitted him to reject the divine character of rabbinic law. It, too, was a creation of a historical epoch and had to be understood in the context of that period. Ordinances that had been devised by the rabbis in earlier centuries to keep the people from idolatry had lost their purpose. The propriety of laws depended on the circumstances of the times in which they were enacted. In debating the authority of talmudic ordinances, one had to ask oneself:

How far it was in the power of any man, or set of men, however learned, and wise, and pious, to bind posterity in matters of conscience?—how far it was even their intention that those ordinances and regulations should permanently remain an integral part of religion under circumstances totally different from those under which they were first enacted?—and whether those pious men, were they now alive, would not see the necessity of abolishing some of them, particularly when those ordinances, instead of proving preservatives to the law, tend to injure it?[48]

Hurwitz was a far more sophisticated and original thinker than any of the other Anglo-Jewish *maskilim*. With his historical approach to rabbinic literature, Hurwitz anticipated the German school of modern Jewish scholarship, although he never appreciated the revolutionary implications of his method (possibly due to his lack of formal training in secular subjects).[49] In terms of immediate impact, however, he was strikingly ineffectual. His influence on the thinking of the Anglo-Jewish elite was, to all appearances, negligible and limited to whatever impression he made on the children of the elite during his tenure as master of the first modern Jewish academy (1799–1821).

In his lack of discernible impact on the outlook of the Anglo-Jewish middle class, Hurwitz was no different than the other few English *maskilim*. Ideas played no great part in shaping the perspective or the activity of the bulk of Anglo-Jewry. The commercial and financial magnates who controlled the institutional life of the community were largely motivated by social considerations. They sometimes borrowed slogans and phrases from the *maskilim*, but these were really nothing more than adornment. This is nowhere more evident than in the series of moderate piecemeal synagogue reforms they instituted in the 1820s and 1830s, prior to the organization of a separatist reformed synagogue in 1840. In altering a number of traditional practices in the worship service, they strove to make their service more decorous rather than more rational, more genteel rather than more theologically correct. Unlike the German reformers, they did not tamper with references to the restoration of the Davidic kingdom or the coming of the Messiah, nor did they introduce cosmetic changes of a radical nature, such as organ accompaniment or prayer in the vernacular, but restricted themselves largely to external improvements of a minor character.

The earliest move to make Jewish worship in England conform more closely to the dominant English pattern came in the mid-eighteenth century when the Great Synagogue ordered its *hazan* to wear canonicals, that is, a long black robe with a pair of white ribbons hanging at the front of the neck.* (A mezzotint of Isaac Polack, *hazan* of the Great Synagogue at midcentury, shows him dressed in such a manner. With his clerical robes, his three-cornered hat, his powdered wig, and his clean-shaven countenance, he is indistinguishable from a minister of the Church of England.) After this innovation, there were no further moves to anglicize Jewish worship until the 1820s, although there was criticism of the indecorous, foreign nature of the Jewish service previous to that time. Around 1800, for example, the anonymous author of *A Peep into the Synagogue* criticized Jewish worship for its lack of true devotion. He complained that almost none of the worshipers were able to understand the prayers they were repeating and, as a consequence, spent their time gossiping and discussing business. He charged that the sale of honors during the service had degenerated into an opportunity for an ostentatious display of wealth, with members of the congregation seeking to outbid each other for "superstitious" privileges. He also attacked the custom whereby persons who had been called to the Torah requested special prayers *(mi she-berakh*s) in honor of relations and friends, since such prayers also required that the persons requesting them offer a contribution to the congregation. The synagogue, he complained, had become an auction room. The Jews, he charged in words that echo a familiar anti-Semitic accusation, seemed to be incapable of accomplishing anything unless money was somehow involved: "Whether you are employed in temporal or spiritual pursuits, money is the moving spirit of all your actions." To make the synagogue "a place of true devotion, solely dedicated to the living God," the author proposed that the sale of synagogue honors and the offering of lengthy *mi she-berakh*s be abolished and that the service be conducted in English.[50] His recommendations, needless to say, were far too radical to gain any kind of hearing; indeed, the overall tone of the

---

*Sephardi rabbis in Holland and England wore clerical gowns and collars from the end of the seventeenth century. The clerical robe and white collar bands only began to appear among German rabbis in the first decades of the nineteenth century. See Alfred Rubens, *A History of Jewish Costume* (London, 1967): 175–94.

tract—strident, tactless, vituperative—was in itself sufficient guarantee that the leaders of the community would ignore, if not damn, its author.

The first serious attempt to make Anglo-Jewish worship more genteel came in 1820. Twenty-two privileged members of the Great Synagogue requested the Committee of the synagogue to limit the offering of *mi she-berakh*s. They felt that the large block of time devoted to these special prayers interrupted "the solemnity which is due to a place of public worship." The congregation hurried through the service "in order to allow time for a system of finance, which, however beneficial in its operation, is certainly inconsistent with decorum and public order," and then passed the time during the *mi she-berakh*s "in levity and idle conversation." Whatever the merit of the proposal, the Committee decided that it would be financially unfeasible to abandon this important source of revenue at a time when the sums needed for poor relief were so great.[51]

Three years later, Isaac Lyon Goldsmid proposed another scheme to improve the tone of the service to the Committee of the Great Synagogue. Goldsmid felt that the exaggerated chanting of the foreign-born *hazanim* in London lacked dignity and that some English-born boys should be trained in a less extravagant cantorial style. A committee of seven persons, with Goldsmid as the chairman, was appointed to consider the matter. Among the members were the *maskilim* Joshua Van Oven and Michael Josephs. The report of the committee admitted that much of the inattention during the service was due to the congregation's inability to understand Hebrew, but it also maintained that the solemnity of the service could be enhanced by introducing an unadorned cantorial style, devoid of "all singing not connected with sacred music." The proposal was much discussed and then finally approved in February 1825. Implementation of the plan, however, was a more difficult task. It was impossible to find a properly qualified English-born *hazan* to train the potential young *hazanim*. The three candidates who were examined in February 1826 were unable to translate correctly the Hebrew prayers into English, and in March it was decided that as there was no one competent in London, another *hazan* would have to be sought on the Continent. The proposal thus ended in failure.[52]

In addition to the above proposals, there were more successful (if less ambitious) moves, both in the Great Synagogue and in the other London congregations, to add an element of formal dignity to the worship service. In 1824, the New Synagogue began prohibiting children from interrupting the reading of the Scroll of Esther on Purim with "Haman clappers," and in 1827 the Hambro Synagogue followed suit. In 1825, the Great Synagogue and the New Synagogue shortened (but did not abolish) the system of lengthy *mi she-berakh*s in the interest of proper decorum and devotion. The Hambro took similar action in 1831 after discussing the issue over the course of the preceding year.[53]

The most sweeping attempt to inject a good dose of English propriety into the service was made in the Spanish and Portuguese Synagogue. In December 1828, the elders of the congregation appointed a five-man Committee for the Promotion and Improvement of Religious Worship. The Committee discussed a number of relatively radical reforms; at one point, they asked the Sephardi *bet din* whether women could join in the chanting, whether instrumental music could be allowed in the synagogue, whether the repetition of the *amidah* (the core of the service) could be dispensed with, and whether the *kaddish* could be repeated a smaller number of times. But when they actually presented their proposals to the elders, they suggested changes that were of a more moderate character: they asked that the gentlemen of the Mahamad remain in the synagogue until the service was completed, that the singing of some psalms be slightly abridged, that all proclamations in the synagogue be in English, and that a sermon be delivered in English on Saturday afternoons (a proposal first made to the elders thirty years earlier by Jacob Mocatta, a member of this committee). In May 1829, the elders approved all of the reforms except for one, that of introducing English sermons. Only after a year and a half of struggle were the reform-minded elders able to muster enough votes to gain passage of this proposal. And even then it was stipulated that every sermon be presented to the Mahamad three days previous to its delivery to ensure that it did not contain "any thing inimical to our religious doctrines or any matter hostile to the established institutions of the country."[54]

Some of the above reforms were designed to make the service more attractive to congregants who no longer understood Hebrew and who were impatient with the length of the traditional service. But most of them, particularly those initiated by the Ashkenazi congregations, were of a cosmetic character; they were concerned with the external appearance of Jewish worship rather than the internal content of Jewish prayer. The men who promoted these reforms were not concerned with making Judaism a rational or more modern religion; what they wanted was a religious service that conformed more closely to English (i.e., Christian) notions of reverence and solemnity. Christian visitors to London's synagogues were extremely critical of "the utmost irreverence and unconcern" they saw there. One visitor found that the synagogue exhibited "an appearance of very little more devotion than the Stock Exchange or the public streets of the metropolis at noon day." Another critic, the Philo-Judaean John A. Q. Brown, noted in 1827 that the Jews in synagogue "repeat the words [of the prayers] like a parrot by rote and yet not understand one word of what they read." He wondered what benefit they gained from attendance at the synagogue to hear a service in a language they did not understand or "two sermons in the year on the subject of fringes and ceremonies in Rabbinical German, which even the wiser amongst the Jewish nation treat with contempt and ridicule."[55] It is inconceivable that the anglicized Jews who promoted these reforms were ignorant of Christian opinion about Jewish worship. To a large degree, their own complaints about Jewish worship were derived from what the non-Jewish world thought—not in the sense that they borrowed them directly, but in the sense that they had internalized the standards of the English upper class and were applying them to their own tradition.

None of the religious reforms introduced in the 1820s were of a radical nature. They were made within the context of traditional Judaism and did not cause a rupture in the basic unity of the Jewish community. In Germany, on the other hand, the reformers were aggressive and strident. They demanded a more radical refashioning of Jewish worship and belief and set up their own synagogues to achieve their goals. Sabbath services in the reform temple in Berlin in the late 1810s and early 1820s lasted only two hours and featured organ music, a German sermon, and German prayers. The Hamburg Temple not only incorporated all of these aesthetic reforms, but went even further and reformed the content of the worship service itself by eliminating prayers for the return to Zion and the restoration of the sacrificial cult in Jerusalem.

By contrast, then, Anglo-Jewish religious reform, at least before 1840, was a quiet and modest affair. Most of the well-to-do members of the community showed little interest in making their Judaism as fashionable or as English as their homes, their dress, or their recreations. Their disinclination to modernize their worship or their beliefs (at least publicly)—and the concomitant passion of their German counterparts to do just that—can be explained in large part by the liberal setting for Jewish acculturation in England. In the German states, the conservative nature of political and social life forced those Jews who desired to enter the larger world to be continually on the defensive. The leaders of German Jewry had to fight a long and bitter struggle to gain the rights and freedoms that English Jews enjoyed without ever having mounted any campaign. The pressure on German Jewish spokesmen constantly to expound the ability of Jews to become good citizens was tremendous. There was a ceaseless ideological assault on Judaism and the Jews, emanating from the most powerful political circles in Germany. German Jews responded to this barrage by publicly demonstrating, in word and deed, that they were worthy of being admitted to German citizenship. The longer and harder they struggled, the more radical their programs and their reforms became. The arena of organized religion, like that of intellectual activity and public manners, was a sphere in which they had to demonstrate their merit.

The pressure in England was milder. There were no public demands for the Jews to prove themselves useful and worthy human beings if they wanted to be granted the privileges of other citizens. The English government, unlike those in some of the German states, took no notice of what went on in the synagogues; it was simply of no interest to them. English Jews quietly adopted the habits of Englishmen because they wanted to feel at home there. They noiselessly abandoned the practices of traditional Judaism because they felt that these practices set them apart from other men and interfered with their pursuit of temporal pleasure and success. The formal character of Judaism and of Jewish worship was pretty much left alone.* Only once did a prominent

*Some confirmation of this thesis may be found in the fact that in the United States, where social and political patterns have more closely resembled those in England rather than those in Germany, attempts to "reform" Judaism in the years

English Jew suggest that it would be necessary to alter Jewish worship in order to gain a political end. In 1831, during the campaign for Jewish emancipation, Isaac Lyon Goldsmid, who was disappointed with the willingness of most Jewish leaders to accept a halfway measure from the government, spoke of establishing a new synagogue and of adopting the form of worship in use in the Hamburg Temple.[56]

For the most part, whatever pressure there was on Anglo-Jewry to conform was felt in the social sphere in the form of slights, derogatory remarks, and unpleasant stereotypes. Middle-class Jews who adopted the genteel fashionability of the English upper class could feel confident they had rid themselves of the traits that created such negative impressions. Unfortunately, the non-Jewish public was not so discriminating as genteel English Jews were and tended to lump all Jews, the well-mannered rich and the disorderly poor, together in one category. Jewish peddlers, pickpockets, old-clothes men, and pugilists—lower-class Jews who had embraced the outlook and the habits of the English poor—provided a cause for great alarm to the Anglo-Jewish elite.

1820 to 1870 followed the moderate, nonideological English course. In America, there were no political incentives to modernize Jewish worship; legal equality already existed. See Leon Jick, *The Americanization of the Synagogue, 1820–1870* (Hanover, N.H., 1976).

5

Peddlers and Hawkers

The acculturation of the Jews of Western and Central Europe has been viewed frequently as if it were a problem that concerned only the Jewish bourgeoisie. The assumption underlying this focus is that the pursuit of wealth and status in the non-Jewish world has had a corrosive effect on the practices and beliefs of traditional Judaism. Few would quarrel with this assumption. It does not follow necessarily, though, that the Jewish poor remained unswervingly traditional in their religious practices and social behavior. This would mean, if true, that the Jewish poor, who were the overwhelming majority of European Jewry in the eighteenth century, remained outside history as passive bystanders, unaffected and unmoved by the changes to which their wealthier coreligionists were responding. That the Jewish masses have been seen as a bastion of traditionalism is in part because the staunchest supporters of traditionalism—those who continued to fill the synagogues or purchase kosher meat, for example—were overwhelmingly from the lower classes. But this may be due less to the insularity of the Jewish poor than to their sheer numbers. As the bulk of the Jewish population, they naturally were the bulk of those who continued to observe Judaism in the traditional fashion.

In England, certainly, the Jewish poor were not immune to the attractions of the non-Jewish world. The street hawkers and old-clothes men of Anglo-Jewry took to many of the patterns of urban life of the social class to which they belonged. This included criminal activity, sexual promiscuity, street violence, and prize-fighting, much to the consternation of the Anglo-Jewish elite. Nervous as they were about their acceptability as English gentlemen, they thus felt compelled to guide the anglicization of the Jewish poor so they would behave in a manner less damaging to the respectability of Jews in general.

That the bulk of Anglo-Jewry were not well-to-do merchants is an ironic commentary on the commercial arguments advanced by some supporters of Jewish settlement. In the years immediately after Cromwell's negotiations with Manasseh ben Israel, some wealthy Sephardim from Holland settled in London, attracted there by the opportunities for commercial success; however, they made up only a very small part of the total Sephardi immigration. Far more numerous were propertyless refugees fleeing the Inquisition in the Iberian peninsula and destitute immigrants from North Africa, Italy, and Holland seeking to escape the poverty of their native lands. Already by the close of the seventeenth century, the number of Sephardi poor posed a serious problem for the Mahamad, the executive committee of the Spanish and Portuguese Synagogue. (At this time there was only one synagogue in London, that of the Spanish and Portuguese Jews, and it assumed responsibility for all the Jewish poor.) In keeping with the custom of Jewish communities everywhere, the Mahamad felt an obligation to care for the Jewish poor who made their way to London, but at the same time it also felt that the financial resources of the congregation were inadequate to care for all those immigrants who sought relief. In 1669, the congregation lodged a complaint with the Lord Mayor about the number of foreign mendicants besetting the synagogue, and in 1682, it decided that Ashkenazi Jews who came to England to beg charity would not receive more than five shillings each and would be shipped back to Amsterdam immediately. In 1692, the Mahamad warned Joseph de la Penha, a wealthy merchant and shipowner of Amsterdam, to stop forwarding poor Jews to London, as the government had just forbidden entry at English ports without a passport costing £3 10s., "a sum which the congregation cannot possibly afford for all the poor would-be immigrants who are detained thereby on entry." In 1705 and 1706, the Mahamad informed the synagogue's agents in Livorno that the congregation was overburdened with poor refugees from Portugal and other places. The following year, in order to deter further migration, the Mahamad ordered that no foreign Jew applying for relief should receive more than forty shillings. When two years later, in 1710, the congregation felt overburdened with destitute Jews from North Africa and Italy, it decided to limit all immigrants to three days of maintenance at the congregation's expense and then to give each of them ten shillings to leave England.[1]

The most concentrated influx of poor Sephardim came in the period 1720–35 as a consequence of renewed activity on the part of the Inquisition in Spain and Portugal. During these years, approximately fifteen hundred New Christians arrived directly from the peninsula—an enormous addition to the local Sephardi community, which numbered only a little more than one thousand persons in 1720. In the minutes of the Mahamad, there is a note from 1726 (a year of particularly virulent Inquisitorial activity) that many Jews were arriving from the Iberian peninsula totally destitute, unable even to pay their fares to the captain who brought them to England. There was an agreement that the synagogue would pay them on their arrival in England; that year, the congregation spent £2,786 on poor relief. In the remaining decades of the eighteenth century, refugees from the peninsula continued to arrive sporadically, although there was no large-scale movement as in the 1720s and the 1730s. A register of 138 Sephardi aliens from 1803—the register did not include those who were wealthy enough to obtain endenization and, hence, is weighted toward the poor—included 6 Jews who immigrated from Spain and Portugal in the 1760s, 1 in the 1770s, 2 in the 1780s, and 1 as late as 1798.[2]

One way in which the London Mahamad tried to cope with the influx of poor Sephardim in this period was to grant them funds to travel to a Sephardi community in the New World, generally Barbados or Jamaica, where presumably it was easier to gain a living.* When, in 1732, the Crown issued a charter for the colonization of Georgia, the Mahamad began making arrangements to

---

*Ironically, it was not uncommon for the Sephardi communites of Amsterdam and Bordeaux to help their surplus poor emigrate to London. See Zosa Szajkowski, "Population Problems of Marranos and Sephardim in France, from the 16th to the 20th Centuries," *Proceedings of the American Academy for Jewish Research* 27 (1958):14.

ship destitute Jews out to the new colony, where debtors of all faiths were being settled. Three leading figures in the Sephardi community, Anthony da Costa, Francis Salvador, and Alvaro Lopez Suasso, became commissioners for the colonization scheme and used the funds they raised from the public to send about forty persons, including two Ashkenazi families, to settle in Savannah.[3]

Ultimately, though, there was little the Mahamad could do to stem the tide of poor Sephardim immigrating to England. Unlike the majority of Jewish communities in pre-Revolutionary Europe, the London community was not an autonomous corporation empowered by the state to exercise administrative and judicial control over its members. The London Jewish community was nothing more than an unorganized collection of voluntary associations: Ashkenazi and Sephardi synagogues, charities, and study groups. In addition to these, there were hundreds—and eventually thousands—of individuals who were identified as Jews and who considered themselves Jews with no affiliation to any Jewish institution. The Mahamad, like the *parnasim* of the Ashkenazi synagogues, had no legal authority to limit the size of the London Jewish community or to control the flow of Jews into the community on even a temporary basis, as was the practice elsewhere in Europe. Given the decentralized nature of English government at this period and the growing opposition to the arbitrary exercise of power by privileged corporations, such controls would have been inappropriate and anachronistic. Possibly the leaders of Anglo-Jewry sensed this, for they never applied to the government for the authority that belonged to their counterparts elsewhere (with the one exception of the abortive Van Oven scheme in 1802, to be discussed in Chapter 7). Even if they had been granted legal responsibility for Anglo-Jewry, it would have been administratively impossible for either the government or the synagogues to police the comings and goings of foreign Jews. London, in particular, was too vast and teeming a place to allow that kind of control. There was no Rosenthaler Gate, as at Berlin, where all Jews entering the city were interrogated before gaining admission. Legally, then, there was nothing any of the Jewish leaders could do to prohibit the immigration of Jews they considered undesirable—undesirable either because they would become a burden on the charitable funds of Anglo-Jewry or because

they would endanger the status of respectable Jews through criminal or other disreputable conduct.

One consequence of the absence of communal control was that
London became a magnet for many poor Sephardim escaping
from poverty in less developed lands. Throughout the eighteenth
and early nineteenth centuries, there was a casual and unorganized, but fairly continuous, flow of Sephardim from the impoverished communities of Italy, Turkey, North Africa, and Gibraltar.
In addition, many Jews who were less than successful in Holland
crossed the Channel to try their luck in England. The 1803 aliens
register from Bevis Marks indicates the origins of the poorer
Sephardim who arrived in the second half of the eighteenth century:[4]

PLACE OF ORIGIN

Holland	41
Italy	27
Morocco, Tunis, and Gibraltar	22
Portugal, Spain, and Brazil	17
Ottoman Empire	12
Hamburg, Vienna, and Poland	12
Bordeaux and Bayonne	7
Total	138

This list does not, of course, include every Sephardi alien in
England in 1803. It is highly probably that just as many did not
bother to register at the Synagogue as did. There is no reason to
suspect, though, that the breakdown according to country of
origin would be any different for those who did not.

In general, this flow was not associated with any specific persecution or particular economic catastrophe, but reflected a widespread deterioration in the economic position of much of the
Sephardi diaspora in the eighteenth century, as well as, perhaps,
a positive perception of the opportunities England offered. The
Italian immigration, from the information available in the aliens
list, appears to have started in the 1760s, and that from North
Africa and Gibraltar began in the 1770s; the immigration from
Holland was fairly constant over the course of the century. There
was a particularly large number of Gibraltarian Jews who arrived
after the evacuation of the population there in 1781 due to the
French siege between June 1779 and February 1783. The reason

most frequently cited for coming to England by those who registered in 1803 was to seek a livelihood. An elderly rhubarb and spice seller, interviewed by the journalist Henry Mayhew around 1850, told how he had left his native town of Mogador, Morocco, when he was about seventeen and sailed to Gibraltar to sell dry goods. After six years there, having earned about five or six hundred dollars, he decided he would do better in England. He told Mayhew that when he was a little child he had heard Jews in his native town say that the Moroccan Jews who sold dried rhubarb in the streets of London had made "plenty of money." Mayhew's informant arrived in London about 1811 and, true to what he had heard, managed by hawking rhubarb to earn enough money in two years to open a dry goods store in Exeter, in partnership with three other Moroccan Jews. This venture ran into trouble after five years because the owners extended credit unwisely and, being unable to speak English very well, were put to the expense of hiring a shop assistant who did. Forced to abandon his store, Mayhew's informant then went back to hawking rhubarb in London and the provinces, traveling as far afield as Wales, Ireland, and Scotland. He concluded his tale by telling Mayhew that he would have been living in ease in his old age at the Jews' Hospital in the Mile End Road had his second wife not been a Christian. As it was, he still received a few shillings from the Hospital before the holidays.[5]

As troublesome as the Sephardi poor were to the synagogue authorities, their arrival in England never became a matter of concern to the non-Jewish public. The popular image of the Sephardi Jew was an opulent stockbroker and that of the Ashkenazi Jew a ragged old-clothes man. This was not because the majority of Sephardim were well-to-do—it should be recalled that the Secretary of Bevis Marks put the number of Sephardi poor at eleven hundred in 1795 (a little more than half the total) —but because the Sephardi poor were, in absolute terms, insignificant in comparison to the number of Ashkenazi poor. Poverty, then, was not an exclusively Ashkenazi problem; it just came to seem so because the Ashkenazi element rapidly overtook the Sephardi group in terms of numbers and because the proportion of lower-class Ashkenazim was probably greater than that of lower-class Sephardim. By 1720 at the latest, the number of Ashkenazim in England had outstripped the Sephardim. At that time, the Sephardi group numbered about 1,050; by 1750, there may have been 2,000 Sephardim, but over the next eighty years, this figure remained fairly constant despite the continual flow of Sephardim from abroad. This was due without doubt to a very high rate of intermarriage; migration to the New World and the marriage of Sephardi women to Ashkenazi men also contributed to keeping this figure from rising.[6]

The Ashkenazi population, on the other hand, grew very rapidly. In 1738, D'Bloissiers Tovey, Principal of New Hall Inn, Oxford, put the number of Jews (that is, Ashkenazim and Sephardim) in England at 6,000. Three years later, while visiting London, the Florentine Jewish diamond merchant Moses Vita Cassuto also estimated the total Jewish population to be 6,000 persons; there is, however, the possibility that he was merely repeating the earlier estimate without citing a source for it. At the time of the Jew Bill controversy, Jonas Hanway wrote that there were 7,000 Jews in England; Philo-Patriae said 8,000. All of these figures were mere guesses. If they were correct, Ashkenazim outnumbered Sephardim by either 2.5 to 1 or 3 to 1 at midcentury. At the end of the century, when the problem of Jewish poverty and criminality caused a public review of the condition of the Jews, the police magistrate Patrick Colquhoun estimated that there were 15,000 to 20,000 Jews in London alone and another 5,000 to 6,000 in the provinces. There is little question, however, that he exaggerated the size of Anglo-Jewry. When the German pastor Frederick Augustus Wendeborn visited England in 1791, he said there were no more than 12,000 Jews in all of England—11,000 of whom lived in London. Of these, 4,000 were Sephardim. This is far too high a figure in light of the demographic calculations made by V. D. Lipman on the basis of the Bevis Marks burial records; it is unlikely that the total Jewish population of London went above 15,000 or so until the 1820s. When Francis Henry Goldsmid calculated the Jewish population of London in 1830 on the basis of burial returns for the London synagogues and the ratio between deaths and the population figures for London as a whole, he arrived at the figure of a Jewish population of 17,986. As the burials of Sephardim were 12 percent of the total, Goldsmid's figures would mean about 2,150 Sephardim in 1830.[7]

Some of the growth of the Jewish population was a result of the natural rate of increase of the native-born element in Anglo-Jewry, but as the Jewish population increased over 2500 percent from 1700 to 1830 and as the native-born were more likely over the years to leave the Jewish community, the major factor was an almost uninterrupted flow of largely destitute Ashkenazi Jews from Holland, the German states, and Poland. As there was no government agency that regulated the entry of aliens, there are no data on the rate of migration. Nevertheless, it is possible to determine the broad contours of the course of Ashkenazi immigration from a variety of impressionistic statements and crude indices. V. D. Lipman has calculated, largely on the basis of the population estimates cited above, that, allowing the maximum for natural increase, about 6,000 Ashkenazim entered England during the first half of the eighteenth century and 8,000 to 10,000 between 1750 and 1815. This would mean about 120 Ashkenazim a year for the first period and about 150 a year for the second period. As immigration was much more difficult in the years of the Revolutionary and Napoleonic wars, the actual number per year before 1793 would have been much higher.[8]

Qualitative evidence indicates that the flow of poor Jewish aliens became especially heavy from the 1770s on. In November 1771, the Earl of Suffolk, Secretary of State, asked Sir John Fielding, the Bow Street magistrate, why there had recently been so many poor Jews on the packet boats from Holland. In 1796, Colquhoun spoke of "the increase . . . of the lower order of the Jews," and in 1802, George Tierney, in introducing the Van Oven scheme for the reorganization of Jewish poor relief to the House of Commons, spoke of an increase in the previous fifty years of Jews resident in England, "a very great proportion of whom are in very indigent circumstances." If the level of Jewish criminal activity in London is some kind of crude index to the level of Jewish poverty, and if the level of Jewish poverty reflects in a general way the influx of foreign poor, then the 1770s can be viewed as the crucial decade in the upswing in Jewish migration from the Continent. For example, in the 1750s, only 18 Jews were sentenced to death or transportation overseas at the Old Bailey; in the 1760s, the number rose to 35, but in the 1770s, 65 Jews were sentenced to death or transportation. In the 1780s, the number dropped slightly to 61, but during the 1790s and the 1800s, when, it will be recalled, migration was far more difficult due to the Revolutionary and Napoleonic wars, the number fell sharply to 37 Jews and 30 Jews respectively. With the return of peace, the number of Jews sentenced to death or transportation at the Old Bailey shot to new highs—89 in the 1810s and 90 in the 1820s.[9]

The increases and decreases in the rate of Jewish crime accord well with the comments of synagogal authorities on the increase of the Jewish poor. In January 1812, at a meeting of representatives of the three City synagogues on the division of financial responsibility for the foreign poor—always a touchy subject—someone remarked that during the war very few foreign Jews had come to England, but that previously the tide could not flow from Gravesend to Billingsgate without there being poor Jewish men and women in the Gravesend boats who had come from abroad. The treasurer of the Great Synagogue added that there had been an increase in the number of Jewish soldiers and sailors who came to England for charity. Two years later, when negotiations on the same subject were again taking place, the Great Synagogue wrote to the Hambro: "The great influx of strangers must baffle all calculation and indeed the increase of foreign poor this present year [i.e., according to the Jewish calendar], of which only two thirds is now expired [June 1814], far exceeds any former year." In October of that same year, the Hambro decided to pay the burial costs of a larger number of destitute Jews due to "the great influx of the poor from different parts abroad since the happy termination of the war." In March 1824, in ordering ten additional sacks of flour for the coming Passover, the Hambro referred to the increase of foreign poor as the reason for increasing their usual order.[10]

The great majority of Ashkenazi Jews entering England in the years 1700 to 1830 came from Germany, with smaller numbers from Holland and Poland. A list of foreign-born Jews living in Plymouth in 1798, which was compiled by the synagogue authorities to comply with the Aliens Act of 1798, gives the place of origin of 58 Jews. Most of them (43) came from Germany; the rest from Bohemia (5), Amsterdam (4), and Poland (6). Those from Germany were primarily from small towns and villages, with only a few from cities of any size or importance; whether this trend was true for the lower-class German Jewish immigration as a whole is uncertain. Fragmentary evidence available for Jews living elsewhere in England does not permit any kind of generalization of this sort. For example: Emanuel Myers, an old-clothes man robbed of two shillings in London in 1783, came from Hanover; Isaac Jacob, who sought aid from Christian missionaries in 1807, grew up in Altona and lived at various places in Germany, including Berlin for three years, before migrating to London; Isaac Marcus, who applied to have his son admitted to a missionary school in 1834, had been born in Potsdam and lived in Paris, where he married a non-Jewish woman; Solomon Joseph, a peddler who converted to Christianity at age 79, was born in Breslau in 1724 and lived in Amsterdam for fifteen years; Abraham Marcus Arnstein, a self-described linen trader who registered as an alien in 1798 at the Westminster Sessions, was born in Giebelstadt, a village in Lower Franconia, later lived in Munster, Westphalia, and arrived in London in 1786; Emanuel Leman, who sold sealing wax and spectacles in Manchester and was converted on his deathbed, was born about 1750 in Würzburg and came to England at age 17. Although these scattered biographical details hardly permit any conclusive statements, they do not suggest that any one area in Germany or any one kind of German Jewish community was the major source of immigration to England.[11]

As the Plymouth aliens list reveals, not all the Ashkenazi immigration stemmed from Germany. In addition to a considerable group from Amsterdam, there were a number of immigrants from Poland, probably far more than has previously been assumed. The records of cases tried at the Old Bailey reveal a large number of immigrants who either used the surname of Polock or Poland or were described in the court records as Polish Jews. In a membership list of the Great Synagogue for the years 1708–50, at least six families can be positively identified as immigrants from Poland. Since only the names of middle-class Jews would appear in such a list, the number of poor Polish Jews must have been many times greater. In the early 1790s, two Polish synagogues were organized, both with a predominantly lower-middle-class and lower-class membership. The Gun Yard Synagogue, founded in 1792, had its roots in a Polish *minyan* that met for some years before this in Gun Square, Houndsditch, and the Polish Synagogue, in Cutler Street, Houndsditch, founded about 1790, grew out of a Talmud study group and *minyan (hevrah shas)*.[12]

Behind the migration of Ashkenazi Jews to England lay the

deteriorating economic position of German Jewry in the eighteenth and early nineteenth centuries. Most of the German states and cities limited the trades that Jews could follow as well as the number of Jews who could reside in any one place.* As the German Jewish population expanded as a result of natural increase as well as migration from Poland, the opportunities for gaining a settlement and earning a living remained constant or even contracted somewhat. As a consequence, many Jews were forced to uproot themselves from their native towns and to seek their livelihoods elsewhere. Many took to the roads permanently, moving in bands from Jewish community to Jewish community, seeking charity. These *Betteljuden,* as they were called, became a major problem for both the secular and Jewish authorities from the end of the seventeenth century, particularly since many of the bands turned to criminal pursuits. Moses Shulvass has estimated that there were at least ten thousand *Betteljuden* in Germany (as compared to a stable population of two hundred thousand Jews) at the end of the eighteenth century. Many of these were Polish Jews who had fled the Haidamak persecutions of the mid-eighteenth century or who were trying to escape the general economic decay of Polish Jewry that had commenced a whole century before, but were now unable to gain permanent residence in a German city or town. A smaller number were social deviants cast out by traditional Jewish communities whose values they had offended—thieves, libertines, sexual offenders, loose women, and the like. Some wealthy English Jews felt that these itinerant bands were a major source of the influx of poor Ashkenazim into London. In 1771, the *parnasim* of the Great Synagogue attributed the upsurge in poor Jews coming to England to "the late disturbances in Poland" and a desire to "share charities distributed by Jews in this kingdom." Toward the end of the century, the anonymous author of *A Peep into the Synagogue* wrote that most of the German Jews who were not born in England had emigrated solely for the purpose of begging.[13]

Not all of those Jews who left Germany were *Betteljuden.* Many

---

*In the early nineteenth century, in the face of economic depression, overpopulation, and popular discontent, the central and southern German states introduced measures, such as marriage restrictions, to restrain the growth of the lower classes in general. Mack Walker, *Germany and the Emigration, 1816–1885* (Cambridge, Mass., 1964), pp. 54–55.

were young men who wished to raise a family and earn a decent living, but realized that they could never do so in Germany, especially since in many localities the number of Jewish marriages per year was limited by law. Of the fifty-eight Jews on the Plymouth aliens list, thirty were between the ages of 20 and 26 when they arrived in England, and nearly all the rest were between 16 and 19 or 27 and 30. Solomon Joseph (1724–1814), a peddler whose biography was recorded by missionaries when he was converted at age 79, left his home in Breslau at age 15 to make his own way in the world. For several years he traveled on the Continent buying and selling small articles, and then he worked for fifteen years in Amsterdam for an innkeeper whom his father knew. When he reached England, he first earned his living by dealing in black beads (for necklaces) and then by buying and selling old clothes. He managed to save some money, but was cheated out of it, so he was forced to hire himself to another Jewish peddler to carry his box of merchandise. He continued to do this until he had saved a few shillings, which he used to purchase Bristol stone buttons. Slowly he expanded his stock of wares and his business so that he was again able to save some money. Eventually he married a Christian woman, a widow whom he had met in the course of his travels.[14]

The biography of Abraham Phillips, a grocer's assistant who sought aid from Christian missionaries in 1809, reveals a similar motivation for leaving his native place. Born at Neuhaus, near Tabor, Bohemia, he was destined for a rabbinic career, but at age 18 gave up his studies and left home so that his father, who had become financially hard pressed, would no longer have to support him. He traveled to Berlin and, supported by charity from Jews there, studied Talmud during the day and German at night. His circle of friends expanded to include "enlightened" Jews and non-Jews, and he began to question, and eventually rejected, traditional Judaism. Sometime around 1805, his advanced views brought him into conflict with some Jews there, and he left for London, arriving in August 1805.[15]

Phillips's experiences not only illustrate the importance of economic considerations in uprooting many young German Jews, but also suggest that in a number of cases, no doubt a minority, the desire to escape the social and intellectual confines of traditional Jewish life was also a powerful motive for immigration.

Abraham Moses Lande, born at Ostrow, Prussia, was sent to school in Breslau, but his father took him home when he began to prefer the company of young Christians. He was then sent to Berlin, where he again formed acquaintances with non-Jews. His father then sent him to Hamburg, but here young Abraham determined to shake off parental authority once and for all and obtained a passport for England, arriving there in May 1805. A very similar pattern is revealed in the early history of the peddler Samuel Harris. Born in Warsaw in 1807, young Samuel first demonstrated a rebellious and skeptical attitude to Jewish tradition when he asked his father some probing questions about Rashi's commentary to the Torah. His father slapped his face and called him *epikoros* (heretic). Later relations between the two of them became so strained that when Samuel was living in someone else's home as an errand boy, his father would not let him come home even to visit his mother. In his early teens he decided to leave Warsaw and engaged himself as a servant to some Jewish merchants going to the Leipzig fair. There he met a Polish Jewish wagoner, who had previously dealt in contraband in Poland but had now found it prudent to flee that country for London by way of Hamburg. Samuel joined him and arrived in London in 1821.[16]

In addition to those Jews who came to settle in England on a permanent basis, there were a small but noticeable number of petty traders who shifted the scene of their activity fairly frequently between England and the Continent. Joseph Isaacs, for example, who was born in Duke's Place about 1724, spent part of his childhood with his mother in Amsterdam and part of the time with his father, a pencil-maker, in London, for whom he worked for nine years. He later hawked knives, buckles, razors, and the like in Holland, France, and Germany. Just before he was sentenced to death in 1744 for robbery, he had been selling leather breeches in Holland. His parents, meanwhile, had migrated to Poland. One of the witnesses at his trial, Jacob Moses, had been hawking goods in the English army camp in Flanders. Henry Simons, a Polish Jew, spent several months in England in 1751 buying secondhand clothing and watches to resell to the Polish nobility. Lazarus Jacobs, who was found guilty of receiving stolen goods in 1777, had lived in France sometime prior to his arrest; his wife and son apparently still lived there. Harvey Nathan, a twenty-eight-year-old linen merchant, traveled in Flanders and Brabant before the French Revolution, selling jewelry, watches, and linen.[17] The relative ease with which these peddlers and petty traders crossed the Channel added to the unsettled character of the London Jewish community. Not only were Jews pouring into London from Germany, Poland, and Holland year after year, constantly reinforcing the immigrant nature of the Jewish community, but some of them were returning to the Continent and then reentering England again. Meanwhile, Jewish peddlers were regularly setting out from London to vend their wares in the English countryside. All these comings and goings added to the difficulty of maintaining social discipline within the Jewish community.

Most Jewish immigrants arrived penniless and unskilled. This is hardly surprising given that the Jewish middle class in Germany had little reason to uproot themselves and Jewish youth in Germany had little opportunity to learn a handicraft. With few real occupational choices available to them, newly arrived Jews turned to the trades they or their families had known in Germany —hawking goods about the streets, buying and selling old clothes, peddling wares in the countryside. A Jew who was asked by Charles Cochrane in the late 1820s how so many poor Jews could earn a living from dealing in old clothes replied that many of them were half-starving but that they had no choice, having been brought up with no particular calling. These trades also possessed the advantage of requiring very little capital with which to commence business. For a few shillings, a street trader could buy enough goods to strike out on his own. In 1812, eighteen-year-old Abraham Levi purchased one hundred lemons to hawk about the streets for only three shillings. An anonymous article in *The Gentleman's Magazine* in 1810 commented on how Jewish old-clothes men traded on a very small capital, setting forth in the morning with only a guinea.[18]

To the poor, Jewish or Christian, these were considerable sums, and raising such a fund was a considerable task. But in this respect, the Jewish poor enjoyed an advantage that the more numerous Christian poor did not: they could sometimes turn to those within their community who had already succeeded for aid in getting themselves started. The Polish-born peddler Samuel Harris recalled in his memoirs how, when he first arrived in

London in 1821, he went to Duke's Place, and the Jews there took up a collection for him so he could set himself up as a peddler. Sometime later, when he lost all he had to a clever Jewish lad who first befriended him and then robbed him, some Jews in Manchester took up a collection for him so he could restock his box. Henry Mayhew was told that several Jewish merchants of substance began trading with small stocks of jewelry that had been charitable donations. Possibly a more common way of giving assistance was for Jewish shopkeepers to supply peddlers with goods on credit. Henry Moses, also known as Zander Falmouth, a substantial shopkeeper in Falmouth in the mid-eighteenth century, accorded credit to Jewish hawkers on the condition that they return every Friday to Falmouth to be part of his *minyan*. On Sunday mornings, they would settle their accounts and furnish themselves with whatever goods were needed for the coming week. In some cases, he advanced them the money to purchase hawking licenses, but in this too he made a stipulation: that the hawkers have their full Jewish name inserted in the license.[19]

In addition to the small amounts of capital they required, these trades possessed other attractions to recent immigrants as well. For those Jews who continued to observe the Jewish Sabbath and holidays, they gave them the freedom to set their own hours and to choose their own day of rest. Equally important, these trades did not require a very substantial knowledge of English. Within a few days of arriving in England, a man could pick up the few phrases he needed to hawk lemons or buttons. As long as he remained within the areas of Jewish settlement in London, all his needs, including a supply of whatever he was hawking, could be provided for by Jews who also spoke Yiddish. When Emanuel Myers, an old-clothes man recently arrived from Hanover, appeared in the Old Bailey in 1783, he was asked, through an interpreter, how he carried on his business without knowing any English. He replied, "There are so many of my country people who generally assist me." He then was asked what he did when they were not around and answered, "I generally make a motion."[20]

Within London, Jews came to monopolize or were strongly associated with certain areas of the street trade. The journalist and social investigator Henry Mayhew, who knew the London street trades as well as any middle-class writer, singled out the trade in oranges and lemons, spectacles, costume jewelry, sponges, rhubarb, lead pencils, and inexpensive framed pictures as "Jewish" trades around 1800. In addition to these, there are frequent references to Jews hawking slippers, sweet cakes, barley sugar, cane straps, glassware, sealing wax, belt buckles, buttons, and the like.[21]

The prominence and high visibility of Jews within the London street trades did not go unnoticed by contemporaries. Fastidious Englishmen and anglicized Jews regretted the proliferation of noisy Jewish street traders and spoke deprecatingly of them. The anonymous author of *A Peep into the Synagogue,* a Jew who was a harsh critic of traditional Jewish culture, bemoaned the absence of Jewish artisans and described how itinerant Jews, newly arrived in London, "embrace the most pitiful and mean employments to procure them food, such as buying and selling old clothes, buckles, buttons, sealing wax, wafers, oranges, lemons, pencils, or such like." Robert Southey complained about the "Hebrew lads who infest you in the streets with oranges and red slippers, or tempt school boys to dip in a bag for gingerbread nuts." For some, Jewish hawkers were a little too insistent in pushing their wares. "In their hopes of sale," commented Mayhew, "they followed anyone a mile if encouraged, even by a few approving glances." A commercial traveler remarked that he could never leave London by stagecoach "without being beseiged by a small army of Jew boys," who offered him "oranges, lemons, sponges, combs, pocket books, pencils, sealing wax, paper, many-bladed pen knives, razors, pocket mirrors, and shaving-boxes—as if a man could not possibly quit the metropolis without requiring a stock of such commodities."[22]

The most characteristic Jewish street trade was the buying and selling of old clothes. At a time when the urban poor were unable to purchase new clothing and had to depend on the cast-offs of the middle and upper classes, this was a thriving and necessary business, although one that suffered from a very bad reputation. Jewish old-clothes men were to be met in streets and squares throughout London, in both the East and West Ends of the metropolis, for the character of the trade required that they buy from the rich, or the servants of the rich, and sell to the poor. In the morning hours they set forth from the East End to trudge the streets of middle-class and aristocratic London, shouting "Old clothes" repeatedly in order to attract the attention of servants with their masters' cast-off clothes to sell. In the afternoon, they carried their morning's purchases to Rag Fair, an open-air market held daily in Rosemary Lane, near Tower Hill, where they bartered or sold what they had bought to other dealers—generally Jews—who kept secondhand shops and repaired the garments for resale. Henry Mayhew thought that at one time there had been as many as one thousand Jewish old-clothes men; Patrick Colquhoun, who thought Jewish old-clothes men tempted servants to pilfer and steal, put their number in the 1790s at two thousand.[23]

The actual number of Jewish old-clothes men in London is relatively unimportant. What is significant is that those who carried on the trade were strikingly visible and highly vocal. Many of them continued to wear the long dark caftan and broad-brimmed hat of Central and East European Jewry. They filled the streets in which they were working with the continuous cry of "Old clothes." As a group, they made an extraordinary impression, generally a negative one, on residents of London—even those who never ventured into Rag Fair—and on visitors from abroad. Coleridge noted, "The two images farthest removed from each other which can be comprehended under one term are, I think, Isaiah—'Hear O heavens and give ear O earth!'—and Levi of Holywell Street—'Old Clothes'—both of them Jews, you'll observe." And an anonymous reviewer of Millman's *History of the Jews* in *The Gentleman's Magazine* in 1830 began with the observation that it was difficult for an Englishman "to separate the idea of Jews from pedlars who cry 'old clothes,' hawk sealing wax, and have a peculiar physiognomical character."[24]

Rag Fair itself was particularly indecorous. Rosemary Lane and the streets leading to it were jammed with buyers and sellers; "a great crowd of dirty ragged people, to the number of some hundreds," made the area practically impassable. A grand display was made of every imaginable item of apparel in every stage of decay, some in tatters, some merely soiled. The secondhand dealers, like those Jews who had secondhand shops in Holywell Street in the Strand, were notorious for their high-powered sales technique. They shouted the virtues of their stock at everyone who passed by and frequently marched out into the street and forcibly took hold of pedestrians by their arms and led them back

James Gillray's stylized portrait of Daniel Mendoza (1763–1836), one of the outstanding prizefighters of the late eighteenth century, credited by historians of the ring with introducing a more "scientific" form of boxing.

ABR.ᵐ GOLDSMID, Esqʳ.

Abraham Goldsmid (1756–1810), loan-contractor, communal magnate and, as this portrait of 1806 by Richard Dighton emphasizes, philanthropist—tucked under Goldsmid's left arm is a list of charitable contributions in the thousands of pounds. For socially ambitious Jewish financiers like Goldsmid, charitable donations to non-Jewish institutions were an important mode of establishing their social respectability.

Polly de Symons (1753–1841), wife of the diamond broker Lyon de Symons and sister of the communal magnates Abraham and Benjamin Goldsmid. Despite the exaggerations imposed by the caricaturist, a stunning example of acculturation to the standards of London fashion among the Anglo-Jewish elite (1801).

A LYONESS.

Solomon Bennett (1761–1838), engraver, polemicist, and bitter critic of Chief Rabbi Solomon Hirschell for his subservience to the Anglo-Jewish elite.

תמונת אד״מ״ו החכם הכולל הגאון הגדול מהו׳ שלמה׳
בן אד׳ מ׳ו הגאון הגדול מהר צבי זצ׳ל׳
א׳ב׳ד דקק אשכנזים בלונדון והמדינה יע״א:
שלשלת היחיכי הגאונים מהו׳ה׳עשי׳ל וחכמצבי זצ׳ל׳זה:

THE REV. SOLOMON HIRSCHELL;
Chief Rabbi of the German and Polish Jews in England.

A formal portrait of Chief Rabbi Solomon Hirschell (1761–1842), engraved in 1808, six years after his arrival in London. Hirschell, who was a traditionalist in most religious matters, nevertheless adopted a mode of dress associated with the Christian clergy—a dark clerical gown with white bands at the neck.

WILL YOU LET ME A LOAN?

Isaac Lyon Goldsmid (1778–1859), one of the few communal leaders to pursue actively full political emancipation, as drawn by Richard Dighton in 1824.

The country home of financier Abraham Goldsmid at Morden, Surrey, as it appeared in 1806—material evidence of the extensive acculturation of the Ashkenazi upper class in the early nineteenth century.

Jewish Theological Seminary of Ameri

Devotion in Dukes Place — or Contractors returning thanks for a Loan.

Pub.d Novem. 6.t 1784 by W. Humphrey N.o 227 Strand

MONEY LENDERS.

By the mid-eighteenth century, Jewish peddlers were a familiar sight in the English countryside, as evidenced by William Hogarth's inclusion of a Jewish peddler with his box of wares in this detail from an engraving of his "Canvassing for Votes," one of four paintings on the 1754 Oxfordshire elections.

Pocket watches, watch chains, stick pins, and shoe buckles are among the items of jewelry carried by the Jewish peddler in this anonymous engraving of 1824. The young lad at the far left of the picture is picking the pocket of the customer who has just purchased a watch. It is unclear whether the artist intends to imply that the pickpocket and the peddler are working as a team.

MO ISAACS

The street trade in dried rhubarb, which was used for medicinal purposes, was dominated by North African Jews, who often appeared in exotic Turkish costume, such as Thomas Rowlandson's rhubarb vendor of 1820.

Thomas Rowlandson's "Old Clothes" of 1820 is only one of many contemporary engravings of the most representative of all Jewish street trades. The pile of used hats on the head of the old clothes man in the foreground and the sacks of old clothes over the shoulders of all three figures were the symbols of the trade.

By 1800, the London street trade in lemons and oranges was associated in the public mind with Jewish hawkers. Francis Wheatley's painting of a Jewish orange man (as reproduced here in an engraving of 1794 by Luigi Schiavonetti) was part of a popular series, "The Cries of London," which included a dozen street trades and their distinctive "cries."

This detail from George Cruikshank's "The Piccadilly Nuisance" of 1818 captures the rough and tumble character of London street life and the association between Jewish street traders and street crime. In the foreground, a Jewish lad picks the pocket of a man asking for directions, while his female accomplice, a fruit seller, stands ready to receive the filched item. On the left, a bearded Jewish street trader collides with a portly gentleman—his goods tumble from his tray, while his right hand removes the gentleman's watch from his pocket.

"Rag Fair" in Rosemary Lane, Houndsditch, was the open-air market for the purchase and sale of old clothes. In this amusing anonymous sketch, all of the sign boards above the stalls bear Jewish surnames. Jewish old-clothes men are recognizable by their bundles, by the piles of hats on their heads and, in some instances, by their long coats and beards.

Jewish Theological Seminary of America

*George Cruikshank's unsympathetic treatment of the manner in which the manage-
ment of the Covent Garden Theatre maintained order during the Old Price Riots
of 1809. Critics maintained that the Jewish prizefighters and ruffians hired to keep
order inside the theatre abused their authority and beat and robbed those who were
demonstrating against the rise in the price of tickets.*

The Jewish poor in the Georgian period had a reputation for rowdiness and tough-ness. In this anonymous engraving of a boisterous tavern scene, a bearded Jew delivers a blow to the mouth of the fellow who has grabbed his beard, while at the doorway a parish watchman, his staff and lantern in hand, has just appeared, drawn by the raucous noise.

The interior of the Great Synagogue in Duke's Place, as drawn by Thomas Rowlandson in 1809.

into their shops. An American visitor to London in 1802 recorded that he was accosted at least fifteen times while passing through Rag Fair. The dealers here, however, were apparently less a nuisance than those in Holywell Street, largely because Rag Fair was not in an area respectable persons frequently visited, but Holywell Street was. A guide book to London published in 1828 told visitors to expect abuse, scurrility, and threats hurled at them if they refused to become purchasers of the "base apparel and ricketty furniture" of the Holywell Street shopkeepers. The author of this guidebook noted that the Jewish shopkeepers there had been reduced at the time to "comparative civility," having been hauled before the Bow Street magistrates in 1824, 1825, and 1826. Still, he warned visitors, their sheer numbers continued to force passersby into their shops, and "persons of keen olfactory nerves get offended in that particular by this sort of forced contact of the doubtfully clean observers of the Pentateuch." Eight years later, Charles Dickens recorded, in his *Sketches by Boz,* how he despised "the red-headed and red-whiskered Jews [in Holywell Street] who forcibly haul you into their squalid houses, and thrust you into a suit of clothes whether you will or not."[25]

Of equal importance to street hawkers and old-clothes men in the economy of the Jewish poor were the itinerant peddlers who roamed the countryside of England. Often having just arrived from Germany or Holland and possessing a very limited knowledge of the English language and of English geography, they made their way into the remotest villages of England, sometimes providing country folk with their first glimpse of a real Jew. Some eventually settled down in the small provincial towns they visited and became shopkeepers, dealing in an expanded range of the goods they had once carried on their backs. But most of them remained itinerant traders, periodically returning to London or, in some instances, to provincial centers to be with their wives and children and to restock their boxes. By the 1740s or the 1750s, at the very latest, Jewish peddlers were a common sight in the provinces, especially in the south of England and in the area around London. By 1772, there were enough Jewish peddlers in England to justify the printing of an annual Yiddish calendar, or almanac, listing the dates of Jewish and English holidays, the dates of important local fairs, and the days on which coaches left London for the provinces.[26]

Detractors of the Jews pictured these itinerant traders as the purveyors of gimcracks and gewgaws. Their stock, according to Robert Southey, consisted of cuckoo clocks, sealing wax, quills, green spectacles, crude plaster of Paris figures, and miserable prints of the king and the queen, the four seasons, the cardinal virtues, the most recent naval victory, the Prodigal Son, the Nativity, the Crucifixion, and so forth. Other more impartial sources indicate, however, that the merchandise sold by these peddlers was a little more substantial than what Southey suggested. The stock of a Sephardi peddler, Jacob Hadida, whose box was stolen in 1824, consisted of shawls, handkerchiefs, dried rhubarb, penknives, pencils, thimbles, other small items, and a wide variety of spices, including nutmeg, cloves, ginger, and mace. The large number of spices in Hadida's stock was typical of Sephardi peddlers. Ashkenazi peddlers, on the other hand, tended to specialize in inexpensive jewelry. The stock of one such peddler, Isaac Solomon, who was assaulted and robbed in 1741 on the road between Rochdale and Manchester, consisted at the time of the following items:

> 2 pairs of carved silver shoe buckles
> 2 pairs of silver tea tongs
> 1 pinchbeck watch chain
> 4 gold rings
> 1 pinchbeck cane head
> 10 pairs of crystal buttons
> 1 silver watch chain
> 3 silver stock buckles
> 1 large silver clasp
> 1 carved silver snuff box
> several pairs of white metal buckles
> several Japan snuff boxes
> several silver thimbles

In addition to the above, he also lost over £18 in English and foreign coins. Abraham Davis, a peddler with a much more substantial business, lost over £180 in goods in 1778 when someone broke into his room in London. His stock included sixty-eight silver watches, ninety gold breast shirt buckles (some set with pearls, some with garnets), forty-eight gold rings set with precious stones, and eighteen pairs of silver shoe buckles. By the 1790s, Mayhew noted, the itinerant jewelry trade was almost entirely in the hands of Jews. In fact, the distribution of inexpensive watches was so closely identified with Jewish peddlers that such watches were referred to as "Jew watches" in the late eighteenth and early nineteenth centuries.[27]

The majority of English Jews in the years up to 1830 probably made their living in one of the three ways just described. It would be misleading, however, to suggest that there was a vast occupational gap, with no intermediary positions whatsoever, between the financiers and merchants of the Anglo-Jewish elite and the peddlers, hawkers, and old-clothes men at the bottom of the occupational ladder, although this is the image some contemporary remarks convey. Economic mobility was not impossible by any means. Some peddlers and hawkers were able to move up the ladder, becoming stall-holders and shopkeepers, and, if they continued to prosper, wholesalers, importers, and manufacturers. The founders of provincial Jewish communities were peddlers who had made good. The "red-headed and red-whiskered" Jews of Holywell Street no doubt had started out as old-clothes men. Mayhew was told of substantial merchants who had begun in the itinerant jewelry trade. Benjamin Hyam, who introduced modern mass-tailoring in Manchester in the 1830s and who owned a chain of thirteen retail outlets by 1851, was the grandson of an immigrant from Hamburg who had started in peddling and then set up as a shopkeeper in Ipswich sometime before 1790. The great-grandfather of Rufus Isaacs (1860–1935), the first Marquess of Reading, a lord chief justice, diplomat, and viceroy of India from 1921 to 1926, was a stall-holder at the regular fruit market in Duke's Place in the first decades of the nineteenth century; his son was a wholesale broker and importer of fruit.[28] London commercial directories of the 1820s list two or three dozen Cohens and Levys with substantial businesses—fabric wholesalers, feather dealers, pencil manufacturers, slopsellers, watchmakers, jewelers, grocers. Sometimes the ascent to middle-class status was accomplished in one generation, as in the case of the merchants referred to by Mayhew; oftentimes, it took two or three, as in the case of the Isaacs and Hyam families; but by no means was it inevitable or widespread. The experience of the Moroccan rhubarb seller whom Mayhew interviewed, who was ending his days in poverty, desperately dependent on the little charity he received at the holidays, was as representative of Anglo-Jewry in the Georgian period as the experience of the Isaacs and Hyam families.

With the passage of time, the size of the Jewish middle class, excluding the small circle of magnates at the top, expanded. The quickening tempo of commercial life in London and the burgeoning manufacturing towns in the provinces provided ambitious immigrants having the appropriate work ethic with ample opportunities for advancement. At the same time, many of the poorest elements within Anglo-Jewry lost their identity as Jews through conversion, intermarriage, or penal transportation to Australia and thus were no longer counted as part of Anglo-Jewry. By 1850, there were no longer any street trades in London still dominated by Jews. Moreover, the absolute number of Jews in any particular trade had fallen from what it had been previously. Yet, Anglo-Jewry as a whole did not lose its lower-class character until well into the Victorian years. At midcentury, contemporaries estimated that at least half of the Jews in England still belonged to the lower class.[29]

The inability of whatever economic mobility that existed to alter the general character of the Anglo-Jewish community before 1830 was in some measure due to the immigrant makeup of the Jewish population. The core of Jewish poor, instead of gradually shrinking as families moved up the economic ladder, kept expanding through a constant influx of destitute immigrants that increased over the years. The achievements of those who escaped poverty, in other words, were largely obscured in the public mind by the poverty of those who were constantly arriving from abroad. This is not, however, a comprehensive explanation of the lower-class status of the bulk of Anglo-Jewry, for poverty did not suddenly evaporate among the second generation, that is, among those who were born in England. Much of it was handed down from one generation to the next. Because economic mobility has frequently characterized Jewish communities in the West freed from the restraints of economic and political discrimination, there is a need to ask if there were restraints of a nonlegal nature that contributed to Anglo-Jewish poverty.

The unstable character of the trades most Jews followed was certainly one crucial element in the transmission of poverty from parents to children. From the life histories referred to above, it is clear that the careers of old-clothes men and peddlers were marked by enormous swings of fortune. Savings could be decimated through a single stroke of bad luck, such as an assault or a break-in, or through a lengthy slump in sales due to the vagaries of the economy. Not being trained in any specialized calling, it was largely impossible for Jews to obtain the kind of employment that provided a steady income. When one trade became depressed, they switched to another, since the training and the outlook required for almost all the trades of the Jewish poor were essentially the same. Isaac Asher, for example, testified at the Old Bailey in 1755 that sometimes he cried "Old clothes," and at other times he traveled the country selling silver and hardware. Alexander Abrahams, who was acquitted of receiving stolen goods the following year, said that he had traveled in the country with hardware and sold anchovies and pickles in the streets of London. When Godfrey Davis was asked at the Old Bailey in 1812 what his occupation was, he replied, "I get my living in the clothes way. I was in the glass way; now times are hard. I cannot afford to be in the glass way."[30]

For the Jewish lower classes of England, two of the most common escape routes from poverty—artisanal training and education—were largely blocked because they could not manage to pay for more than a few years of education for their children and were equally unable to have them apprenticed. (The social institutions that performed these functions for the Jewish poor elsewhere in Europe and later in the United States—Jewish charity schools and state schools—only came into existence relatively late in Anglo-Jewish history, and then they touched the lives of only a very small number of children. See Chapter 7.) Despite a religious tradition that extolled the virtues of learning, it was common for the children of the Jewish poor to be put to work by their parents at a very early age, as was the practice of the non-Jewish poor. Whatever education they received was devoted to learning the Hebrew liturgy and possibly some passages from the Bible. Only the well-to-do could afford to keep their children in school for more than three or four years. For families with five to ten children, it was essential that eight- and nine-year-olds assist in supporting the family. Ikey Solomons (1785–1850), who became the most notorious fence in Regency London, hawked oranges and lemons at age eight or nine; the "Jew peddler" of a popular song of that title sold men's hair rollers at age eight and a half. In another popular song of the early nineteenth century, "The Happy Jew," the subject of the song recalled that he had gone out into the world to make a living at a tender age because his father had died. Having later married and had children of his own, he, in turn, sent them out into the streets: "There's Sammy sells slippers in St. Paul's Churchyard—Joey cries heart-cakes in Cheapside—Becky sells oranges at the Mansion House—and little Isaac carries about *Dutch* sealing wax made in Duke's Place." The missionary Joseph Samuel Frey related in his memoirs the story of a boy who had been orphaned at age two and who was put out to sell sweetmeats at age eight by his grandmother and aunt, who had charge of him. When he turned ten, they refused to give him any further protection because they considered him capable of making his own living. He moved out, found lodgings of his own in Petticoat Lane, and began hawking lozenges in the streets.[31]

Even in families that were not in desperate straits, families in which the father was a small shopkeeper or artisan, for example, it was rare to educate children past the age of eleven or twelve. Daniel Mendoza, the greatest prizefighter of the late 1780s and early 1790s, recalled that even though his family was in "the middling class of society," his father placed him and his numerous brothers and sisters in different employments very early in life. Daniel had received the rudiments of an English education at a "Jew's school," including English grammar, writing, and arithmetic, but before he was thirteen, he was sent to live with a glass cutter, to whom he was to be bound apprentice if it appeared they were mutually satisfied after a trial period. As things turned out, Daniel quarreled with the son of his potential master, and thrashed him and left. Before turning to fighting as a career, he worked for a fruiterer and greengrocer, a tea dealer, and a tobacconist.[32]

The exposure to secular learning Mendoza received in the 1770s was in no way typical of the education of the children of the Jewish lower classes. It was highly exceptional, although it became less so with the passage of time, and reflected the Sephardi and middle-class background of his family. And as unusual as it was, it was not advanced enough to guarantee him access to a career he could not have obtained otherwise. The bulk of the children of the Jewish poor received far less instruction than he, and what little they did obtain was devoted almost exclusively to the study of Hebrew. Their consequent ignorance in both Jewish and secular matters was considered a communal scandal and disgrace and frequently remarked upon by critics inside and outside the Jewish community.

The inability of the Jewish lower classes to apprentice their sons to either Jewish or Christian masters is a more complex issue than that of their general inability to provide them with much education. Early nineteenth-century reformers like Joshua Van Oven thought that the ceremonial restrictions of Judaism made it impossible for a Jewish lad to be bound apprentice to a Christian master, since no master would want to lose the work of his apprentice on the Jewish Sabbath and festivals. Only in a few instances, Van Oven noted, had handsome premiums induced Christian masters to submit to these inconveniences. The assumption underlying this explanation is that the majority of the Jewish poor were strictly orthodox, an assumption open to question. But even if it were true that religious considerations kept most Jewish parents from apprenticing their children to non-Jewish masters, it would not be the most basic reason. For there were Jewish artisans—pencil-makers, glass cutters, engravers, watchmakers, jewelers, tailors, hatters, shoemakers, pastry cooks, confectioners, pen and quill makers—to whom Jews could be apprenticed. And the articles binding Jewish children to Jewish masters generally contained provisions exempting them from work on the Sabbath and the festivals. The most crucial obstacle to the Jewish poor in providing a better future for their children was not their religion but their inability to pay the required fees, a disability from which all the poor suffered. When Michael Jacobs was bound apprentice in 1767 to Mordecai Levy, a glass engraver, for seven years, Levy received a premium of six guineas. In 1795, when Naphtali Hart was bound apprentice to Marco Ozeley, a jeweler, for seven years, his father paid Ozeley £42.[33] These sums were well beyond the means of the average street trader or old-clothes man.

There is also reason to believe that the economic position of Jewish artisans was not particularly secure and that this may have dissuaded some parents from binding over their children to learn a craft. The Hebrew printer Levy Alexander thought that Van Oven's scheme to train more Jewish artisans was foolhardy and utopian: the few Jewish artisans already plying their trades had difficulty in finding enough work, and more Jewish shoemakers and glass cutters would only flood an already overcrowded market. In 1795, Jacob Isaacs explained to a jury at the Old Bailey that he had stolen a boy's coat and a pair of breeches from a Jewish tailor he knew because he had a sick father and mother at home who were "starving for want." He was a hatter by trade and said he could not obtain any work. The experiences of Michael Jacobs, an apprentice glass engraver, also indicate that possession of a handicraft was no guarantee of economic security. Jacobs served Levy for three years, but after his master's business fell off, he was sent out to hawk glasses in the streets. When he fell ill from overexposure, Levy would not care for him, as he was obligated to do by the indentures, and Jacobs was sent home to his mother, who either would not or could not take care of him. Jacobs was ill for nine weeks and would have starved if a friend had not taken up a collection for him. After he recovered, he returned to Levy to resume his training, whereupon Levy told him to go about his business, as he had quit his trade and sold his tools. Jacobs then complained to the *parnasim* of the Great Synagogue, who adjudged that Levy should pay one half the expenses of the lad's illness; this accomplished nothing, since their decision was unenforceable. Finally, Jacobs obtained some relief by taking Levy before a Justice of the Peace for Middlesex.[34]

Beyond the specific issue of the inability of most Jews to obtain a secular education or to become artisans, there lies the larger problem of the general orientation of the Jewish poor to the value of sustained work and economic achievement. Not all of the poverty that characterized Anglo-Jewry is attributable to the immigrant status of such a large proportion of the community or to the inability of young Jews to obtain artisanal training. Economic success in the modern world usually requires a state of mind that inculcates the habits of diligence, industry, and frugality. This kind of orientation, commonly referred to as the bourgeois work ethic, aided many Jews over the course of the Georgian period, including some freshly arrived from the Continent, to work their way up into the middle class. But just as many immigrants came with a very different orientation to the value of ceaseless economic activity. They arrived with a precapitalistic, lower-class disdain for both the work ethic and the personal morality of respectable folk. They were, from the vantage point of the Anglo-Jewish bourgeoisie, lazy, irresponsible, feckless, and immoral. Contemporary observers argued that it was not merely the inability to become artisans that was responsible for so much Jewish poverty. The pseudonymous Philo-Judaeis pointed out that the Christian poor, who had no ceremonial obstacles to learning a trade, still remained poor. For him, the crux of the matter was an attitudinal question: how to inculcate the principles of virtue and habits of industry in "such a licentious crew." Levy Alexander agreed with him: making poor Jews productive and useful meant overcoming "the hereditary and deeply rooted prejudices of a nation." This required, in his mind, a great length of time, at least three or more generations.[35] Over the course of the nineteenth century, a middle-class orientation came to dominate most of Anglo-Jewry, but as the following chapter will make clear, that "triumph" did not occur before 1830.

6

Pickpockets and Pugilists

The Jewish poor in Georgian England were in many respects very similar to the non-Jewish poor. They lived in accordance with a system of values and priorities that often clashed with the morals and the manners of polite society. They absorbed, on a selective basis, the less-inhibited habits of their immediate non-Jewish neighbors, rather than the standards of country gentlemen, and pursued anglicization in their own distinctive manner rather than as the well-to-do Anglo-Jewry, thus threatening the latter's respectability. Many embraced the rough-and-tumble ways of English street life with alacrity, including a taste for the rougher amusements of English life, and disregarded traditional Jewish notions of ethical conduct. A few displayed streaks of violence and cruelty so disruptive of the calm of the community that the Anglo-Jewish elite had to intervene in the affairs of the poor.

One major consequence of the lower-class orientation of so many English Jews was that a very visible portion of the community engaged in criminal activity, either on an occasional basis or as a full-time occupation. Some of the crimes with which Jews were associated in the public mind were closely related to the trades in which they were concentrated. For example, as dealers in secondhand merchandise of every description, they frequently purchased stolen goods, for receiving stolen goods was a branch of criminal activity inseparable from the trade in secondhand goods. Most of the crimes for which Jews were actually apprehended, however, such as picking pockets, shoplifting, and breaking and entering, in no way reflected either the occupational makeup of the community or their immediate historical experience as Jews. Crimes such as these were the outgrowth of poverty in general; in other words, because the majority of English Jews belonged to the lower class, they contributed to the problem of crime in London.

Some of the crimes Jews committed were a direct consequence of the dire poverty in which they lived. Assuming the testimony of the accused who appeared at the Old Bailey to be true, it was want that moved many of them to break the law. Abraham Abrahams (age 36, married, the father of two children), who was sentenced to death in 1794 for stealing twenty-two yards of linen, pleaded poverty. Solomon Nathan, age 16, who was transported to Australia for life in 1824 for shoplifting nine handkerchiefs, pleaded distress. That same year, Henry Hart, age 14, was ordered to be whipped for stealing a sheet. He told the court he did it from hunger, having lost his job and having been turned out of his father-in-law's house.[1]

In addition to those who stole to keep from starving, there were scores of Jews whose entire livelihoods depended on the fruits of illegal activity—pickpockets, housebreakers, receivers, forgers, brothel-keepers, and swindlers. There were also hundreds of otherwise employed lower-class Jews who broke the law occasionally when a particularly good opportunity for extra gain presented itself. In short, there was no one pattern of Jewish criminal behavior, but a variety of motives and modes.

Before the 1760s, Jewish criminal activity was not regarded as an acute social problem, either by the notables of the Jewish community or by the critics of the Jews. There was, as far as it is possible to know, little Jewish criminal activity before these years, no doubt because there were few Jews, respectable or otherwise, in England. In the 1730s, the first decade for which it is possible to obtain any information, there were only four Jews convicted at the Old Bailey—two for stealing from their masters, one for forging an acceptance to a bill of exchange, and one for burglary.[2] In the next decade, there was a considerable jump in the number of convictions—to eighteen—including one for stealing some of the ritual silver from the Great Synagogue, but not enough of a leap to attract any public comment. Still, it is impor-

tant to remember that the number of Jews who actually committed crimes was far, far greater than the number of those eventually convicted. The rate of apprehension and conviction in Georgian London, particularly before the establishment of stipendiary
magistrates offices in 1792, was abysmally low. London was a
notoriously unsafe city. The threats to property and person were
as great, if not greater, than in the most dangerous American
cities today. Those individuals who appeared in court to answer
for their crimes represented only the tip of an iceberg of criminal
activity. Abraham Pass, who was sentenced to death in 1743 for
burglary, confessed during the course of his trial to at least
twenty other burglaries, none of which he had been apprehended
for.[3]

During the Jew Bill controversy of 1753, the Jews were rarely
charged with being a criminal element. If there had been a noticeable number of Jews who were criminals, it is hard to imagine that
the opponents of Jewish naturalization would not have exploited
this issue to the fullest extent possible. Charges of this nature
were made, but only infrequently; they can hardly be considered
a dominant motif in the anti-Jewish campaign. Still, they are
worth examining for what they reveal about the character of
Jewish criminal activity at midcentury. The pseudonymous pamphleteer J. E. charged the Jews with three kinds of crimes: (1)
receiving stolen goods, (2) sweating and filing coins (reducing
their weight by wearing away their surface and their edge respectively), and (3) thievery.[4] Taking the latter two charges first, there
is little evidence from the Old Bailey in the 1740s and 1750s to
corroborate the accusation that these were areas in which English
Jews distinguished themselves. The charge of sweating and filing
coins was made against English Jews in the preexpulsion period
and was frequently repeated on the Continent during the medieval and early modern periods. It is very possible that J. E., whose
opposition to Jewish naturalization rested largely on the traditional religious objection of the Jews being deicides and blasphemers, was unhesitatingly borrowing accusations from another
time and another place as if they were eternally valid.

The first charge J. E. made—that the Jews were receivers of
stolen goods—was not a baseless accusation. From the middle of
the eighteenth century through the 1830s, and probably beyond,
Jews were among the most active fences in London. Victims

desiring to recover stolen goods and thieves trying to dispose of them assumed they would find what they wanted in the Jewish quarter. In November of 1743, a woman who had stolen a gold watch approached Abraham Jacobs in Rag Fair, where he had gone to buy a pair of shoes, and asked him if he were a Jew. When he replied that he was, she told him that she had a gold watch she wanted to get rid of and that she wanted him to help her find someone to buy it. She assumed, in other words, that any Jew she met in that part of London would know where to find a buyer for a stolen watch. The same assumption also appeared in the testimony of a shopkeeper who, in 1769, had watches worth £200 stolen from his shop in Cornhill. After discovering the break-in, he "thought it most likely they might be heard of in Duke's Place. I went there to Mr. Howard, who keeps a coffee house, and told him the case, and told him if he found any such things offered with such names and numbers, I should be obliged to him if he would let me know."[5]

The reputation Jews had as receivers of stolen property derived from the belief that, as dealers in all kinds of secondhand goods, they were willing to purchase anything offered to them—an assumption that was basically correct. Even old-clothes men and shopkeepers who were not professional fences would purchase things in the normal course of business that they undoubtedly knew were stolen. The following testimony by a witness, Jacob Isaacs, at the Old Bailey in 1769, well illustrates this point:

> I follow all kinds of business, and deal in watches, rings, or anything. The prisoner came to me, and asked me if I would buy some velvets. I said I had not money to buy such a thing. . . . I said I could not buy it without I went to Henry Lion. I went and told him of it, but said, I do not know whether it was come by honestly or not. He said, do not mind that; if it is worth the money, buy it. He gave me fifteen guineas to buy it.

The very same outlook was attributed to the Jews in the patter to a popular song from the early nineteenth century, "Mister Reubens Cohen and Mr. Nab":

> Steal, pe tamed! if a cood pargain came to my fingers vat right have I to ax a yentleman how it vas come into his hand. If I vas deal mit a tief, must I make a rogue of myself by axing him to tell me vat I buy stolen coods? No, no, py Cot! . . . Nobody vat

is curious can made a cood pargains honestly. Dat is not my vay; never ax questions—it spoils every ting at arl vat is trade mit an honest yentleman vat lives at his fingers' ends by his.[6]

In charging the Jews of London with being receivers of stolen goods, J. E. and others frequently pointed out that their connections abroad allowed them to ship stolen goods of exceptional value out of the country. J. E. remarked that "if anybody could bring him, they'd buy the devil and send him to Holland." John Lancaster, who was executed at Tyburn in 1748, testified that the fence he dealt with, Levi Chitty, exported all the stolen goods he brought to him to Holland. At the Old Bailey in 1757 it was charged that there was a Jew who "was worth from four or five thousand pounds, whose chief employ was to buy stolen goods and send them to Holland." Henry Fielding, who as a London magistrate knew the criminal world as well as any man in the ruling class, wrote in 1751 of some notable Jewish receivers who carried on their business in an almost public manner and regularly shipped goods to Rotterdam, where they had warehouses and agents.[7] With a constant flow of Jews between Holland and England, and with such close family and business ties, it is not surprising that Jews were active in disposing of stolen goods abroad.

Not many years after the controversy over the Jew Bill, Jewish criminal activity reached such a pitch that it became a matter of concern to the leaders of Anglo-Jewry. In the 1760s, the number of Jews sentenced to death or transportation at the Old Bailey jumped to thirty-five—almost double what it had been in the previous decade—and then in the 1770s it rose to sixty-five. The first sign of concern on the part of the Anglo-Jewish elite over the increase came in 1766. According to the antiquary William Cole, "the poor, vagabond Jews in and about London were come to such a pitch in thieving, cheating, robbing, and pilfering, that the Government began to take notice of it. . . . the greater Jews thought proper to give a check to such a scandal, which ultimately rebounded upon themselves, and might, if suffered to go on to greater lengths, be of consequence to their own peaceful settlement." Aside from an overall increase in the amount of Jewish crime, the exact character of the events that led the government to act are unknown. It is certainly reasonable to speculate that testimony like the following at the Old Bailey in October 1765 played a role. Robert Byfield, an accused thief, told the court about Abraham Terachina, a well-known fence: "This Jew used to encourage us to do so; he used to give us diamonds to cut windows, and he said, if we got in trouble, he would bail us. He has encouraged several little boys to thieve." It is not known how the government intended to crack down on Jewish criminals. What is known is that in the spring of 1766 the *parnasim* of the Great Synagogue, Naphtali Franks and Naphtali Hart Myers, possibly with the assistance of others, used their influence within the Jewish community to gain information about Jewish receivers and then passed this information on to Sir John Fielding, the Bow Street magistrate who worked closely with the government. At the same time, in order to dissociate themselves further from "those few infamous receivers of stolen goods about Duke's Place and Houndsditch," the Great Synagogue excommunicated several Jewish criminals, and Franks and Myers published an exchange of letters with Fielding in the *Public Advertiser* of 31 May, in which Fielding thanked them for their concern and assistance.[8]

The leaders of Anglo-Jewry may have succeeded in reducing the level of Jewish crime for a few months, but there was very little they could do over the long run. Aside from providing the magistrates with leads that their position enabled them to obtain, they had no means of exerting control over or disciplining their wayward coreligionists. They could withhold charity from those they wanted to punish, but that action would only affect the small number of poor who regularly received relief from the synagogue. They could also refuse to give them synagogal honors and a Jewish burial, but it is hardly likely that men like Abraham Terachina were swayed by considerations such as these. Whether they were English-born or not, Jewish criminals and other similarly disreputable Jews were not dependent on the authorities of the Jewish community for protection. They could not lose their right to dwell in London, as was frequently the case in the German states. They could offend public morality, Jewish and Christian, as much as they liked without having anything to fear from the Chief Rabbi or the *parnasim*. Like everyone else, their only concern was to avoid apprehension by the state, and this, by and large, they managed to do quite successfully.

There is every indication that the tempo of Jewish criminal

activity picked up after the crackdown of 1766. Within the year, Joseph Phineas, a barber's boy, broke into the Great Synagogue and stole a silver cup and a silver caster. In 1769, Abraham Terachina, described by a witness at the Old Bailey as "a notorious receiver of stolen goods," was still unapprehended. But the most telling evidence of the futility of the *parnasim*'s intervention in 1766 came in testimony Sir John Fielding gave in April 1770 before a committee of the House of Commons looking into a rise in the number of burglaries in London. In the course of his remarks, Fielding explained that housebreakers had previously taken their loot to non-Jewish pawnbrokers and silversmiths, but that his office had taken to notifying them immediately of stolen goods so that it no longer became possible for burglars to dispose of their goods in this fashion. Instead, they now went directly to Jewish receivers, who melted down the plate, knocked the stones out of their original settings, and otherwise destroyed the distinguishing marks of whatever they bought so as to make them untraceable. He also told the committee that his office had successfully detected several receivers in Duke's Place and was offering a reward of five guineas for further apprehensions. It can be no coincidence that during the same week the Great Synagogue advertised in the newspapers it was offering a reward for the detection of receivers of stolen goods.[9]

Once again the necessarily restricted efforts of the synagogal authorities to deter crime met with complete failure. The 1770s witnessed almost a 100 percent increase over the previous decade in the number of Jews sentenced to death or transportation at the Old Bailey. Moreover, at the very beginning of the decade, the entire community became subject to abuse when public outrage over Jewish criminals crystallized around the so-called Chelsea murder case. The story of this case has never been told in any detail before, and it is worthwhile to do so here,[10] both for what it reveals about the gravity of Jewish criminal activity from the 1770s on and for what it discloses about the seriousness of the threat posed to the well-being of the entire community by this activity.

On the night of 11 June 1771, a gang of nine Jews broke into the house of a Mrs. Hutchins in the King's Road, Chelsea, then a rural area. In the course of robbing the house, they shot and murdered a servant who tried to resist. The Bow Street magistrate's office was informed of the break-in and murder in the early hours of 12 June. In an unusual move, the government, at the request of Sir John Fielding, agreed to offer a reward of £50 for information leading to the arrest of the gang. Details about the crime were published in a number of newspapers, but there was no immediate response. Then, sometime in the early autumn of the same year, Daniel Isaacs, a member of the gang who had fallen on hard times, applied for charity to the Great Synagogue. Naphtali Hart Myers, one of the *parnasim,* not knowing his true identity at this time, refused to give him anything because he believed that Isaacs had left Holland, where he might have earned an honest living, and come to London to take advantage of the Great Synagogue's reputed largesse. Later, when Isaacs heard of the rewards being offered by the Secretary of State and the City of London, he decided to turn King's evidence, and returned to Myers, making known to him the identities of the gang's members. Myers then took Isaacs to Fielding, who, on hearing his story, decided that the gang should be rooted out and prosecuted at government expense—instead of by the victim, as was normally the practice—because they were "so extraordinary a gang and have raised such a terror."

By the first week in November, two members of the gang had been picked up, along with two receivers, for their role in another break-in committed by the gang at a Mrs. Deighton's in Wormley, Hertfordshire, in February. At the same time, Fielding had reward posters describing the gang distributed throughout the country—another unprecedented move—by the Post Office and the Customs and Excise. By 9 November, all but one of the principals in the case had been taken; however, a number of "suspicious" Jews continued to be apprehended in different parts of England. At Truro, for example, the mayor committed Solomon Levi, age 28, and Simon Levi, also age 28, to prison because they appeared to have no visible means of support. They claimed to be peddlers, but were traveling without licenses and had no boxes of goods with them. Solomon Levi said he had peddled goods in and about London for several years, but had made away with money that he owed to the man who had extended him credit. Neither Levi, it turned out, had anything to do with the Chelsea murder, but their detention in Truro was characteristic of the atmosphere of suspicion and hostility created by the case.

The gang responsible for the Chelsea murder was composed largely of hardened criminals who had operated on both sides of the English Channel. The leaders of the band were Asher and Levi Weil. The former had been in England only two years and required an interpreter when he appeared in court; the latter was a surgeon and apothecary who had studied medicine, so it was said, at Leiden. He recruited several Jews from Holland at one point to strengthen the group operating in England. Solomon Lazarus, another member who turned King's evidence, had previously been sentenced to hang for passing false money in an English army camp on the Continent, but had been pardoned by the Marquess of Granby. A number of women also appear to have been associated with the gang. There was Phoebe, a twenty-four-year-old German Jew, "tall and rather lusty, fairish complexion for a Jewess," and Fanny, the wife of Hyam Lazarus, a member of the gang, and the current mistress of another member, Aaron (or Abraham) Linevil. Not one of the band, apparently, was a practicing Jew. When they were being examined by Sir John Fielding and Solomon Porter began abusing Isaacs, Sir John told him to stop, as it would do him no good to revile his brother Jew. Porter immediately burst out: "He a Jew? He's no Jew; he is more Christian as Jews." Porter, Lazarus, and the brothers Weil were hanged at Tyburn on 9 December, and the rest, excepting those who turned King's evidence, were deported to Holland or made to stand trial for other offenses.

The Chelsea murder case, in itself not a particularly violent act by the standards of the time, served as a focal point around which a large amount of latent and diffuse anti-Jewish sentiment was able to crystallize. Anglo-Jewry as a body stood convicted. According to the barrister William Jackson, "A Jew could scarcely pass the streets, but he was upbraided with the words, 'Hutchins' and 'Chelsea,' and many of them were pulled by the beards, while those who ought to have taken the insulters into custody stood calmly by and triumphed in the insult." According to the London *Chronicle,* "a great number of Jews" fled the kingdom to escape the hostility that had been aroused. Horace Walpole quipped, a few days after the hangings at Tyburn, that Almack's Club in Pall Mall, which was noted for its extravagant gambling, was "in a very languishing way" because "it is not so easy *to borrow a Jew,* now so many are hanged or run away." The public uproar made such an impression on men's minds that it was remembered decades later. The radical tailor Francis Place, who was born in 1771, wrote many years later that every Jew was implicated in public opinion and that the prejudice and ill will created by the case did not cease for many years. " 'Go to Chelsea' was a common exclamation when a Jew was seen in the streets and was often the signal of assault." Over half a century later, Cobbett was still using the Chelsea case as a stick with which to beat the Jews. Although he was only eight years old at the time, "the thing was so much talked of in the country" that he never forgot it, remembering even the name of the person in whose house the murder was committed. In recalling those events, he did, however, add some details that were not originally there. He imagined that the Jewish gang had mutilated the body of the male servant in a manner insulting to human nature (did he mean they castrated him?) and that the government had forbidden the Jews, for their own safety, to travel more than so many miles from St. Paul's.[11]

The immediate response of the leaders of Anglo-Jewry to the Chelsea case was to aid the government in apprehending the gang. According to one newspaper account, "The Synagogue itself expended a very large sum to promote the ends of public justice." Then, after the gang was apprehended, the *parnasim* of the Great Synagogue inserted an announcement in the London papers distancing themselves from the gang by branding them "a set of foreign miscreants who stain our religion by calling themselves Jews," pledging to assist the civil magistrates in every way, imploring the honest members of the community to do likewise, and promising to refuse Jewish criminals burial or any other religious ceremonies. The last part of the statement was also intended "to deter every Jew from receiving stolen goods or concealing such or harboring any persons guilty of any theft." On 7 December, two days before the execution of Lazarus, Porter, and the Weils, a formal ban of excommunication was pronounced against the guilty at the Great Synagogue. At the same time that they moved to clear the name of the Jewish community, the *parnasim* also asked the government, through Fielding, to place restrictions on the migration of poor Jews from the Continent. They realized, quite correctly, that the unregulated flow of lower-class Jews between England and Holland seriously contributed to the problem of Jewish criminality. As poor Jews, like "the industrious poor of all nations," could obtain free passage on the king's cross-channel packet boats, the *parnasim* wanted the government to require them, before embarking for England, to produce statements certifying that they needed to travel to England on business or that they were likely to find employment there. In December 1771, the Earl of Suffolk ordered that no Jews be permitted to board the packet boats unless they paid the regular fare. For reasons unknown, the regulation was not put into effect until 10 October 1774, when a General Post Office directive stipulated that "Jews are in no instance to be admitted on board [the packet boats] without paying the full passage money of 12/ 6d. each."[12] As there was no drop in the 1770s and thereafter in the rate of Jewish immigration to England, in the level of Jewish poverty, or in the extent of Jewish criminality, it is very probable that the regulation was never conscientiously enforced.

The concern of the Anglo-Jewish elite over the rise in the level of Jewish criminal activity was in many ways justified. In the words of the Hebrew printer Alexander Alexander, writing in 1775, "the very name of a Jew doth become so stigmatised that the good do suffer for the bad." This fear was realised in the indiscriminate hooliganism that followed the Chelsea murder case and in a number of proposals (some of which were described previously) to institute collective responsibility for Jewish criminal activity. In a letter to Lord North that appeared in the *Morning Post* on 6 December 1775, A True Englishman proposed a special tax of two guineas a year on every Jew in England. He felt that the Jews were not contributing their fair share to the well-being of the nation, that they were an unproductive and injurious body of people. "The greatest part of them live like gentlemen by receiving stolen goods. . . . nine-tenths of the burglaries are occasioned by them. A housebreaker the moment he hath got his booty of plate or other valuables goes to the Jews . . . and for plate in particular their melting pots are always ready to prevent a discovery." A similar proposal, grounded on the same assumptions, was advanced by Richard King at the end of the decade in *The Frauds of London Detected.* King believed that "the many horrid and shocking murders and burglaries they have committed" required legislative action, particularly as the Jews abused the judicial system, taking advantage of its leniency to escape punishment. The only way to restore to the English nation the huge sums the Jews had taken from them through criminal acts was to fine the Jewish community as a whole. "Let them be taxed, and severely too, they can afford it, they have money in plenty, ease them of some part of the burden they groan under, and therewith lighten the burden of taxes imposed upon ourselves. Retaliation is commendable in this case and ought forthwith to be put in practice against them."[13]

The upswing in Jewish criminal activity that began in the late 1760s and early 1770s continued to rise over the next five decades. As was mentioned earlier, only during the Revolutionary and Napoleonic wars, when immigration from Germany and Holland was extremely difficult, was there a sharp drop. In the 1780s, sixty-one Jews were sentenced to death or transportation at the Old Bailey; in the 1790s and the 1800s, the numbers dropped to thirty-seven and thirty respectively. Some portion of this decline was a result of a shift in the pattern of sentencing during the wars; fewer prisoners were sentenced to transportation due to a shortage of ships to carry them to Australia. But with the coming of peace, the numbers shot up again to eighty-nine in the 1810s and to ninety in the 1820s.

The overwhelming majority of Jews who received these extreme sentences committed offenses that were in no way associated in the public mind with Jews. They were tried for shoplifting, or for burglary, or for stealing from carts and warehouses —crimes characteristic of the poor in general. An increasingly large number of Jews, however, were convicted of crimes that came to be seen as the special province of Jews—passing bad coins and picking pockets, for example. At the same time, Jews also came to be identified as the major perpetrators of various frauds and swindles in the world of commerce. They became notorious, for example, for staging fraudulent bankruptcies and laying false claims before the Commissioners of Bankrupts. During a discussion of the bankruptcy laws in the House of Commons in May 1817, J. J. Lockhart, M.P., charged that in London the principal claimants of fictitious debts before the Commissioners of Bankrupts were Jews, citing in particular the example of one Jew who had sworn himself the creditor of a bankrupt to the amount of £5,000, but upon examination by the Commissioners, had been found to have had not one shilling owed him. Lockhart went on to claim that Jews had no reverence for any oath not taken before a rabbi—a charge that prompted a public denial from Chief Rabbi Hirschell. Several witnesses who appeared before the House of Commons Select Committee on the Bankrupt Laws that same year revealed there were Jews who made a living from arranging false bankruptcies. These persons would draw up fictitious bills of exchange to show the "debts" owed to them by the bankrupt and would manage to be appointed assignees to the bankrupt. They would then prevent a fair investigation of the conduct and accounts of the bankrupt and would allow the weight of the debt to be taken up by largely fictitious claims, to the detriment of the legitimate creditors of the bankrupt. In such "Jew commissions," as they were known, the bankrupt would claim he kept no account books or would produce books manufactured for him for the occasion. So assiduous about their work were these dealers in bankruptcy that they regularly attended commissions of bankruptcy "for the purpose of seeing how frauds are detected, that they might more minutely practice them hereafter without the possibility of detection; thereafter, you never find a commission executed, if it is a commission of any moment at all, but Jews are there, receiving their education."[14]

Another form of commercial chicanery associated with Jews—in this case, as in the former, more with Jews of some means than with those from the lowest ranks—was that known as swindling: obtaining goods from manufacturers or merchants on false credit and then absconding before detection of the fraud, or declaring bankruptcy and arranging to swap the real claims with false ones. One guide to London morals and manners, published in 1781, credited Jews with having introduced swindling into England in the early 1760s and singled out the years around 1770 as a period in which swindling was "in its meridian of glory." In a case tried in the Court of King's Bench in 1819, four Jewish swindlers were convicted of having cheated respectable merchants out of goods worth more than £50,000 by having set themselves up as opulent merchants in order to gain the trust of the commercial world and then having obtained large quantities of goods on credit. In Manchester, two years earlier, Noah Lodolski, a newly arrived immigrant, and two local Jewish shopkeepers attempted to defraud Manchester textile firms of goods worth £25,000 on the security of two trunks that supposedly contained "Birmingham goods" but in fact were filled with bricks.[15]

Jews were also frequently associated with various stratagems for selling shoddy goods at inflated prices by misrepresenting their true worth. One common ruse was the mock auction, at which the prices of articles of inferior quality were driven up by bidders working for the auctioneer. In 1817, at a time when the English watchmaking trade was depressed, witnesses told a House of Commons committee that shoddy watches manufactured by Jews were frequently sold at such auctions. A more elaborate ruse was developed for selling inexpensive watches in the streets of London. Two Jews, one in the dress of a sailor, would stage an argument in tones loud enough to attract the attention of passersby. The Jew would attempt to buy the watch of the "sailor," who would claim to have paid £12 or £14 for it and would refuse to sell it to the Jew, as he had cheated him previously, or because he did not want to sell it to any "damned Jew." The "sailor," having just come ashore and being short of money, would then offer to sell the watch to someone nearby who he thought was a likely target. The "sailor" would entreat this person to buy it, and then the Jew would approach and whisper that he would buy the watch from the customer if he bought it from the "sailor," as well as give him a guinea or so for his trouble. He would then disappear, telling the customer to meet him at such-and-such place later on. If the stratagem worked, the customer would then buy a watch worth from ten to twenty-five shillings for £6, £7, or £8. Later, when he went to look for the Jew, he would of course have disappeared. So widespread had this confidence trick become in 1817 that the Lord Mayor of London felt compelled to issue a warning not to buy watches from strangers in the street. A variation on this technique was employed by two Jews in Manchester in 1821 to sell a grocer a bundle of used clothes, worth less than £1, for £7. One of the Jews, in the guise of a liveried footman, offered the clothing to the grocer, while the other, posing as a peddler, forced the price up by bargaining with the footman. Of course, not all efforts to sell shoddy goods were so elaborate. Much more common was the simple misrepresentation of the goods being offered, such as selling trinkets of brass or another yellow metal as gold jewelry. A Jewish peddler in a popular song from the early nineteenth century boasted of selling "good gold rings of copper gilt," "sealing wax of brick-dust," and "pencils without lead."[16]

In one area of criminal activity—receiving stolen goods—Jews remained especially active, coming to control, with the passage of time, an even greater share of the field. One of the first relatively objective surveys of crime in the metropolis, that published by Patrick Colquhoun in 1796, put special emphasis on the place Jews occupied in the disposal of stolen goods. After describing the role of old-clothes men in purchasing small articles pilfered by servants and apprentices, Colquhoun drew attention to a feature of fencing that had not yet received public notice. He pointed to a class of Jewish scrap-metal dealers with single-horse carts who purchased stolen goods (copper bolts, nails, spikes, old iron, cordage, etc.) in the seaports and conveyed them to London, where they disposed of them to receivers with shops there. A more detailed survey of criminal life, conducted in the early 1830s by W. A. Miles, found that Jews were the biggest fences in London and that Christian fences played only a subsidiary role. The police superintendents and officers who supplied Miles with his information thought that the major fences remained in constant communication with agents abroad to whom they shipped stolen goods. These fences, some of whom lived in respectable houses and even kept shops in the West End, also purchased stolen goods from old-clothes men who had themselves previously bought the goods from young thieves in the street.[17]

There was, then, by the first decades of the nineteenth century, a kind of occupational hierarchy among receivers of stolen goods. At the bottom of the ladder were street traders, especially old-clothes men, who purchased the loot of petty criminals; at the top, the seemingly respectable general dealers with their well-stocked shops and their networks of agents throughout the country and on the Continent, men of some substance who through diligent effort had risen from the ranks of the poor; and somewhere in between, the itinerant junk men with their one-horse carts who served as a conduit for stolen goods from the provinces into London.

As noted earlier, the heavy concentration of Jews in the trade in secondhand goods was in large part responsible for their prominence as receivers of stolen goods. In a similar manner, but to a lesser extent, the clustering of lower-class Jews in street trades, which required them to be constantly making change, was

responsible for their notoriety in passing bad coins. For reasons
not clear, coining and issuing counterfeit money was not an activity in which Jews engaged to any noticeable extent before the
1790s. There were no convictions of Jews at the Old Bailey for
any offenses involving counterfeit coins, including their manufacture and distribution, before 1782. Then, from the 1790s on,
orange and lemon sellers began to appear fairly regularly at the
Old Bailey for passing bad coins. In 1795, *The Times* warned its
readers that "at this season the Jew fruitmen should be particularly guarded against." A guidebook to London from 1813 issued
a similar caveat to the unwary: "Itinerant vendors of fruit, especially the Jews, are constantly in the habit of *smashing,* or ringing
the changes, viz., changing the good money given them for bad."
The ploy used by these fruit vendors was to offer their oranges
and lemons at a low enough price to entice buyers to purchase
several pieces of fruit so that they would have to pay for them
with a silver coin. On being paid, the vendors would judiciously
examine the coin, rubbing it with both their thumbs to test its
authenticity. As they did so, they would contrive to substitute a
counterfeit coin for the good one with which they had been paid.
Then they would return the bad coin to the purchaser, asking him
to give them one about which they had no doubts. If they were
fortunate, they would be able to repeat this process two or three
times and take in two or three good coins in the course of one
transaction.[18]

The passing of bad coins was not the only aspect of the trade
in base money in which London Jews participated. The skills of
engravers, calligraphers, seal engravers, and watchmakers were
occasionally employed in the manufacture of silver and copper
coins and, less frequently, bank notes. Others acted as middlemen, selling base coins to street criminals who would actually put
them into circulation. Only in one other branch of the trade,
however, did Jews achieve any notoriety—the highly visible one
of repurchasing bad shillings that shopkeepers and others had
unwittingly accepted. According to Colquhoun, several of the
middlemen in the base coin trade held a kind of market every
morning, attended by forty to fifty Jewish boys, at which they
supplied the boys with counterfeit halfpennys. The boys then
spent the day walking the streets of London, crying "Bad shillings." With the bad halfpennys that had been advanced to them,

they would purchase bad shillings at the rate of about threepence each. At the end of the day, they repaid the dealers who supplied them, clearing from five to seven shillings each, an extravagant sum by the standards of the time. The dealers then resold the bad shillings to counterfeiters who speedily recolored them and introduced them again into circulation at their full nominal value. The boys, added Colquhoun in a moralistic vein, threw their earnings away during the night in riot and debauchery and returned penniless in the morning to their old trade.[19]

This was not an isolated instance of juvenile crime in Anglo-Jewry. Boys of twelve and thirteen, many of them the associates of hardened criminals twice their age, were frequently to be seen in the prisoner's dock at the Old Bailey. In September 1771, eleven-year-old Lazarus Solomons stood trial for picking a gentleman's pocket in the Cornhill. He was working with an older woman to whom he passed the linen handkerchief he had retrieved. He was found guilty and transported to the American colonies for seven years. Philip Marks, age 14, was described at the trial of Levy Cohen in February 1802 (he was charged with counterfeiting Bank of England notes) as "the thieving boy who lives with Cohen." He had already been in prison several times, as well as flogged, for stealing and picking pockets. In February 1814, Henry Wolf, age 12, was sentenced to death for stealing a threepence knife, and Moses Solomon, age 9, also sentenced to death (but recommended for mercy) for breaking into a house and stealing a pair of shoes. The offense for which Jewish boys and young men most frequently stood trial, aside from the usual lot of shoplifting and burglary charges, was picking pockets. The nimbleness of youth made them well suited for the task of removing billfolds, watches, and handkerchiefs from the pockets of gentlemen who lingered a moment too long in front of a shop window or who let themselves become too distracted by street fights or passing processions. The notorious Ikey Solomons was arrested for the first time, when, at age 25, he was caught picking the pocket of Thomas Dodd at a meeting of Westminster voters in New Palace Yard. Like other young criminals, Jewish and non-Jewish, he later graduated to crimes that required less agility.[20]

Juvenile crime in London was not, by any means, restricted to the Jewish community. It was a prominent feature of lower-class urban life that cut across religious lines. In the case of the Jewish community, however, there were social patterns symptomatic of Anglo-Jewish life that particularly encouraged it. The Jewish poor sent their children out into the streets to work at a very young age; not having received any training in a handicraft, they had to earn something by whatever means they could, and the morality of the streets, assuming it was different from that of the home, was easily absorbed. The temptations to turn to criminal pursuits were constant and many; the chances of apprehension and conviction were slim. Countervailing forces that in other Jewish communities discouraged social deviance were not present in Anglo-Jewry. The leaders of the community were unable to exert social control over those who abandoned the norms of the community.* In a metropolis as vast and teeming as London, Jewish youth who turned to crime found enough companionship outside the bounds of respectable Jewry that they probably experienced little sense of shame. The overly protective, tight-knit Jewish family, the prime instrument of socialization among middle-class Jews in the modern period, was not characteristic of lower-class Jewish life in London. The children of the Jewish poor, like the children of the non-Jewish poor, were on their own from a very early age; they had to survive by their wits in a physically and economically harsh world.

The story of Hyam Isaacs, as recounted by the missionary Joseph Samuel Frey in his memoirs, illustrates the temptations to which young men without training or family to fall back on were subjected. Born in Ipswich in 1794, Isaacs was left by his parents in the care of his grandfather when he was eighteen months old. At fourteen, he and his grandfather moved to London, due to the latter's ill health, and eventually the grandfather entered the Spanish and Portuguese Jews' Hospital and died. Isaacs then worked as a delivery boy for a quack doctor, receiving board, lodging, and one shilling per week. He remained in this position about eighteen months, but in the end the mother of the quack

---

*The higher rate of female criminality in London, as opposed to the countryside, during this period reflects the same absence of traditional restraints on behavior. Women who lived in London, especially the large number in lodgings, were less protected and less sheltered than those in rural settings. They encountered a wider range of society and were more vulnerable to enticements, dangers, and economic privations. See J. M. Beattie, "The Criminality of Women in Eighteenth Century England," *Journal of Social History* 8 (1975): 80–116.

doctor turned him out, she being a very observant Jew and he far less strict. Within a matter of weeks, he was reduced to near starvation. One evening, as he was walking near the London docks, a gang of pickpockets grabbed him and tried to force him to join them. He refused and they roughed him up. After a few hard weeks with very little to eat, he found his way to the Jews' Chapel, where he was given food and shelter.[21]

In those instances in which the children of the Jewish poor rejected the traditional values of their parents and embraced those of the English lower classes, their parents' immigrant background was undoubtedly crucial. The experience of immigration frequently demoralizes those who uproot themselves from their native country to begin life over again somewhere else. Jews who migrated to London from the small towns and villages of Germany and Poland no doubt found the task of settling down in a metropolis of London's size (a city of nine hundred thousand in 1800) a trying experience. There was no compact, tight-knit Jewish community to ease the pains of transition. The values and patterns of traditional Jewish life would have seemed more out of place in London than in Frankfurt or Altona, where contacts between Jews and non-Jews were more restricted and formalized. The children of Jewish immigrants to London must have found their parents' bewilderment and, in some cases, demoralization, unsettling. The virtues of traditional Jewish life probably seemed to them less than appropriate for survival in the competitive jungle of urban life. The instances of boys from religiously observant homes turning their backs on the values of their parents to plunge into a life of crime are numerous. For example, a son of Benjamin Levi, *shammash* (beadle) of the Great Synagogue, was transported for seven years in 1756 for stealing a silver mug from a pub in Aldgate High Street. In October of the following year, Abraham Bareive was transported for seven years for stealing three dozen silk handkerchiefs and eighteen yards of cloth. About the time the crime was committed, Abraham's father, Nathan, was in the Sephardi synagogue for the Rosh Hashanah service.[22]

The tragic consequences of the disorientation engendered by the immigration experience are well illustrated in the story of Joseph Jacob and his son Feibel. In the mid-1760s, Joseph Jacob was living with his family in some comfort in Jever in Oldenburg, Germany. When another Jew whose note he had signed went bankrupt, he, as the endorser, lost all that he had. In 1768 or 1769, he moved to London; how he made a living there is not known. In July of 1771, he was elected *hazan* and *shohet* for the Jewish community in Dover. That same month his fifteen-year-old son and another Jewish lad took a linen handkerchief worth tenpence from the pocket of a gentleman viewing a public ceremony in the Guildhall. In December, Feibel was sentenced to seven years' transportation to British North America. In desperation, his father wrote a cousin of his, Meyer Josephson, living in Reading, Pennsylvania, to plead with him to see that Jews there bought the boy, for he did not want him to live among non-Jews. He told his cousin that Feibel had always been a good boy and always shown respect for authority. Perhaps, the father suggested, the boy had been misled.[23]

In not every instance was crime something that had to be learned away from the home. Many Jewish immigrants had lived outside the framework of traditional Jewish life for some time prior to their settling in London, often as *Betteljuden,* and in the course of their wanderings had taken to the low habits of vagabonds and itinerant hucksters. As a general rule, the Jews who migrated to England were those who did not have a materially secure existence in the communities they abandoned, and they were thus somewhat predisposed to adopt standards different from those of respectable, property-owning Jews. In families such as these, criminal activity was a way of life passed on from one generation to the next. In 1814, for example, it was said that Hyam Isaacs of 50 Cable Street, Wellclose Square, was a well-known receiver of stolen goods and a brothel-keeper, and that his son Isaac was a fence and his daughter Elizabeth a brothel-keeper. In 1816, Levi Abrahams, age 32, was sentenced to death at the Old Bailey for stealing; his daughter Sarah, age 16, was transported for fourteen years for receiving stolen goods; and his sister-in-law Esther Jonas, age 23, was also sentenced to death for receiving stolen goods. That same year, Sir Daniel Williams, a magistrate in Whitechapel since 1796, told a House of Commons committee that there had been an increase in the number of Jewish juvenile offenders and that frequently these young criminals were "trained up to such pursuits by their relatives and connexions." In 1825, Henry Worms, age 57, and his son Morris, age 14, were both found guilty of receiving stolen goods.[24]

In addition to having a reputation for unquestionably illegal activities, Jews achieved notoriety for their association with certain other callings that, although not necessarily criminal, were far from respectable and often held in great disrepute. During the first decades of the nineteenth century, and especially during the years of the Napoleonic Wars, Jews in London and the port towns frequently acted as crimps, that is, agents who supplied the East India Company and the Royal Navy with sailors. Crimping had a disgraceful reputation because of the questionable methods crimps used to procure sailors. Jewish crimps, according to a guide to London's dangers published in 1818, approached sailors as soon as they came ashore, advanced them small amounts of money—or the equivalent in shoddy watches, buckles, hats, and jackets—and provided them with food and lodging, all charged at extravagant rates. The sailors, thus in debt to the crimps, were then kept in a kind of confinement until their ships were ready to receive them. An equally unpopular occupation was the keeping of sponging houses (detention houses for debtors). When Charles Dickens's father was arrested for debt in November 1834 by Shaw and Maxwell, wine merchants, he was put in Abraham Sloman's sponging house at 4 Cursitor Street, off Chancery Lane—in all likelihood the model for Solomon Jacobs's sponging house in Dickens's "Passage in the Life of Mr. Watkins Tottle" (1835) in his *Sketches by Boz.* In William Thackeray's *Vanity Fair,* first published in 1848 but set in the period of the Napoleonic Wars, Rawdon Crawley is confined to Mr. Moss's sponging house in Cursitor Street at the suit of Mr. Nathan, to whom Colonel Crawley owed £136 6s. 8d.[25]

The hoary association of Jews with moneylending—a source of social disharmony for centuries—also persisted in the Georgian period, although it appears to have been limited largely to lending to members of the aristocracy who lived beyond their means. Charles James Fox, a compulsive gambler and a consistent loser who was capable of losing £10,000 in a night, made good his losses by borrowing sums at high rates from Jewish moneylenders. George Walpole, the third Earl of Orford, was in debt to Jewish moneylenders. His uncle Horace Walpole, having taken charge of his nephew's financial affairs when he showed signs of insanity, wrote to a friend in 1773, "I live in town to hear of mortgages and annuities, and do not wonder that Titus was

called the delight of mankind, for he put *the Jews* to the sword."
According to Walpole, it was common for "youths of brilliant
genius" who ran up large debts at cardplaying to borrow from
Jews "at vast usury." The two eldest sons of the first Lord Foley
contracted gambling debts of close to £220,000 before the death
of their father and only met their obligations by borrowing from
Jewish moneylenders.[26] Jews who lent money to dissolute sons of
aristocrats were, of course, not from the same social rank as Jews
who picked pockets or passed bad coins. They were men of
substance, not street criminals living a hand-to-mouth existence.
But, like common criminals, they were following a profession that
aroused popular disgust, and they thus contributed in their own
way to the disreputability of Anglo-Jewry as a whole.

The precise extent of Jewish criminality will always remain
unknowable. The majority of English Jews, including the very
poorest, were probably no more dishonest or no more virtuous
than their English counterparts. But to minds accustomed to
thinking in a stereotypical fashion about Jews, to minds that
subsumed every individual Jew under the larger category of "the
Jews," it seemed that criminality within the Jewish community
was coterminous with the entire Jewish community. If Christian
tradition taught that "the Jews" without exception were eternally
damned for rejecting Jesus, then it was not difficult to believe that
"the Jews" were a people with deep-seated criminal instincts.
Some observers, in discussing Jewish criminals, tried to make a
distinction between them and the respectable portions of Anglo-
Jewry. Richard King, for example, in his *Modern London Spy* of
1781, wrote that he did not mean to arraign the whole Jewish
people although the evidence against a good many of them was
very strong. But his disclaimer, buried in the midst of several
dozen highly charged sentences about the nefarious crimes that
"the Jews" committed, was unlikely to counteract the general
effect of the whole piece. Patrick Colquhoun also attempted to set
the well-to-do Jews of London apart from the mass "who exist
chiefly by their wits." He recognized that there was a responsible
and virtuous upper class who "cannot but view with horror and
distress the deplorable condition and horrible depravity of so
large a proportion of the lower ranks of their own society" and
urged them to undertake the reform of the numerous Jewish
youths "who are at present rearing up in idleness, profligacy, and

crimes." But here, too, the sheer weight of the evidence he mustered worked against making careful distinctions. Indeed, at one point Colquhoun suggested that there was a uniform code of (corrupt) commercial ethics to which all Jews adhered: "From the orange boy and the retailer of seals, razors, glass, and other wares in the public streets to the shop-keeper, dealer in wearing apparel, or in silver and gold, the same principles of conduct too generally prevail."[27]

Colquhoun's statement about a uniform code to which all Jews gave allegiance contained the germ of an idea that in others was developed into a blanket condemnation. This was the notion that there was a great chain of Jewish criminality that stretched from the meanest street tough to the wealthiest stockbroker, with each in his own fashion being an expression of the same criminal essence.* The idea first entered into public discourse in the late 1760s, following the above-mentioned crackdown on Jewish receivers. The Rev. William Cole wrote at the time that, despite the early successes the magistrates and the synagogal authorities had had in apprehending receivers, they were unlikely in the long run to make any real headway. It was highly improbable, he thought, "that a people, ragged, wretched, poor and miserable, thieves by education, as well as necessity, who come into this country by shoals, and have nothing to subsist on but their wits [and] the charity of the synagogue," could be changed. "Such a race, *who are everywhere the same,* I mean brokers, *from the highest to the lowest,* would always continue to be pawnbrokers, that is, the receivers of stolen goods, or extortioners and usurers, wherever they happen to be settled" [emphasis added]. A few years later, in 1774, when the public was agitated by the Chelsea murder case—when the "wicked ingenuity" of the Jews was never greater—a correspondent to the *London Magazine* called on Parliament to pass special legislation to restrain the Jews. The whole people, he argued, were corrupt because their religion was unprincipled and their education unsocial. As a consequence, they felt no obliga-

---

*The notion of a uniform code of behavior among Jews was not peculiar to England. In Germany, Adolf von Knigge's 1788 guide to proper conduct attributed a cunning mind and an unscrupulous willingness to exploit that cunning for profit to Jewish bankers at the top and to Jewish peddlers and petty traders further down the social ladder. See Jacob Katz, *Out of the Ghetto* (Cambridge, Mass., 1973), pp. 81–82.

tion to obey the normal criminal laws, which were thus rendered ineffective. A particularly scurrilous pamphlet that appeared in 1809, *An Essay on the Commercial Habits of the Jews,* treated Jewish stockbrokers and Jewish receivers as the adherents of a uniform code of behavior. To be associated with the following description of the area of Jewish settlement in the East End could hardly have flattered the Anglo-Jewish elite:

> The number of intricate lanes and alleys near Whitechapel and other parts of the town, entirely occupied by these miscreants and their associates, render them formidable to the officers of justice, and at the same time impervious to the public eye. From these depositories of filth and iniquity, the approach of morning sends them in herds over the whole face of the capital, and when admitted into the houses of the inhabitants, they carry with them that knavery and contamination, the seeds of which lie scattered in their own disorderly dwellings.[28]

The "knavery" of the Jewish lower classes was not the only source of acute embarrassment with which their acculturation provided the Anglo-Jewish elite. The areas of Jewish settlement in the eastern parts of the metropolis were not isolated enclaves; Jews and non-Jews of the same social class shared the same neighborhoods and frequently the same buildings or rooming houses. They jostled each other in the streets, where so much of the business of daily life was conducted, in public houses, at fairs, and in open spaces. The Jewish poor, not surprisingly, came to adopt a good many of the tastes and habits of those people in whose midst, quite literally, they dwelled. For example, almost all of them eventually gave up the traditional Jewish garb of Central and Eastern Europe. By the first decades of the nineteenth century, many had taken to a flashy style of dress that respectable folk looked down on. When Ikey Solomons's wife, Ann, a fence in her own right, appeared in court in 1827, *The Times* commented that what she was wearing was quite fashionable, with nothing of the tawdry about it, and that this was unusual for "the Israelitish tribe" who preferred "tinsel on the back and the more substantial matter in the pocket." The "Jewish" narrator of a popular song of the same period acknowledged the Jews' penchant for glittery garb, but boasted that this was to be preferred to a taste for liquor:

Dey call us dashers, but never mind their clack,
'Cause to dress, not to drink, sirs, we have the knack;
Dey puts theirs on the stomach, and we on the back!

As these few lines suggest, lower-class acculturation was a selective process, one that did not encompass a wholesale exchange of one style of living for another. Drunkenness was never a problem for the Jewish community in the way that it was for the Irish, for example. There was, no doubt, much more heavy drinking than would have been permitted in a tightly controlled Jewish community in Germany—Moses Davis, for example, was found dead in his room in Petticoat Lane from extreme intoxication in 1809—but it never reached the point where critics damned the Jews for insobriety.[29]

The lives of the Jewish poor in London were distinguished by a lack of the rigid self-restraint characteristic of smaller, more socially isolated Jewish communities elsewhere. They expressed their joy, their resentment, and their anger in ways similar to those of their immediate neighbors but unacceptable to the magnates of the community. Physical violence and verbal abuse were considered by many as appropriate means of self-expression and self-defense. When, for example, in 1810, a sea captain applied to the East India House for an apprentice of his who had run away, he was physically attacked by Jewish crimps who supplied the East India Company. About fifty of them, including one Samuel Solomons, who allegedly persuaded the boy to quit his ship, kicked and shoved the captain about as he emerged from the building, forcing him eventually to release his grip on the boy. The previous year, when George Eades went to collect a sum of money Angel Benjamin owed to his father, two of Benjamin's brothers assaulted him "in a most violent and outrageous manner," temporarily blinding him; a grand jury indicted them, but it was found impossible to bring them to trial since they were itinerant peddlers who were usually traveling in distant parts of the country. That same year, a quarrel broke out at Bow Fair between some Jewish butchers and some Irishmen when an Irish laborer accused a Jew of cheating him. In the ensuing fracas, the Jews managed to trounce the Irish, but the latter returned later in the evening with reinforcements to continue the dispute. Marching together in one body, armed with bludgeons, they repeatedly shouted "No Jews, No Jews" and threatened to kill "every bloody Jew" they met. Fortunately for the Jews, the anger of the Irish was deflected when someone in the crowd yelled out "England Forever!" The Irish then turned on the English, a riot between these two groups followed, and in the end the Tower Hamlets Militia had to be called out to restore order.[30]

Whenever it was tactically possible, the Jewish lower classes responded to aspersions on their national character by resorting to the same means of protest the rest of the London poor employed. The most notable example of this kind of popular protest from below was the reaction of Jews to an anti-Jewish slur in a play of Thomas Dibdin, *Family Quarrels*, which opened on 18 December 1802. Prior to the first performance, a song from the play about three Jewish whores circulated in an inexpensive booklet of popular songs. A large number of Jews were grossly offended and bought tickets to the opening performance in order to make their dissatisfaction known. Trouble occurred, however, before the offensive song was even heard. In the second act, one of the characters, on being offered some goods by another character disguised as a Jewish peddler, replied, "I never deal with your people." The Jews in the audience instantly raised a clamor and kept it up until the end of the act so that it was impossible to hear a single sentence. They continued to protest in a similar fashion during the remainder of this performance and several succeeding ones. The reaction of the press to the behavior of the Jews was one of outrage and disbelief. They could not understand why the Jews were insulted. The references to which they objected were harmless jokes. Lawyers, physicians, Frenchmen, Italians, the Scots and the Irish were the subjects of stage humor. Were the Jews any different? asked the *Monthly Mirror:* "What prescriptive right [have] these men . . . to except to the universally-admitted license of the stage to place in a humourous, and even ludicrous, point of view the peculiarities, local and characteristic, which discover themselves in the common intercourse of men and manners?" The *Monthly Mirror* and other journals and newspapers denounced the arrogance of the lower-class Jews who protested. Indeed, the *Monthly Mirror* warned them they might be going too far in making use of the liberties the English allowed them and reminded them of the resentment that had been created by the Chelsea murder case thirty years earlier when, according to the *Monthly Mirror*, "none of their race durst, for a long time, venture beyond the purlieus of Houndsditch, without experiencing, in some degree, the effects of popular fury."[31]

The lack of bourgeois restraint with which these lower-class Jews denounced their enemies was characteristic of the exuberant behavior of the Jewish poor in many spheres of life. Both those who remained wedded to traditional Judaism and those who did not resembled their lower-class neighbors in being remarkably unself-conscious about what others, particularly their "betters," thought of them. This attitude carried over even into the area of religious practices. Many Jews, for example, took to celebrating Simhat Torah, a particularly joyful festival, in a manner combining the customs of Central Europe (in which gunpowder was exploded as part of the holiday celebration) and those of Guy Fawkes Day, which was celebrated at approximately the same time of the year. On the evening of the holiday, between five and six o'clock, several hundred men and boys would gather in Broad Court, Duke's Place, to set off fireworks (firecrackers, rockets, and serpents) before going on to the synagogues in the immediate area. The disturbance they created was considerable. One year, Porter Ridout, a distiller whose house and wine vaults were in Broad Court, became so angered that he picked up a sword and chased a boy into a synagogue. In 1784, Ridout again became outraged at the noise and disorder and sent for the beadle of the parish and a constable to disperse the crowd. The beadle tried to find some Jewish constables to help him, "knowing their people could disperse them better than ours," but none could be found. Then Ridout, the beadle, and the non-Jewish constable waded out into the mob to try to grab hold of those who were setting off the fireworks, for they feared that some of the buildings might be set on fire. The mob, however, overwhelmed them, pinning Ridout and the constable to the ground and giving them a good thrashing. Ridout managed to free himself and rushed back to his house, only to discover that his assailants had torn his pockets open and robbed him of £14 6s. Fearing for his life, or so he told the court, he grabbed a blunderbuss, rushed upstairs, threw open a window, and fired indiscriminantly into the crowd, killing thirteen-year-old Moses Lazarus, a barber's boy, and wounding several others.[32]

A London newspaper in 1811 reported another "considerable disturbance" in Duke's Place in which physical violence was employed to settle a dispute. A Jewish baker there, to whom the Jews of the neighborhood brought their puddings and pies for baking on Friday afternoons, was in the habit of allowing the dishes to continue cooking after the commencement of the Sabbath and of then handing them over to their owners. A complaint was made to one of the rabbis, who went to the baker's shop one Friday just before sundown and fixed three seals on the entrance to the oven so that it could not be opened until sundown the next day. A short time later, the Jews whose dishes were baking showed up, and the baker explained what had happened and said that he dare not open the oven, for, clearly, he feared that he could not openly defy the rabbi. One of the owners, however, was not going to let the authority of the rabbinate ruin his Friday evening meal. He knocked the baker down, broke off the seals, and opened the oven, whereupon "it was found that his pudding was at the back and that many dishes must be removed before the identical one could be come at. The owners of the different dishes, taking advantage of this circumstance, ran away with their property."[33]

One of the most interesting signs of the extent to which lower-class Jews adopted the habits and tastes of their peers was the passion with which they took to prizefighting, both as spectators and as participants. From the 1760s through the 1820s, at least thirty Jews were active enough in the ring to merit inclusion in the standard accounts of boxing compiled in the nineteenth century. These included the greatest fighter of the period, Daniel Mendoza (1763–1836), who was credited by early historians of the sport with introducing a more "scientific" form of boxing (one that emphasized finesse and agility rather than brute strength), and other equally well-known, although less distinguished, champions such as Dutch Sam (1775–1816); his son, Young Dutch Sam (1801–43); Aby Belasco, (1797–1824); and Barney Aaron, (1800–50), or "The Star of the East," as he was known. These men were great heroes to the Jews of London. Their victories, in which the Jewish poor could vicariously participate, were credited by at least one contemporary with reducing the number of attacks on Jews in the streets. According to the radical tailor Francis Place, "About the year 1787 Daniel Mendoza, a Jew, became a celebrated boxer and set up a school to teach the art of boxing as a science, the art soon spread among the young Jews and they became generally expert at it. The consequence was in a very few years seen and felt too. It was no longer safe to insult a Jew unless he was an old man and alone." An etching from around 1800 by an unknown artist depicts a Jewish peddler in a pub knocking out an adversary who has seized him by the beard, to the delight of the rough-looking crowd seated drinking around a large table. Even a few Jewish women took to fighting for money. In 1795 a boxing magazine reported a well-fought match in a field near the New Road in London between Mary Anne Fielding and "a noted Jewess of Wentworth Road" who was seconded by Daniel Mendoza. Fielding knocked the Jewess down over seventy times, with the fight lasting an hour and twenty minutes.[34]

Important matches were rallying points for ethnic pride and the occasions of much heavy wagering. When Mendoza fought, he was always billed as "Mendoza the Jew." One thousand Jews, according to Henry Lemoine, were present at Odiham in Hampshire for the first Mendoza–Humphries fight in January 1788. An etching of their second meeting, published in May 1789, carried an inscription that compared Mendoza's victory to David Levi's polemical triumphs. The Christian pugilist, went the inscription, proved himself "as inferior to the Jewish hero as Dr. Priestley when opposed to the Rabbi [*sic*], David Levi." When Aby Belasco met Patrick Halton at Harpendon Common in Hertfordshire in April 1823, one journal referred to the match as "Pork and Potatoes, or Ireland versus Judea." After the fight, brawling broke out among the Irish and Jewish spectators. A day or two later, a dinner was given at Howard's Coffee House in Aldgate to honor Belasco, and according to one contemporary account, "all the sheenies of importance attended." Jews bet heavily on their own fighters. When Lazarus the Jew Boy dislocated his shoulder in a match with Ballard in 1816, it was "to the utter 'weeping and gnashing of teeth' of the Jews, who were cleaned out in the most alarming manner." Dutch Sam, whose principal patron was Ephraim Jacobs, could always find Jewish money "to back him upon any pugilistic occasion.[35]

In the eyes of prizefighting enthusiasts, who were largely confined to the two extremes of the social hierarchy—the lower classes and the landed classes—the achievements of Jewish prizefighters were evidence of the normalcy of the Jewish people. But to the reform-minded middle classes, Jewish boxers were, on the contrary, further evidence of the ruffianism and the dissoluteness that seemed characteristic of the Jewish poor. From the mid-eighteenth century, these middle class "improvers" had been particularly active in suppressing the popular and often violent recreations of the English lower classes as part of their more general campaign to impose on all of English society a bourgeois orientation to work and play. Jewish prizefighters, who were probably no more or no less disreputable than other boxers, shared in this general condemnation. They were stigmatized as ruffians and brutes. Knapp and Baldwin's *New Newgate Calendar* (1809–10) remarked that "of late years" the Jews were becoming "the bullies of the people of London." "The disgraceful practice of pugilism, revived by Mendoza on their part, has greatly increased as well their depredations as their audacity." Marianne Thornton recalled that when her father, an important member of the Clapham Sect, was once campaigning for Parliament in Southwark, "Mendoza the Jew boxer" was part of the mob demonstrating against him. He kept shaking his fist at Thornton and crying "No popery! No popery!" (Thornton was in favor of Catholic emancipation; Mendoza in all likelihood had been hired to raise a clamor.) A few boxers distinguished themselves as rakes and purveyors of illicit pleasures after their fighting careers came to an end. Aby Belasco became "a keeper of low gambling houses, night houses, supper rooms, and such like resorts of midnight and morning debauchery," which brought him into repeated conflicts with the law. Young Dutch Sam became the intimate companion of two aristocratic rakes who were sowing their wild oats, and eventually he died from the "excesses" of such dissolute living.[36]

One event in particular managed to fix the image of Jewish boxers as audacious ruffians and bullies—this was their participation in the Old Price Riots of 1809. The Theatre Royal in Covent Garden, having burned down the previous year, reopened in a new building on 18 September 1809 with a rise in the price of tickets and a reduction in the number of inexpensive seats. At every performance during the first week after reopening, the audiences protested the rise with catcalls, hisses, rattles, whistles, and trumpets, so that it was impossible to hear a syllable uttered.

Toward the end of the first week in October, the clamor not having died down, the management hired a number of Jewish pugilists and rowdies, including Daniel Mendoza and Dutch Sam, to keep order inside the theater. They also gave Mendoza and Dutch Sam a large number of free passes to distribute to their friends in order to lace the audience with promanagement forces. Persons who hissed or shouted were challenged to a fight or roughed up. The audiences responded with even greater vehemence than before. During the second week in October, the air was filled with shouts of "Turn out the fighting Jews," "Old Clothes," "Lemons and Oranges," "Any Bad Shillings?" and so on, and placards were displayed with slogans such as, "Oppose Shylock and the Jews," "The Covent Garden Synagogue—Mendoza the Grand Rabbi," and "Shall Britains be subdued by the wandering tribe of Jerusalem?" On one night, a dozen or so Jews outside the theater faced a party of Old Price demonstrators armed with sticks, and a pitched battle was narrowly avoided. On another occasion, the Jews the management had hired staged a sham fight in the saloon of the theater, and while they were going at it, another team of Jews picked the pockets of those who had gathered to watch the fight. The negative impression produced by the whole affair led the Chief Rabbi, Solomon Hirschell, to remove the names of one hundred "itinerant" Jews from the charity list of the Great Synagogue for six months and to threaten them with excommunication if they persisted. Meanwhile, the management realized that the tactic of hiring Jewish pugilists had backfired and by 15 October at the latest discontinued it. The disturbances continued until the middle of December, when the management finally agreed to reduce pit prices and to open some private boxes to the ordinary public.[37]

In the mid-1810s another opportunity for denouncing Jewish disreputability appeared with the entry of corruption into prizefighting. The lively betting that accompanied important matches eventually made it attractive to unscrupulous promoters to know the outcome of a match before it was fought. Jews were among the backers who became notorious for fixing prizefights, although, from what scanty evidence survives, it appears they received a disproportionate share of the blame for the unsavoriness that became attached to it. George Borrow's strange autobiographical romance *Lavengro*, which was published in 1851 but recounts episodes from the early decades of the century, charged Jews with having "planted rottenness in the core of pugilism." William Cobbett made the same charge in 1830, accusing them of having taken control of prizefighting as soon as it became "a sort of base gambling." Even a leading journal of the sporting world, *The Annals of Sporting and Fancy Gazette,* which was not normally hostile to Jews, issued a blanket warning to its readers in 1824 to avoid all dealings with Jews in prizefighting matters: "Never trust a Jew in a battle; nor bet on a match made by a Jew, at a Jew's public house, or by his connivance."[38]

The breakdown of traditional Jewish values among the poor was particularly acute in the realm of sexual discipline and family life. The social pressure to conform to community norms, which had reinforced the halakhic regulation of sexual conduct in the autonomous *kehillot* of the Continent, was missing in England. From the 1750s at the very latest, cohabitation with non-Jews, outside of marriage, became a frequent occurrence. Jacob Levi, who burglarized the home of Sarah Fernandes Nunes in 1764, had previously lived with her non-Jewish servant girl, Sarah Beardsley, who had a child by him. Solomon Solomons, who was observant enough to be in the synagogue on a *shabbat* in April 1764, was living with a washerwoman who was not his wife. Isaac Lazarus, who was sentenced to be transported for seven years for stealing twenty-four pounds of cheese from a warehouse in 1773, was living at the time with Sarah Gardner, a non-Jew, although he also had a wife and a child. In 1798, when Abraham Samuels appeared as a witness at the Old Bailey and was asked if he was a Jew, he first replied, "I am not an Englishman." Pressed to answer the question in a less ambiguous way, he explained, "My mother is a Jewess, but I don't know what my father is." In 1827, the wife of Saul Cohen asked the authorities of Bevis Marks to aid her in obtaining a Jewish divorce from her husband, who was living in Chepstow in Monmouthshire, married bigamously to a Christian woman. They gave her brother £9 to travel to Chepstow to arrange the divorce. Two years later, Mary Denney, a non-Jew, wrote to the Mahamad to denounce Moses Delangy, a Sephardi, with whom she had been living for the past five years and by whom she was the mother of a three-week-old child. Delangy had been to see her only once since the birth of their child and had told her at that time that he was to be married to a young Jewish woman who had a dowry of £250 coming to her from a Sephardi charity, but that he did not love this woman and intended to leave her after getting hold of her money. He had promised to return to Mary if she would move with him to the country. Mary blamed Moses for all her troubles, since she had had a good place as a servant girl until he had seduced her.[39]

The attitude of many lower-class Jews to the very institution of marriage was much more casual than Jewish law allows. Relationships were entered into and then sundered without having recourse to the religious ceremonies that in Judaism are intended to guarantee the purity of family life. Around the year 1803, the wife of Moses Cohen Peixotto had an affair with an acquaintance of his. While Peixotto was away from London, this fellow robbed him of all he owned and ran off with his wife. Peixotto apparently never divorced her, but sometime around 1818 began living with a German Jewess, Clara Levy. He explained that "as man was not created for himself," he formed "a connection" with her "by betrothing her to be my wife in the presence of special witnesses." They had three children together and in 1822 asked the Haham to marry them. The Mahamad, however, refused its permission. That same year, Jacob Nunes Martines (Jacob Martin) and Fanny Solomons, who had been living together in Chatham in Kent for some time and had had several children, agreed to be properly married after the congregation there persuaded them to do so. In 1824, Levi Abrahams married a non-Jew in her mother's rooms in Bath. He claimed that there were other Jews present and that they were married according to his religion, although there is nothing to indicate that she had converted prior to the "ceremony." In 1823, the New Synagogue refused Rebecca Levy's request for charity because she was not legally married to the Jew with whom she was living.[40]

In an attempt to prevent the marriage of persons forbidden by Jewish law to marry (but obviously would have anyway), the Great Synagogue began requiring in 1826 that all prospective marriages be recorded in a register at the synagogue seven days prior to their taking place. It was hoped that anyone who had information regarding any irregularities would contact the Chief Rabbi or the Secretary. The necessity of instituting a practice that so clearly copied the Anglican custom of posting banns indicates the concern with which the synagogue authorities viewed the irregu-

lar nature (in terms of Jewish law) of many marriages. One incident in particular was responsible for this regulation, and it merits telling for all it says about the character of much lower-class
sexual behavior. In March 1826, Aby, the *shammash* of the Great
Synagogue, applied to the Chief Rabbi for permission for Emanuel Simmons and Rachel Belasco to marry. They had been living
together for a number of years, had three children, and now
wished to marry according to Jewish law. The Chief Rabbi ordered Aby to investigate their background and current situation
and to report back to him in a few days. Aby informed Hirschell
several days later that he had learned that the couple kept a
whore house. Hirschell agreed to give them permission to marry
if they gave this up, which the prospective bridegroom swore they
would do, adding that they were going into the lemon business.
A few days after the ceremony was performed, it was discovered
in the record book of the *bet din* that Simmons's brother had
previously been married to the Belasco woman and that they had
been divorced in 1810. According to Jewish law, marriage with
a brother's former wife is forbidden, and the issue of such a
marriage are considered bastards. Aby, it turned out, had mis-
represented the matter to Hirschell; as he later admitted, "She
was connected with both and they say the children are also from
both."[41]

The behavior of the Jewish lower classes in London was not
extraordinary by the standards of the time. Whoring, thieving,
rioting, and drinking were an integral part of lower-class life-
patterns everywhere in Europe. But as the Jews were a minority
whose relations with the majority were often governed by deep-
rooted irrational assumptions, the noisy street hawkers and swag-
gering prizefighters and brazen brothel-keepers among them
suggested to respectable non-Jews that such behavior was characteristic of Jewry as a whole. The reality of course was that the
Jewish lower classes were no different than the English lower
classes: there were saints as well as sinners. But the majority very
rarely ever saw the saints, in large part because they spoke with
the same accent as the sinners, lived in the same sections of town
as the sinners, worked in the same trades as the sinners, and
hence were invisible to non-Jewish eyes. The Anglo-Jewish elite
believed that their own status suffered from the existence of such
a large bloc of unruly Jews, and from the late 1780s on they

initiated a number of schemes to reform the manners and the morals of this group. But their definition of disreputability included more than criminality and promiscuity: it included many aspects of lower-class Jewish life that were merely un-English. Thus, many of the saints were, in their eyes, as unacceptable as receivers of stolen goods or brothel-keepers. Their goal was to remake the Anglo-Jewish poor in their own image.

7

Reforming the Jewish Poor

The Jewish poor were an embarrassment and a threat to the Anglo-Jewish elite. Well-to-do Jews who were eager to be accepted as gentlefolk believed that the disreputable character of much of lower-class Jewish life made their social ascent more difficult, if not impossible. The very word *Jew* was considered a term of disparagement, a synonym for a knave, a usurer, or a cheat. This prejudicial way of thinking, according to the surgeon Joshua Van Oven, derived from "the constrained and deplorable state of the poor alone"[1]—an assumption shared by the Anglo-Jewish elite as a whole. The communal magnates felt that in order to promote their own interests they had to curb the disreputable behavior of the Jewish poor, but they also realized, by the 1780s at the latest, that paternalistic intervention on an ad hoc basis was ineffectual. They did not enjoy the social or legal authority to force the poor to comply with their wishes. In the past, the most they had been able to do was to aid the magistrates in apprehending a few criminals. The mass of the Jewish poor remained unreformed.

In the last decades of the eighteenth century, the leaders of Anglo-Jewry came to see the problem of lower-class disreputability in a new light. They came to view the problem of Jewish criminality as a social question and proposed to cure it by attacking it at its foundations—in their minds, the lack of useful skills and of a proper work ethic among the Jewish poor. They proposed to make the poor more productive and more respectable by refashioning the younger generation—by taking the children of the Jewish poor off the streets and putting them in modern Jewish schools where they would learn artisanal skills and English manners. They reasoned that if the children of the poor remained uneducated they would succumb "to all the temptations and profligacy with which this great metropolis abounds, and must inevitably fall early victims to vice and crime; thus reflecting indelible disgrace on the community to which they belong."[2] Beginning in 1788 with the modernization of the Ashkenazi Talmud Torah and continuing for the next four decades, the Anglo-Jewish elite established a series of institutions and programs to educate, in the broadest sense of the term, the Jewish poor.

For most of the eighteenth century, whatever formal schooling the children of the Jewish poor received was limited to a few years of study in a *heder*, a one-room school where they were taught to read a few elementary Hebrew texts. The quality of education in the *hadarim* was low. The language of instruction was Yiddish, a language many English-born children knew imperfectly or not at all. The mode of instruction required the children to learn verses and chapters from the Bible by rote, memorization rather than comprehension being the immediate objective. The majority of teachers were recent immigrants, temperamentally and pedagogically unsuited to teaching a native-born generation. Moreover, there was no supervision from above on the part of either the chief rabbinate or the *parnasim*. Low standards flourished because the *hadarim* were small-scale, unregulated private enterprises.

The Anglo-Jewish elite, whose children were educated by private tutors, in modern Jewish boarding schools, or in Christian schools, developed a strong aversion to the *hadarim* not only because they did nothing to prepare the Jewish poor for the workaday world, but also because they failed to accomplish their own professed objective—the teaching of Hebrew. The *maskil* Hyman Hurwitz, who ran a modern Jewish school at Highgate from 1799 to 1821 and who published a systematic Hebrew grammar for children in 1807, claimed that scarcely twenty out of a hundred Jewish youth could read Hebrew with any grammatical correctness after completing their schooling and that fewer still could understand the Bible without the aid of an English translation. An anonymous Jewish source described a typical *heder* of the second decade of the nineteenth century in the following scornful manner:

> In a second-floor back room, or more frequently in a back attic, sat an aged man, past labour, who, having a beard, was dignified with the high-sounding title of rabbi. Around this aged teacher, in such fetid chamber, with the thing called a *bed* in the corner, sat, or rather squatted, a number of ill-clad and, with but few exceptions, dirty children, who were being taught Hebrew, and to translate some portions of the Pentateuch and prayer book, in a jargon composed of various portions of the languages of the countries which the said Rabbi might have visited during his migration from the land of his birth—Poland. The consequence was that a large proportion of our working-class grew up in a lamentable state of ignorance, but few, if any, having been able to read, write, or understand the vernacular tongue.[3]

The primary objection of the Anglo-Jewish elite to the traditional form of Jewish elementary education, however, was that it did not provide the poor with marketable skills. There were, after all, only a limited number of opportunities for the unskilled to earn an honest living in the street trades, and such occupations did nothing to boost the status of the Jewish community as a whole. The first attempt to modify the character of Jewish education came in 1788, when the governors of the Ashkenazi Talmud Torah (wealthy merchants and brokers such as Abraham and George Goldsmid, their brothers-in-law Daniel Eliason and Lyon de Symons, Eliezer Isaac Keyser, E. P. Salomons, Levy Barent Cohen, and Samson Gompertz) reorganized the school along nontraditional lines. The Talmud Torah had been founded in 1732 to provide an advanced Hebrew education to a small number of Jewish boys whose parents would otherwise be unable to pay for such schooling. Instruction was limited to traditional Hebrew texts. When the governors reorganized the school, they reduced the amount of time devoted to Hebrew and added three secular subjects: reading, writing, and arithmetic. Implicitly, this represented a rejection of the traditional belief that the mastery of rabbinic texts was the foundation of a Jewish education. The study of the Talmud, moreover, was not retained as a required subject, but made an elective for those "whose capacity will admit." Thus, rabbinic learning was dethroned and pride of place given to more "practical" and elementary subjects. In January 1803, only a few months after having arrived in England, Chief Rabbi Solomon Hirschell complained to the governors of the school that the study of Talmud was being neglected. They agreed with him, but pleaded poverty: the limited funds of the charity made it impossible to provide more advanced training. Their response was somewhat disingenuous; had they felt that talmudic learning was essential, the money could have been found. Their true feelings about the value of rabbinic learning were more openly expressed in the way in which they conducted the school. For example, they awarded two silver medals annually, one for the best Hebrew scholar and one for the best English scholar—there being no indication that the former was considered more prestigious than the latter. The boys who were selected to receive these awards delivered speeches, in Hebrew and English respectively, at the annual dinner of the Talmud Torah's benefactors. Until 1812, the Hebrew speech was a talmudic discourse on a halakhic theme. In that year, the governors decided it would be more appropriate if the speech consisted of a moral explication of some scriptural verse or sentiment.[4]

The objectives of the reformed Talmud Torah were not limited to providing students with a rudimentary knowledge of Hebrew and English. Equally important—indeed, if not more so—was its extra-academic goal: improving "the morals of the boys that they may become useful members of society." The Talmud Torah was to turn out well-mannered, potentially productive young men who would not disgrace the Jewish community. To this end, the committee that oversaw the management of the school investigated the character of prospective students, as well as that of their parents, before admitting them. Illegitimate children and children whose parents could not satisfactorily prove the legality of their marriage were barred outright. Great emphasis was placed on instilling in the boys the virtues of cleanliness and orderliness. On several occasions, the parents of a number of boys were summoned to appear at the Talmud Torah and were reprimanded for not keeping their children clean and their clothing in good repair. In 1806, when the Committee found that the boys were about the streets on the Sabbath and that "many irregularities" resulted from this, they decided to keep them occupied at the school part of the day by having the Hebrew master give them "religious and moral lessons." To help the boys acquire an honest trade, the Committee apprenticed them to masters of good character within six months after their thirteenth birthday, at which time they left the school; this in itself is evidence that serious rabbinic scholarship was not a paramount concern of the Talmud Torah, for students in traditional communities customarily entered a more advanced stage of talmudic training at this point in their lives. Most of the boys were apprenticed to tailors, glass cutters, watch finishers, and pencil-makers, with a handful being bound to Jewish merchants in the West Indies. One boy, Levy Joseph, who was awarded a silver medal for good conduct, was helped in obtaining passage in 1807 to Charleston, South Carolina.[5]

The reformation of the Ashkenazi Talmud Torah was not a large-scale project. The school itself, which was supported exclusively by voluntary contributions from the rich, never accepted many students and was limited to the children of the so-called respectable poor. In 1793, there were eighteen boys; in 1803, twenty-one boys. The improvement of the poor in general, who numbered in the thousands, required a much grander effort. In 1795, Benjamin and Abraham Goldsmid launched a campaign to raise funds for a major poor-relief scheme, the details of which are unknown. Within a few weeks, they raised approximately £12,000, among both Christians and Jews, with the former, largely banking friends of the Goldsmids, contributing almost half the total. Widespread concern over criminality and poverty allowed the brothers to collect another £8,000 over the next two years, so that by 1797 they were able to invest £20,000 in Imperial three percents. At this point, the various backers of the scheme quarreled (the subject of their disagreement is not known), and the Goldsmids became disgusted and withdrew their attention from the project, leaving the principal to gather interest for the next ten years, that is, until the Jews' Hospital was opened in 1807.[6]

Before the Goldsmid project was realized, Joshua Van Oven proposed an even more ambitious scheme to control Jewish poverty and criminality—the creation of a communally financed, government-supported agency for the relief and the control of the Jewish poor. The immediate impetus for the scheme came from the publication of the enlarged sixth edition of Patrick Colquhoun's *Treatise on the Police of the Metropolis,* which first appeared in 1796. Colquhoun's unflattering remarks about the Jews of London, which were quoted in the previous chapter, doubtless made anglicized Jews uncomfortable. Although Colquhoun indicated at one point that there was a respectable Jewish middle class distinct from the mass of lower-class Jews, he was not always careful about making such distinctions and frequently spoke of "the Jews" as a uniform and undifferentiated body. In March 1801, after having met with Colquhoun privately, Van Oven published a letter to the police magistrate to defend his poorer coreligionists and to set before the public his scheme to improve their condition. Van Oven explained, as did Jewish and non-Jewish reformers everywhere in Europe (e.g., the Prussian bureaucrat Dohm and the French physiocrat Mirabeau), that the degeneracy of the Jews was due exclusively to the circumstances into which intolerance and oppression had forced them. Through the centuries, they had been barred from acquiring artisanal skills; even under the tolerant conditions of life in England, their religious practices prevented them from apprenticing their children to Christian masters. The influx of poor Jews into England during the previous half-century had placed a heavy burden on the financial resources of the synagogues, who generally acted independently of each other in matters of poor relief. Jews who became utterly destitute could not turn to the workhouses and hospitals maintained by the parishes and private foundations because they made no provision for the observance of the dietary laws and Jewish holidays. (On this point, Van Oven erred: some Jews did enter parish workhouses.) What was needed, Van Oven concluded, was a comprehensive, systematic, communitywide approach to Jewish poor relief.[7]

The scheme Van Oven proposed in his published letter to Colquhoun called for the establishment of a Jewish poor relief board to be invested by Parliament with quasi-governmental powers. The board was to be authorized "to put the existing laws in force with respect to idle and disorderly persons, to enquire into the circumstances of the poor and render occasional relief, to investigate the situation of foreign Jews who came to settle in this country without an evident means of procuring a livelihood and have power to pass them back if judged proper." The board was also to be empowered to appropriate a certain percentage of the poor rates that Jews paid to the parishes in which they lived or to tax directly all Jews for the maintenance of the poor. The funds raised in this manner, along with the amounts already distributed by the synagogues on an ad hoc basis, were to be distributed by the board, which would assume responsibility for the relief of all the Jewish poor in London. The institutional center of Jewish poor relief activity was to be a house of industry and hospital, "the whole arranged on a strict Judaic plan with respect to prayers, education, and diet."[8] The scope of the scheme was startlingly ambitious: with the power to tax Jewish ratepayers and the authority to jail and deport foreign-born Jews it considered undesirable, the board was to take on many of the governmental functions exercised by the autonomous *kehillot* of premodern Europe. In its desire to systematize the distribution of charity, it looked to the future; in its desire to gain governmental authority for its activities and to make the support of those activities obligatory rather than voluntaristic, it hearkened back to the past.

With Colquhoun's support, Van Oven took his project to Abraham Goldsmid. Goldsmid, in turn, interested his friends and relations in the scheme and eventually passed it on to Henry Addington, Chancellor of the Exchequer, with the hope of gaining Parliamentary approval. According to the plan as it was then formulated, the board was to consist of twelve Ashkenazi representatives; four Sephardi representatives; two Aldermen of the City of London; two magistrates for the counties of Middlesex, Kent, Essex, and Surrey; and the presidents of the four City synagogues. The board was to be empowered to erect four buildings: a home for the aged and the infirm, a hospital for the sick, a school to train children as artisans, and a workhouse for the vagrant poor and the able-bodied poor who were not willing to work. It was also to have police powers with regard to the foreign-born Jewish poor. The financial arrangements were left much the same as Van Oven had originally proposed, except that it was now stipulated that the parishes would hand over to the board 50 percent of the rates paid by their Jewish residents. The board was also to be authorized to borrow up to £10,000.[9]

The leadership of the Ashkenazi synagogues supported the measure, the Hambro declaring, for example, "that the poor and sick and aged Jews, as also the youths of both sexes, require a better and more extensive aid than is at present offered them."

But the Sephardim strenuously opposed it for both social and financial reasons. They objected in the first instance to being considered part of the same "political" body as the Ashkenazim. In a petition they submitted to Parliament in March 1802 in order to be excluded from the provisions of the scheme, they stressed that "the Spanish and Portuguese Jews and the German Jews always considered each other as they actually are separate and distinct bodies." In short, like the acculturated Sephardim of other West European states, they did not want to be associated in the public mind with the poorer and less-anglicized Ashkenazim. An equally important consideration, possibly the decisive one, was that their inclusion in such a plan would be financially disadvantageous. The Sephardim, on the whole, were a wealthier body than the Ashkenazim and would consequently be forced to contribute a disproportionate amount of the funds to support the project, especially since the Sephardi poor were such a small percentage of the total Jewish poor and already were "well provided for" with "suitable establishments," a claim that was not altogether true. As the Sephardim explained in their petition to Parliament, "the Portuguese and German Jews cannot make the supporting their poor a cause in common with each other, because their poor not bearing equal proportions, what would result a benefit to one would be an act of injustice and oppression to the other, independently of the Portuguese poor being already provided for."[10]

Bevis Marks was not alone in publicly declaring its opposition to the Van Oven scheme. Voices from outside the Goldsmid circle protested the bid of the Anglo-Jewish elite to gain such extensive control over the Jewish poor. The anonymous pamphleteer Philo-Judaeis compared the proposed board to the Directory in Paris, declared such a delegation of power "repugnant to our constitution," and predicted that Parliament would never approve such a measure. The printer Levy Alexander also saw the Van Oven scheme as an attempt of the rich to impose "the iron hand of power on the weaknesses of the poor." He warned his poorer brethren of the mischievous measure about to be inflicted on them, "for should the synagogues obtain the wished-for power, what will be the consequences only time can show." One immediate consequence he was sure of: the financial burden would fall most heavily on the already overtaxed artisan and shopkeeper class, since the rich were so few. Philo-Judaeis agreed: the scheme would impose a hardship on the frugal and industrious part of the community, who already groaned under the pressure of parliamentary and parochial taxes. He also thought that no scheme would be capable of reforming the habits of adult Jews:

> How can it be expected that your proposed Directory with limited powers . . . will be able to restrain such a licentious crew; and inculcate the principles of virtue and habits of industry, in persons of such a description as your beggars are? especially after they are reinforced by a fresh importation of alien Jewish vagabounds who may migrate hither, in order to seek what *they* may deem an asylum from penury and vagrancy.

The only effective solution to the problem of Jewish poverty and criminality, he argued, was to inculcate moral precepts in the younger generation, to impel Jewish children to habits of industry early in their development. To this end, he proposed that a school for Jewish youth be established with the money raised by the Goldsmids in the previous decade. In such an institution, the children of the poor could be taught Hebrew, English, and arithmetic, as well as a bourgeois orientation to work.[11]

The Van Oven scheme, now with the backing of Abraham Goldsmid and his friends, was brought before Parliament, but never advanced beyond the first stage in the legislative process. On 25 February 1802, George Tierney presented to the House of Commons a petition from "the German Jews resident in London" setting forth the need for a strong Jewish poor relief measure. The petitioners requested that power be given them "to regulate and maintain their poor, and to promote industry and a knowledge of useful and productive labour among them" so that they might become "more useful members of society." But Tierney did not move to bring in a bill that would incorporate the Van Oven proposals. He moved simply to lay the petition on the table, indicating that at some future date he would move to refer it to a committee and only after that would introduce a bill. This was the last time anything was heard in Parliament of the Van Oven scheme. The Sephardim had already taken steps to dissociate themselves from the measure and had ordered their solicitor to draft a clause to be inserted in the intended legislation excluding them from its provisions. The withdrawal of the wealthiest and most anglicized segment of the community no doubt damaged the chances of any bill concerning the Jews becoming law. But the inability of the Ashkenazim to obtain legislative approval for their scheme was due probably to a more fundamental reason: the disinclination of Parliament to grant such extensive powers to a private group of men. For it is inconceivable really that the English ruling class, with its suspicion of centralized authority, would have authorized the creation of a quasi-autonomous Jewish government within English society. The Van Oven scheme looked to the past for a solution to Jewish poverty and criminality, and thus had one strike against it from the start. At a meeting of its Ashkenazi backers on 22 April 1802 at Coachmakers Hall, "the affair was given up."[12]

The next attempt to reform the Jewish poor—a more modest venture—was also a more successful one, at least in an institutional sense. In 1807, a group of Ashkenazi magnates, headed by Asher Goldsmid, established the Jews' Hospital in the Mile End Road with the funds raised in the previous decade by Abraham and Benjamin Goldsmid. The Hospital consisted of two separate departments—an old-age home, whose purpose was exclusively charitable, and a trade school, which was, in terms of its programs and its goals, an extension of the Talmud Torah and the abortive Van Oven scheme. The committee of ten that founded the Hospital consisted of Asher Goldsmid, three Goldsmid brothers-in-law (Daniel Eliason, Nathan Solomons, and Lyon de Symons), the *maskilim* Joshua Van Oven and Moses Samuel, Dr. Joseph Hart Myers, Leyon Levy, E. I. Keyser, and Gotchal Levien. Six of the ten had been actively involved in the reorganization of the Talmud Torah in 1788, as had Asher Goldsmid's brothers, George and Abraham. Not surprisingly, the trade school reflected the same orientation as the Talmud Torah; the one important difference was that it placed less emphasis on formal education and more on practical training. The objective of the Hospital was to keep Jewish children in their early teens from the temptations of London street life, while training them to be productive citizens. Hebrew instruction was limited to two hours a day and consisted of nothing more advanced than the reading of the prayer book and selections from the Bible; slightly less time, one and a half hours, was given over to English and arithmetic. The bulk of the school day, two hours in the morning and two hours in the afternoon, was devoted to teaching the children practical skills. In the workshops of the Hospital, the boys were taught shoemaking, chairmaking, and cabinetmaking. The girls were taught to knit, wash, iron, cook, do needlework, and clean house. When the children left the Hospital—the boys at age 12 or 13, the girls at age 15—they were apprenticed to skilled artisans, in the case of the boys, or put into domestic service, generally in Jewish homes, in the case of the girls.[13]

Like the Talmud Torah, the Jews' Hospital was as much concerned with forming the character of its wards as it was with preparing them for a useful trade—perhaps more so, since those who entered the Hospital were less academically inclined and less disciplined than those who were admitted to the Talmud Torah. The school of the Jews' Hospital was a total institution: the children, who were referred to as inmates, lived there on a permanent basis. When they entered the school, their parents signed over legal responsibility for the children to the Hospital. They could not come and go as they pleased, but were subject to a prisonlike regimen that kept them confined within the walls of the institution. When Joshua Van Oven visited the school in June 1814, he found several boys absent from the shoe shop and, on inquiring, discovered that they were washing themselves to go to Bow Fair. In the visitors book in which the governors of the Hospital recorded their impressions, he expressed doubts as to whether this was proper. In 1823, when it was discovered that the wall at the bottom of the boys' playing field was in such poor condition that the boys could climb over it easily, the governors decided to raise the height of the wall and to fix iron spikes along the top. Disobedience, disorderly conduct, and mischief were sternly punished. Instances of boys being flogged, put on bread and water, and expelled were not uncommon.[14]

From the perspective of the school's benefactors and managers, stern measures were necessary. The boys who were admitted to the school, although drawn from the ranks of the so-called respectable poor, were an undisciplined, if not rowdy, lot. They brought with them lower-class habits and attitudes unacceptable to the respectable portion of Anglo-Jewry. Even their accents required mending, "a rather difficult task," as Amelia Solomon noted when she visited the school in 1813. Mrs. Solomon went on to remark that before the children could be taught anything, "they have much to unlearn. They, necessarily from their previous situations, bring with them many habits which must be eradicated entirely before they can receive any real education." Refashioning the children of the Jewish poor was not an easy task; they clung stubbornly to their old habits and often did not show a proper regard for the new ones the school was teaching them. When M. Isaacs visited the school in 1817, he was shocked by the appearance of Barnet Solomons. "He was walking in the boys' ground in *rags* and *dirt,* and had I unfortunately introduced any strangers I would have tended to impress them with ideas far different than what I anticipated. . . . [He was] in appearance like a *common beggar in rags.*" It was Isaacs's belief that the boys were allowed too much freedom in respect to their dress. He suggested that the headmaster make a daily examination of the boys and of the state of their clothing, for if they became "habituated to cleanliness from early example, they would gradually emanate from their present system."[15]

A small minority proved altogether intractable and had to be expelled and, in some cases, handed over to the magistrates for punishment. In November 1822, for example, the school successfully prosecuted two boys who refused to accept the school's discipline. Morris Naphtali was sentenced to eleven days in jail for assault and Moses Levy to one month in solitary for being a disorderly apprentice. The boys returned to the Hospital upon being released, but did not remain there very long. In 1823, the Levy boy fled the Hospital and enlisted in the service of the East India Company, and the Naphtali boy was expelled for continuing to resist the school's discipline. That same month, another boy, Phillip Cohen, was expelled for having pawned some sheets and a pair of shoes belonging to the Hospital. The governors of the Hospital handed him over for prosecution to a police magistrate, and he was sentenced to one month of hard labor in the Clerkenwell House of Correction.[16] Cohen was extremely fortunate that the school chose to prosecute him for pawning illegally (a relatively minor offense) rather than for stealing. If he had been found guilty of the latter crime, he might have been hanged or transported for life.

An essential aspect of reforming the children of the Jewish poor was providing them with instruction in ethics and morals.

From the school's inception, the master was assigned the task of delivering an ethical discourse every Sabbath. But this practice fell into neglect, and in 1820 a committee suggested that an English sermon again be delivered on the Sabbath and the festivals in order to rouse the inmates "to a due sense of the religious, moral [and] social duties they have to perform." Another method of instilling morality in the children was formal classroom instruction in ethics and theology. When Amelia Solomon visited the school in July 1812, she noted with pleasure that the girls had learned Maimonides' thirteen articles of faith. She felt, however, that their "moral education" was still "very deficient," and proposed to remedy this by providing the girls with didactic children's books. Instruction in the theological tenets of Judaism was not sufficient: "*Moral* education is absolutely indispensable to render them fit members of society and a credit to this excellent institution." Rachel Hart, who visited the school soon after Mrs. Solomon, agreed with the latter that the moral education of the children was deficient, attributing much of the deficiency to the lack of proper books. She noted in the Lady Visitors' Book, "Moral books should also be allowed them, as the lower classes of the Jews require much cultivation. Those who take the trouble to advance their education will find themselves repaid by the improvement of the rising generation." Providing such books was not an easy task. At the time, there were no English-language books written specifically for Jewish children, so the school was compelled to use Christian books, with the objectionable christological passages crossed out, to teach universal ethical principles.[17]

In 1818, a wealthy Jewish woman published anonymously a ninety-five-page manual of Jewish beliefs and practices for the girls of the Jews' Hospital. *The Jewish Preceptress,* as the guide was called, was geared explicitly to "children in an humble station." Aside from some rather general remarks about the necessity of strictly observing the Sabbath and other Jewish rites, there was little said about how those rites were to be observed. The bulk of the text was given over to descriptions of the moral benefits of religion in general, to the spiritual rewards of Jewish practices in particular, and to exhortations to morality and obedience. The ethical exhortations in particular demonstrate the extraeducational objectives of ventures like the Jews' Hospital. Under such headings as "On our Duty to our Superiors," "On Gratitude," "On Humility," "On Truth," and others, *The Jewish Preceptress* taught its lower-class readers, most of whom were destined to be servants, the virtues necessary for success in domestic service. The girls were told that it was "the indispensable duty of a servant to be industrious, economical, careful, and attentive." A servant who was lazy, wasteful, impertinent, or who was a liar or a gossip was "equally as dishonest as if she had actually committed theft." Above all, *The Jewish Preceptress* sought to inculcate the virtue of industriousness. Idleness was "the mother of vice," "a perverter of moral virtue and the sure destroyer of health and even comfort," that is, the creator of all the poverty and criminality that besmirched the reputation of the Jewish community. Industrious activity, on the other hand, held the social order together:

> it is admirable to observe the regular gradations of industry, by which the three classes of society, the great, the middling, and the poor, are united. The peasant labors for his immediate subsistence, and his industry procures him the means. The labor of the mechanic, and the ingenuity of the artist, are rewarded by the purchase of their industry by the affluent. The affluent, in their turn, are occupied by the peculiar duties of *their* station. The Statesman in the Cabinet, the Soldier in the Field, the Sailor on the Ocean. Nor is even the Sovereign exempt from toil: the welfare of his subjects, and the interests of his empire, continually *employ* him; and in proportion as a Monarch is the father of his people, in proportion are his cares enlarged.[18]

The capacity of the Jews' Hospital to rescue the children of the poor from potential disrepute, although greater than that of the Talmud Torah, was still limited. When the school opened in 1807, it housed only 10 boys and 8 girls. Over the next two decades, the number of students expanded considerably. In 1821, there were 47 boys and 29 girls. The growth of the institution was in part due to the ability of the original backers to obtain the support of wealthy Christians and to make the annual fund-raising dinner an important social event within the Jewish community. In the 1810s, the annual dinner at the City of London Tavern attracted three to four hundred subscribers every year. Like the Talmud Torah, however, the Jews' Hospital touched the lives of only a small number of persons in relation to the size of the entire Jewish population. In 1844, Henry Faudel calculated that since its inception the Hospital had apprenticed 135 children (or 3 2/3 children per year) and placed another 88 children in domestic service. It is hard to imagine that the 3 2/3 children who entered the handicrafts every year made much of an impact on the moral tone and occupational makeup of the Jewish lower class. Moreover, of those who were trained at the Jews' Hospital, "a very large portion are not following their trades," Faudel charged. The workshops of the Jews' Hospital did not provide training commensurate to that given by private tradesmen. The boys who left the school were unable to compete and experienced great difficulty in obtaining employment. The impact of the Jews' Hospital was also limited by the fact that, like the Talmud Torah, it imposed rigid eligibility requirements. Only the children of persons who had lived in London for at least ten years and who belonged to one of the three Ashkenazi synagogues in the City were considered proper objects of the charity. Male candidates, moreover, were required to be able to read the Hebrew prayer book, with preference given to those who could also read English.[19] Thus, those who were most in need of help, those who were most likely to give the community a bad name (the poorest, the least anglicized, and the most recently arrived) were automatically barred from receiving assistance. The governors of the institution obviously felt that there was a need for moral and occupational reform even among the so-called respectable poor and that their first obligation was to those families who had a claim on the City synagogues. No doubt they also feared that if they imposed no residency requirements their charity would act like a magnet and attract even larger numbers of impoverished Jews from abroad.

The desire to upgrade the social and economic status of the Jewish poor was not the only one at work in the establishment of the school department of the Jews' Hospital. An additional motive was the fear that the Jewish poor would send their children to the free schools being organized by the London Missionary Society's Jewish Committee (the predecessor of the London Society for Promoting Christianity Among the Jews). The conversionist activities of the Rev. Frey and his associates, no matter how pathetic they may seem in historical perspective, troubled the leaders of Anglo-Jewry. In January 1807, Solomon Hirschell delivered two Sabbath sermons warning the community about the proposal of Christian missionaries to open a free school for Jewish children. Abstracts of the sermons were printed in Hebrew and English and distributed in the Jewish quarter. A deputation from the Great Synagogue called on Joseph Hardcastle, Treasurer of the London Missionary Society, a few days after Hirschell's second sermon, to express "their intention to obstruct the execution of the plan by every means in their power." Notwithstanding these protests, the London Missionary Society proceeded to open its free school that month, with an enrollment of about a dozen children. Nine months later, there were still only about a dozen children. Although this school, Frey's first effort, was not a success, it is still reasonable to conclude that the threat it posed was a motive in opening the Jews' Hospital in June of the same year.[20]

The successor organization to the Jewish Committee of the London Missionary Society, the London Society for Promoting Christianity among the Jews, was more successful in attracting Jewish children to its schools, admitting 219 pupils in the years 1809–14. During this period, some Jewish parents also began sending their children to the charity schools operated by the National School Society (in practice, a Church of England auxiliary) and the British and Foreign School Society (a voluntary association supported by Dissenters, Evangelical Anglicans, and some secular radicals). In 1816, for example, there were two Jewish students at the British and Foreign Society school in the Horse Ferry Road, a few at the National Society school in Whitechapel, and four at the National Society school in North Street.[21] Although these schools were not conversionist in aim, their instructional material was suffused with Christian symbols and beliefs. The willingness of the Jewish poor to send their children to schools such as these, as well as those of the London Society, demonstrates how desperate they were to obtain some kind of education for their children. The Talmud Torah and the Jews' Hospital accepted only a handful of children each year. Those who could not gain admission to either of these institutions and were unable to pay the fees of a private school had few alternatives: with no state schools, they either had to enroll in a Christian charity school or forego a secular education altogether.

In 1811, in response to the enrollment of Jewish children in Christian schools and as part of their continuing effort to upgrade the Jewish poor, the governors of the Talmud Torah began to discuss expanding the institution to include a free school for several hundred boys. In June 1812, through the initiative of Joshua Van Oven, it was decided to establish a school for the poor based on the Lancastrian monitorial system of the British and Foreign Society schools (a labor-saving method of teaching by rote, then very much in vogue, that utilized students, coached by the master, to teach other students). The Jews' Free School, as the new institution was called, opened its doors in the spring of 1817; within a few weeks, the enrollment jumped from 102 boys to 184. By June, there were 220 boys, and by the end of 1818, the number of applicants so outstripped the number of places that it was decided to erect a larger school and to admit girls as well. The new school building in Bell Lane, Spitalfields, was dedicated in June 1822, and six months later there were 447 students enrolled. By August of the following year, there were over 550.[22]

The establishment of the Jews' Free School was the Anglo-Jewish elite's most concerted effort to educate and discipline the Jewish poor. It enjoyed wide support within the Jewish community—there were 210 subscribers to the original fund—and attracted Christian gentlemen to its annual fund-raising dinners. In his review of London charities in 1822, Anthony Highmore, a solicitor and secretary of the London Lying-in Hospital, spoke glowingly of the school's accomplishments. Many poor boys had already been rescued by the order and discipline of the school from the consequences of ignorance; those who would have turned their talents to infamy and fraud had been saved by salutary instruction.[23] No doubt Highmore was correct: the Jews' Free School did offer an escape out of poverty. The education it provided was rudimentary—reading, writing, arithmetic, and Hebrew—but it was enough to hold out the possibility of entering a trade other than hawking or peddling. The discipline and values it imposed, if internalized, were capable of saving the young from the temptations of London street life and of propelling them toward bourgeois respectability.

The adult Jewish poor received far less attention from the reformers than did the children. In all likelihood, the Anglo-

Jewish elite felt there was little they could do to change the habits of the older generation and thus concentrated their efforts on the more malleable young. They did make one effort, however, to offer working men and women the same kind of moralizing education that was being provided to their children—in the context of a free night school for adults—but this did not prove to be a long-lived project. The immediate impetus for this venture in adult education was the establishment of a school for Jewish women by the Philo-Judaean Society early in 1828. The Ladies' Association of the Society founded the school to teach reading and writing, but the leaders of the Great Synagogue denounced the project as a conversionist ploy and threatened to deny a Jewish burial to women who attended. Having become aware, though, of a desire on the part of some of the Jewish poor for self-improvement, a group of Ashkenazi leaders, including the *maskilim* Joshua Van Oven, Michael Josephs, and Selig Newman, established an association (*Hevrat Or Torah* [The Light of Torah Society]) to sponsor a free school for adults. With the blessing of the Chief Rabbi, the school opened in the spring of 1828 with classes meeting four nights a week in the building of the Jews' Free School. The courses were generally well attended, and at the end of July the committee that managed the school expanded the program by introducing a series of Sabbath afternoon lectures in English. The night school program, however, lasted only six months due to a lack of support from the respectable part of the community. According to a newspaper account that appeared a quarter of a century later:

> It was objected to on account of the school being held at the *Free* School; again a grave objection was taken in the dislike of many to mix with persons of doubtful character; again, the elder took exception to, and were abashed to learn with the younger children; and lastly, the lecturers (though eminently qualified in every respect) could not give that regular attention which the subject required to be systematically carried out.

The Sabbath afternoon lecture series was more fortunate and continued to operate as late as March 1830.[24]

The ability of the Anglo-Jewish elite to promote the *embourgeoisement* of the Jewish lower class was limited by their financial resources and by the voluntary nature of Jewish institutions. As the number of poor Jews who attended the modern schools was never very great, always remaining a small minority within the Jewish lower class as a whole, the contribution of the *maskilim* and their programs to the modernization of Anglo-Jewry was, at the very most, a modest one, and possibly of no real consequence at all. The very gradual movement of the bulk of the Anglo-Jewish population from poverty to respectability over the course of the nineteenth century (before the mass influx of Eastern European Jews at the end of the century) was a process over which the Anglo-Jewish elite had little control.

An awareness of the limited impact of these modernizing schemes on the long-term course of Anglo-Jewish history derives only from historical hindsight and must not be allowed to obscure the importance assigned to such programs at the time. To the Anglo-Jewish elite and to their non-Jewish well-wishers, the task of educating and thereby upgrading the Jewish poor was both necessary and humanly attainable. The education of the poor was a traditional concern of the rich. At the same time, reforming the manners and the morals of the Jewish poor and providing them with marketable skills were not entirely acts of disinterested philanthropy. These were tasks designed to make the world more hospitable toward Jews of all ranks, including those with great wealth and correspondingly great social ambitions.

The desire to refashion the character of the Jewish lower class was not peculiar to the Anglo-Jewish elite, but was a central concern of well-to-do, acculturated Jews everywhere in Western and Central Europe in the years 1750 to 1850. In the German states in particular, as Jacob Katz has noted, "the most extensive and conspicuous efforts" of the *maskilim* were in the field of education. It was clear to them that "any attempt at remolding the Jewish mentality would have to start with reforming the old institutions." Modern Jewish schools for the poor opened in Berlin in 1781, in Breslau in 1791, in Dessau in 1799, in Seesen in 1801, in Frankfurt in 1804, in Wolfenbuttel in 1807, and in Kassel in 1809. In their emphases, the new schools differed from place to place: some offered instruction in only the rudiments of reading, writing, and arithmetic; others stressed commercial subjects and training in the handicrafts; while one, the Wolfenbuttel school, added Latin and Greek to the curriculum so students could prepare themselves for gymnasium. The one characteristic that bound them all together was that they deemphasized the study of traditional Jewish texts and featured some kind of training for entry into the non-Jewish world.[25]

Efforts to discipline the poor were also an important concern of propertied Englishmen in this period. The hundreds of charity schools established in the first half of the eighteenth century, largely under the sponsorship of the Society for Promoting Christian Knowledge, sought to immunize the children of the poor against the dangers of Popery and to drill in habits of industry and sobriety, in addition to providing a rudimentary education. "They were not intended to be centers for mental training," David Owen explained in his history of English philanthropy, "but 'pious nurseries' for godly discipline. In these the children of the poor would receive religious instruction and social conditioning, from which they would emerge as industrious, sober, and docile members of a society which saw them as future hewers of wood and drawers of water. Submission and gratitude to their benefactors, these were the qualities which the teaching was designed to inculcate."[26] The Sunday School movement, which began in the 1780s as an effort to save children who worked in the factories from vice and idleness, expanded in the troubled decades after the French Revolution because men of property feared the revolutionary potential of an unschooled and undisciplined lower class. The free schools operated by the Sunday School Society, the National School Society, the British and Foreign School Society, and other religious groups aimed at training docile, God-fearing youngsters who would be content with their low station in life.

In their concern for social discipline, the Jewish schools were very similar to their Christian counterparts. But there was also an important difference as well. The Anglo-Jewish poor were not a potentially revolutionary class and were not viewed as such by the Anglo-Jewish elite. They were politically apathetic and hardly constituted a threat to the established order. The discipline the Jewish magnates sought to impose was designed to promote their own status rather than to protect their property. The schools they established did not aim to keep the poor in their place, but proposed to do just the opposite: to remove the Jewish poor from London's streets and turn them into respectable artisans, clerks, and domestic servants, or possibly even better. Social mobility was a key objective, not the preservation of the socioeconomic status quo. For it was only through the *embourgeoisement* of the entire community—or so some believed—that their own integration into English society could be secured.

8

Integration and Intermarriage

The entry of foreign- and native-born Jews into English life over the course of the Georgian period rested on their prior acculturation to the patterns of the majority. But this acculturation, no matter how thoroughgoing, did not necessarily guarantee unrestricted access to English social circles or voluntary associations. It was not an automatic ticket of admission to English society. Social acceptance was a favor that was bestowed, not a prize that could be earned. Acting like an English gentleman, of course, was a prerequisite for being accepted as an English gentleman and for being admitted to genteel circles, but the proper behavior did not always bring about the desired results. Ultimately, the personal tastes and social prejudices of Englishmen determined the pace of Anglo-Jewish integration, for it was the host population that controlled access to those circles and groups Jews wished to penetrate.

The extent and the tempo of Anglo-Jewish integration over the course of the Georgian period are difficult to gauge with any precision. The entry of the Jews into the life of the English nation was not a massive assault played out in the public arena. Unlike the battle for the removal of civil disabilities, there were no decisive landmarks. The social integration of Anglo-Jewry consisted of innumerable interpersonal exchanges with the non-Jewish world. The private and undistinguished nature of most of these transactions (e.g., carousing in public houses, attending charity dinners, gossiping in coffee houses, socializing at costume balls and dinner parties, doing business in shops, warehouses, and in the streets, etc.) has blurred their historical significance and at the same time impeded the reconstruction of the course of Anglo-Jewish integration. Yet these mundane, face-to-face meetings, when taken in toto, constitute the stuff of concrete social reality. It is these encounters—rather than the reflective or polemical writings of a handful of self-conscious observers—that constitute the entry of the Jews into English society.

The sphere in which Jews and non-Jews at all levels of society met most frequently was the world of commerce. Itinerant peddlers, no less than merchant bankers or diamond brokers, came into contact on a daily basis with non-Jews. Such marketplace meetings, however, were generally of an instrumental and formal character; they did not bring the whole personality of the participants into play, but only a part of it.[1] They did not require, in other words, that the buyer and the seller evaluate each other's worth as human being and fit companion. Thus, the frequency with which Jews and non-Jews met in the marketplace cannot be taken as an indicator of the integration of Anglo-Jewry. Indeed, for centuries, Jews and Christians had been doing business with each other without any kind of rapprochement between the two groups, the primary motive having been, as it was also in Georgian England, the possibility of striking a mutually satisfying agreement. Moreover, it might be argued that some contacts in the economic sphere obstructed, rather than promoted, the process of integration. English gentlemen who were accosted daily in the streets by importunate Jewish hawkers could not have been moved by this experience to welcome any Jew, regardless of his manners and his wealth, into the intimate surroundings of their homes. Similarly, the experiences non-Jews had with Jewish orange men who passed bad coins, with Jewish peddlers who sold shoddy watches at inflated prices, and with Jewish salesmen who pulled customers bodily into their shops were hardly conducive to promoting integration.

Despite the discord of commercial encounters such as these and the widespread diffusion of uncomplimentary beliefs about Jews in general, social contacts between Jews and non-Jews became increasingly common over the course of the eighteenth and early nineteenth centuries. At all levels of society, from very early in the eighteenth century, small groups of anglicized Jews began to forge social relationships with their non-Jewish peers. Highly acculturated Sephardi brokers, ensconced in their newly purchased Thames-side homes to the west of London, entered into the social life of the neighborhood's fashionable set. Horace Walpole's voluminous correspondence contains numerous references to the Sephardim who mingled in these circles. He noted with pleasure the gifts of fruit given him by the army commissary Abraham Prado (d. 1782), who lived on Twickenham Common and was celebrated throughout the area for his knowledge of gardening and for the fine fruits he produced. In October 1778, he invited to a party at his famous home, Strawberry Hill, "three Jews of Abraham's standing and seven Sarah's who still talk of the second temple." In June 1780, in a letter to the Countess of Upper Ossory, he praised "an exceedingly pretty fire-work" in honor of the King's birthday that he had seen at the Thames-side home of Raphael Franco, a diamond and coral merchant. Isaac D'Israeli, writing in 1833, recalled that in the previous century "the Salvadors, the Francos, the Mendezes were . . . the ornaments of fashionable drawing rooms."[2]

In a very small number of families, non-Jewish friends and acquaintances—particularly those of the younger generation— were as numerous as Jewish ones. The four-hundred-odd pages of testimony given in a breach of promise case in 1734 between the young rake and libertine Jacob Mendes da Costa and his cousin, the wealthy young widow Catharine da Costa Villareal, reveal a pattern of social relationships in which Jews and non-Jews mingled frequently on a familiar and informal basis. When Abraham Mears published a descriptive account of Jewish customs for Christians in 1738, he assumed that his educated readers numbered Jews among their acquaintances. In the preface to his work, for example, he noted that if his readers wanted to know whether he had described accurately the customs of the Jews, "I can only refer them to resort to the Jewish Gentlemen and Ladies of their acquaintance at the times and seasons herein mention'd when such ceremonies are to be performed." When Mears came to describe the *matzot* that are eaten at Passover, he wrote that it was not necessary to give a detailed description of "their Passover cakes" since "the shape and form of their cakes is well known to everybody."[3]

Ashkenazim who amassed great fortunes in commerce and finance appeared in upper-class Christian circles at a later date than their Sephardi predecessors. This was due, in part, to the relative absence of wealthy Ashkenazim before the last decades of the eighteenth century (for wealth, above all, was the first prerequisite for outsiders desiring entry into upper-class English life) and, in part, to the social and cultural background of the Ashkenazim, who, having lived only among uneuropeanized Jews for several centuries, were unprepared to mix comfortably with upper-class Englishmen. Still, there were a few individuals who seem to have moved quite easily into the social life of the English countryside at a relatively early date, the Franks being a notable example. An unknown gentleman at Isleworth wrote around mid-century to a friend in London,

> M——s H——t [Moses Hart] and A——n F——s [Aaron Franks] at the last vestry held here, mingled with the rest without opposition, though two clergymen and Justice B—— were present. No less than a coach-load of them [Jews] last Thursday assembled at a clergyman's house very near us to play cards.

Aaron Franks' nephew, Moses Franks (1718–89), was on visiting terms with his neighbor Horace Walpole. When he died at his country home at Teddington, Thomas Pitt, the first Lord Camelford, wrote to a friend, "Poor General [Spencer] Cowper regrets extremely the loss of his neighbor Moses Franks, who was one of the few he cultivated." Indeed, the Franks were so successful in making their way into non-Jewish circles that they had virtually disappeared as Jews by the end of the eighteenth century.[4]

In general, however, Ashkenazim were not to be found moving in elite English circles until the "arrival" of the Goldsmid brothers at the very end of the century. With the fortune and the recognition they gained in government loan-contracting from 1795 on, Abraham and Benjamin Goldsmid went about making a place for themselves in non-Jewish society. Through generous contributions to non-Jewish charities and lavish entertaining at their country homes, they set out to win the acceptance of their non-Jewish peers. At the annual dinner of the Society for the Deaf and Dumb in 1810, for example, Abraham Goldsmid gave £700 out of a total of £3,000 subscribed that evening. Benjamin was particularly generous in contributing to and raising funds for the Naval Asylum at Paddington Green, an orphanage established in 1798, amidst much public fanfare, to maintain and educate the children of sailors fallen in battle. Benjamin contributed £2,000 personally and, by 1806, had raised another £2,600 within the Jewish community. Such generosity did not pass without notice from the detractors of the Jews, who discerned more than a philanthropic impulse in such lavish charity-giving. The anonymous author of *The Commercial Habits of the Jews* thought that many persons had been misled by these ostentatious displays of liberality and warned his readers that wealthy Jews never parted with a farthing without some very potent reason. The Goldsmids were out to buy popularity for themselves:

> One of these gentlemen [Abraham Goldsmid] (who, it must be confessed, if we remove out of the consideration the rapidity and manner in which his immense property has been acquired, *has* been liberal in his charitable donations) has been exhibited in the windows of the printshops, with scrolls of paper dangling out of his pockets, enumerating the whole of his splendid gifts of this sort. The indelicacy of this exhibition is sufficiently obvious; but our contempt and disgust are excited when we learn, that it was not the result of gratuitous adulation, but a wretched design and plot upon the admiration of the publick.[5]

The Goldsmid brothers were as lavish in entertaining non-Jews as they were in contributing to their charities. To celebrate Nelson's victory at the Battle of the Nile in 1798, Benjamin gave a fete at his Roehampton estate that was, in the words of a contemporary,

> in the most splendid style possible, beyond anything that was ever attempted anywhere else. . . . his Mansion was most splendidly illuminated with fireworks. Music and dancing prevailed in the house, with Masques &c. and intervals of refreshments which amused his visitants near 24 hours.

His brother Abraham often entertained his neighbor Admiral Nelson and Nelson's mistress, Lady Hamilton, at his country home, and on one occasion, George III and Queen Charlotte unexpectedly dropped in for a meal. Benjamin received the Prince of Wales in a splendid fashion at Roehampton one afternoon, but scandalized the more orthodox members of the Jewish community since the Prince had selected the Jewish Sabbath for his visit and Goldsmid had not wanted to offend him by suggesting another day. The daily papers, wrote John Francis in his *Chronicles and Characters of the Stock Exchange* (1850),

> bore an almost daily testimony to their munificence. . . . the grandeur of an entertainment to royalty was recorded. . . . Entertainments to princes and ambassadors reviving the glory of the Arabian nights, were frequent; and galleries, with works of art worthy [of] the magnificence of a Medici, graced their homes. They were awhile Fortune's chief and most especial favorites.[6]

To a large degree, the Goldsmids succeeded in making a place for themselves in fashionable circles. The English upper class was not overly fastidious about socializing with new money and was certainly not averse to being wined and dined on a magnificent scale by parvenus, even Jewish parvenus. Some persons of respectable birth were even willing to reciprocate and to invite the Goldsmids to their homes. According to Levy Alexander, when Benjamin Goldsmid and his wife Jessie first established themselves at Stamford Hill (that is, in the late 1780s before moving to Roehampton) they gained

> the friendship of all the gentlefolks for many miles round the spot and *reciprocal* [emphasis added] visits were as frequent as the return of day, each being emulous to become more and more agreeable to the strangers, till the most complete union was formed in all the neighbouring villages of Tottenham, Edmonton, and several miles round with this family.

When Benjamin Goldsmid died in 1808—he hanged himself from a silk cord that he had used to lift his heavy, gout-ridden body from bed in the morning—an obituary in *The Universal Magazine* lauded him and his brother for having set the trend of wealthy Jews giving to Christian charities. When Abraham also committed suicide two years later—he shot himself in the throat —the obituary in *The Times* was fulsome in its praise of his generosity and kindness:

> There are not many men who have ever performed more kind acts in social life, or more liberal ones in what may be esteemed his public one, than Mr. Abraham Goldsmid; no one indeed,

of any class of description, ever became tolerably well known to him, without improving their fortunes, in some degree, by the connexion; so that the list of those whom gratitude, or the sense of kindness received in one way or other, had bound, or ought to have bound, to him was almost endless.[7]

The triumphs of the brothers Goldsmid were, however, by no means unqualified ones. Their entry into the non-Jewish world of fashion and wealth did not signify their full incorporation into that world. Their suicides, indeed, may very well have been the partial result of the insecurity and the anxiety of living on the margins of fashionable society, never knowing whether they had made it into the inner circle or not. Although their wealth demanded that other men of wealth and influence recognize them, it could not purchase their unalloyed acceptance and approval. To one observer, writing in 1809, "the present *taste* for Judaic *fêtes* and *coteries,* in which our princes and nobles are not ashamed to participate" was a fashion of the moment, a fad, like styles in dress, "subjected to the caprices of the . . . *beau monde.*" That the *beau monde* ever warmly received the Goldsmids into their midst, making them an integral part of their comings and goings, is doubtful. As long as the Goldsmids remained Jews, their integration remained incomplete. A short time before Benjamin Goldsmid's death, his eldest son, age 19, acknowledged this situation by converting to Anglicanism. "In relation to these circumstances, probably, the deceased father once said, if common rumour be not fallacious, that he should be the last Jew of his family." He was correct. His widow and his other six children, who were described at the time of his death as "by no means strict in their observance of the customs of their people," were converted four years later.[8]

By formally abandoning their Jewish identity, Jessie Goldsmid and her children publicly acknowledged that there were limits to the social acceptability of even the wealthiest Jews. The *beau monde* might be willing to tolerate Jews in its midst on occasion, but it was not yet prepared to grant them unqualified access and full-hearted approval. Horace Walpole may have invited his Jewish neighbors to his home, but he did so with a feeling of condescension, with the sense that he was doing a favor for persons socially inferior to him. As he wrote to a friend in 1778,

You may perhaps think that some of the company were not quite of dignity adequate to such a high festival, but they were just the persons made the most happy by being invited; and as the haughtiest peers stoop to be civil to shopkeepers before an election, I did not see why I should not do, out of good nature, what the proudest so often do out of interest.

Five decades later, when the integration of Anglo-Jewry was much more advanced, the author of a guide to English manners and morals complained about the penetration of Jews into fashionable gambling and sporting circles:

Moses has crept into all circles; from the ring to the peerage and baronetage, the stage, the race-course; and our clubs are tinged with the Israelitish mixture: they may *lend* money, but they cannot lend a lustre to the court, or to the gilded and painted saloons of the *beau monde*. [9]

The reservations that well-bred Englishmen had about *nouveaux riches* Jews, although not made part of any public debate, brought grief and distress to ambitious Jews, who, unlike their German counterparts, did not expose their wounded hearts to the world, but remained silent and contented themselves with the limited socializing that did occur. Even the Sephardi elite, much heralded by historians of the present century for their acceptability to Englishmen, suffered some of the sorrows of unrequited love. Samson Gideon, the most prominent financier of the mid-eighteenth century, found his ascent on the social ladder blocked by what a contemporary termed "the delicacy of the English nobility." Gideon, who had married a Christian and had had each of his children baptized a few days after birth, hoped to use his enormous wealth to found a family that would merge into the landed aristocracy. Not having himself formally renounced Judaism, he focused all his ambitions on his eldest son, also called Sampson (but spelled with a *p*). "The first object of his policy," wrote a correspondent to *Town and Country Magazine* in 1786, "was family connection." But in seeking to find a wife of aristocratic stock for his son, he found his own Jewish origins "an insurmountable impediment, and the New Christian [the son] was repeatedly rejected for no other reason than because his father was an Old Jew." Gideon then sought an alliance among a less exclusive group of men, members of the liberal professions, "and found a learned law lord [Sir John Eardley Wilmot, Lord Chief Justice of the Court of Common Pleas] who, not possessing the same prejudices which had influenced the lay tribe of patricians, consented to a matrimonial connection between his daughter and our hero."[10]

Benjamin Disraeli recalled that his paternal grandmother suffered terribly from the rebuffs she encountered from her Christian neighbors in the country. Her husband, Benjamin D'Israeli, who had arrived in England from Ferrara in 1748, had commenced business as an importer of Italian goods, especially straw bonnets. He had also begun speculating in stocks and shares, eventually becoming a partner in a successful firm of stockbrokers. In the late 1760s or early 1770s, he took a large country house at Enfield in Middlesex, where according to his famous grandson, he and his wife seemed to have been friendly enough with some of their English neighbors. Sarah D'Israeli, the daughter of a rich City merchant, was not, however, content with her position in country society. She did not like to mix with Jews, but neither did she find the unqualified welcome she desired from the English: "She was so mortified by her social position that she lived until eighty without indulging in a tender expression," her grandson wrote. "She foresaw for her child [Isaac] only a future of degradation."[11]

The successes and the rebuffs wealthy Jews met with in entering elite English circles were the experiences of a tiny minority within Anglo-Jewry, for the obvious reason that only a small group of Jewish families had the wealth to attempt to enter those circles, even as late as the 1820s. The vast majority of Jews in England at any time in the years 1700–1830 were hardly comfortable enough materially to dream of making a place for themselves in upper-class society. This does not mean there was no social interaction between Jews and non-Jews below a certain income level; quite the contrary. As will be made clear later, informal social contacts between nonaffluent Jews and non-Jews occurred more regularly and with less effort than at the top of the social hierarchy. Moreover, not all Jews—even anglicized ones— desired to mix on intimate terms with their non-Jewish peers. At any point in the eighteenth or early nineteenth centuries, a high proportion of the Jews living in England—it is impossible to be any more precise—had been born abroad. Their experiences on the Continent did not incline them to reach out for social ties to the non-Jewish world. Those who had learned to speak English did so haltingly, so that even if they had desired to seek non-Jewish companionship they would have been seriously handicapped. Most Jews, foreign- and native-born, were content to satisfy their social needs within the Jewish community. Those who had acquired English tastes and manners were not necessarily propelled outside their own group; they could find satisfactory companionship among their equally acculturated peers. That this was so should not be surprising, since most persons in religiously and ethnically diverse societies rarely go outside their own group for their closest personal relationships, but instead form them with those whose habits are familiar to them and with whom they naturally feel comfortable and at ease.

With the passage of time, though, the minority of English Jews whose aspirations lay outside the Jewish community became increasingly larger. This was due, in part, to the expansion of the Jewish upper middle class and, in part, to an increase in the number of Jews who had developed cultural, intellectual, and professional needs that could only be satisfied within the non-Jewish world. For those who sought fame and fortune, advancement and promotion, acceptance and intimacy in the non-Jewish world, and who would not be satisfied with anything less than they thought they merited, their Jewishness eventually became a burden—something that had to be thrown off and abandoned. As James Picciotto, a pioneer historian of Anglo-Jewry, aptly observed in the 1870s:

> in all communities there are men of keen feelings, of restless energy, of ambitious minds, and withal, of weak convictions. To these individuals, the condition of a Jew [during the last quarter of the eighteenth century and the first quarter of the nineteenth] entailed continual humiliations, disappointments, and miseries. To remain on a dead level with those around them, hopeless of ever soaring higher in the social sphere, must have proved gall and wormwood to many Israelites in olden days. The mart, the exchange, the Synagogue, the domestic circle, did not suffice for their aspirations.

For those Jews who wanted no limitations placed on their advancement or their children's, the only solution was to be converted, or to marry a non-Jew and raise one's children as Christians, or to have one's children baptized before they reached adulthood. "Baptism," Picciotto continued, "promised the rich [Jew] the realization of his ambitious dreams: place, honor, power, social considerations."[12]

Baptism was, then, in Heine's words, "a ticket of admission" to many exclusive areas of English life. Isaac D'Israeli, who moved on the periphery of several literary circles but was, according to his biographer, "never fully accepted in any English social circle," was determined that his children would not inherit his own indeterminate status. In July 1817, a year after his father died and several months after his formal break with Bevis Marks, Isaac had his three boys and one girl baptized. Neither he nor his wife, Maria Basevi, ever formally abandoned Judaism, and Isaac maintained a keen enough interest in Jewish affairs to produce *The Genius of Judaism* in 1833. Of course, Isaac did not have definite careers marked out for his children when he took this step —the eldest child, Sarah, was only fifteen at the time. He was motivated, rather, by the more general belief that they would find life easier and more pleasant if unencumbered by any formal attachment to Judaism. Still, there were before him already the examples of two baptized Sephardim who had merged with the landed gentry and entered Parliament: Sampson Gideon the younger represented Cambridgeshire in Parliament from 1770 to 1780, and Manasseh Masseh Lopes (1755–1831), the son of a wealthy West Indian merchant who had settled in England about the middle of the eighteenth century and set himself up as a country gentleman at Clapham, was elected to Parliament in 1802 and served there until 1829, except for the two years he spent in prison for electioneering bribery and corruption. In the previous century, the prominent German-born physician, Dr. Meyer Loew Schomberg (1690–1761) had also taken similar steps to promote the careers of his six sons. Schomberg, who was active in London from about 1720 until his death, worked diligently to build up a large and profitable practice. According to Boswell, "Fothergill, a Quaker, and Schomberg, a Jew, had the greatest practice of any two physicians of their time." By the time Schomberg published his denunciation of moral hypocrisy in the London Jewish community *(Emunat omen,* 1746), he was already alienated from Jewish tradition. He sent his sons to English schools, including Merchant Taylors' and St. Paul's, and then into prestigious institutions that required adherence to the Church of England. Solomon entered the Middle Temple to study for the bar; Alexander, the Navy; Henry, the Army; and Isaac, Trinity College, Cambridge. Only Moses, a notary in partnership with two observant Sephardim, remained within the Jewish community. Ralph, a physician in Bath who married a Christian and had his children baptized, may, like his father, never have formally embraced Christianity.[13]

Young men and women whose ambitions outstripped those of their parents often took themselves to the baptismal font in the belief that this would ease their way in the world. Such was the case, for example, with Sir Francis Palgrave (1788–1861), barrister, constitutional historian, antiquarian, and first archivist of what is now the Public Record Office. Palgrave's father was Meyer Cohen, a wealthy stockbroker; his mother, Rachel, a daughter of Gotchal Levien, one of the twelve licensed Jewish brokers and an active supporter of Jewish charities and schools. As the son of a prosperous stockbroker, Francis was educated at home by a private tutor and at an early age demonstrated a capacity for and interest in scholarly matters. His life of ease was shattered, however, when war with France and the threat of invasion caused a sharp slump on the stock exchange, leaving his father a much poorer man. With the family fortune gone, he was articled, at age 16, as a clerk to a firm of solicitors. But the education he had received and the interests it had kindled pushed him to seek companionship outside the Jewish community. He contributed many articles to the minor journals of the day, frequented a circle of writers that included Sir Walter Scott, and in 1821 was elected a Fellow of the Royal Society. Several years before this date he was baptized, and when in 1823 he married Elizabeth Turner, daughter of a partner in Gurney's Bank and also a man with antiquarian interests, he obtained a royal license to change his name from Cohen to Palgrave, the name of his wife's mother's family. There were now no impediments to his integration into English society. In 1827, he was called to the bar by the Inner Temple, in 1832 knighted, in 1834 appointed Keeper of the Records at the Chapter House at Westminster Abbey, and in 1838 made the first Deputy Keeper of the Public Records. Palgrave's break with his family and with his past was almost a complete one, his only remaining link being the financial support he gave to his destitute father until the latter's death in 1831. A sister-in-law of Palgrave recalled that "for upwards of 30 years of his married life he never alluded to his own previous name or religion. I well remember the first time of his withdrawing the curtain which hid that part from our view, his speaking of that elderly cousin (Miss Levien) and of his father and his own name (which signified Priest) and of his being of the tribe of Levi."[14]

The key factor in moving Palgrave away from the Jewish community—the nature of his personal makeup aside—was his desire to participate in an intellectual culture outside the boundaries of Jewish life. Having been given the education of an English gentleman by an indulgent and proud father, and having responded to this education with enthusiasm and ability, he had to look, as a consequence, beyond his family's friends and acquaintances for social and intellectual companionship. For within the Jewish community there were no secular intellectual coteries. With a few exceptions, the Anglo-Jewish elite, especially the Ashkenazim, did not provide its sons with a broadly based secular education. A few years at a private school or with a private tutor were deemed sufficient for the sons of most stockbrokers and diamond merchants. Moses Montefiore was sent to school for only a few years and then, as a young lad, apprenticed to a firm of provision merchants in the City. The education of David Ricardo ended when he was thirteen, after having spent two years in Amsterdam with his father's relatives. He never studied any political economy or any scientific subjects as a youth and only acquired a knowledge of these areas after his marriage. According to Maria Edgeworth, Ricardo once told her, "My father gave me but little education. He thought reading, writing, and arithmetic sufficient because he doomed me to be nothing but a man of business; he sent me at eleven to Amsterdam to learn Dutch, French, and Spanish." The first Anglo-Jewish engineer, Jacob Samuda (1811–44), destined by his parents for a mercantile career, was educated at Leopold Neumegen's school at Highgate (Neumegen had taken over Hyman Hurwitz's modern Jewish school when the latter retired in 1821) and was put into a counting house in his early teens. Because Samuda displayed a bent for mechanical pursuits and a dislike for the routine of the commercial life, his father placed him, when he was fifteen or sixteen, with an engineer with whom he completed his apprenticeship. The actuary and mathematician Benjamin Gompertz (1779–1865) was almost entirely self-taught. Intended by his father, a successful diamond merchant, to follow a purely mercantile profession, he made his start in life on the stock exchange. Even if there had been a demand on the part of the Anglo-Jewish elite for higher education, there would have been no way of meeting that demand. Oxford and Cambridge were closed to Jews; a university education only became possible for Jewish youth after the establishment of the nonsectarian University College, London, in 1827 by a group of prominent non-Anglicans, including Isaac Lyon Goldsmid. As Henry Lemoine summed up the situation in a letter to *The Gentleman's Magazine* in 1810: "An English Jew starts into life a very ignorant or uninformed being. . . . Born and bred to commercial transactions, his knowledge is confined to such topics; and all his leisure is spent in the amusements of the town, visiting, or walking, but always with an eye to business."[15]

Had Francis Palgrave been "born and bred to commercial transactions," he probably would have remained Francis Cohen, for unless he became very rich and began to entertain soaring social ambitions, he would have been satisfied with the amusements of Jewish society. It was an interest in matters outside the range of Jewish life as it had been lived previously that pulled him and other bright young men away from the confines of the Jewish community. Jews who broke new ground and made careers for themselves outside the world of commerce—as artists, littérateurs, actors, and musicians, for example—in effect declared that their closest associates would be non-Jews. John Braham, né Abraham (1774–1856), the outstanding tenor in England in the first three decades of the nineteenth century, began his career singing in the Great Synagogue, but left to sing on the stage when he was thirteen. In 1802, Nancy Storace, a singer and actress and for many years his partner on the stage, bore him a son, who eventually took orders in the Anglican Church. In 1816, Braham married a Miss Bolton of Arwick, a union which produced six children, all of whom were raised in the Church of England. The career of the musical composer and singing teacher John Barnett (1802–90) displayed a similar pattern. His father, a jeweler in Bradford who had migrated from Prussia and anglicized his name, Bernhard Beer, to Barnett Barnett, articled him at age 11 to the proprietor of the Lyceum Theatre in London (a non-Jew), who agreed to provide him with musical instruction in return for his services as a singer. Because his father chose for him a career in a field outside the world of business, his links with the Jewish community were weakened, although his uncle, Aaron Barnett, was *hazan* of the Hambro Synagogue. In 1837, he married the youngest daughter of the cellist Robert Lindley.[16]

Not all anglicized Jews with non-Jewish cultural and intellectual interests felt pressured into renouncing or abandoning their links with the community into which they had been born. Many were content with a limited or restricted kind of acceptance and were too closely tied to the Jewish community to allow their ambition to lead them to apostasy. There was, moreover, enough of a tolerant spirit in literary and scientific circles, as well as in some fashionable circles, to admit Jewish participants who did not demand a full and unqualified acceptance. Isaac D'Israeli, it will be recalled, never abandoned Judaism. In the eighteenth century, a number of Sephardim, some of whom were educated at Portuguese universities before fleeing the peninsula, were elected Fellows of the Royal Society: the physicians Isaac de Sequeria Samuda (elected in 1723) and Jacob de Castro Sarmento (1729); the wealthy merchants Alvaro Suasso (1735), Anthony da Costa (1736), and Joseph Salvador (1759); and the eminent naturalist and antiquary Emanuel Mendes da Costa, who served as Librarian and Secretary of the Royal Society until he was dismissed for embezzlement. Mendes da Costa's extensive knowledge of minerals and fossils gave him entrée to country homes and drawing rooms not always open to moneyed Jews. In 1747, for example, when the Duke of Richmond had a grotto built in the garden of his country home, Greenwood Park, he asked Mendes da Costa to come down to study the fossils in the grotto. Martin Folkes, President of both the Royal Society and the Antiquarian Society, extended the invitation on behalf of the Duke and assured Mendes da Costa he would not feel uncomfortable there:

> The Duke being the most humane and the best man living, you need be in no difficulty about your eating, here being all sorts of fish, and every day the greatest variety of what you may feed on without breach of the Law of Moses, unless the lobsters of Chichester should be a temptation, by which a weaker man might be seduced. Here is also a Chaplain, I should suspect

originally of your Nation, for he talks Hebrew almost naturally, and will not wish to harm you any more than myself.

Three weeks later Folkes again wrote to Mendes da Costa reemphasizing the point he had made previously:

> His Grace is very sorry the duties of your religion, which every good man is well attached to [the High Holidays], prevent your coming hither just at this time. . . . Your living you need be in no pain about, as we have not had a single dinner without plenty of what the strictest Laws of Moses would allow you, though at the same time we have eat barbecued shols, and other abominations to your nation; but we are all citizens of the world, and see different customs and different tastes without dislike or prejudice, as we do different names and colours.[17]

The entry of educated Sephardim into religiously neutral cultural spheres from very early in the eighteenth century rested on their long-standing acculturation to non-Jewish patterns of life. Not unexpectedly, few Ashkenazim moved in such circles until many decades later. The polemicist David Levi (1742–1801) was friendly with the hack writer and bookseller Henry Lemoine, who supplied him with materials for his controversy with Joseph Priestley. In the 1780s, Lemoine, Levi, and other minor literati gathered frequently for dinner at the home of the bookseller George Lackington in Chiswell Street. Solomon Bennett, whose quarrels with the Anglo-Jewish establishment in the 1810s inclined him to seek companionship outside the Jewish community, was, in his own words, "honored with some literary friends of the first rank and amiable characters in the metropolis." Hyman Hurwitz was part of Coleridge's circle at Highgate. Benjamin Gompertz was a member of the Mathematical Society of Spitalfields, a contributor to several scientific journals, and a Fellow of the Royal Society from 1819.[18] None of these men, however, chose occupations that led away from the Jewish community: Levi was a shoemaker and then a hat dresser; Bennett, an engraver; Hurwitz, the master of a Jewish school; Gompertz, a stockbroker and then an actuary for the Alliance Assurance Company, founded in 1824 by his brother-in-law Moses Montefiore and Nathan Rothschild. Their secular diversions took them into the non-Jewish world, but their occupational concerns brought them back again to the Jewish community.

The admission of unconverted Jews to scientific bodies and literary circles must, however, in no way be interpreted as the burgeoning of unqualified toleration. The principles that animated these groups were religiously neutral, but the men who joined these associations, being flesh and blood, were subject to all the social prejudices of the age. Their willingness to admit talented Jews into their midst was not a judgment about the character of Jews in general or even about the nonintellectual characteristics of those they admitted. They recognized merit, but merit—then, as now—only counted for as much as prejudice and whim would allow it. In 1763, when Emanuel Mendes da Costa was considering whether to run for the office of Librarian of the Royal Society, the historian and biographer Thomas Birch warned him, "Your religious profession may possibly be a prejudice to you with some persons," but encouraged him to offer himself as a candidate nevertheless, "since you have shown yourself so useful a member of the Society, and are capable of doing great service to it in the office now vacant." Benjamin Gompertz's eccentric younger brother Lewis (1784–1861) was one of the founders of the Society for Preventing Cruelty to Animals and its energetic Secretary from 1826 to 1832, though in 1832 the Committee of the SPCA decided that the organization should be exclusively Christian and tossed Gompertz out. Henry Lemoine and David Levi belonged to the same social-literary set, and Lemoine and Levy Alexander collaborated on a memoir of Benjamin Goldsmid, but this did not prevent Lemoine from saying uncomplimentary things about Jews in general in letters to *The Gentleman's Magazine* and in a sketch of Manasseh ben Israel in his *Eccentric Magazine*. The public-spirited men who were invited to Isaac Lyon Goldsmid's home and with whom he was associated in a number of reformist enterprises (e.g., Henry Brougham, Thomas Babington Macaulay, Robert Owen, James Mill, Samuel Gurney, Thomas Campbell) were not necessarily unambiguous admirers of the Jews. Macaulay's feelings (as indicated in Chapter 3) were highly ambivalent.[19]

The mixed reception acculturated Jews received when they participated in spheres of activity outside their own community drove many of them to change their religious identity. The stigma attached to Jewishness, while not strong enough to keep them out of gentile circles altogether, had not weakened sufficiently to allow them free and easy access. As doubts and reservations lingered on about their true acceptability, apostasy became the usual escape for those who could not bear even the smallest measure of exclusion or contempt.

Deserting Judaism rarely posed any serious religious problems for ambitious Jews. The Church of England imposed no regular obligations; the traditional beliefs and practices of Judaism had been abandoned long before. One religion was as good as another, given a secular orientation to life. A more important source of tension for those who broke with Judaism was their relationship to relatives, parents especially, who remained behind. For to accept Christianity was to do more than to reject Judaism: it was to turn one's back on a network of family and social relationships that were independent of ritual and doctrine. Thus, because apostasy had extradoctrinal implications of great psychological importance, many persons who might have considered conversion early in life delayed doing anything until after the death of a parent or a spouse. Only in the year after his father's death did Isaac D'Israeli formally break with Bevis Marks and take his children to be baptized. After Judith Levy's husband, the fabulously wealthy diamond merchant Elias Levy, died in 1748, she gave up her house in Wellclose Square in the Jewish quarter and moved to Albemarle Street in fashionable, non-Jewish Mayfair. Having inherited her husband's fortune and eventually her father's (her father was Moses Hart, the dominant figure in the Ashkenazi community in the first half of the century), she launched herself into fashionable society, coming to prefer "the company of female Gentiles to that of the Hebrew ladies, merely on account of the superior elegances and politeness of the former." She spent her summers at different watering places, and "in the winter she visited masquerades, balls, etc. and introduced her daughter to the Duchess of N[orthumberlan]d's routes, then a noted match-maker, who delighted in procuring great fortunes for younger brothers of quality." Daughter Isabella's dowry caught the fancy of the third son of the Earl of Aboyne, the Hon. Lockhart Gordon, and the couple were married in April 1753 in the Church of England. When David Franks (1720–94) wrote from Philadelphia in 1775 to his brother Moses in England that he proposed to send his son Moses to London to study for the bar (a step that would have required his adherence to the Church of England), Moses replied that it was "highly imprudent to attempt it while Mr. A——Franks is living. He never would admit a step of that sort in any of his family so avowedly, nor would any of us venture to countenance it, as it would highly insense him. Therefore, it is necessary to give up the thought at present." Mr. A——Franks was Aaron Franks (1685/92–1777) of Isleworth and London, a brother-in-law of the above-mentioned Elias Levy, a son-in-law of Moses Hart, the uncle of David and Moses Franks, and, significantly, a pillar of the Great Synagogue. As patriarch of the Anglo-American Franks clan, his religious sensibilities were not to be insulted. His nephew David had married a non-Jew, but there is no evidence that he ever formally accepted Christianity; in any case, he lived in the wilds of North America. Moses cautiously advised his brother that "in its proper time"— after their uncle Aaron's death—"your son shall (if he chooses it) come here for the purpose aforesaid."[20]

With many of the marriages contracted between upper-class Jews and Gentiles, the wealth the Jewish partner brought to the marriage was undoubtedly the key element in securing the union. The younger sons of the aristocracy and the gentry were barred by the laws of entail and primogeniture from inheriting any portion of the family's estate, and unless their fathers made other provisions for their financial security (such as providing them with clerical livings or leaving them other forms of property), they were forced to make their own way in the world. Well-dowered Jewish daughters, like Isabella Levy, were attractive to younger sons with few prospects for advancement. Catherine da Costa Villareal, who achieved notoriety from a breach of promise suit brought by her cousin, married William Mellish of Blyth, Nottinghamshire, the younger son of a country squire, in 1735. A generous outlay of her money sent him to the House of Commons as M.P. for Retford, Nottinghamshire, in 1741. In one rare instance, a truly magnificent dowry even purchased a titled husband, although the title was then an Irish one. In 1757, Samson Gideon married his daughter Elizabeth, age 18, to the second Viscount Gage, age 39, with a portion of £40,000. In mixed marriages such as these, commented Jacob Mocatta at the end of the century, "happiness is not often the result, and I do not doubt but the more prevalent incentive of the other party is the fancied opulence of the Jews."[21]

Not all of the social relationships forged between Jews and non-Jews rested on as opportunistic grounds as those described above. Close relationships between Jews and non-Jews in which the Jewishness of the former did not complicate the relationship did spring up, although not with such frequency as to be a defining characteristic of Jewish-Gentile relations as a whole. Marriages between Jews and non-Jews did take place in which ambition and material gain were not the primary goals. David Ricardo's marriage to Priscilla Wilkinson, the daughter of a Quaker physician whose house in Bow was not far from the Ricardos's, presupposed a previous degree of informal social intercourse in which love could blossom. The marriage was opposed by both families and, thus, obviously did not originate in either family's longing for an improvement in their fortunes.

Marriages of this sort were relatively uncommon among the Jewish and gentile upper classes. In part, this was due to the nonromantic character of marriage in upper-class life. For the wealthy, marriage was far more an alliance of two families than the union of two individuals. It was too important a matter to be left to the vagaries of love. Family finances had to be repaired or strengthened, political connections forged or reinforced. The formal, or structured, nature of upper-class socializing also worked to inhibit the growth of romantic love between Jews and Gentiles of property. Social intercourse at the top was by invitation only; social activity was limited by and large to set occasions and set times. Outside the drawing room, the music room, and the ballroom, casual encounters and chance meetings, especially for women, were infrequent. This kind of life-style did not provide fertile ground for the growth of informal relationships between persons of different backgrounds.

At the opposite end of the social scale, a very different set of circumstances prevailed. The Jewish poor and the Jewish petite bourgeoisie lived on very close physical terms with their non-Jewish peers. They lodged in the same narrow streets and crowded courts, frequently in the same buildings. Miserable housing drove them, as it did all the poor of London, into the streets, the public houses, the theaters, and the open spaces of the East End in search of entertainment and diversion—a pursuit, needless to say, that was not governed by the rigid conventions of upper-class socializing. Poor Jews who had abandoned or never known Jewish tradition drank, whored, and fought with non-Jews in a free and easy way that would have been the envy of the Franks or the Goldsmids. The records of cases tried at the Old Bailey portray a degree of intimate socializing among the Jewish and non-Jewish poor not found among the rich: Moses Levi, a diamond cutter, having a glass of wine at the Crown and Horseshoe, Drury Lane, with his friends Mrs. Cox and Mrs. Mason (1735); Rachel Levi, onetime mistress of Baron Suasso, becoming drunk on rum and brandy at the house of Sarah Chapman (1735); Sarah Jacobs, whose husband beats her but is now away from London, having a beer in a public house in Harrow Court with William Steers, whom she met in the street only a few minutes earlier (1755); Joseph Jacobs, on trial for armed robbery, producing two non-Jewish women who lodge in the same house as his mother as character witnesses (1770); Moses Marks, a pencil-maker, celebrating the impending marriage of his close friend Harriet Wilson by drinking away the night before her marriage in her company (1799); John Levy, a silversmith, drinking and playing cards with non-Jewish friends at the Cart and Horse, Goswell Lane (1816).[22]

Intimate and sustained socializing between the Jewish and non-Jewish poor was a common enough occurrence to lead to close cooperation in criminal endeavors. Integrated teams of pickpockets, housebreakers, and shoplifters, while never coming to constitute a majority of the cases, appeared with increasing frequency from the 1770s. In September 1770, for example, Joseph Josephs was sentenced to death for armed robbery along with Mary Ann Ryan and James Simpson. Seventy-three-year-old Israel Phillips and a non-Jewish woman, age 32, were sentenced to transportation for seven years in April 1790 for shoplifting seventeen yards of muslin. In February 1812, Jonas Solomon, age 17, Abraham Nathan, age 50, and two non-Jews were transported for seven years for stealing three reams of paper. Solomon Levy, age 19, and his non-Jewish partner, age 22, were sentenced to seven years transportation in October 1813 for stealing a chest of tea from a delivery cart.[23]

An even more arresting indicator of the extent to which intimate integration was possible outside of elite circles was the not uncommon phenomenon of mixed marriages in which the non-Jewish partner, usually a woman, chose to convert to Judaism.

When Joshua Sarfaty de Pinna requested permission from the Mahamad in 1824 to marry formally a convert with whom he had been living for some years, they refused on the grounds that she had been converted in England and that this was contrary to the terms of settlement by which the Sephardim had been readmitted to England. Several months later, in June 1825, Joseph Nunes Martines, whose dispute with the Mahamad over their refusal to bury a child of his, distributed a handbill in which he claimed that this dispute would lead "to an exposure of how many Christian females have been made Jewesses in London contrary to Law."[24] Mixed marriages contracted by respectable Jews almost always ended with the apostasy of the Jewish partner or with the eventual baptism of his or her children. Among the less prosperous, where the drive for status was less acute, non-Jewish partners did not risk a dramatic fall in their personal standing if they chose to convert.

Only a minority of all mixed marriages, however, resulted in a gain to Anglo-Jewry. Jews without money who selected marital partners from outside their own community had to have already acquired the customs and the habits of their neighbors and to have abandoned the rites and the doctrines of traditional Judaism. Their connection to the Jewish group having been weakened previously, they often chose to identify themselves with the majority community after marriage. This choice, it can be hypothesized, was also dictated by a desire to escape the common opprobrium attached to the Jews as a group. For although the mode of life of the propertyless classes encouraged greater face-to-face contact between Jews and non-Jews, popular hostility was as pronounced as in elite circles. Not surprisingly, then, most mixed marriages ended in the total absorption of the Jewish partner or his children into the Christian population.

Again, it must be emphasized that any discussion of integration as intimate and as thoroughgoing as that described above pertains to a minority, although a noticeable one, within Anglo-Jewry. The immigrant character of the bulk of the Jewish lower classes at any point in the eighteenth century or the early nineteenth century prohibited a high degree of integration for the community as a whole. Indeed, most Jews outside the elite, regardless of the accommodations they had made to English life, preferred to seek companionship within their own community.

The hostility of the non-Jewish world, in tandem with a natural proclivity to associate most closely with persons sharing the same behavioral patterns, worked to hold acculturated Jews together. A typical manifestation of this pattern of group behavior was the formation of Masonic lodges composed entirely or primarily of Jews.

English Freemasonry, from its origins in the early eighteenth century, was nondenominational, seeking to provide a neutral meeting ground for enlightened men from all Christian sects, but it was not necessarily non-Christian. Christian symbols and prayers permeated the ritual. Nevertheless, as early as the 1730s, well-to-do Sephardim began to be admitted to the English lodges. The appeal that Freemasonry exerted on acculturated Jews in these early decades is not difficult to discern: it held out the possibility of intimate companionship with respectable Christians, and offered an escape from the drudgery of everyday life into a glamorous world of exotic ritual. By the middle of the century, the demand for admission to the English lodges on the part of Sephardim and Ashkenazim, rich and not-so-rich, had grown to the point that "Jewish" lodges began to appear; that is, lodges in which the majority of members were Jewish, the ritual was adapted to Jewish usage, the dietary laws were observed, and meetings were rescheduled if they conflicted with Jewish holidays. These Jewish lodges catered almost exclusively to Jewish shopkeepers and artisans. The Anglo-Jewish elite, being few in number, continued to seek admission—obviously for reasons of status—to non-Jewish lodges where they would come in contact with prominent members of society. With increasing pressure for admission on the part of lower-middle-class Ashkenazim, some English lodges took explicit steps to bar Jews from membership. When a Jew was proposed for membership in the Lodge of Friendship in 1752, the brothers voted against accepting him and decided that in the future no Jew should even be proposed for membership. In the Lodge of Tranquility in 1793, "It was agreed by the Brothers the better to avoid imaginary insult if any of them inadvertently should recommend a Jew that he could not be admitted as a Brother on any pretence whatever in future." In 1796, Mount Moriah Lodge decided that "No Isrelite Should become a Member of this Lodge." Overt discrimination such as this, along with the centripetal pull of ethnic identity, spurred the creation of Jewish lodges. By the first decades of the nineteenth century, there were at least six Jewish lodges in London: Lodge of Israel No. 280, Lodge No. 253, Lodge No. 221, Lodge of Judah No. 277, Lodge of Joppa No. 319, and Hiram Lodge No. 355. Their members were drawn exclusively from the lower echelons of the Jewish commercial world. The Lodge of Judah in 1818, for example, included a hatter, a pencil-maker, a silversmith, a tobacconist, a navy agent, a slopseller, an oil merchant, a victualler, a jeweler, a watchmaker, a musician, and a self-declared "gentleman."[25]

The course of Anglo-Jewish integration was not a linear or progressive one, with each decade bringing greater opportunities for larger numbers of Jews to participate in English life. As the expansion of predominantly Jewish Masonic lodges at the end of the Georgian period indicates, the passage of time did not always bring a decrease in anti-Jewish sentiment or a substantial weakening of Jewish cohesiveness. Social prejudices against the entry of Jews into certain circles were not substantially weaker in 1800 than they were in 1750. If they had been, socially ambitious Jews would not have continued to abandon their identity to gain the acceptance of the majority society. The constant exodus of individuals from all ranks of the Jewish community over the course of the eighteenth and early nineteenth centuries testifies to the persistence of objections to the integration of Jews qua Jews into English life. The obstacles to integration that remained, however, were increasingly social ones of a snobbish nature. Unconverted Jews were not welcome as intimate members of fashionable society at any time before the Victorian period, but they were allowed to participate in an expanding number of religiously neutral charities, scientific bodies, literary circles, and reform associations. The entry of upper-middle-class Jews into these circles, as well as the expansion of social relationships between Jews and non-Jews outside respectable society, led eventually to a new self-perception on the part of many Jews about what it meant to be a Jew and a citizen of a liberal state at the same time.

9

Jewish Citizens in a Liberal State

The anglicization of the Jews in England and their integration into English life gradually produced a shift in the way Jews perceived their place within the English state. The pioneers of the Resettlement and the leading figures of the first decades of the eighteenth century, like countless generations before them, saw themselves as a distinct people, as an alien group of foreign stock. They thought of themselves as Jews first and rarely—if ever—as Englishmen, or as members of the English nation, or as citizens of the English state. Their primary allegiance was to the Jewish group because their primary sense of identity derived from membership in that group. The state protected them to a degree unparalleled elsewhere in Europe and allowed them to enjoy many of the rights of native-born Christian citizens; thus, they proclaimed their loyalty to the state. But the political life of the state—indeed, public life in general—remained a matter of little concern to them except insofar as it affected the privileges they enjoyed.

With the passage of time, this attitude toward public life began to change. From the end of the eighteenth century, many Jews of middle-class origin began to identify themselves more closely with the country in which they had been born and with its inhabitants. Their sense of identity expanded to include a sense of Englishness as well as a sense of Jewishness. This kind of identification, which eventually came to define modern Jewish consciousness everywhere in Western and Central Europe and was the product of the dual processes of acculturation and integration, has been traced in the preceding chapters. As Jews acted increasingly like Englishmen and as they multiplied their contacts with Englishmen, they began to think of themselves as Englishmen and as Jews, or, at least, they began to act as if they were no longer strangers in England but native inhabitants at ease in their homeland. The belief that life in the Diaspora was life in exile, a belief that had held sway for centuries, lost its appeal to all but a minority of the very traditional. Jews from all levels of the social hierarchy no longer behaved as if they were barely tolerated guests who dared not offend their hosts. This reorientation in Jewish self-consciousness eventually led a small minority of English Jews to demand full political emancipation.

The first three or four generations of English Jews after the Resettlement, regardless of their level of acculturation, never entertained any thoughts about belonging to the English nation. The Jewish Naturalization Bill the Anglo-Jewish elite won from the Pelham ministry in 1753 did nothing to alter the political status of the community as a whole; the benefits it conferred were economic rather than political. The factional political life of mid-century England, with its scramble for the spoils that control of the state apparatus brought, was of no interest to the magnates of Anglo-Jewry. Indeed, political involvement was seen as something that potentially threatened the security of the Jewish community. As an anonymous pamphleteer wrote in 1753, "They are the only people that can be said to be of no party, because they will offend none, lest that party which they should offend should take revenge upon them whenever the time comes that they are the prevailing party." As the legal basis for Jewish settlement in England rested on unclear and ill-defined grounds, it was thought best to avoid antagonizing any political faction. For as long as the Jews felt they had no self-evident, natural right to live and work in England like the Christian inhabitants of the country, they acted as if whatever privileges they did enjoy could be withdrawn or curtailed arbitrarily by an antagonized political foe—as if their residence in England, like that of medieval Jewish communities, was conditional on their good behavior. When a treaty was being negotiated at Paris in 1783 to bring an end to the war with the American colonies, the Board of Deputies of British Jews hesitated to send a congratulatory address to George III on the declaration of peace. It was felt that "peace or war being political concerns, addressing would be taking a part in matters we ought to avoid." They decided that an address would be proper only "when the subject relates to the King's person or family." Four years later, when the leaders of the Jewish community of Rome wrote to the Sephardi congregation in London about the possibility of settling a large number of Roman Jews in England and asked about the status of Anglo-Jewry, Bevis Marks replied in language that clearly revealed its perception of Anglo-Jewry's political position: the Jews in England enjoyed *previligios* (as opposed to rights), consisting of "the free exercise of our religion and the security of our property." As late as 1819, the bylaws of the Sephardi congregation prohibited members from taking any part in political questions or voting in elections;[1] interestingly, the prohibition was first made in 1688, the year of the Glorious Revolution.

English Jews, with a handful of exceptions, remained aloof from political activity throughout the turbulent years of the American War of Independence, the French Revolution, and the Napoleonic conquest of the Continent. At a time when ideological concerns were reanimating British political life, and hitherto politically disenfranchised groups were demanding radical reforms of the established order, Anglo-Jewish writers were reemphasizing the loyalty and the political quiescence of their coreligionists. The religious polemicist David Levi reassured his readers in 1795 that "we never enter into the political disputes of the different nations among whom we dwell, but indeavour strictly to abide by the admonition of the prophet Jeremiah, 'And seek the welfare of the city where I have sent you into exile, and pray to the Lord on its behalf, for in its welfare you will find your welfare.' [Jer. 29:7]" He strove to convince his audience that at a time when revolutionary upheaval on the Continent was bringing an end to the medieval status of the Jews, Anglo-Jewry remained firmly apolitical. Throughout the history of the Diaspora, he wrote, the Jews had never been involved "in any rebellion, sedition, or treasonable practices towards the different governments where they have resided, not withstanding the most unexampled oppressions and cruelties." The same theme was taken up by L. Cohen of Exeter in 1807 in an attack on the Sanhedrin convened by Napoleon in Paris. Cohen accused the reformers in the Sanhedrin of bargaining away the cherished religious beliefs of Judaism for French citizenship. In particular, he singled out the Sanhedrin's adoration of Napoleon as a messianic redeemer and its rejection of "our fond hopes of being reinstated to our former splendour, or greater" in the Land of Israel. The Jews of England, he maintained, who did not enjoy the status of full citizens, were better off than those in France. "We are happy under the British government as we can reasonably expect to be [while living in exile], since we enjoy here every blessing, as much as any other Jews in Europe." Cohen expressed Anglo-Jewry's loyalty to the Crown, its readiness to pay strict obedience to the laws, and its resolve not to interfere in any political matters. Isaac D'Israeli, writing in the *Monthly Magazine* in August 1807, also disavowed any sympathy on the part of English Jews for Napoleon's Jewish schemes: "After due enquiry, I can assert that the Jews in this country have never communicated with this Sanhedrim; its principles can never be those of an English Hebrew, whose shoulders were never scarred by that yoke of degrading servitude which the French, the German, and the Italian Hebrews have been doomed to endure."[2]

This emphasis on the loyalty of the Jewish community to the established order was generated by a justifiable concern for the security of the community during the decades of domestic reaction when England was at war with France and her allies. On the Continent, Jews were associated in the rhetoric of conservative writers and statesmen with the forces of revolution because the fall of the old order eventually had forced the emancipation of the Jews. In England, this association was not widespread, but it was made frequently enough to put Anglo-Jewry, already the target of an intensified xenophobia, even more on the defensive. Writing in 1830, G. R. Clarke, the historian of Ipswich, noted that in the early part of the French Revolution "the Jews were unjustly suspected of being favourable to republican opinions; and, on the 14th of September, 1793, a tablet was put up in this chapel [the synagogue in Ipswich], exhibiting, in the Hebrew language, a form of prayer for the king and royal family, evincing their attachment to their sovereign, and their anxiety to be considered as peaceable and loyal subjects of the realm." In Manchester, Portsmouth, and possibly in other provincial towns, "suspicious"

Jewish peddlers of foreign birth were deported under provisions of the Aliens Act of 1793. A number of caricatures from the period portrayed Jews as supporters of Napoleon. Cruikshank's "Easier to say than do" (1803), for example, showed Napoleon scraping England off the map with the assistance of a Dutchman, a Spaniard, and a Jew.[3]

The number of English Jews who took an active part in political life during these decades of heightened political consciousness (1770–1815) was minuscule. In addition to John King, né Jacob Rey (whose checkered career was described in Chapter 4), there appear to have been only a few Jews who showed any interest in the growing wave of democratic radicalism. In the 1790's, Emanuel Nunes Carvalho (born 1771) "identified himself with a democratic party" that favored "the American principles of government," according to a memoir written by his nephew in 1875, and as a consequence, he nearly became involved "in serious troubles." Carvalho left London in 1799 to serve as rabbi to the Sephardi congregation in Barbados. In June 1794, a government spy sent the police magistrate Patrick Colquhoun a list of fifteen persons "suspected to be inimical" to the government; among them was a Mr. Cohen, a banker's clerk. At a meeting of the Society of the Friends of the People, a moderate reform group with upper-class support, on 9 May 1792 at the London Coffee House, there was a Mr. Benjamin among the thirty-one persons present.[4] Further research might reveal another nine or ten similar examples, but even then such isolated instances hardly would permit one to speak of Jewish political activity.

This lack of interest in English political life on the part of middle-class Jews extended even to their own political status as second-class "citizens." At a time when the leaders of the Prussian and French Jewish communities were campaigning for the rights of citizenship (that is, from the 1780s through the 1810s), the Anglo-Jewish elite remained silent about the legal disabilities from which Anglo-Jewry suffered—the inability to vote (legally) in parliamentary elections, to hold municipal office, to sit in the House of Commons, to take a degree at Oxford or Cambridge, and to operate a retail business in the City of London. Indeed, the first attempts to improve the legal status of English Jews were initiated by Evangelical "philo-Semites" rather than by Jews themselves.

One possible explanation for this apparent apathy is that even anglicized Jews still felt that they constituted a separate community, living in exile in a foreign country, and that they therefore had no real interest in gaining the right to participate fully in English political life. This explanation, although certainly applicable to earlier generations of English Jews, hardly applies to the Anglo-Jewish elite at the end of the eighteenth century and after. The intensity with which well-to-do Jews went about adapting themselves to the customs and the styles of English life does not bespeak a desire for separateness and a sense of alienation. It is difficult to believe that the Anglo-Jewish upper class had any real sense of living in exile, although they may have given lip service to such a notion in their prayers. As a Jewish convert remarked in 1838, "There are very few of Abraham's descendents that really concern themselves about [the coming of the Messiah and the return to the Land of Israel]. I have heard many Jews say that they would prefer continuing to reside in this country rather than return to Judea, should the restoration take place in their days."[5] A more plausible reason for the passivity of Anglo-Jewry in regard to its own civil disabilities was the reactionary political climate of the two decades immediately following the French Revolution. Political reforms in the air in the 1770s and the 1780s had to be shelved in the 1790s when the very idea of reform became associated with treason and sedition. With Catholics and Dissenters remaining unemancipated owing to this repressive atmosphere, it would have been sheer foolhardiness to press for greater rights for the Jews at the time.

The decisive explanation for the inactivity of the Anglo-Jewish elite, however, has little to do with either Anglo-Jewry's own sense of religioethnic distinctiveness or with the general political climate, but with the character of the legal disabilities besetting Anglo-Jewry. English Jews did not suffer grievously from being second-class citizens, a status they shared in common with other non-Anglicans. England had no anti-Jewish statutes, with the exception of the City of London's ban on baptized Jews acquiring the freedom of the City. There were no laws specifically barring Jews from particular occupations, or restricting the size of Jewish settlements, or regulating the management of Jewish communal organizations, or imposing burdensome and humiliating taxes on Jews, either collectively or individually. In short, the Jews of

England were not rightless aliens who had to fight to be recognized as citizens. The legal obstacles to their acquisition of full political rights were the christological oaths required of all Englishmen who wished to participate in public life. English Jews, on the whole, had little interest in fighting these oaths because they had little interest in entering government service, the ancient universities, or the Inns of Court to study for the bar. The aspirations of most English Jews were limited to success in the world of commerce and finance. The right to sit in Parliament or to hold the office of Lord Mayor of London or to take a degree at Oxford was a luxury they could do without. As long as they were able to live and work freely without governmental harassment, they were content to leave the governing process to the traditional rulers of England. In other words, Jewish emancipation in England was not crucial to the material well-being of the Jewish community in the way it was in Germany, France, and Italy, where discriminatory statutes made the life of the Jews a difficult and often hazardous struggle for survival. The need for emancipation in England, in short, was not the same as elsewhere in Europe.

Thus, the long campaign to win for English Jews complete political emancipation (1829–58) failed to attract the active support of the bulk of Anglo-Jewry. In the early 1850s, a "Hebrew gentleman" told Henry Mayhew "that so little did the Jews themselves care for 'Jewish emancipation,' that he questioned if one man in ten, actuated solely by his own feelings, would trouble himself to walk the length of the street in which he lived to secure Baron Rothschild's admission into the House of Commons." Among the Jewish hawkers and old-clothes men Mayhew met, there was "a perfect indifference to, and nearly as perfect an ignorance of, politics." The London correspondent of a New York Jewish newspaper reported in 1850 that Anglo-Jewry as a body was "quite indifferent" about Jewish emancipation and that only a few ambitious individuals cared whether Jews could sit in Parliament. In 1841, the Bishop of London, C. J. Blomfield, told the House of Lords that he had made "many enquiries on the subject" and had found "very few of the great body of the Jewish people who cared anything at all about the success of the measure." This indifference to the outcome of the emancipation campaign was not limited to the Jewish poor and petite bourgeoisie.

Lewis Levy (1786–1856), the greatest farmer of turnpike tolls in
the 1820s and 1830s—he was known popularly as "Turnpike"
Levy and was worth £250,000 when he died—stated in a petition
to the House of Commons in April 1830 that he did not desire
to have the franchise nor to be admitted to a seat in Parliament
and that all his Jewish friends were equally indifferent. All he
asked of Parliament was that they make a declaratory law removing all doubts as to the ability of Jews to hold landed property.[6]

In addition to the indifferent majority, there was a very small
minority of observant Jews who opposed emancipation for religious reasons. This group, which was neither very vocal nor very
influential, feared that emancipation would lead to a weakening
of Jewish tradition by forcing Jews who entered public life to
violate specific religious laws. The colonial entrepreneur Moses
Levy, for example, was a vocal opponent of moves to gain political emancipation. For him, the price Jews would have to pay for
political privileges would be too great.

> Is a Jew a true Jew [he asked] when he obtains the privileges
> of a money-making citizen, or an office at the expense of the
> observance of the Sabbath? For certainly if he, as a citizen,
> accepts of an office, he must discharge its duties on Saturday
> as well as on any other day. Jews, then, who for the sake of mere
> lucre, would trample under foot this sacred command, are
> virtually no Jews; and what are they? Nothing; or mere money-
> making animals.

Levy cited evidence from Holland and France, where Jews had
been made equal citizens in the 1790s, to prove that Judaism had
suffered. True, individual Jews had prospered and attained positions of eminence in those countries, but their triumphs had in
no way benefited the Jewish community. Such persons no longer
believed in the peoplehood of Israel or in the return to Zion. In
France, "religion mournfully sits as solitary amongst them now
as it ever did, when they were considered no better than serfs."
In Holland, secularly educated Jews stayed away from the synagogue. Levy also adduced a reason for opposing emancipation
that non-Jewish opponents of equality for the Jews everywhere in
Europe always invoked: the Jews were incapable of becoming
Englishmen—they could not "amalgamate" into the English nation. It was against the laws of nature for any human being "to

have two springs of action." Just as a person could not be a
Dutchman and an Englishman at the same time, likewise a Jew
could not be an Englishman. The Hungarian-born rabbi Joseph
Crool (1760–1829), who served congregations in Manchester
and Nottingham in the first decades of the century and then
taught Hebrew in an unofficial capacity at Cambridge, opposed
the granting of political equality because it ran counter to the
traditional belief that the Jews were in exile and must await redemption in their own land at the hands of God. Like Levy, he
feared that political ambitions would seduce Jews from their
faith. In particular, he thought that the entry of Jews into Parliament and the social contacts they subsequently would establish
with Christian gentlemen would lead to their conversion. (This,
incidentally, was exactly what many Evangelicals were hoping
for.) Chief Rabbi Solomon Hirschell also had serious reservations about the advisability of greater Jewish integration into
English life and may, at heart, have been opposed to emancipation altogether, but he was too much the dependent of magnates
like Nathan Rothschild and Isaac Lyon Goldsmid to oppose their
efforts. When Goldsmid asked Hirschell in 1836 for his endorse-
ment of a tract on Jewish emancipation, Hirschell replied that it
was not within his power to take a hostile position toward it,
although he feared that those who entered government service
would be forced to transgress the commandments. The Bishop
of London reported in 1841 that "many of the higher and more
religious Jews entertain most serious doubts whether they could
receive the privileges thus to be conferred on them."[7]

Those who actively campaigned for the removal of all Jewish
disabilities were a small but influential minority within the ranks
of Anglo-Jewry. Although their first attempts to obtain parliamentary relief met with failure, they ultimately succeeded, in the
mid-Victorian period, in removing all legal barriers to Jewish
integration. For our purposes, however, the importance of these
early efforts lies less in what they eventually led to than in what
they reveal about the aspirations of emancipation's promoters at
the end of the Georgian period.

The chief promoters of Jewish emancipation in 1829 and
the early 1830s—Isaac Lyon Goldsmid, Nathan Rothschild, and
their relations and close associates—were wealthy men for whom
second-class status was hardly an affliction, at least in a material

sense. But it was an onerous burden for them in a way it was not for other Jews. Having acclimatized themselves to the life of the English upper class, having embraced many of the social and cultural concerns of other men of property, and having formed personal relationships with non-Jews, they had come to think of themselves as Englishmen as well as Jews and had come to see their fate as tied up with the fate of the English nation. Hence, public life became a matter of concern for them—as it was for other wealthy men—whereas it remained a matter of indifference to less anglicized, less wealthy, and less integrated Jews. But as the right to participate in public life was withheld from them, they found themselves marked off from their non-Jewish peers in a manner that was psychologically burdensome. They had achieved so much in the material world and had made themselves so much like other Englishmen that the remaining barriers to full participation in English life, regardless of the actual benefits their removal would confer, came to be regarded as unbearable. As Tocqueville explained in *The Old Regime and the French Revolution,* a grievance that has been patiently endured for a long time only comes to seem intolerable when the possibility of removing it occurs to men. "For the mere fact that certain abuses have been remedied draws attention to the others and they now appear more galling; people may suffer less, but their sensibility is exacerbated." From the beginning of the campaign, Isaac Lyon Goldsmid and his son Francis Henry refused to consider a piecemeal approach to Jewish emancipation because they believed such an approach implied that the Jews were content with fewer rights than Dissenters or Roman Catholics.[8] After Parliament had extended political rights to Roman Catholics in 1829, Jews remained the only politically disadvantaged religious minority. This no doubt intensified the stigma of belonging to such a group. The success of Catholic emancipation suggested to Goldsmid and his friends that the time had come to push for full rights for Jews. Unfortunately, they did not realize that the passage of Catholic emancipation was due more to a concern with political and social unrest in Ireland and, hence, with placating Irish political demands, than with any abstract enthusiasm for absolute religious equality.

The decision to promote Jewish emancipation also reflected a new awareness about the possibility of living simultaneously as

Jews and as full citizens in a liberal state. Before the 1820s, the pervasiveness of anti-Semitic stereotyping and the refusal of many circles to receive unconverted Jews warmly had convinced many socially ambitious Jews that the only way to participate fully in English society was to abandon their Jewishness altogether. Conversion, in other words, was for many the only sure road to integration. Now a small group of equally ambitious Jews was declaring that it was possible to live in England as a citizen and as a Jew without having to give up one's Jewishness. Encouraged by the success of Roman Catholic emancipation, they declared their determination to maintain their identity as Jews and at the same time to enjoy the full benefits of citizenship. Unlike previous generations of ambitious Jews, they chose to fight, rather than to retreat to the baptismal font, in order to advance their claims to acceptance. This change in the outlook of a small group of influential, well-to-do Jews was due to the increasingly liberal nature of English social structure and political culture and to the high degree of acculturation and integration they permitted. The demand for Jewish emancipation, in other words, rested on a successful record of anglicization, a degree of religious toleration unique in Europe, and a more limited, but still substantial, record of integration.

Enthusiasm for political emancipation was not the only sign that English Jews were feeling more at home in England. There were other indicators—ones that reflected the attitudes of a broader spectrum of Anglo-Jewry—that Jews were becoming more secure about their place in English society and less fearful of intolerance. Among the surest indicators of this growing sense of security was the willingness of some Jews to engage in religious disputes with Christians and the eagerness of an even wider group to defend actively the honor of the Jewish community.

In the medieval and early modern periods, Jewish leaders tried to avoid public disputations; such confrontations were usually staged by the authorities from the outset in such a way as to result in a victory for Christianity, and any meaningful rebuttal on the part of the Jews to Christian charges would, by enraging Christian sensibilities, inevitably endanger the Jewish community. Even as late as 1769, a privileged Jew like Moses Mendelssohn felt he had to refuse to reply to the challenge of the Swiss theologian Johann Caspar Lavater, because of, among other reasons, the delicate position of Prussian Jewry. As "a member of an oppressed people that had to implore the ruling nation for patronage and protection," he felt that to attack the Christian religion would be to demonstrate a lack of gratitude to the Christian rulers who protected the Jews.[9] The official leaders of Anglo-Jewry, especially the Sephardim, also exercised caution about publicly offending the sensibilities of Christians and tended at all times to discourage public defenses of Judaism or the conversion of Christians to Judaism. The Sephardim believed that at the time of the Resettlement the government had stipulated that they might not make proselytes or do anything to offend the established religion. Although no documentary evidence of any such conditions has survived, the Elders and the Mahamad believed that such stipulations had been made and acted accordingly. The first bylaws of the congregation from 1663 forbade the circumcision of non-Jewish men and the ritual immersion of non-Jewish women. They also barred Jews from disputing with Christians on religious matters, since to do so would be to "disturb the liberty which we enjoy and to make us disliked." In 1751, after a group of Norwegians had arrived in London with the intention of embracing Judaism, the Mahamad appealed to the *parnasim* of the Great Synagogue and the Hambro Synagogue to cooperate in refusing to convert them. "Being persuaded you will join with us in all things that tend to preserve our present happy toleration," Bevis Marks asked the Ashkenazi synagogues to forbid their members from assisting in these or any other conversions; whether they ever took place is unknown. In 1829, when the Sephardim were considering a number of reforms in their worship service, they hesitated to introduce English sermons out of the fear that such sermons, if they touched on doctrinal matters, might offend the Church of England. So concerned were they that this innovation might violate the conditions of the Readmission that they sought the legal opinion of Dr. Stephen Lushington (a Whig reformer, Member of Parliament, and judge of the consistory court of London) to determine whether any acts of Parliament were in force that precluded the Jews from preaching sermons in the English language. Lushington replied that there were no practical impediments to such an innovation, but he admitted that the technical legal position of Judaism was "very anomalous and difficult to be defined." Statutes embodying "antiquated principles of intolerance" had not been repealed, although they "would not now be endured by any of our Courts, and yet it is impossible to point out how or to what extent they have been modified."[10]

Ashkenazim outside the moneyed elite were far less reticent in coming to the defense of the Jewish religion. In 1787, David Levi, a learned shoemaker and hat-dresser, responded to Joseph Priestley's *Letters to the Jews* on the evidence for Christianity with a one-hundred-page defense of Judaism. Levi noted in his opening remarks that most of the learned men among the Jews had declined to answer Priestley because they were deficient in the English language and because the leaders of the community opposed Jews entering into public religious debates. Levi remarked that he saw no danger to the Jewish community in investigating theological issues in the enlightened atmosphere of his time. His willingness to speak out in defense of his religion, however, defied the accepted wisdom of the Anglo-Jewish elite. A Christian critic of the aggressive conversionary tactics of the London Society observed in 1809 that it was wrong to provoke the Jews to a discussion of religious questions since they conceived it to be their duty to decline. He explained that out of a sense of gratitude for the kind treatment they had experienced in England they avoided public debates in which they were liable to wound the feelings of their hosts. Two years later, Henry Lemoine wrote in the pages of *The Gentleman's Magazine* that the Jews were not "polemics" and were adverse "to meddle in any disputes where the religion of the country is concerned." When Levi responded to Thomas Paine's *The Age of Reform* in 1797, Lemoine wrote, "the community [i.e., its leaders] was in the greatest terror . . . fearing the civil authority or ecclesiastical law would be moved against him and bring serious consequences upon themselves." In December 1827, at a meeting to protest the persecution of Russian Jews, M. E. Levy charged that the moneyed Jews of London had absented themselves because they were too preoccupied with their own fashionable amusements and because they were "in dread of exciting any hostile feelings in persons possessed of power."[11]

David Levi's polemical defense of Judaism in the 1780s and 1790s was an isolated display of confidence in English toleration. Several decades later, many more Jews felt it was possible to enter into public disputations on religious subjects without invoking the wrath of the government or the populace. At a meeting of the Philo-Judaean Society on 8 March 1827, Selig Newman, a Hebrew teacher, debated the Rev. Joseph Woolf, an apostate, on the Hebrew proof texts for Jesus' messiahship. The majority of persons at the meeting were Jews. When Woolf made some derogatory remarks about Judaism in the course of his presentation, the Jews in the audience created an uproar, drowning out Woolf's voice and refusing to allow him to finish. At times, the chairman was able to restore order momentarily, but once the Jews in the audience were again able to hear what Woolf was saying (e.g., that the whole Jewish people were eternally damned) the uproar resumed. More harmonious were a series of weekly meetings between Evangelical Christians and Jews in 1827 and 1828, held first at Salvador House in Bishopsgate and later at the King's Head Tavern in the Poultry. The topics discussed included the interpretation of prophecy, the relationship of the oral to the written law, and the messianic passages of the Old Testament. In heated but tolerant exchanges, Jews quoted from the New Testament and Christians invoked the opinions of Maimonides. The Anglo-Jewish elite, however, remained opposed to such proceedings. In December 1829, for example, the directors of the Jews' Free School reprimanded the assistant master of the school, H. A. Henry, for attending meetings of the Philo-Judaean Society and participating in their debates.[12]

The dread with which the Anglo-Jewish elite viewed the activities of religious polemicists did not extend to a policy of total passivity in the face of hostility to Judaism. In countering the aggressive tactics of the London Society, the leaders of Anglo-Jewry demonstrated an awareness that they had a right to protect the integrity of the community from conversionary onslaughts. As mentioned earlier, when the first missionary school for Jewish children was opened in 1807, the *parnasim* of the Great Synagogue sent a delegation to Joseph Hardcastle, Treasurer of the London Missionary Society, to express their intention to thwart the Society's missionary efforts. Isaac Lyon Goldsmid protested to the Duke of Kent, the Patron of the London Society, on at least two occasions, once in April 1813 and once in December 1814, about activities of the Society that, to his mind, violated the principle of religious freedom. Goldsmid's first letter was persuasive enough for the duke to stress, at a London Society dinner in May 1813, that the Society's new facilities in Bethnal Green would be operated on a purely voluntary basis and that no attempt would be made to interfere with or offend the Jewish community.[13]

The most persuasive evidence, however, that London Jews felt free enough and secure enough to defend their honor as Jews is the treatment that street traders, shopkeepers, and artisans accorded to apostates and to missionaries. Without a thought for the sensibilities of Christians, these lower-class and lower-middle-class Jews subjected those they perceived as traitors and as enemies of their community to a barrage of physical and verbal abuse. A Mr. Cooper, who took upon himself the task of being "a proclaimer to the Jews" around 1804, "was imprudent enough to attempt an harangue in Duke's Place; the children of Israel rose upon him, tore him from his pulpit, and it was with difficulty that he escaped without personal injury." The missionary activities of the apostate Samuel Joseph Frey aroused such enmity that a Mr. Helmore, who previously had been able to distribute tracts in the streets of the Jewish quarter, began to fear for his personal safety and in 1809 had to cease his activity there. The directors of the London Society declared in 1811 that "more than once [Frey had] been endangered by a few hundred Jews of the lower order attending at the Jews' Chapel." They feared for his life, which they felt to be threatened by "the lower order of Jews."[14]

Apostates whom the London Society had converted and who continued to ally themselves with the London Society—largely for opportunistic reasons—fared even worse. Ostracized socially and deprived of employment within the Jewish community, they frequently became the targets of physical violence and harassment. In 1809, when Barnard Jacobs of Petticoat Lane visited the Jews' Chapel, his neighbors broke his windows, smashed his furniture, and swore they would murder him. For a time the London Society felt compelled to furnish him with the protection of a constable, but one day he went out into the street by himself and was soundly trounced. In 1812, when a boy who was under the protection of the London Society was assaulted in the street by a Jew, the Society circulated handbills offering a reward of £20 for the conviction of the offender.[15]

In another incident, Elizabeth Harris, a Jewess of Holywell

Street, who lived with James Tweedy, a Christian, became the target of a campaign of intimidation by her Jewish neighbors because she was, according to her sister, intimate with a Christian and had become pregnant by him. They made loud noises and knocked violently against the wall of her bedroom in order to terrify her. When she went into labor early on a Sunday morning in September 1818, they began hooting and howling in the street outside, "Now we shall have the young Tweedy." They pulled down the iron bars of the window shutters and rattled them on the stones of the street. At intervals throughout the day, they resumed the howling and the knocking. When she gave birth at about three in the afternoon, one of them called out, "Now is your time, boys, she has got a young Tweedy." The noise then became more violent than before. They continued to harass her in this manner for at least another ten days. At last they were arrested and indicted for conspiracy.[16] At no time, however, did the Jewish community as a whole suffer for the intemperate behavior of a few. Individuals were punished by the law for assault and disturbing the peace and other standard criminal offenses, but not for insulting the established religion.

Of course, not all of the energy that went into the persecution of missionaries and apostates and wayward women such as Elizabeth Harris can be attributed to a zeal for orthodoxy. The Jewish poor, as mentioned, were hardly a bastion of piety and religiosity. No doubt the possibility of settling old debts or of letting off a little steam motivated many of those who rose to the defense of the Jewish religion. In any case, the motives of Jews who challenged Christian intruders are not the issue. What is crucial is that, regardless of motivation, Jews acted in a manner that revealed no particular concern for the fact that they were threatening Christian religious interests. Their lack of restraint recalls the previously described behavior of Jewish theatergoers who raised a clamor at successive performances of Thomas Dibdin's *Family Quarrels* in 1802 because the play cast aspersions on their national character.[17] Although the London press denounced these rowdy Jews for abusing the liberties allowed to them and warned that such arrogance, if continued, would arouse a furious popular reaction, there appear to have been no untoward consequences.

The abandon that lower-class Jews displayed in persecuting their enemies was a direct reflection of the decentralized, liberal character of the English state. The policing powers of the state were incapable of restraining the petty violence of lower-class urban life. The organized Jewish community—in reality an amalgam of independent, weak, voluntaristic organizations—was powerless in controlling the behavior of any of its members. Furthermore, the Jewish poor could "insult" Christianity with impunity because the Christian rulers of England, even if they had been capable of policing the Jewish poor, were not really concerned about such "insults." The free exchange of religious ideas was becoming an established habit in the early decades of the nineteenth century. Men were at liberty to pick and choose their religious doctrines as they pleased. The principles of the unregulated marketplace of commodities were being transferred to the marketplace of religion. The world of the sacred, moreover, had lost much of its hold. Behavior that had been "insulting" to earlier generations had become a matter of indifference to their more worldly descendants.

The sense of security that underlay the brazen behavior of the Jewish poor was the functional equivalent of the sense of identification with the English nation that underlay the campaign for Jewish emancipation. Both permitted Jews to risk or demand what had been forbidden to them, what had been beyond the reach of their hands and the grasp of their imaginations for centuries. By the early decades of the nineteenth century, English Jews were beginning to behave as if they lived in England by right rather than by sufferance. No longer content with a limited toleration that guaranteed their safety in return for docility and obsequiousness, they were beginning to demand that they be treated as equal citizens in every respect. Many, indeed, were behaving as if they already enjoyed that equality. Some among the very wealthy were asking that their status be made consistent with the principles of liberalism that increasingly were coming to dominate the conduct of public policy. Their Jewishness, they were arguing, was a category of personal identification solely and, hence, a matter of no concern to the state.

10

From Tradition to Modernity

The passage from tradition to modernity for Anglo-Jewry was a multidimensional experience. For Jews born in Germany, it meant the journey, in a literal sense, from the relative calm and security of small town life to the bustling anonymity of urban life —indeed, of the greatest urban center in Europe at the time. For Jews from everywhere, it meant the journey from a quasi-autonomous corporate community, isolated culturally and socially from the surrounding population, to a decentralized Jewish community, with no legal standing in the eyes of the state, organized solely on the basis of voluntary participation. This passage from the restraints of communal control to the freedoms of a permissive and tolerant society was closely linked to another major transformation. The political setting for Jewish life was no longer the centrally directed absolutist state of Central Europe, with its interventionist regulatory impulse, but the emerging liberal state, with its guarantees of individual rights.

In religious terms, Judaism ceased to be an all-embracing civilization, a way of life, a point of orientation by which to measure all other values and activities. It became, instead, a religion— something that affected the individual English Jew in a much less definitive way than it had his ancestors. Judaism as a religion became one concern, one element, one interest among many in the lives of most English Jews.

This diminution in the impact of Judaism on the totality of

Jewish life was matched by a growing sense among many English Jews that religion per se was no longer a necessary ingredient in their lives. Many became apathetic or careless about the performance of ritual and attendance at synagogue because the world seemed to them to have become a less sacred place. If they still believed that God existed, his existence did not impinge on them in any immediate way, affecting them instead only in a very remote manner.

The modernization of Jewish life in England not only included its desacralization but a breakdown in the barriers—both self-imposed and externally erected—that had separated Jews from non-Jews. The passage from tradition to modernity meant that tradition was no longer a sufficient guide to living in the modern world. The intellectual and cultural interests of English Jews expanded to include the arts and the learning of the non-Jewish world. What had once been scorned and ignored was now pursued avidly. New forms of socializing, new modes of recreation, and new ways of seeking honor and recognition became common among rich and poor Jews alike. For the rich in particular, the desire for approval and acceptance by the non-Jewish world became a passion, at times an all-consuming desire. Within a generation in many cases, Jewish brokers and merchants transformed themselves into English country gentlemen. It is difficult to imagine a more dramatic shift in values. For centuries, Jews had sought status and honor within their own group by cultivating those attributes their culture esteemed, especially those associated with Torah-learning and piety. Now, in the absence of legal barriers to integration, they looked beyond their own group for values and ideals and nurtured hopes that their acculturation would lead to their social integration.

The disappearance or modification of traditional beliefs and practices during the Georgian period was a social transformation not confined to the Jewish community alone. Profound cultural adjustments were forced on Englishmen of all backgrounds by the rapid changes associated with the agricultural and industrial revolutions. Local customs, popular recreations, regional dialects, the remnants of pagan superstitions—all began to give way during these years to the rationalizing and homogenizing forces of modernity. Older patterns of paternalistic social behavior were weakened by the penetration into the countryside of a market economy and an individualistic capitalist ethos. Tens of thousands of men and women from the provinces poured into London in the Georgian years. Like Jewish immigrants from small towns and villages in Central Europe, they too found themselves in a startlingly harsh and unfamiliar environment and were forced to adapt themselves to new conditions in a new world.

The particularistic practices of other religious minorities in England also underwent modification as non-Anglican Christians sought a modicum of social and political acceptance and as the piety and rigor of earlier generations waned. Quakers, for example, who in the eighteenth century were sharply set apart from the rest of Englishmen by their habits, their dress, and their kinship ties, had shed their distinctive outward signs by the end of the nineteenth century. They, too, lost large numbers of members to the Established Church over the course of the nineteenth century as their wealthiest members abandoned the tight-knit family networks of Quaker society to gain status in the larger world beyond. Catholicism, a minority religion in England frequently more despised than Judaism, sought to tone down its doctrinal distinctiveness in order to gain political emancipation. English Catholics, in an attempt to convince others of their loyalty to the state, adopted a position of extreme cisalpinism, denying temporal authority to the Pope in Rome and rejecting the doctrine of papal infallibility.

For Jews, however, the passage from tradition to modernity was probably less smooth than for most other groups. It meant a transformation in every imaginable sphere of life—religious, dietary, linguistic, educational, social, political, and so on. Judaism and Jewish identity survived the transformation, but they were not what they had been in the premodern world. Only one aspect of Jewish life remained fairly constant—the occupational structure of Jewry. Despite the hopes and the pleas of Jewish modernizers, the overwhelming bulk of English Jews, and Jews elsewhere in Europe as well, remained concentrated in the world of commerce for generations. This strain of continuity, though, was untypical.

By the close of the Georgian period, Jewish life in England had been transformed more radically than elsewhere in Europe at this time. The bulk of German Jewry, Alsatian Jewry, and possibly Dutch Jewry was still traditionally inclined. The *maskilim*, reformers, and apostates of the northern European cities were the exception, not the rule. The extensive changes that occurred in England were due in part to the immigrant nature of the community. There was no ancient community in London at the beginning of the modern period, with a well-entrenched leadership and long-established customs of learning, charity, and piety. Those Jews who settled in London had already uprooted themselves from traditional communities elsewhere and were hardly predisposed to accept again the restraints of religious law and communal control. The major force, though, for the transformation of tradition at all levels of Jewish society was the unprecedented degree of toleration Jews found in Georgian England. Never before, except for the tiny Jewish communities in North America, had Jews lived with so few restraints. The state took hardly more interest in Jews than it did in other citizens. The Jewish community itself, in the sense of a corporate body with authority over the individual, simply did not exist.

English Jews abandoned tradition—or, rather, aspects of it—because they no longer found it meaningful, because they wanted to feel at home in England and mix more closely with their surroundings, and because there were no external constraints to encourage its maintenance. Their abandonment of traditional patterns was not, however, predicated on an elaborate intellectual rejection of traditional belief and on the creation of a new system of thought. There was no need, as in the German states, to convince the government that the Jewish group was capable of citizenship. There was no ongoing public campaign of public hostility to Jewish integration that called for an apologetic response. Thus, most well-to-do English Jews felt no necessity to promote a modernized form of Judaism, that is, a Judaism stripped of nationalist and irrational elements and bolstered with an overlay of abstract universalist ethics.

Whatever pressure to conform there was came not from the absence of political equality but from the lack of full social acceptability. Jews whose ambitions transcended the limits of the Jewish group undoubtedly sensed they were considered deficient in whatever was needed for gentility. Thus, some radically anglicized themselves in order to overcome their limitations, while others obviously felt that only the extreme step of conversion was capable of overcoming their alienation from the dominant group.

In one sense, then, the rapid anglicization of the community was not so much due to hostility as to the absence of hostility. For it was the possibility of moving closer to the non-Jewish world—a possibility Jews began to entertain only as obstacles to integration disappeared—that spurred on the desire for greater conformity.

The personal advantages English Jews reaped from the increasingly liberal character of English society were balanced by the threats this society posed for the survival of Judaism and the Jewish people. For if Georgian England provided welcome relief to Jews as individuals after centuries of persecution on the Continent, it did not encourage the survival of the Jewish people in a collective sense as a distinct cultural and religious group. Judaism, whether in terms of religious observance, traditional learning, theology, or modern scholarship, did not flourish in the tolerant atmosphere of eighteenth- and nineteenth-century England. Indeed, in the West it was only in Germany, where hostility was the most intense and, of course, where Jewish settlement had never been completely disrupted since its origins, that truly important contributions were made to Jewish thought. Freedom, then, was both good for the Jews and bad for the Jews at the same time. This, however, should not be a surprising conclusion. For who today still believes that history advances without ambiguity?

lots of people

Appendix, Abbreviations, Bibliography, Notes, and Index

Appendix: Statistics on Jewish Crime

The nature and extent of Jewish criminal activity in Georgian England can only be gauged in a very rough and approximate way. Most criminals in London went unapprehended, largely due to the absence of an effective police force, and many crimes went unreported, again because there was no government agency to which victims could turn for assistance. Moreover, as it fell to the victim rather than to the government to prosecute, many criminals also went free because their victims, either out of a fear of reprisal or a lack of money, failed to bring them to justice. Hence, whatever figures can be extracted from court records will reveal only a portion of the total amount of criminal activity, and probably a small portion at that.

The most complete record of criminal proceedings for London in the eighteenth and early nineteenth centuries is the series of printed volumes recording the cases tried at the Old Bailey in the City of London, *The Whole Proceedings upon the King's Commission of Oyer and Terminer and Gaol Delivery for the City of London and also the Gaol Delivery for the County of Middlesex.* Serious offenses committed in both the City of London and the County of Middlesex were tried before juries at the Old Bailey. Lesser offenses were dealt with by police magistrates, justices of the peace, and elected officials of the City of London, sitting in a variety of courts, often with overlapping jurisdictions. The records of these courts have either not survived, are not complete, or are inaccessible to the historian. Since the bulk of the Anglo-Jewish community lived and worked within the jurisdiction of the courts sitting at the Old Bailey, a very representative sampling—if not the majority—of Jewish criminals who were brought to trial in England appeared there.

Jews who appeared at the Old Bailey, either as witnesses or as defendants, were not officially designated as Jews in the published records. Thus, there is a problem in pulling out the Jewish cases. In some instances, a Jew was referred to as a Jew by a witness or an attorney, or the question of his Jewishness arose in the course of testimony (in regard to observing the Sabbath, for example, or taking an oath); I had no problem with cases such as these. In the majority of cases, however, I identified Jewish criminals by their names. (Anglo-Jewish names in the Georgian period, it should be noted, bear little resemblance to American Jewish names today.) Whenever there was a serious question regarding the Jewishness of a convicted criminal (usually when his last name was Harris or Phillips—common Anglo-Jewish names—but his first name was not distinctively Jewish) and there was no supporting material to indicate that he was Jewish (such as his occupation, his residence, or the names of his friends), I did not consider him to be Jewish. Thus, the figures below, in all likelihood, underrepresent the number of Jews convicted at the Old Bailey.

Naturally, I could not include in this study Jews who were acquitted of the crimes with which they were charged. Strictly speaking, they were not criminals. I have little doubt, however, that in many instances of acquittal the defendants were as guilty as humanly possible and that they managed to escape conviction, like mobsters and white-collar criminals today, by exploiting loopholes and technicalities in the legal system. This is one more reason that the figures below underrepresent serious crimes committed by Jews.

The figures I have arrived at do not provide a definitive picture of Jewish criminal activity. They do illustrate that Jewish crime was not inconsequential, they do provide concrete evidence to support the subjective observations of contemporaries, and they do offer a way of measuring rises and falls in the rate of Jewish criminal activity over the years.

JEWS CONVICTED AT THE OLD BAILEY

Years When Sentenced	Death	Transportation	Other (prison term, fine, whipping, etc.)	Total
1730–39	1	0	1	2
1740–49	8	6	1	15
1750–59	1	17	0	18
1760–69	1	34	1	36
1770–79	16	49	9	74
1780–89	19	44	31	94
1790–99	5	33	30	68
1800–09	5	25	16	46
1810–19	29	60	36	125
1820–29	7	84	52	143
TOTAL	92	352	177	621

The question naturally arises how these figures compare with figures for the non-Jewish population. Unfortunately, there are no figures with which to make this comparison. The only index available is that provided by J. S. Levi and G. F. J. Bergman in their popular account of Jewish convicts in Australia, *Australian Genesis: Jewish Convicts and Settlers, 1788–1850* (London, 1974). From a study of the records of convicts actually transported to the penal colonies in Australia, they conclude that out of 145,000 persons transported from 1788 to 1852 at least 1,000 were Jews. The largest number of Jewish convicts to arrive in one year— 1818—was 28 out of a total of 2,550. (Not all persons sentenced to transportation were actually sent out of England. Before 1818, more than two-thirds never got farther than the ship hulks anchored at Portsmouth and Woolwich. In the 1820s this trend reversed, and at least two-thirds were actually transported. A. G. L. Shaw, *Convicts and the Colonies: A Study of Penal Transportation from Great Britain and Ireland to Australia and Other Parts of the British Empire* [London, 1966], p. 150.)

The figures presented by Bergman and Levi indicate that Jewish crime was insignificant within the context of crime throughout the entire United Kingdom and Ireland. However, since the Jewish population was concentrated in London, such a comparison is meaningless. The only significant comparison would be one with figures for the London area alone, and such figures, as I have indicated, are not available. In one sense, it is not really important to know the actual contribution of Jews to the overall crime rate. More important is the fact that non-Jews thought it was high and that the Anglo-Jewish elite responded to accusations about Jewish criminality as if they were true.

Abbreviations

ASPS   Archives of the Spanish and Portuguese Synagogue, London

AUS   Archives of the United Synagogue, Adler House, London

CF   Colyer-Fergusson Collection, Jewish Museum, Woburn House, London

DNB   *Dictionary of National Biography*

GM   *The Gentleman's Magazine*

JH   The Jews' Hospital, Norwood Homes for Jewish Children Collection, Anglo-Jewish Archives, Mocatta Library, University College, London

JSS   *Jewish Social Studies*

LBJRE   London Board of Jewish Religious Education, Woburn House, London

LMS   London Missionary Society, Archives of the Council for World Mission, School of Oriental and African Studies, University of London

LSPCJ   London Society for Promoting Christianity among the Jews

MJHSE   *Miscellanies of the Jewish Historical Society of England*

OB   *Old Bailey Sessions Papers; or, The Whole Proceedings upon the King's Commission of Oyer and Terminer and Gaol Delivery for the City of London and also the Gaol Delivery for the County of Middlesex*

PRO   Public Record Office, London

PAAJR   *Proceedings of the American Academy for Jewish Research*

TJHSE   *Transactions of the Jewish Historical Society of England*

Bibliography

PRIMARY SOURCES

Archival Documents

Anglo-Jewish Archives, Mocatta Library, University College, London: Norwood Homes for Jewish Children Collection, minute books and visitors books of the Jews' Hospital.

Archives of the Council for World Mission, School of Oriental and African Studies, University of London: Correspondence and miscellaneous papers of the Jewish Committee of the London Missionary Society.

Archives of the Spanish and Portuguese Synagogue, London: Minute books, correspondence, and miscellaneous papers of the Elders and the Mahamad.

Archives of the United Synagogue, Adler House, London: Minute books of the Great, the Hambro, and the New Synagogues.

Board of Deputies of British Jews, Woburn House, London: Minute books of the Board of Deputies.

Bodleian Library, Oxford: Church Mission to the Jews Collection (London Society for Promoting Christianity among the Jews), minute books and certificates of candidates for the Jewish schools.

City of London Record Office: Minutes of the Sessions of the Peace, Journals of the Court of Common Council, miscellaneous papers of the Court of Common Council and the Court of Aldermen.

Greater London Record Office, Westminster: Westminster and Middlesex Sessions Papers.

Historical Society of Pennsylvania, Philadelphia: Tench Coxe MSS, correspondence with members of the Franks family.

Jewish Museum, Woburn House, London: Colyer-Fergusson Collection, scrapbooks of newspaper clippings on Anglo-Jewish history and personalities collected by Sir Thomas Colyer-Fergusson.

London Board of Jewish Religious Education, Woburn House, London: Minute books of the Jews' Free School.

Mocatta Library, University College, London: Lucien Wolf's historical notes.

Public Record Office, London: Returns of Friendly Societies (F.S.1 and F.S.2), correspondence on the Chelsea murder case (S.P. 37/8).

University College, London: Isaac Lyon Goldsmid Collection.

Printed Materials—Books and Pamphlets

An Address to the Friends of Great Britain: Occasion'd by the Debates among the People, and the "Answer to Considerations on the Bill for Naturalizing the Jews." London, 1753.

Adler, Marcus N. *Memoir of the Late Benjamin Gompertz.* London, 1865.

Adventures of that Notorious Fence and Receiver of Stolen Goods, Isaac Solomons. London, 1829.

Alexander, Alexander. *A Key to Part of the Hebrew Liturgy.* London, 1775.

Alexander, Levy. *Answer to Mr. Joshua Van Oven's Letters on the Present State of the Jewish Poor in London.* London, 1802.

———. *The Axe Laid to the Root, or, Ignorance and Superstition Evident in the Character of the Rev. S. Hirschell.* London, 1808.

———. *Hebrew Ritual and Doctrinal Explanation of the Whole Ceremonial Law, Oral and Traditional, of the Jewish Community in England and Foreign Parts.* London, 1819.

———, [and Lemoine, Henry]. *Memoirs of the Life and Commercial Connections of the late Benj. Goldsmid, Esq., of Roehampton.* London, 1808.

Allen, John. *Modern Judaism, or a Brief Account of the Opinions, Traditions, Rites, and Ceremonies of the Jews in Modern Times.* London, 1816.

Ambler, Charles. *Reports of Cases Argued and Determined in the High Court of Chancery.* 2nd ed. London, 1828.

Anichini, P. *A Few Remarks on the Expediency and Justice of Emancipating the Jews.* London, 1829.

An Answer to the "Considerations on the Bill to Permit Jews to be Naturalized." n.p., [1753].

An Apology for the Naturalization of the Jews. London, 1753.

Archaicus [pseud.]. *Admonitions from Scripture and History, from Religion and Common Prudence, Relating to the Jews.* London, 1753.

Austin, William. *Letters from London Written during the Years 1802 & 1803.* Boston, 1804.

Azulai, Haim Yosef David. *Sefer maagal tov* [The Good Path]. Edited by Aron Freimann. Jerusalem, 1934.

Badcock, John. *A Living Picture of London for 1828.* London, 1828.

———[Jon Bee]. *Slang: A Dictionary of the Turf, the Ring, the Chase, the Pit, of Bon-Ton, and the Varieties of Life.* London, 1823.

Ballard, Joseph. *England in 1815.* Boston and New York, 1913.

Bat Yisrael [pseud.]. *Letter to Mr. Frey.* London, 1810.

Bennett, Solomon. *Netzah Yisrael: The Constancy of Israel.* London, 1812.

———. *The Present Reign of the Synagogue of Duke's Place Displayed.* London, 1818.

Blizard, William. *Desultory Reflections on Police, with an Essay on Preventing Crimes and Amending Criminals.* London, 1785.

Boaden, James. *Memoirs of the Life of John Philip Kemble.* 2 vols. London, 1825.

Borrow, George. *Lavengro.* London, 1904.

Boswell, James. *The Life of Samuel Johnson, LL.D.* London, 1867.

Brayley, E. W.; Brewer, J. N.; and Nightingale, J. *A Topographical and Historical Description of London and Middlesex.* 5 vols. London, 1810–1816.

Britannia [pseud.]. *An Appeal to the Throne against the Naturalization of the Jewish Nation.* London, 1753.

Browne, Halblot Knight [Camden Pelham]. *The Chronicles of Crime, or, The New Newgate Calendar.* 2 vols. London, 1891.

By-stander [pseud.]. *A True State of the Case Concerning the Good or Evil which the Bill for the Naturalization of the Jews May Bring upon Great Britain.* London, 1753.

The Case of Mr. Anthony Da Costa with the Russia Company. [London], 1728.

Cibber, Theophilus. *The Harlot's Progress.* London, 1733.

Clarke, G. R. *The History and Description of the Town and Borough of Ipswich.* Ipswich and London, 1830.

Clegg, W. *The History and Conversion of Samuel Harris.* Bradford, 1833.

Cobbett, William. *Rural Rides.* Edited by George Woodcock. Baltimore, 1967.

[Cochrane, Charles]. *Journal of a Tour Made by Senor Juan de Vega, the Spanish Minstrel of 1828–29, through Great Britain and Ireland.* 2 vols. London, 1830.

Cohen, L. *Torat Emet: Sacred Truths Addressed to the Children of Israel Residing in the British Empire, containing Strictures on the Book Entitled, The New Sanhedrin, and Observations on some of the Proceedings of the Grand Sanhedrin.* Exeter, [ca. 1807].

Cohen, Shalom ben Jacob. *Elements of Faith for the Use of Jewish Youth.* Translated by Joshua Van Oven. London, 1815.

Coleridge, Samuel Taylor. *Collected Letters of Samuel Taylor Coleridge.* Edited by Earl Leslie Griggs. 6 vols. Oxford, 1966–71.

A Collection of the Best Pieces in Prose and Verse Against the Naturalization of the Jews. London, 1753.

Colquhoun, Patrick. *A Treatise on the Commerce and Police of the River Thames.* London, 1800.

———. *A Treatise on the Police of the Metropolis.* 5th ed. London, 1797.

Corry, John. *A Satirical View of London.* 2nd ed. London, 1803.

The Crisis, or, an Alarm to Britannia's True Protestant Sons. London, 1754.

A Daughter of Israel [pseud.]. *The Jewish Preceptress, or, Elementary Lessons*

Written Chiefly for the Use of the Female Children Educated at the Jews Hospital. London, 1818.

Defoe, Daniel. *A Tour Thro' the Whole Island of Great Britain.* 2 vols. Edited by G. D. H. Cole. London, 1927.

Dibdin, Thomas. *The Reminiscences of Thomas Dibdin.* 2 vols. London, 1827.

Dickens, Charles. *The Letters of Charles Dickens.* Edited by Madeline House and Graham Storey. 3 vols. to date. Oxford, 1965–.

––––––. *Sketches by Boz.* London, 1866.

[D'Israeli, Isaac]. *The Genius of Judaism.* London, 1833.

––––––. *Vaurien, or, Sketches of the Times.* 2 vols. London, 1797.

Dowling, Frank R. *Fistiana, or, The Oracle of the Ring.* London, 1841.

Edgeworth, Maria. *Letters from England, 1813–1844.* Edited by Christina Calvin. Oxford, 1971.

Egan, Pierce. *Boxiana.* 5 vols. London, 1812–29.

The Encyclopedia of Wit. London, 1804.

An English Israelite [pseud.]. *A Letter to the Parisian Sanhedrin.* London, 1808.

Espinasse, Isaac. *Reports of Cases Argued and Ruled at Nisi Prius in the Courts of King's Bench and Common Pleas.* 6 vols. London, 1793–1807.

An Essay on the Commercial Habits of the Jews. London, 1809.

The Expediency of a General Naturalization of Foreign Protestants and Others. London, 1751.

Faudel, Henry. *A Brief Investigation into the System of the Jews' Hospital.* London, 1844.

[Feltham, John]. *The Picture of London for 1813.* 14th ed. London, 1813.

Ferguson, James, ed. *The British Essayists.* 45 vols. London, 1819.

Fielding, Henry. *The Works of Henry Fielding.* 10 vols. London, 1806.

Francis, John. *Chronicles and Characters of the Stock Exchange.* Boston, 1850.

Frey, Joseph Samuel C. F. *Narrative of the Rev. Joseph Samuel C. F. Frey.* 4th ed. New York, 1817.

Goldsmid, Francis Henry. *Remarks on the Civil Disabilities of British Jews.* London, 1830.

Gooch, Elizabeth Sarah Villa Real. *The Life of Mrs. Gooch.* 3 vols. in 1. London, 1792.

Goodman, Tobias. *An Address to the Committee of the London Society for Promoting Christianity among the Jews.* London, 1809.

––––––. *Emunat Yisrael: The Faith of Israel.* London, 1834.

Grégoire, Henri. *An Essay on the Physical, Moral, and Political Reformation of the Jews.* London, 1791.

Grove, Joseph. *A Reply to the Famous Jew Question.* London, 1754.

Haggard, John. *Reports of Cases in the Consistory Court of London Containing the Judgments of Sir William Scott.* 2 vols. London, 1822.

Hanway, Jonas. *A Review of the Proposed Naturalization of the Jews.* London, 1753.

Henderson, Andrew. *The Case of the Jews Considered.* London, 1753.

Hershkowitz, Leo, and Meyer, Isidore S., eds. *The Lee Max Friedman*

Collection of American Jewish Colonial Correspondence: Letters of the Franks Family, 1733–1748. Waltham, Mass., 1968.

Highmore, Anthony. *Philanthropia Metropolitana: A View of the Charitable Institutions Established in and near London, Chiefly during the Last Twelve Years.* London, 1822.

———. *Pietas Londinensis.* 2 vols. London, 1810.

Home, Henry. *An Introduction to the Art of Thinking.* 4th ed. Edinburgh, 1789.

Hone, William. *The Everyday Book and Table Book.* 3 vols. London, 1826–41.

Howitt, William. *The Northern Heights of London.* London, 1869.

Hurwitz, Hyman. *Elements of the Hebrew Language.* London, 1807.

———. *A Grammar of the Hebrew Language.* 4th ed. London, 1850.

———. *Hebrew Tales: Selected and Translated from the Writings of the Ancient Hebrew Sages, to which is prefixed an Essay on the Uninspired Literature of the Hebrews.* London, 1826.

J. E., Gent. [pseud.]. *Some Considerations on the Naturalization of the Jews.* London, 1753.

Jackson, William. *The New and Complete Newgate Calendar, or, Malefactor's Universal Register.* 2nd ed. 8 vols. London, 1818.

The Jews Impartially Consider'd. London, 1754.

John Bull [pseud.]. *The Laughing Philosopher.* London, 1825.

Kidd, William. *London and Its Dangers.* London, [ca. 1835].

King, Richard. *The Complete Modern London Spy.* London, 1781.

———. *The Frauds of London Detected.* London, n.d.

Knapp, Andrew, and Baldwin, William. *The New Newgate Calendar.* 5 vols. London, 1826.

Lamb, Charles. *Essays of Elia.* 1st series. New York, 1845.

Laws of the Great Synagogue, Duke's Place, London. London, 1827.

A Letter Addressed to the Overseers of the Portugueze Jewish Synagogue, in Bevis-marks, London, upon Their Extraordinary Conduct in the Dispute between Mr. Ximenes and Mr. Joshua Lara. London, 1772.

A Letter to the Publick on the Act for Naturalizing the Jews. London, 1753.

Levi, David. *A Defense of the Old Testament, in a Series of Letters Addressed to Thomas Paine.* London, 1798.

———. *Letters to Dr. Priestly in Answer to Those He Addressed to the Jews.* London, 1787.

———. *A Succinct Account of the Rites and Ceremonies of the Jews.* London, 1783.

The Life and Exploits of Ikey Solomons. London, 1829.

Locke, John. *The Works of John Locke.* 10 vols. London, 1823.

Loewe, Louis L., ed. *Diaries of Sir Moses and Lady Montefiore.* 2 vols. London, 1890.

The London Guide and Stranger's Safeguard against the Cheats, Swindlers, and Pickpockets that Abound within the Bills of Mortality. London, 1818.

London Society for Promoting Christianity among the Jews. *Historical*

Notices of the London Society for Promoting Christianity among the Jews.
London, 1850.

————. *The Obligations of Christians to Attempt the Conversion of the Jews.* 2nd
ed. London, n.d.

————. *Report of the Committee to the First Half Yearly Meeting of the London
Society for Promoting Christianity among the Jews.* London, 1809.

A Looking-Glass for the Jews, or, The Credulous Unbelievers. London, 1753.

Lyon, Angel [pseud.]. *A Letter from Angel Lyon to the Right Honourable Lord
George Gordon on Wearing Beards.* London, 1789.

Lysons, Daniel. *The Environs of London: An Historical Account of the Towns,
Villages, and Hamlets within Twelve Miles of the Capital.* 6 vols. London,
1792–1811.

Macaulay, Thomas Babington. *The Letters of Thomas Babington Macaulay.*
Edited by Thomas Pinney. 3 vols. to date. Cambridge, 1974–.

Malcolm, James Peller. *Anecdotes of the Manners and Customs of London
during the Eighteenth Century.* London, 1808.

Marks, David Woolf, and Löwy, Albert. *Memoir of Sir Francis Henry Goldsmid, Bart., Q.C., M.P.* London, 1879.

Marks, E. P. *The Key to the Sacred Language.* London, 1818.

Marks, Henry John. *Narrative of H. J. Marks, formerly a Jew, now a Follower
of the Lord Jesus Christ.* London, 1838.

Mayhew, Henry. *London Labour and the London Poor.* 3 vols. London, 1851.

Mears, Abraham [Gamaliel ben Pedahzur]. *The Book of Religion, Ceremonies, and Prayers of the Jews, as Practiced in their Synagogues and Families.*
London, 1738.

Mendoza, Daniel. *Memoirs of the Life of Daniel Mendoza.* Edited by Paul
Magriel. London, 1951.

Miles, W. A. *Poverty, Mendicity, and Crime.* Edited by H. Brandon. London,
1839.

Mills, John. *The British Jews.* London, 1853.

[Mocatta, Jacob]. *An Appeal to the Elders of the Spanish and Portuguese Jews.*
London, [ca. 1800].

Moritz, Carl Philip. *Journeys of a German in England in 1782.* Translated
and edited by Reginald Nettel. London, 1965.

*The Motives to the Senseless Clamour against the Act concerning Jews Exposed and
the Act Set in a True Light.* London, 1753.

Mottley, John [Robert Seymour]. *A Survey of the Cities of London and Westminster.* 2 vols. London, 1734–35.

Murphy, Arthur. *The Works of Arthur Murphy.* 7 vols. London, 1786.

Nichols, John. *Illustrations of the Literary History of the Eighteenth Century.* 8
vols. London, 1817–58.

Norris, Henry Handley. *The Origins, Progress, and Existing Circumstances of
the London Society for Promoting Christianity Amongst the Jews.* London,
1825.

Oldenburg, Henry. *The Correspondence of Henry Oldenburg.* Edited by A.
Rupert Hall and Marie Boas Hall. 9 vols to date. Madison, Wis.,
1965–.

The Other Side of the Question: A Collection of What Hath Yet Appeared in Defence of the Late Act in Favour of the Jews. London, 1753.

Parker, George. *A View of Society and Manners in High and Low Life.* 2 vols. London, 1781.

Pasquin, P. P. *Jewish Conversion: A Christanical Farce.* London, 1814.

A Peep into the Synagogue, or a Letter to the Jews. London, n.d.

Pellatt, Apsley. *Brief Memoir of the Jews in Relation to their Civil and Municipal Disabilities.* London, 1829.

Pereira, Moses Gomez. *The Jew's Appeal on the Divine Mission of Richard Brothers and N. B. Halhed, Esq., to Restore Israel and Rebuild Jerusalem.* London, 1795.

Perseverans [pseud.]. *A Letter to the English Israelite.* London, 1809.

Pettigrew, Thomas Joseph. *Memoirs of the Life and Writings of the Late John Coakley Lettsom.* 3 vols. London, 1817.

Phillips, Richard. *Modern London: The History of the Present State of the British Metropolis.* London, 1804.

Philo-Judaean Society. *The First Report of the Philo-Judaean Society.* London, 1827.

———. *The Second Annual Report of the Philo-Judaean Society.* London, 1828.

———. *The Third Annual Report of the Philo-Judaean Society.* London, 1829.

Philo Judaeis [pseud.]. *A Letter to Abraham Goldsmid, Esq., Containing Strictures on Mr. Joshua Van Oven's Letters on the Present State of the Jewish Poor.* London, 1802.

Philo-Patriae [pseud.]. *Considerations on the Bill to Permit Persons Professing the Jewish Religion to be Naturalized by Parliament, in Several Letters from a Merchant in Town to his Friend in the Country.* London, 1753.

———. *Further Considerations on the Act to Permit Persons Professing the Jewish Religion to be Naturalized by Parliament, in a Second Letter from a Merchant in Town to his Friend in the Country.* London, 1753.

The Proceedings at Large in the Arches Court of Canterbury between Mr. Jacob Mendes Da Costa and Mrs. Catharine Da Costa Villa Real. London, 1734.

Pughe, William Owen [David Hughson]. *London: An Accurate History and Description of the British Metropolis and its Neighbourhood.* 6 vols. London, 1805–9.

Reasons against the Bill Now Depending in Parliament, Intituled, A Bill for Inlarging and Regulating the Trade to the Levant Seas. [London], 1744.

Reasons Offered to the Consideration of Parliament for Preventing the Growth of Judaism. London, n.d.

[Reid, William Hamilton]. *The New Sanhedrin, and Causes and Consequences of the French Emperor's Conduct Towards the Jews.* London, 1807.

Report of the Proceedings at the Late Public Meeting of the Jews. London, 1827.

Ricardo, David. *The Works and Correspondence of David Ricardo.* Edited by Piero Sraffa. Cambridge, 1951–. Vol. 10, Biographical Miscellany, 1955.

[Romaine, William]. *An Answer to a Pamphlet Entitled, "Considerations on the Bill to Permit Persons Professing the Jewish Religion to be Naturalized."* London, 1753.

———. *A Full Answer to a Fallacious Apology Artfully Circulated through the Kingdom in Favour of the Naturalization of the Jews.* 2nd. ed. London, 1753.

———. *A Modest Apology for the Citizens and Merchants of London who Petitioned the House of Commons against Naturalizing the Jews.* London, 1753.

Roth, Cecil, ed. *Anglo-Jewish Letters, 1158–1917.* London, 1938.

Rules and Regulations for the Management of the Jews' Hospital, Mile End. London, 1808.

Rules Framed for the Management of the Orphan Charity School, Known by the Name of Hevra Kadisha Talmud Torah, Belonging to the German Jews. London, 1788.

Rutt, John Towill. *Life and Correspondence of Joseph Priestley.* 2 vols. London, 1831–32.

Sailman, M. *The Mystery Unfolded.* London, 1817.

Samuel, Moses. *An Address from an Israelite to the Missionary Preachers.* Liverpool, 1827.

———. *Memoirs of Moses Mendelssohn, the Jewish Philosopher, including the Celebrated Correspondence on the Christian Religion with J. C. Lavater, Minister of Zurich.* 2nd. ed. London, 1827.

Saussure, César de. *A Foreign View of England in the Reigns of George I and George II: The Letters of Monsieur César de Saussure to his Family.* Translated and edited by Madame Van Muyden. London, 1902.

Silliman, Benjamin. *A Journal of Travels in England, Holland, and Scotland.* 3rd ed. 3 vols. New Haven, Conn., 1820.

Sketch of a Speech Delivered by the President at the Second General Meeting of the Subscribers to the New Spanish and Portuguese Jews Charity School on July 1, 1821. [London, 1821].

Smeeton, George. *Doings in London, or, Day and Night Scenes of the Frauds, Frolics, Manners, and Depravities of the Metropolis.* 10th ed. London, n.d.

de Sola, Abraham. *Biography of David Aaron de Sola.* Philadelphia, 1863/64.

Southey, Robert [Don Manuel Alvarez Espriella]. *Letters from England.* 3 vols. 2nd ed. London, 1808.

———. *Selections from the Letters of Robert Southey.* Edited by J. W. Warter. 4 vols. London, 1856.

Stanhope, Philip Dormer. *The Letters of Philip Dormer Stanhope, 4th Earl of Chesterfield.* Edited by Bonamy Dobree. 6 vols. New York, 1968.

Starkie, Thomas. *Reports of Cases Determined at Nisi Prius in the Courts of King's Bench and Common Pleas.* 3 vols. London, 1817–23.

Stirling, A. M. W. *The Letter-Bag of Lady Elizabeth Spencer-Stanhope.* 2 vols. London, 1913.

Swanston, Clement Tudway. *Reports of Cases Argued and Determined in the High Court of Chancery.* 3 vols. London, 1821–27.

Tacitus [pseud.]. *Copy of a Letter Taken Out of the Whitehall Journal, Tuesday, January 1, 1722–23.* London, 1723.

Tama, Diogene. *Transactions of the Parisian Sanhedrin.* Translated and with an introduction by F. D. Kirwan [pseud.]. London, 1807.

Tegg, Thomas. *The Rise, Progress, and Termination of the O. P. War.* London, 1810.

Toland, John. *Reasons for Naturalizing the Jews in Great Britain and Ireland.* London, 1714.

Tovey, D'Blossiers. *Anglia-Judaica, or, The History and the Antiquities of the Jews in England.* Oxford, 1738.

The Trial of John Kinnear, Lewis Levy, and Mozely Woolf, Indicted with John Meyer and others, for a Conspiracy. London, 1819.

A Trip from St. James's to the Royal Exchange. London, 1744.

Tucker, Josiah. *A Letter to a Friend Concerning Naturalizations.* London, 1753.

—————. *Reflections on the Expediency of Opening the Trade to Turkey.* London, 1753.

—————. *A Second Letter to a Friend Concerning Naturalizations.* London, 1753.

The Universal Songster, or, Museum of Mirth. 3 vols. London, 1834.

Van Oven, Barnard. *An Appeal to the British Nation on Behalf of the Jews.* London, [ca. 1830].

—————. *Emancipation of the Jews.* London, 1830.

Van Oven, Joshua. *Letters on the Present State of the Jewish Poor in the Metropolis.* London, 1802.

—————. *A Manual of Judaism.* London, 1835.

Wade, John. *A Treatise on the Police and Crimes of the Metropolis.* London, 1829.

Walpole, Horace. *Memoirs of the Reign of King George II.* 3 vols. London, 1846.

—————. *The Yale Edition of Horace Walpole's Correspondence.* Edited by W. S. Lewis. 39 vols. to date. New Haven, Conn., 1937–.

Wendeborn, Frederick Augustus. *A View of England Towards the Close of the Eighteenth Century.* 2 vols. London, 1791.

[Westmacott, C.M.] *The English Spy.* 2 vols. London, 1825–26.

Weston, Edward. *Some Reflections upon the Question Relating to the Naturalization of Jews, Considered as a Point of Religion.* London, 1754.

The Whole Proceedings upon the King's Commission of Oyer and Terminer and Gaol Delivery for the City of London and also the Gaol Delivery for the County of Middlesex. 76 vols. London, 1729–1834.

Winstanley, Thomas. *A Sermon Preached at the Parish-Church of St. George, Hanover Square, Sunday, October 28, 1753.* London, 1753.

Witherby, Thomas. *An Attempt to Remove Prejudices Concerning the Jewish Nation by Way of Dialogue.* 2 parts. London, 1803–4.

—————. *A Vindication of the Jews, by Way of Reply to the Letter Addressed by Perseverans to the English Israelite.* London, 1809.

Wraxall, Nathaniel William. *The Historical and the Posthumous Memoirs of Sir Nathaniel William Wraxall, 1772–1784.* Edited by Henry B. Wheatley. 5 vols. London, 1884.

Zeh ha-kuntras nikra olam hadash olam hafukh [A New World, A World Turned Upside Down]. London, 1789.

Printed Materials—Newspapers and Journals

The Annals of Sporting and Fancy Gazette.
The Annual Register.
Cobbett's Weekly Political Register.
The Eccentric Magazine.
The Gentleman's Magazine.
The Hebrew Intelligencer.
The Jewish Chronicle.
The Jewish Expositor and Friend of Israel.
The Jewish Repository.
The London Gazette.
London Magazine.
The Monthly Magazine.
The Monthly Mirror.
The Monthly Repository.
The Morning Chronicle.
The New Wonderful Museum and Extraordinary Magazine.
The Observor.
The St. James Chronicle.
The Times.
The Universal Magazine.
The Voice of Jacob.
The World.

SECONDARY WORKS

Anglo-Jewish History

Abrahams, Dudley. "Jew Brokers of the City of London." *MJHSE* 3 (1937): 80–94.

Adler, Elkan Nathan. *London.* Jewish Communities Series of the Jewish Publication Society. Philadelphia, 1930.

Barnett, Arthur. "Solomon Bennett, 1761–1838, Artist, Hebraist and Controversialist." *TJHSE* (1951–52): 91–111.

———. *The Western Synagogue through Two Centuries, 1761–1961.* With a foreward by Cecil Roth. London, 1961.

Barnett, Lionel D., ed. *Bevis Marks Records: Contributions to the History of the Spanish and Portuguese Congregation of London.* Pt. 1. London, 1940.

———, ed. *El Libro de los Acuerdos: The Records and Accompts of the Spanish and Portuguese Synagogue of London from 1663 to 1681.* Oxford, 1931.

Barnett, Richard D. "The Correspondence of the Mahamad of the Spanish and Portuguese Congregation of London during the Seventeenth and Eighteenth Centuries." *TJHSE* 20 (1959–61): 1–50.

———. "Haham Meldola and Hazan de Sola." *TJHSE* 21 (1962–67): 1–38.

————. "Samuel Montefiore's Diary." In *Explorations: An Annual on Jewish Themes,* edited by Murray Mindlin. London, 1967.

Bermant, Chaim. *The Cousinhood.* New York, 1971.

Cohen, Abraham. *An Anglo-Jewish Scrapbook, 1600–1840: The Jew through English Eyes.* London, 1943.

Cohen, Norman. "Non-religious Factors in the Emergence of the Chief Rabbinate." *TJHSE* 21 (1962–67): 304–13.

Cranfield, G. A. "The London Evening Post and the Jew Bill of 1753." *The Historical Journal* 8 (1965): 16–30.

Diamond, A. S. "Problems of the London Sephardi Community, 1720–1733—Philip Carteret Webb's Notebooks." *TJHSE* 21 (1962–67): 39–63.

Duschinsky, Charles. *The Rabbinate of the Great Synagogue, London, from 1756–1842.* 1921. Reprint. Westmead, Farnborough, Hants., 1971.

Emanuel, Charles H. L. *A Century and a Half of Jewish History: Extracted from the Minute Books of the London Committee of Deputies of British Jews.* London, 1910.

Emden, Paul H. "The Brothers Goldsmid and the Financing of the Napoleonic Wars." *TJHSE* 14 (1935–39): 225–46.

————. *Jews of Britain: A Series of Biographies.* London, 1944.

Ettinger, Shmuel. "Yehudim ve-Yahadut be-einei ha-Deistim ha-Angliim be-meah ha-shmoneh-esrei" [Jews and Judaism in the Eyes of the English Deists in the Eighteenth Century]. *Zion* 29 (1964): 182–207.

Finberg, Hilda F. "Jewish Residents in Eighteenth Century Twickenham." *TJHSE* 16 (1945–51): 129–35.

Finestein, Israel. "Anglo-Jewish Opinion during the Struggle for Emancipation (1828–58)." *TJHSE* 20 (1959–61): 113–43.

Fisch, Harold. *The Dual Image: The Figure of the Jew in English and American Literature.* New York, 1971.

Gaster, Moses. *History of the Ancient Synagogue of the Spanish and Portuguese Jews.* London, 1901.

Glassman, Bernard. *Anti-Semitic Stereotypes without Jews: Images of the Jews in England, 1290–1700.* Detroit, 1975.

Goodman, Paul. *Moses Montefiore.* Philadelphia, 1925.

Henriques, H. S. Q. *The Return of the Jews to England: A Chapter in the History of English Law.* London, 1905.

Henriques, Ursula. "The Jewish Emancipation Controversy in Nineteenth Century Britain." *Past & Present,* no. 40 (July 1968): 126–46.

Huhner, Leon. "David L. Yulee, Florida's First Senator." *Publications of the American Jewish Historical Society* 25 (1917): 1–29.

————. "Moses Elias Levy, An Early Florida Pioneer and the Father of Florida's First Senator." *The Florida Historical Quarterly* 19 (1941): 319–45.

Hyamson, Albert M. *The London Board for Shechita, 1804–1954.* London, 1954.

————. *The Sephardim of England: A History of the Spanish and Portuguese Jewish Community. 1492–1951.* London, 1951.

Isaacs, Gerald Rufus. *Rufus Isaacs: First Marquess of Reading.* New York, 1940.

Jewish Historical Society of England. *Migration and Settlement: Proceedings of the Anglo American Jewish Historical Conference . . . July 1970.* London, 1971.

Kobler, Franz. *The Vision Was There: A History of the British Movement for the Restoration of the Jews to Palestine.* London, 1956.

Krusin, Henry M. *History of the Lodge of Tranquility.* London, 1937.

Landa, Myer J. "Kitty Villareal, the Da Costas and Samson Gideon." *TJHSE* 13 (1932–35): 271–91.

Levin, Salmond S. "The Origins of the Jews' Free School." *TJHSE* 19 (1955–59): 97–114.

Lipman, Vivian D., ed. *Three Centuries of Anglo-Jewish History: A Volume of Essays.* London, 1961.

Marcus, Jacob Rader. "Shed a Tear for a Transport: The Sad Fate of Feibel, the son of Joseph Jacob of Jever." In *Raphael Mahler Jubilee Volume.* Edited by Shmuel Yeivin. Merhavia, Israel, 1974.

Patinkin, Don. "Mercantilism and the Readmission of the Jews to England." *Jewish Social Studies* 8 (1946): 161–78.

Perry, Thomas W. *Public Opinion, Propaganda, and Politics in Eighteenth Century England: A Study of the Jew Bill of 1753.* Cambridge, Mass., 1962.

Picciotto, James. *Sketches of Anglo-Jewish History.* Edited by Israel Finestein. London, 1956.

Rosenberg, Edgar. *From Shylock to Svengali: Jewish Stereotypes in English Fiction.* Palo Alto, Calif., 1960.

————. *Tabloid Jews and Fungoid Scribblers.* New York, 1972.

Roth, Cecil. *Essays and Portraits in Anglo-Jewish History.* Philadelphia, 1962.

————. *The Great Synagogue, London, 1690–1940.* London, 1950.

————. *A History of the Jews in England.* 3rd ed. Oxford, 1964.

————. "The Lesser London Synagogues of the Eighteenth Century." *MJHSE* 3 (1937): 1–7.

————. *The Rise of Provincial Jewry: The Early History of the Jewish Communities in the English Countryside, 1740–1840.* London, 1950.

Rubens, Alfred. *Anglo-Jewish Portraits: A Biographical Catalogue of Engraved Anglo-Jewish and Colonial Portraits from the Earliest Times to the Accession of Queen Victoria.* London, 1935.

————. "Anglo-Jewry in Caricature, 1780–1850." *TJHSE* 23 (1969–70): 96–101.

————. *A Jewish Iconography.* London, 1954.

————. "Portrait of Anglo-Jewry, 1656–1836." *TJHSE* 19 (1955–59): 13–52.

Samuel, Edgar R. "Dr. Meyer Schomberg's Attack on the Jews of London." *TJHSE* 20 (1959–61): 83–111.

Shaftesley, John M. "Jews in Regular English Freemasonry, 1717–1860." *TJHSE* 25 (1973–75): 150–69.

————. *The Lodge of Israel No. 205, 1793–1968.* London, 1968.

————, ed. *Remember the Days: Essays on Anglo-Jewish History Presented to Cecil Roth.* London, 1966.

Sharot, Stephen. "Secularization, Judaism, and Anglo-Jewry." *A Sociological Yearbook of Religion in Britain* 4 (1971): 121–40.

Stein, Siegfried. *The Beginnings of Hebrew Studies at University College.* London, 1952.

————. "Some Ashkenazi Charities in London at the End of the 18th and the Beginning of the 19th Centuries." *TJHSE* 20 (1959–61): 63–81.

Susser, Bernard. "Social Acclimatization of Jews in Eighteenth and Nineteenth Century Devon." In *Industry and Society in the South-West,* edited by Roger Burt. Exeter, 1970.

Sutherland, Lucy Stuart. "Samson Gideon: Eighteenth Century Jewish Financier." *TJHSE* 17 (1951–52): 79–90.

Tobias, J. J. *Prince of Fences: The Life and Crimes of Ikey Solomons.* London, 1975.

Van der Veen, H. R. S. *Jewish Characters in Eighteenth Century England.* 1935. Reprint. New York, 1972.

Vereté, Meir. "Raayon shivat Yisrael ba-mahshavah ha-Protestantit be-Angliyah ba-shanim 1790–1840" [The Idea of the Restoration of Israel in Protestant Thought in England, 1790–1840]. *Zion* 33 (1968): 145–79.

Wilensky, Mordecai. *Shivat ha-Yehudim le-Angliyah be-meah ha-sheva esreh* [The Return of the Jews to England in the Seventeenth Century]. Jerusalem, 1943.

Williams, Bill. *The Making of Manchester Jewry, 1740–1875.* Manchester, 1976.

Wolf, Lucien. *Essays in Jewish History.* Edited by Cecil Roth. London, 1934.

————. *Manasseh ben Israel's Mission to Oliver Cromwell.* London, 1901.

Woolf, Maurice. "Joseph Salvador, 1716–1786." *TJHSE* 21 (1962–67): 104–37.

Zimmels, H. J.; Rabbinowitz, J.; and Finestein, Israel, eds. *Essays Presented to Chief Rabbi Israel Brodie on the Occasion of his Seventieth Birthday.* 2 vols. Jews' College Publications, New Series, no. 3. London, 1967.

English History

Albert, William. *The Turnpike Road System in England, 1663–1840.* Cambridge, 1972.

Atherton, Herbert M. *Political Prints in the Age of Hogarth: A Study of the Ideographic Representation of Politics.* Oxford, 1974.

Babington, Anthony. *A House in Bow Street: Crime and the Magistracy, London, 1740–1881.* London, 1969.

Beattie, J. M. "The Criminality of Women in Eighteenth Century England." *Journal of Social History* 8 (1975): 80–116.

———. "The Pattern of Crime in England, 1660–1800." *Past & Present*, no. 62 (February 1974): 47–95.

Best, G. F. A. "Popular Protestantism in Victorian Britain." In *Ideas and Institutions of Victorian Britain: Essays in Honour of George Kitson Clark*, edited by Robert Robson. London, 1967.

———. *Temporal Pillars: Queen Anne's Bounty, the Ecclesiastical Commissioners, and the Church of England.* Cambridge, 1964.

Blake, Robert. *Disraeli.* New York, 1968.

Capp, B. S. *The Fifth Monarchy Men: A Study in Seventeenth Century Millenarianism.* London, 1972.

Clifford, James L., ed. *Man versus Society in Eighteenth Century Britain.* Cambridge, 1968.

Cohn, Norman. *The Pursuit of the Millennium.* London, 1970.

Curtis, L. P., Jr. *Anglo-Saxons and Celts: A Study of Anti-Irish Prejudice in Victorian England.* Bridgeport, Conn., 1968.

———. *Apes and Angels: The Irishman in Victorian Caricature.* Washington, D. C., 1971.

Derry, John W. *Charles James Fox.* London, 1972.

Dickson, Peter G. M. *The Financial Revolution in England: A Study in the Development of Public Credit, 1688–1756.* New York, 1967.

Ford, John. *Prizefighting: The Age of Regency Boximania.* Newton Abbot, Devon, 1971.

Forster, E. M. *Marianne Thornton: A Domestic Biography, 1797–1887.* New York, 1956.

Garrett, Clarke. *Respectable Folly: Millenarians and the French Revolution in France and England.* Baltimore, 1975.

George, M. Dorothy. *London Life in the Eighteenth Century.* Harmondsworth, Middlesex, 1965.

Gilley, Sheridan. "Protestant London, No-Popery, and the Irish Poor, 1830–60." *Recusant History* 10 (1969–70): 210–30; 11 (1971–72): 21–46.

Henriques, Ursula. *Religious Toleration in England, 1787–1833.* Toronto, 1961.

Hill, Christopher. *Antichrist in Seventeenth-Century England.* London, 1971.

———. *Society and Puritanism in Pre-Revolutionary England.* London, 1969.

———. *The World Turned Upside Down: Radical Ideas during the English Revolution.* New York, 1973.

Kramnick, Isaac. *Bolingbroke and His Circle: The Politics of Nostalgia in the Age of Walpole.* Cambridge, Mass., 1968.

Leslie-Melville, R. *The Life and Work of Sir John Fielding.* London, 1934.

Malcolmson, Robert W. *Popular Recreations in English Society, 1700–1850.* Cambridge, 1973.

Manning, Bernard. *The Protestant Dissenting Deputies.* Edited by Ormerod Greenwood. Cambridge, 1952.

Manuel, Frank E. *Isaac Newton, Historian.* Cambridge, Mass., 1963.

Miles, Henry Downes. *Pugilistica: The History of British Boxing.* 3 vols. Edinburgh, 1906.

Mingay, G. E. *English Landed Society in the Eighteenth Century.* London, 1963.

Norman, E. R. *Anti-Catholicism in Victorian England.* London, 1968.

Ogden, James. *Isaac D'Israeli.* Oxford, 1969.

Owen, David. *English Philanthropy, 1660–1960.* Cambridge, Mass., 1964.

Quinlan, Maurice J. *Victorian Prelude: A History of English Manners, 1700–1830.* 1941. Reprint. Hamden, Conn., 1965.

Reid, J. C. *Bucks and Bruisers: Pierce Egan and Regency England.* London, 1971.

Robson, L. L. *The Convict Settlers of Australia.* Melbourne, 1965.

Rothblatt, Sheldon. *Tradition and Change in English Liberal Education: An Essay in History and Culture.* London, 1976.

Rudé, George. *Hanoverian London, 1714–1808.* Berkeley and Los Angeles, 1971.

———. *Paris and London in the Eighteenth Century: Studies in Popular Protest.* New York, 1971.

Shaw, A. G. L. *Convicts and the Colonies: A Study of Penal Transportation from Great Britain and Ireland to Australia and other parts of the British Empire.* London, 1966.

Stephen, Leslie. *History of English Thought in the Eighteenth Century.* 2 vols. New York, 1962.

Stromberg, Roland N. *Religious Liberalism in Eighteenth-Century England.* Oxford, 1954.

Sykes, Norman. *Church and State in England in the Eighteenth Century.* Cambridge, 1934.

Thomas, Keith. *Religion and the Decline of Magic.* New York, 1971.

Thompson, Edward P. *The Making of the English Working Class.* London, 1965.

Tobias, J. J. *Urban Crime in Victorian England.* New York, 1972.

Toon, Peter, ed. *Puritans, The Millennium and the Future of Israel: Puritan Eschatology, 1600–1660.* Cambridge, 1970.

Ward, W. R. *Religion and Society in England, 1790–1850.* London, 1972.

Welch, Charles. *Modern History of the City of London.* London, 1896.

General Jewish History

Altmann, Alexander. *Moses Mendelssohn: A Biographical Study.* Philadelphia, 1973.

Baron, Salo W. "The Modern Age." In *Great Ages and Ideas of the Jewish People,* edited by Leo W. Schwarz. New York, 1956.

———. *A Social and Religious History of the Jews.* 1st ed. 3 vols. New York, 1937.

Blumenkranz, Bernhard, ed. *Histoire des Juifs en France.* Toulouse, 1972.

Eliav, Mordecai. *Ha-hinukh ha-Yehudi be-Germanyah biymei ha-haskalah ve-*

ha-emantzipatziyah [Jewish Education in Germany during the Period of Enlightenment and Emancipation]. Jerusalem, 1960.

Glanz, Rudolf. *Geschichte des Niederen Jüdischen Volkes in Deutschland.* New York, 1968.

Gordon, Milton M. *Assimilation in American Life: The Role of Race, Religion and National Origins.* New York, 1971.

Hertzberg, Arthur. *The French Enlightenment and the Jews.* New York, 1968.

Katz, Jacob. *Emancipation and Assimilation: Studies in Modern Jewish History.* Westmead, Farnsborough, Hants., 1972.

————. *Jews and Freemasons in Europe, 1723–1939.* Translated by Leonard Oschry. Cambridge, Mass., 1970.

————. *Out of the Ghetto: The Social Background of Jewish Emancipation, 1770–1870.* Cambridge, Mass., 1973.

Meyer, Michael A. "Where Does the Modern Period of Jewish History Begin?" *Judaism* 24 (1975): 329–38.

Necheles, Ruth F. *The Abbé Grégoire, 1787–1831: The Odyssey of an Egalitarian.* Westport, Conn., 1971.

Poliakov, Léon. *Histoire de l'antisémitisme.* 3 vols. Paris, 1955–68.

Pollack, Herman. *Jewish Folkways in Germanic Lands, 1648–1806.* Cambridge, Mass., 1971.

Ravid, Benjamin. "The Legal Status of the Jewish Merchants of Venice, 1541–1638." *The Journal of Economic History* 35 (1975):274–79.

Scholem, Gershom. *Sabbatai Sevi: The Mystical Messiah.* Translated by R. J. Zvi Werblowsky. Princeton, 1973.

Shohet, Azriel. *Im hilufei tekufot: reishiyt ha-haskalah be-Yahadut Germanyah* [Beginnings of the Haskalah among German Jewry]. Jerusalem, 1960.

Shulvass, Moses A. *From East to West: The Westward Migration of Jews from Eastern Europe during the Seventeenth and Eighteenth Centuries.* Detroit, 1971.

Sokolow, Nahum. *History of Zionism.* 2 vols. London, 1919.

Stern, Selma. *The Court Jew: A Contribution to the History of the Period of Absolutism in Central Europe.* Translated by Ralph Weiman. Philadelphia, 1950.

Toury, Jacob. *Kavim le-heker keniysat ha-Yehudim la-hayyim ha-ezrahiim be-Germanyah* [Prolegomena to the Entrance of the Jews into German Citizenry]. Tel Aviv, 1972.

Trachtenberg, Joshua. *The Devil and the Jews: The Medieval Conception of the Jew and its Relation to Modern Antisemitism.* New York, 1966.

Yerushalmi, Yosef H. *From Spanish Court to Italian Ghetto—Isaac Cardoso: A Study in Seventeenth Century Marranism and Apologetics.* New York, 1971.

Unpublished Dissertations

Grinstein, Hyman B. "The American Synagogue and Laxity of Religious Observance, 1750–1850." M.A. thesis, Columbia University, 1935.

Martin, R. H. "The Pan-Evangelical Impulse in Britain, 1795–1830, with Special Reference to Four London Societies." D.Phil. diss., Oxford, 1974.

Quinn, P. L. S. "The Jewish Schooling Systems of London, 1656–1956." Ph.D. diss., University of London, 1958.

Rumney, J. "The Economic and Social Development of the Jews in England, 1730–1860." Ph.D. diss., University of London, 1933.

Scult, Melvin M. "The Conversion of the Jews and the Origins of Jewish Emancipation in England." Ph.D. diss., Brandeis University, 1968.

Shachar, Isaiah. "Studies in the Emergence and Dissemination of the Modern Jewish Stereotype in Western Europe." Ph.D. diss., University of London, 1967.

Reference Works

Hyamson, Albert M. "The Jewish Obituaries in The Gentleman's Magazine." *MJHSE* 4 (1942): 33–60. "Corrigenda." *MJHSE* 5 (1948):-212–13.

Jacobs, Joseph, and Wolf, Lucien. *Bibliotheca Anglo-Judaica: A Bibliographical Guide to Anglo-Jewish History.* London, 1888.

Lehmann, Ruth P. *Anglo-Jewish Bibliography, 1937–1970.* London, 1973.

_____. *Nova Bibliotheca Anglo-Judaica: A Bibliographical Guide to Anglo-Jewish History, 1937–1960.* London, 1961.

Matthews, W. *British Autobiographies: An Annotated Bibliography of British Biographies Published or Written before 1851.* Berkeley, 1955.

_____. *British Diaries: An Annotated Bibliography of British Diaries Written between 1442 and 1942.* Berkeley, 1950.

Roth, Cecil. *Magna Bibliotheca Anglo-Judaica: A Bibliographical Guide to Anglo-Jewish History.* New ed. London, 1937.

United Synagogue, London. *Archives of the United Synagogue: Report and Catalogue by Cecil Roth.* London, 1930.

Notes

CHAPTER 1

1. This account of the expulsion and the so-called "middle period" in Anglo-Jewish history follows Cecil Roth, *A History of the Jews in England,* 3rd ed. (Oxford, 1964), chs. 4 and 5.

2. H. S. Q. Henriques, *The Return of the Jews to England, Being a Chapter in the History of English Law* (London, 1905); Lucien Wolf, *Manasseh ben Israel's Mission to Oliver Cromwell* (London, 1901); Mordecai Wilensky, *Shivat ha-Yehudim le-Angliyah be-meah ha-sheva esreh* [The Return of the Jews to England in the Seventeenth Century] (Jerusalem, 1943); Cecil Roth, "The Mystery of the Resettlement," in *Essays and Portraits in Anglo-Jewish History* (Philadelphia, 1962); Bernard Glassman, *Anti-Semitic Stereotypes without Jews: Images of the Jews in England, 1290–1700* (Detroit, 1975), chap. 5.

3. Roth, "Mystery of the Resettlement," pp. 98–102.

4. Don Patinkin, "Mercantilism and the Readmission of the Jews to England," *JSS* 8 (1946):161–78.

5. Edgar R. Samuel, "The First Fifty Years," in *Three Centuries of Anglo-Jewish History: A Volume of Essays,* ed. V. D. Lipman (London, 1961), pp. 28, 41.

6. Samuel, "The First Fifty Years," p. 28; Roth, *History of the Jews in England,* pp. 168–71; Wilensky, *Shivat ha-Yehudim,* ch. 9, "Ha mifneh be-yahas la-Yehudim be-hugei ha-Royalistim" [The Turning Point in the Royalist Relationship to the Jews].

7. Samuel, "The First Fifty Years," pp. 36–37; Roth, *History of the Jews in England,* pp. 180–83.

8. Roth, *History of the Jews in England,* pp. 163, 167; Wilensky, *Shivat ha-Yehudim,* pp. 116–19.

9. Dudley Abrahams, "Jew Brokers of the City of London," *MJHSE,* pt. 3 (1937): 82, 92–94; the petition is quoted in Robert Seymour, pseud. [John Mottley], *A Survey of the Cities of London and Westminster,* 2 vols. (London, 1734–35), 2:408–9. Mottley does not give the name of the petitioner or the date of the petition, but from internal evidence it can be dated sometime after 1703.

10. Paul Goodman, *Moses Montefiore* (Philadelphia, 1925), p. 31; Apsley Pellatt, *Brief Memoir of the Jews in Relation to their Civil and Municipal Disabilities* (London, 1829), p. 25. Pellatt also mentioned that cases had occurred in which brokers had revenged themselves on Lord Mayors. By threatening to expose certain dealings, "sums have been disgorged and paid back to the broker."

11. *The Times,* 15 May 1830; Cecil Roth, "The Lord Mayor's Salvers," in *Essays and Portraits,* pp. 108–12.

12. Charles Welch, *Modern History of the City of London* (London, 1896), p. 162; *The Case of Mr. Anthony Da Costa with the Russia Company* (n.p., 1728); Roth, *History of the Jews in England,* pp. 205–6; *Reasons against the Bill Now Depending in Parliament, Intituled, A Bill for Inlarging and Regulating the Trade to the Levant Seas* (n.p., 1744).

13. Lucy Sutherland, "Samson Gideon and the Reduction of Interest, 1749–50," *Economic History Review* 16 (1946):15–29; idem, "Samson Gideon: Eighteenth Century Jewish Financier," *TJHSE* 17 (1953):79–90; Maurice Woolf, "Joseph Salvador, 1716–1786," *TJHSE* 21 (1962–67):104–37; Thomas W. Perry, *Public Opinion, Propaganda, and Politics in Eighteenth Century England: A Study of the Jew Bill of 1753* (Cambridge, Mass., 1962), pp. 17–22.

14. Philo-Patriae, pseud., *Considerations on the Bill to Permit Persons Professing the Jewish Religion to be Naturalized by Parliament* (London, 1753), p. 52.

15. John Toland, *Reasons for Naturalizing the Jews in Great Britain and Ireland* (London, 1714), pp. 6, 39, 42. It would be interesting to know whether Toland received any compensation or encouragement from Jewish merchants in composing this. I have come across nothing to indicate this might have been the case. Toland mentioned (p. 48) that he intended to bring out an English translation of Simone Luzzatto's *Discorso circa il stato de gl'Hebrei,* an important apologetic work, first published in Venice in 1638, which stressed the economic utility of the Jews. His familiarity with the *Discorso* would account for his knowledge of Jewish commercial activity in the Mediterranean and of certain Jewish customs and attitudes.

16. *The Expediency of a General Naturalization of Foreign Protestants and Others* (London, 1751), pp. 5, 10, 12.

17. Arthur Murphy, "The Temple of Laverna," *Gray's Inn Journal,* no. 18 (17 February 1752), in *The Works of Arthur Murphy,* 7 vols. (London, 1786), 5:149–58. Reprinted in *The Craftsman,* 16 June 1753, and in *A Collection of the Best Pieces in Prose and Verse Against the Naturalization of the Jews* (London, 1753).

18. Sutherland, "Samson Gideon: Jewish Financier," passim; John Eardley Wilmot, "A Memoir of the Life of Samson Gideon Esq. of Spalding Co. Lincoln and Belvedere, Kent," in *Illustrations of the Literary History of the Eighteenth Century,* ed. John Nichols, 8 vols. (London, 1817–58), 6:279, 283; Isaac Kramnick, *Bolingbroke and His Circle: The Politics of Nostalgia in the Age of Walpole* (Cambridge, Mass., 1968), ch. 2; Peter G.M. Dickson, *The Financial Revolution in England: A Study in the Development of Public Credit, 1688–1756* (New York, 1967), passim.

19. Philo-Patriae, pseud., *Further Considerations on the Act to Permit Persons Professing the Jewish Religion to be Naturalized by Parliament* (London, 1753), p. 36; Jonas Hanway, *A Review of the Proposed Naturalization of the Jews* (London, 1753), p. 67; [William Romaine], *Answer to a Pamphlet Entitled "Considerations on the Bill to Permit Persons Professing the Jewish Religion to be Naturalized"* (London, 1753), p. 77; Edgar Samuel, "The Jews in English Foreign Trade—A Consideration of the 'Philo-Patriae' Pamphlets of 1753," in *Remember the Days: Essays on Anglo-Jewish History Presented to Cecil Roth,* ed. John M. Shaftesley (London, 1966), p. 131; Joshua Van Oven, *Letters on the Present State of the Jewish Poor in the Metropolis* (London, 1802), p. 7; Levy Alexander, *Answer to Mr. Joshua Van Oven's Letter on the Present State of the Jewish Poor in London* (London, 1802), p. 24. For a full discussion of the Jewish poor, see ch. 5.

20. A. S. Diamond, "Problems of the London Sephardi Community, 1720–1733—Philip Carteret Webb's Notebooks," *TJHSE* 21 (1962–67):40, 60; Daniel Lysons, *The Environs of London,* 6 vols., (London, 1792–1811), 3:482.

21. Andrew Henderson, *The Case of the Jews Considered* (London, 1753), p. 6; Josiah Tucker, *A Letter to a Friend Concerning Naturalizations* (London, 1753), p. 7; *An Apology for the Naturalization of the Jews,* in *The Other Side of the Question, Being a Collection of What Hath Yet Appeared in Defence of the Jews* (London, 1753), p. 17; *DNB,* s.v., "Tucker, Josiah."

22. G. E. Mingay, *English Landed Society in the Eighteenth Century* (London, 1963), pp. 279–81; Edward Thompson, quoted in Christopher Hill, *Reformation to Industrial Revolution,* The Pelican Economic History of Britain, vol. 2 (Harmondsworth, Middlesex, England, 1969), p. 268; David S. Landes, *The Unbound Prometheus: Technological Change and Industrial Development in Western Europe from 1750 to the Present* (Cambridge, 1969), pp. 54, 66.

23. Jacob Viner, "Man's Economic Status," in *Man Versus Society in Eighteenth Century Britain: Six Points of View,* ed. James L. Clifford (Cambridge, 1968), p. 24; G.F.A. Best, *Temporal Pillars: Queen Anne's Bounty, the Ecclesiastical Commissioners, and the Church of England* (Cambridge, 1964), pp. 118–19.

24. *An Apology for the Naturalization of the Jews* (London, 1753), pp. 15–16, 23; *The Crisis, or, An Alarm to Britannia's True Protestant Sons* (London, 1754), pt. 2, p. 31; Henderson, *Case of the Jews,* pp. 6–7; *An Address to the Friends of Great Britain* (London, 1753), p. 7; Translator's Preface,

Henri Grégoire, *An Essay on the Physical, Moral and Political Reformation of the Jews* (London, 1791), p. iii.

In his "Letter Concerning Toleration" (1689), Locke limited the jurisdiction of the magistrate exclusively to civil concerns: life, liberty, health, and property. "The power of civil government relates only to men's civil interests, is confined to the care of the things of this world, and hath nothing to do with the world to come." "The business of laws is not to provide for the truth of opinions, but for the safety and security of the commonwealth, and of every particular man's goods and person." "The commonwealth embraces indifferently all men that are honest, peaceable, and industrious." *The Works of John Locke,* 10 vols. (London, 1823), 6:10, 13, 40, 52.

25. Josiah Tucker, *A Second Letter to a Friend Concerning Naturalizations* (London, 1753), pp. 12–14, 21–22.

26. *A Letter from a Clergyman in the Country to his Friend in Town,* in *The Other Side of the Question,* pp. 38–39; *A Looking-Glass for the Jews, or, The Credulous Unbelievers* (London, 1753), pp. i–v; *The Crisis,* pt. 2, p. 30.

27. Henderson, *Case of the Jews,* pp. 6–7.

28. *The Mirror of Parliament* 2 (1830):1783.

29. *The Rise, Fall, and Future Restoration of the Jews,* p. 41, quoted in [William Hamilton Reid], *The New Sanhedrin* (London, 1807), p. 105; Reid, *New Sanhedrin,* pp. 106–7; William Jackson, *The New and Complete Newgate Calendar,* 2nd ed., 8 vols. (London, 1818), 5:24. The latter work first appeared in 6 vols. in 1795.

30. Translator's Preface, Grégoire, *Reformation of the Jews,* p. iv; Pellatt, *Brief Memoir,* p. 28; Thomas Witherby, *An Attempt to Remove Prejudices Concerning the Jewish Nation by Way of Dialogue* (London, 1804), pp. 43–46; Toland, *Reasons for Naturalizing,* p. 18; Jon Bee, pseud. [John Badcock], *Slang: A Dictionary of the Turf, the Ring, the Chase, the Pit, of Bon-Ton and the Varieties of Life* (London, 1823), p. 95.

31. The account that follows is based largely on Roland M. Stromberg, *Religious Liberalism in Eighteenth Century England* (Oxford, 1954); Norman Sykes, *Church and State in England in the Eighteenth Century* (Cambridge, 1934); W. R. Ward, *Religion and Society in England, 1790–1850* (London, 1972); Best, *Temporal Pillars;* Gerald R. Cragg, "The Churchman," in Clifford, *Man Versus Society.*

32. Sheldon Rothblatt, *Tradition and Change in English Liberal Education: An Essay in History and Culture* (London, 1976), pp. 96–97; Best, *Temporal Pillars,* pp. 69–70; James Boswell, *The Life of Samuel Johnson, LL.D.* (London, 1867), p. 222; Perry, *Public Opinion, Propaganda, and Politics,* p. 49.

33. Roth, *History of the Jews in England,* p. 153; Perry, *Public Opinion, Propaganda, and Politics,* p. 18; *Hansard's Parliamentary Debates,* 2nd ser. (1820), 2:473.

34. Ursula Henriques, *Religious Toleration in England, 1787–1833* (London, 1961), pp. 183–84.

35. George Rude, *Hanoverian London, 1714–1808* (Berkeley and Los Angeles, 1971), pp. 107, 109, 224; idem, "The Gordon Riots: A Study of the Rioters and their Victims," in *Paris and London in the Eighteenth*

Century: Studies in Popular Protest (New York, 1971), pp. 201–21, 268–92; Edward P. Thompson, *The Making of the English Working Class* (London, 1965), pp. 68–69, 73–74. For further examples, see Bernard Manning, *The Protestant Dissenting Deputies,* ed. Ormerod Greenwood (Cambridge, 1952), pt. 2, ch. 1.

These are only the most well-known instances of popular religious hostility exploding in physical violence; the number of examples could be multiplied many times over. In all of the above cases, irrational religious sentiments were not the only force at work. The fact that the mob frequently operated in a selective fashion, moving against the property of well-to-do Catholics or Unitarians rather than indiscriminately cracking open any Catholic or Unitarian head that appeared in the street, suggests that social resentment and economic grievances contributed to the fury of the rioters. The recognition of underlying discontents in religious outbursts should not, however, be allowed to obscure the elementary fact that religion and ethnicity (in the case of anti-Irish disturbances) provided the framework, at the very minimum, for expressing this discontent.

36. Sheridan Gilley, who has written at length about "No Popery" sentiment in Victorian England, concludes that the Roman Catholic Church was "the living embodiment of every un-English vice, the national anti-type which defined all manner of native virtue, and as such was loathed before 1830 by Englishmen of all shades of theological opinion and of none at all." Sheridan Gilley, "Protestant London, No-Popery, and the Irish Poor, 1830–60," pt. 1, *Recusant History* 10 (1969–70); 213; Christopher Hill, *Antichrist in Seventeenth Century England* (London, 1971), passim; G. F. A. Best, "Popular Protestantism in Victorian Britian," in *Ideas and Institutions of Victorian Britain,* ed. Robert Robson (New York, 1967), pp. 120–21. There has been little work done explicitly on anti-Irish and anti-Catholic prejudice in Georgian England. On Victorian England, in addition to the above, see the following: L. Perry Curtis, Jr., *Anglo-Saxons and Celts: A Study of Anti-Irish Prejudice in Victorian England* (Bridgeport, Conn., 1968); idem, *Apes and Angels: The Irishman in Victorian Caricature* (Washington, D.C., 1971); E. R. Norman, ed., *Anti-Catholicism in Victorian England* (London, 1968); and pt. 2 of the above cited article by Gilley, *Recusant History* 11 (1971–72):21–46.

37. *The Crisis,* pt. 1, p. 2, pt. 2, p. 30; *A Looking-Glass for the Jews,* pp. iv–v; Philo-Patriae, *Considerations,* pp. 41–45.

38. Best, "Popular Protestantism," p. 121.

CHAPTER 2

1. Ruth F. Necheles, *The Abbé Grégoire, 1787–1831: The Odyssey of an Egalitarian* (Westport, Conn., 1971), pp. 12–13; Baruch Mevorach, "Hareka lifniyyat Lavater le-Mendelssohn" [The Background to Lavater's Appeal to Mendelssohn], *Zion* 30 (1965):158–70.

2. Norman Cohn, *The Pursuit of the Millennium* (London, 1970), p. 29.

The first chapter of this work, "The Tradition of Apocalyptic Prophecy," contains a succinct account of the sources and early development of Christian millenarianism.

3. Cohn, *Pursuit of the Millennium,* pp. 77–78.

4. The links between conversionist philo-Semitism and moves to readmit the Jews and to relieve Jewish disabilities have not gone unnoticed. The "philo-Semitic" component in the Readmission controversy has been dealt with by Mordecai Wilensky in his *Shivat ha-Yehudim* and, much earlier in this century, by Nahum Sokolow in his *History of Zionism,* 2 vols. (London, 1919), vol. 1, chs. 7 and 8. Sokolow has also described the revival of schemes to restore the Jews to Zion during the Napoleonic era, ch. 15, as has Meir Vereté, "Raayon shivat Yisrael ba-mahshavah ha-Protestantit be-Angliyah ba-shanim 1790–1840" [The Idea of the Restoration of Israel in Protestant Thought in England, 1790–1840], *Zion* 33 (1968):145–79. The outpouring of conversionist sentiment in 1753 has generally gone unnoticed. Only Melvin Scult, in his unpublished Ph.D. dissertation, "The Conversion of the Jews and the Origins of Jewish Emancipation in England" (Brandeis University, 1968), has developed this point. Scult has also described the role that the conversionists played in the parliamentary campaigns for the relief of Jewish disabilities, although he does not treat the far more critical role they assumed in the struggle to allow Jews to take up the freedom of the City of London. A major shortcoming of all these works is that they fail to assess critically the actual impact of the ideas they are discussing; they do not indicate what social and political elements within English society championed Jewish resettlement, naturalization, and emancipation on conversionist grounds, nor do they adequately explore the changing political fortunes of such sentiments over a two-century period.

5. B. S. Capp, *The Fifth Monarchy Men: A Study in Seventeenth Century English Millenarianism* (London, 1972), pp. 33–34; Christopher Hill, *Antichrist in Seventeenth Century England* (London, 1971), pp. 9–32; Wilensky, *Shivat ha-Yehudim,* p. 4.

6. Wilensky, *Shivat ha-Yehudim,* p. 5; Christopher Hill, *Society and Puritanism in Pre-Revolutionary England* (London, 1969), pp. 196–97; Franz Kobler, *The Vision Was There: A History of the British Movement for the Restoration of the Jews to Palestine* (London, 1956), pp. 18–20; Peter Toon, "The Latter Day Glory," in Toon, ed., *Puritans, The Millennium and the Future of Israel: Puritan Eschatology, 1600 to 1660* (Cambridge, 1970), pp. 32–34.

7. Christopher Hill, *The World Turned Upside Down: Radical Ideas during the English Revolution* (New York, 1973), pp. 30, 70, 74; Capp, *Fifth Monarchy Men,* pp. 38–39.

8. B. S. Capp, "Extreme Millenarianism," in Toon, *Puritans,* pp. 66–67; idem, *Fifth Monarchy Men,* p. 190; Hill, *Antichrist,* p. 114; Scult, "Conversion of the Jews," pp. 43–44.

9. Roth, *History of the Jews in England,* pp. 149–50, 285; Wilensky, *Shivat ha-Yehudim,* pp. 69, 74–75; Hill, *Antichrist,* p. 115; idem, *Society and Puritanism,* p. 196; Capp, "Extreme Millenarianism," p. 74; idem, *Fifth Mon-*

archy Men, pp. 201–2; Clarke Garrett, *Respectable Folly: Millenarians and the French Revolution in France and England* (Baltimore, 1975) p. 184.

10. Hill, *Society and Puritanism,* p. 197.

11. On the equation of the Jews with the forces of Satan, see Joshua Trachtenberg, *The Devil and the Jews: The Medieval Conception of the Jew and its Relation to Modern Antisemitism* (New York, 1966).

12. Gershom Scholem, *Sabbatai Sevi: The Mystical Messiah,* trans. R. J. Zvi Werblowsky (Princeton, 1973), pp. 101–2, 339–52, 543–45, 547–48, 942–43.

13. Samuel Pepys, *The Diary of Samuel Pepys,* ed. Henry B. Wheatley, 8 vols. (London, 1924), 5:212–13.

14. Henry Oldenburg, *The Correspondence of Henry Oldenburg,* ed. A. Rupert Hall and Marie Boas Hall, 9 vols. to date (Madison, Wisconsin, 1965–), 2:637.

15. Quoted in Cecil Roth, ed., *Anglo-Jewish Letters, 1158–1917* (London, 1938), pp. 50–51.

16. Quoted in Kobler, *The Vision,* p. 38. See also Frank E. Manuel, *Isaac Newton, Historian* (Cambridge, Mass., 1963), ch. 9.

17. Kobler, *The Vision,* pp. 38–51; Vereté, "Raayon shivat Yisrael," pp. 145–79; Garrett, *Respectable Folly,* passim.

18. Perry, *Public Opinion, Propaganda, and Politics,* pp. 17–22.

19. Philo-Patriae, *Considerations,* p. 8. Edgar Samuel, in an article that appeared in the Cecil Roth *Festschrift,* argued that the author of this tract was Joseph Salvador, the most zealous promoter of the Jew Bill within the Jewish community. This attribution, which has been made by other historians of Anglo-Jewry, rests on the assumption that only someone who was very close to the Sephardi community and had a remarkable familiarity with the financial affairs of the Salvador family could have produced a pamphlet with the details and examples of *Considerations* and Philo-Patriae's other work, *Further Considerations.* There is no reason to challenge this assumption, but it does not necessarily follow that Salvador was the author of the pamphlets. The conversionist sentiments of Philo-Patriae hardly seem compatible with someone who chose to remain a Jew and obtain his privileges through legislative relief, rather than through baptism. Salvador may have provided the author with certain details, since they were both seeking the same short-term goal, but I do not see how to reconcile his authorship or financial sponsorship of the pamphlets with their decidedly Christian attitude to the conversion of the Jews. Samuel, "The Jews in English Foreign Trade," pp. 123–43.

20. Thomas Winstanley, *A Sermon Preached at the Parish Church of St. George, Hanover Square, Sunday, October 28, 1753* (London, 1753), pp. 12–14.

21. Romaine, *Answer to a Pamphlet,* p. 27.

22. Henderson, *Case of the Jews,* p. 17; Philo-Patriae, *Considerations,* p. 88.

23. Edward Weston, *Some Reflections upon the Question Relating to the*

Naturalization of Jews, Considered as a Point of Religion (London, 1754), p. 41; Philo-Patriae, *Further Considerations*, p. 4.

24. *An Address to the Friends of Great Britain* (London, 1753), p. 17; Henderson, *Case of the Jews*, pp. 15, 18.

25. Weston, *Some Reflections*, p. 30; By-stander, pseud., *A True State of the Case Concerning the Good or Evil which the Bill for the Naturalization of the Jews May Bring upon Great Britain* (London, 1753), pp. 13, 15; *A Letter to the Publick on the Act for Naturalizing the Jews* (London, 1753), pp. 13–14.

26. Josiah Tucker, *A Second Letter to a Friend Concerning Naturalizations* (London, 1753), p. 42, and *A Letter to a Friend Concerning Naturalizations* (London, 1753), p. 12; *A Looking-Glass for the Jews, or, The Credulous Unbelievers* (London, 1753), p. vii.

27. Perry, *Public Opinion, Propaganda, and Politics*, pp. 140–48.

28. *GM* 29 (1759):269–70.

29. For a discussion of these works, see Vereté, "Raayon shivat Yisrael," pp. 162–66.

Garrett, in a comparative study of millenarianism in France and England, stresses the much greater informal acceptance that millenarianism gained in Protestant England, "where pamphlets, sermons, treatises, and tracts on millenarian themes circulated freely during the eighteenth century," and points out that the educated and respectable classes of eighteenth-century England never repudiated the assumptions of the previous century's millenarianism. Garrett believes that the relative weakness of French millenarianism was due to the fact that "Roman Catholic theology continued to follow St. Augustine's doctrine that biblical prophecies should be understood spiritually and not literally." *Respectable Folly*, pp. 21, 122.

30. Roth, *Anglo-Jewish Letters*, pp. 202–4; Vereté, "Raayon shivat Yisrael," pp. 149–51. For the political implications of the millenarian fantasies of this period, see Thompson, *English Working Class*, pp. 116–18.

31. Thompson, *English Working Class*, p. 118; Vereté, "Raayon shivat Yisrael," p. 152; Garrett, *Respectable Folly*, p. 188; Moses Gomez Pereira, *The Jew's Appeal on the Divine Mission of Richard Brothers and N. B. Halhed, Esq., To Restore Israel and Rebuild Jerusalem* (London, 1795).

32. Vereté, "Raayon shivat Yisrael," p. 154; John Towill Rutt, *Life and Correspondence of Joseph Priestley*, 2 vols. (London, 1831–32), 2:409–10.

33. LSPCJ, *Report of the Committee to the First Half Yearly Meeting of the LSPCJ* (London, 1809), p. 7; *The Monthly Repository* 2 (1807):650.

34. Diogene Tama, *Transactions of the Parisian Sanhedrim* [sic], trans. and with a preface by F. D. Kirwan (London, 1807), pp. iii, xiv–xv. According to *The Monthly Repository* 2 (1807):653, Kirwan was a pseudonym, "a mere bookseller's name." I have been unable to find any information about F. D. Kirwan in the standard reference works.

35. *GM* 80, p. 1 (1810):556–57.

36. [Isaac D'Israeli], "On the Late Installation of a Great Sanhedrim of the Jews in Paris," *Monthly Magazine* 24, pt. 2 (1807):34–38, and "Acts of the Great Sanhedrim at Paris," ibid., pp. 134–36, 243–48.

37. *GM* 69, pt. 1 (1799):501–2; Vereté, "Raayon shivat Yisrael," p. 154.

38. Ward, *Religion and Society in England,* pp. 44–45.

39. John Walsh, "Religion: Church and State in Europe and the Americas," in *War and Peace in an Age of Upheaval, 1793–1830,* ed. C. W. Crawley, The New Cambridge Modern History, vol. 9 (Cambridge, 1965), p. 165.

40. Joseph Samuel C. F. Frey, *Narrative of the Rev. Joseph Samuel C. F. Frey,* 4th ed. (New York, 1817), pp. 50, 62, 71.

41. LSPCJ, Minute Book, August 1808–September 1810, Dep. CMJ c.5, entries for 4, 11, and 20 August 1808, Bodleian Library, Oxford; LMS, memoir from Frey to the Jewish Committee, 19 October 1807; R. H. Martin, "The Pan Evangelical Impulse in Britain, 1795–1830: With Special Reference to Four London Societies" (D. Phil. diss., Oxford University, 1974), pp. 324–29.

42. Henry Handley Norris, *The Origins, Progress, and Existing Circumstances of the LSPCJ* (London, 1825), p. 2; Scult, "Conversion of the Jews," pp. 206–14.

43. S. G. Checkland, *The Gladstones: A Family Biography, 1764–1851* (Cambridge, 1971), p. 164.

44. M. Sailman, *The Mystery Unfolded* (London, 1817), p. 7; Bat Yisrael, pseud., *Letter to Mr. Frey by a Daughter of Israel* (London, 1810), p. 6; P. P. Pasquin, *Jewish Conversion: A Christanical Farce* (London, 1814), pp. 4–5. Jews were prominent among the subscribers to Sailman's exposé.

45. *Quarterly Review* 68 (1839):183; *Jewish Repository* 1 (June 1813): 244; Bat Yisrael, *Letter to Mr. Frey,* p. 6; Sailman, *Mystery,* p. 48; Norris, *Origins,* pp. 54, 88; LSPCJ, Minute Book, September 1810–February 1815, Dep CMJ c.6, entry for 28 January 1812; *Historical Notices of the LSPCJ* (London, 1850), p. 3; Scult, "Conversion of the Jews," p. 196.

46. *The Trial of John Kinnear, Lewis Levy, and Mosely Woolf* (London, 1819), p. 164.

47. Moses Samuel, *An Address from an Israelite to the Missionary Preachers* (Liverpool, 1827), p. 6.

48. Sailman, *Mystery,* p. 20; Bat Yisrael, *Letter to Mr. Frey,* p. 6; LSPCJ, Minute Book, August 1808–September 1810, Dep. CMJ c.5, entry for 13 March 1810 and Minute Book, September 1810–February 1815, Dep. CMJ c.6, entry for 28 May 1811, Bodleian Library, Oxford.

An anonymous Jewish correspondent wrote to *The Gentleman's Magazine* in 1810 that the London Society had acquired "a few foreign itinerant Jews" and "a few children, the most part of whom are the fruits of illicit love, of Jewish fathers and Christian mothers." *GM,* vol. 80, pt. 2 (1810):235.

49. LSPCJ, *The Obligations of Christians to Attempt the Conversion of the Jews,* 2nd. ed. (London, n.d.), p. 11; *Morning Chronicle,* 27 June 1827; *An Appeal to the Humanity of the English Nation in Behalf of the Jews* (Dunstable, 1812), pp. 30–31.

50. *The First Report of the Philo-Judaean Society* (London, 1827), p. 10;

The Third Annual Report of the Philo-Judaean Society (London, 1829), p. 20.

51. *The First Report of the Philo-Judaean Society,* pp. 11–12, 14; *The Times,* 15 May 1828.

52. *The Jewish Expositor and Friend of Israel* 12 (February 1827): 80. *House of Commons Journal* 82 (25 July 1826–22 January 1828):601, 83 (29 January 1828–18 December 1828):452; *The Second Annual Report of the Philo-Judaean Society* (London, 1828), p. 13.

53. I have reconstructed the course of the Saul brothers' case from the information included in the dozen or so petitions they sent to the Court of Common Council and the Court of Aldermen. These petitions may be found in the papers of these bodies in the City of London Record Office.

54. The Court of Aldermen was a notoriously illiberal body. When the Saul brothers' case was incidentally mentioned in the course of the Commons debate on the repeal of the Test and Corporation Acts, the Benthamite Joseph Hume charged that the jails were filled with men whom the Court of Aldermen had prosecuted and added that, if the law allowed it, the Court would revert to the fire and the faggot. *Hansard Parliamentary Debates* (Commons), 2nd. ser., 18 (1828):307.

55. *The World,* 4 July 1827; *The Second Annual Report of the Philo-Judaean Society,* p. 12; Pellat, *Brief Memoir of the Jews,* pp. 26–27.

56. *DNB,* s.v., "Pellatt, Apsley"; *The Times,* 20 June, 2 July 1829, 15 May 1830; *The World,* 2 January 1828.

57. Roth, *History of the Jews in England,* pp. 252–53; Ursula Henriques, *Religious Toleration in England, 1787–1833* (London, 1962), p. 190; *The Mirror of Parliament* 2 (1830):1238.

58. Moses Elias Levy (d. 1854) of Park Lane, Knightsbridge, was a fascinating figure, a promoter of colonial schemes and an active religious polemicist. His American career has been well documented by Leon Huhner, but his activity in London has hitherto gone unrecognized. For the latter, see the concluding chapter of this work. For biographical details and other aspects of his career, see Huhner, "David L. Yulee, Florida's First Senator," *Publications of the American Jewish Historical Society* 25 (1917):1–29, and "Moses Elias Levy, An Early Florida Pioneer and the Father of Florida's First Senator," *The Florida Historical Quarterly* 19 (1941):319–45. Moses Elias Levy is not to be confused with the Moses Levy of Great Alie Street in the City, who petitioned Parliament in 1827 for the removal of Jewish disabilities. Moses Elias Levy was opposed to Jewish emancipation because he feared that greater integration would lead to a weakening of religious practices.

59. *The World,* 31 October, 5, 12, 26 December 1827; *Report of the Proceedings of the Late Public Meeting of the Jews* (London, 1827), pp. 3–4; *The Second Annual Report of the Philo-Judaean Society,* p. 15.

60. *The World,* 2 January 1828.

CHAPTER 3

1. On the persistence of anti-Semitism during the so-called "middle period" in Anglo-Jewish history, see Bernard Glassman, *Anti-Semitic Stereotypes without Jews: Images of the Jews in England, 1290–1700* (Detroit, 1975).

2. See, for example, Toland, *Reasons for Naturalizing,* p. 19; William Romaine, *A Modest Apology for the Citizens and Merchants of London who Petitioned the House of Commons Against Naturalizing the Jews* (London, 1753), pp. vii, 9, 12–14; idem, *Answer to a Pamphlet,* passim; Archaicus, pseud., *The Rejection and Restoration of the Jews* (London, 1753), p. 35; Britannia, pseud., *An Appeal to the Throne against the Naturalization of the Jewish Nation* (London, 1753), pp. 4–5, 17–18; *St. James Chronicle,* 13–15 November 1804; William Kidd, *Kidd's London Directory and Amusement Guide* (London, [ca. 1835]), "London and All its Dangers," p. 12.

3. Britannia, *Appeal to the Throne,* pp. 4–5; Romaine, *Modest Apology,* p. vii; idem, *A Full Answer to a Fallacious Apology Artfully Circulated through the Kingdom in Favour of the Naturalization of the Jews,* 2nd ed. (London, 1753), p. 6.

4. *Westminster Journal,* 7 July 1753, quoted in *Collection of the Best Pieces,* p. 59; *An Answer to the Considerations on the Bill to Permit Jews to be Naturalized* (n.p., [1753]), pp. 11, 31; Romaine, *Answer to a Pamphlet,* p. 56; idem, *Modest Apology,* pp. 6–7; Archaicus, pseud., *Admonitions from Scripture and History, from Religion and Common Prudence, Relating to the Jews* (London, 1753), p. 22; *Some Remarks on the Jewish Apology for a Late Act,* in *Collection of the Best Pieces,* pp. 34–38; Hanway, *Review of the Proposed Naturalization,* pp. 27–28, 33, 42.

5. Isaiah Shachar, "Studies in the Emergence and Dissemination of the Modern Jewish Stereotype in Western Europe," (Ph.D. diss., University of London, 1967), pp. 88–89, 414–16.

6. Philo-Patriae, *Considerations,* p. 59; *The Crisis,* pt. 2, pp. 3–4; *The Motives to the Senseless Clamor against the Act Concerning Jews Exposed and the Act Set in a True Light* (London, 1753), pp. 6–7.

In a similar manner, the *Daily Advertiser* of 16 June 1753 commented: "Christianity, a word we had of half an age scarce heard pronounced, except by a few unfashionable preachers, has for some weeks past thundered from innumerable mouths, been hung up in capitals amidst the ribbald immorality of newspapers, and rung in every ear throughout the kingdom. The inconsiderate many had forgotten there was such an establishment, till the cunning few could make it useful for their purposes."

7. *Motives to the Senseless Clamor,* p. 2.

8. Philip Dormer Stanhope, *The Letters of Philip Dormer Stanhope, 4th Earl of Chesterfield,* ed. Bonamy Dobree, 6 vols. (New York, 1968), 5:2062–63; Horace Walpole, *Memoirs of the Reign of King George II,* 3 vols. (London, 1846), 1:357–58; E. J. B. Rathery, ed., *Journal et mémoires du Marquis d'*

Argenson (Paris, 1866), 8:133–34; Shachar, "Studies in the Modern Jewish Stereotype," pp. 152–54.

9. Carl Philip Moritz, *Journeys of a German in England in 1782*, trans, and ed. Reginald Nettel (London, 1965), pp. 181–82; *St. James Chronicle*, 13–15 November 1804; Don Manuel Alvarez Espriella, pseud. [Robert Southey], *Letters from England*, 2nd ed., 3 vols. (London, 1808), 3:144; John Bull, pseud., *The Laughing Philosopher* (London, 1825) pp. 392–93. On the curses on the twelve tribes, see Trachtenberg, *The Devil and the Jews*, pp. 50–52, and Yosef H. Yerushalmi, *From Spanish Court to Italian Ghetto—Isaac Cardoso: A Study in Seventeenth Century Marranism and Jewish Apologetics* (New York, 1971), pp. 131–32.

10. *The Mirror of Parliament* 2 (26 March 1830–29 May 1830):1240, 1778; *Hansard's Parliamentary Debates*, 3rd ser., 18 (1833):50.

11. *The Mirror of Parliament* 2 (26 March 1830–29 May 1830):1783.

12. Keith V. Thomas, *Religion and the Decline of Magic* (New York, 1971), chs. 18 and 22.

13. For this account, I have relied on Shmuel Ettinger, "Yehudim ve-Yahadut be-einei ha-Deistim ha-Angliim be-meah ha-shmoneh-esrei" [Jews and Judaism in the Eyes of the English Deists in the Eighteenth Century], *Zion* 29 (1964):182–207; Léon Poliakov, *Histoire de l'antisémitisme*, 3 vols. (Paris, 1955–68), *De Voltaire à Wagner*, vol. 3, bk. 1, ch. 1; Leslie Stephen, *History of English Thought in the Eighteenth Century*, 2 vols. (New York, 1962), pp. 72–73, 118–25, 141; Edmund Burke, *Reflections on the Revolution in France* (London, 1964), p. 86. For a similar kind of secular anti-Semitism among the *philosophes* of France, see Arthur Hertzberg, *The French Enlightenment and the Jews* (New York, 1968), ch. 9.

14. *GM*, vol. 80, pt. 1 (1810):558; William Shakespeare, *The Merchant of Venice*, act 3, sc. 1., lines 62, 65; *The Encyclopedia of Wit* (London, 1804), pp. 109, 432–33.

15. Thomas Witherby, *An Attempt to Remove Prejudices Concerning the Jewish Nation by Way of Dialogue* (London, 1803), p. 2; *Reasons Offered to the Consideration of Parliament for Preventing the Growth of Judaism* (London, n.d.), pp. 8–9 [the edition in the library of the Jewish Theological Seminary, New York, is undated; Roth's *Magna Bibliotheca Anglo-Judaica*, p. 214, lists editions from 1738 and 1753]; *The Universal Songster, or, Museum of Mirth*, 3 vols. (London, 1834), 1:262; Charles Stuart, *The Distressed Baronet*, 1787, quoted in Edgar Rosenberg, *Tabloid Jews and Fungoid Scribblers* (New York, 1972), p. 34.

16. *The Commercial Habits of the Jews* (London, 1809), pp. 13–31.

17. Britannia, *Appeal to the Throne*, p. 22; Archaicus, *Admonitions*, pp. 25–26; letter from Old England to the *London Evening Post*, 24 May 1753, in *Collection of the Best Pieces*, p. 11–12. This last cited pamphlet contains a number of selections in which the fear of a Jewish take-over is strongly expressed.

18. Quoted in Perry, *Public Opinion, Propaganda, and Politics*, p. 101.

19. *Commercial Habits of the Jews*, pp. 22–23, 27–29.

20. William Cobbett, *Rural Rides*, ed. George Woodcock, (Baltimore,

1967), pp. 34, 37, 150; idem, *Cobbett's Weekly Political Register* 69 (1830): 730, 734.

21. *Hansard's Parliamentary Debates*, 3rd ser., 24 (1834):722; *Commercial Habits of the Jews*, p. 8; Henry Hunt, *To the Radical Reformers Male and Female of England, Scotland, and Ireland*, 2 vols. (London. 1821–22), p. 8. I am indebted to Roger Draper for the references to Lord Malmesbury and "Orator" Hunt.

22. *Hansard's Parliamentary Debates*, n.s., 23 (1830):1344; Cobbett, *Rural Rides*, pp. 119–20.

23. William Cobbett, *Rural Rides*, ed. G. D. H. Cole and M. Cole, 3 vols. (London, 1930), 1:313; *Universal Songster*, 2:61; Richard Sheridan, *Moses and Shadrac, or, A Specimen of Jewish Education*. The play was never published. The only known copy is a MS in the Larpent Collection at the Huntington Library, San Marino, California. It was probably written in early 1780 and was first acted at the Drury Lane Theatre on 19 April 1784. Quoted in H. R. S. Van der Veen, *Jewish Characters in Eighteenth Century English Fiction and Drama* (1935; reprint ed., New York, 1972), pp. 277–78.

24. *Morning Chronicle*, 15 September 1801; Richard Cumberland, *The Observer*, no. 38, in *The British Essayists*, ed. James Ferguson, 45 vols. (London, 1819), 38:252–53.

25. *St. James Chronicle*, 13–15 November 1804; Kidd, "London and All its Dangers," p. 12; Samuel Taylor Coleridge, *Table Talk*, 8 July 1830, quoted in Edgar Rosenberg, *From Shylock to Svengali: Jewish Stereotypes in English Fiction* (Palo Alto, California, 1960), p. 56.

26. Herbert M. Atherton, *Political Prints in the Age of Hogarth: A Study of the Ideographic Representation of Politics* (Oxford, 1974), pp. 85, 210–12.

27. Thomas Babington Macaulay, *The Letters of Thomas Babington Macaulay*, cd. Thomas Pinncy, 3 vols. to datc (Cambridgc 1974–), 2:36; Horace Walpole, *The Yale Edition of Horace Walpole's Correspondence*, ed. W. S. Lewis, vol. 10, pt. 2, *Horace Walpole's Correspondence with George Montagu*, ed. W. S. Lewis and Ralph S. Brown, Jr. (New Haven, 1941), pp. 106–7; Charles Lamb, "Imperfect Sympathies," in *Essays of Elia*, 1st ser. (New York, 1845), pp. 75–76. This essay first appeared in the early 1820s in *The London Magazine*.

28. Nathaniel Wraxall, *The Historical and the Posthumous Memoirs of Sir Nathaniel William Wraxall, 1772–1784*, ed. Henry B. Wheatley, 5 vols. (London, 1884), 5:121; *The Annual Register for 1806* (London, 1807), p. 458 [I am indebted to Navah Haber-Sheim for bringing this reference to my attention]; Cecil Roth, *The Great Synagogue, London, 1690–1940* (London, 1950), pp. 162–63.

29. Moritz, *Journeys of a German*, p. 105.

30. Tacitus, pseud., *Copy of a Letter Taken Out of the Whitehall Journal, Tuesday, January 1, 1722/23* (London, 1723); *GM* 17 (1747):568–69; *Morning Post*, 6 December 1775; *Reasons for Preventing the Growth of Judaism*, p. 21.

31. Charles Ambler, *Reports of Cases Argued and Determined in the High Court of Chancery*, 2nd ed. (London, 1828), p. 228.

32. Clement Tudway Swanston, *Reports of Cases Argued and Determined in the High Court of Chancery*, 3 vols. (London, 1821–1827), 2:485, 492–93, 527.

33. Diamond, "Problems of the London Sephardi Community," p. 50; *The Universal Magazine* 9 (January–June 1808):453; *Reasons for Preventing the Growth of Judaism*, pp. 13–14; *The Mirror of Parliament* 2 (26 March 1830–29 May 1830):1781; Alfred Rubens, *A Jewish Iconography* (London, 1954), p. 38; Isaac Lyon Goldsmid to the Duke of Wellington, 9 May 1828, Goldsmid MSS, University College, London.

34. Henry Mayhew, *London Labour and the London Poor*, 3 vols. (London, 1851), 2:129; *GM* 23 (1753):588.

35. *OB* 9 (1757):230–32; *The Annual Register for the Year 1769* (London, 1770), p. 93; *GM* 46 (1776):189; Minutes of the Mahamad, 9 October 1818–21 September 1824, MS 111, entry for 11 May 1824, ASPS.

36. *The Annual Register for the Year 1763*, quoted in William Connor Sydney, *England and the English in the Eighteenth Century*, 2nd ed., 2 vols. (Edinburgh, 1891), 2:213; CF, "Various"; G. R. Clarke, *The History and Description of the Town and Borough of Ipswich* (Ipswich and London, 1830), p. 319.

37. Henry John Marks, *Narrative of H. J. Marks*, intro. Charles B. Tayler (London, 1838), p.v.

38. *OB* 45 (1803):286–95; LSPCJ, Hebrew Schools, Certificates of Candidates, Dep. CMJ c.114/2, Bodleian Library, Oxford; MS diary of J. L. Mallet, entry for 24 June 1830, quoted in Piero Sraffa, ed., *The Works and Correspondence of David Ricardo*, 11 vols. (Cambridge, 1951–55, 1973), 10:16; Henry Home, *An Introduction to the Art of Thinking*, 4th ed. (Edinburgh, 1789), p. 131.

CHAPTER 4

1. Yerushalmi, *Spanish Court to Italian Ghetto*, p. 44.

2. The overwhelming majority of the material I have uncovered on the acculturation of the Anglo-Jewish middle class reflects the experiences of Jewish men. Obviously, the process of acculturation extended to Jewish women as well. I have been unable to discover historical evidence that can tell us very much about the changes in behavior and attitude of well-to-do Jewish women. There is, however, a large body of material about the acculturation of *poor* Jewish women, for which see ch. 6.

3. Tacitus, *Letter*; César de Saussure, *A Foreign View of England in the Reigns of George I and George II: The Letters of Monsieur César de Saussure to his Family*, trans. and ed. M. Van Muyden (London, 1902), pp. 328–29; Charles Duschinsky, *The Rabbinate of the Great Synagogue, London, from 1756–1842* (London, 1921), pp. 9–10; Angel Lyon, pseud., *A Letter from Angel Lyon to the Right Honourable Lord George Gordon on Wearing Beards*

(London, 1789), p. 7; *Zeh ha-kuntras nikra olam hadash ve-nikra olam hafukh* [A New World, A World Turned Upside Down] (London, 1789), pp. 10, 14–15; New Synagogue, Minute Book F, 1820–24, entry for 19 May 1822, AUS.

4. Duschinsky, *Rabbinate of the Great Synagogue*, p. 15; Alfred Rubens, *Anglo-Jewish Portraits: A Biographical Catalogue of Engraved Anglo-Jewish and Colonial Portraits from the Earliest Times to the Accession of Queen Victoria* (London, 1935), pp. 114–15; Bernard Susser, "Social Acclimatization of Jews in Eighteenth and Nineteenth Century Devon," in Roger Burt, ed., *Industry and Society in the South-West* (Exeter, 1970), p. 52.

5. Cecil Roth, "The Jew Peddler—An 18th Century Rural Character," in *Essays and Portraits*, p. 132; *Olam hadash*, p. 10; Great Synagogue, Minutes of Vestry Meetings, 1825–51, entries for 22 May 1826, 8 January 1827, and 17 February 1827, AUS.

6. Romaine, *A Modest Apology*, p. 9; Southey, *Letters from England*, 3: 151; Kidd, "London and All its Dangers," p. 12; [Isaac D'Israeli], *Vaurien, or Sketches of the Times*, 2 vols. (London, 1797), 2:222–23.

7. Ralph Schomberg to Emanuel Mendes da Costa, 1761, in Nicholas, ed., *Illustrations of the Literary History*, 4:768; [C. M. Westmacott], *The English Spy*, 2 vols. (London, 1825–26), 1:346–47; Asher Goldsmid to Isaac Lyon Goldsmid, 13 June 1822, Goldsmid MSS, University College, London; A. M. W. Stirling, ed., *The Letter-Bag of Lady Elizabeth Spencer-Stanhope*, 2 vols. (London, 1913), 1:342.

The Times of 2 April 1794 reported that "a young son of Levi" was a considerable debtor to one of the faro clubs in St. James Square, but "not finding it convenient to pay what is not recoverable by law, he no longer appears in those fashionable circles."

8. Daniel Defoe, *A Tour Thro' the Whole Island of Great Britain*, 2 vols., ed. G. D. H. Cole (London, 1927), 1:382–83; Roth, *The Great Synagogue*, p. 50; *A Catalogue of Pictures of Moses Hart, Esq., which Will Be Sold By Auction, Wednesday, 23 March 1757;* Hilda F. Finberg, "Jewish Residents in Eighteenth Century Twickenham," *TJHSE* 16 (1945–51):129–35; "Jewish County Families," London *Jewish Chronicle*, 24 May 1889; Haim Yosef David Azulai, *Sefer maagal tov* [The Good Path], ed. Aron Freimann (Jerusalem, 1934), p. 31; Chaim Bermant, *The Cousinhood* (New York, 1971), pp. 19–21; Levi Alexander, [and Henry Lemoine], *Memoirs of the Life and Commercial Connections of the late Benjamin Goldsmid, Esq., of Roehampton* (London, 1808), pp. 94–100; Paul H. Emden, *Jews of Britain: A Series of Biographies* (London, 1944), p. 96.

According to *The Gentleman's Magazine*, vol. 82, pt. 1 (1812), pp. 673–74, Henry Lemoine, a hack writer and bookseller, and a friend of the controversialist David Levi, wrote Alexander's life of Goldsmid "under the particular inspection of a Jewish printer," i.e., Levi Alexander. "Mr. Lemoine remarked to his friends that he was, against his own representations and advice, in a manner compelled to insert several ridiculous traits, relative to Mr. Goldsmid, in this publication." This probably refers to Goldsmid's extramarital sexual life.

9. James Ogden, *Isaac D'Israeli* (Oxford, 1969), pp. 6–7.

10. Roth, *The Great Synagogue*, pp. 153–54; Albert M. Hyamson, *The Sephardim of England: A History of the Spanish and Portuguese Jewish Community, 1492–1951* (London, 1951), p. 217; Bermant, *The Cousinhood*, pp. 42–43, 45, 48–49; Sraffa, *Works of David Ricardo*, 10:36–37; *The Hebrew Intelligencer*, 1 January 1823.

11. Rubens, *Anglo-Jewish Portraits*, p. 129; Theophilus Cibber, *The Harlot's Progress* (London, 1733), p. 10; *Brittannia's Fortune-Teller* (London, 1753); Henry Fielding, *Miss Lucy in Town*, in *The Works of Henry Fielding*, 8 vols. (London, 1771), 3:289.

12. *A Trip from St. James's to the Royal Exchange* (London, 1744), p. 218; Meyer Schomberg, *Emunat omen* [The True Faith], trans. Harold Levy, printed in Edgar R. Samuel, "Dr. Meyer Schomberg's Attack on the Jews of London," *TJHSE* 20 (1959–61):103.

13. Woolf, "Joseph Salvador," pp. 111, 116; [Henry Lemoine], "Authentic Memoirs of Baron Ephraim Lopes Pereira D'Aguilar," *The New Wonderful Museum and Extraordinary Magazine* 1 (1803):143–44, 148; Richard D. Barnett, "Samuel Montefiore's Diary," in *Explorations: An Annual on Jewish Themes*, ed. Murray Mindlin (London, 1967), p. 260; Alexander, *Memoirs of Benjamin Goldsmid*, pp. 51–80, esp. p. 79; Guardians of Faith, MS bylaws, 1832, FS 1/443, and *Rules of a Friendly Society called the United Israelites* (London, 1835), FS 1/486A, PRO.

14. Leo Hershkowitz and Isidore S. Meyer, eds., *The Lee Max Friedman Collection of American Jewish Colonial Correspondence: Letters of the Franks Family (1733–1748)* (Waltham, Mass., 1968), pp. 7–8; Duschinsky, *Rabbinate of the Great Synagogue*, pp. 15–16; *Olam hadash*, p. 7; *The Times*, 28 October 1802. Interestingly, this story was picked up by *The Mercury and New England Palladium* of Boston, Mass., and reprinted on 25 January 1803.

15. MS minute book of Hevra Kadisha de-Talmud Torah, entry for 17 February 1803, in the possession of Salmond S. Levin, London; Lucien Wolf, "Lady Montefiore's Honeymoon," in *Essays in Jewish History*, ed. Cecil Roth (London, 1934), pp. 248, 250; Hambro Synagogue, MS record of meetings between the Hambro and the Great Synagogue, 1812, in Copy Book of Letters Despatched, 1808–14, AUS; Albert M. Hyamson, *The London Board for Shechita, 1804–1954* (London, 1954), pp. 11, 16.

16. New Synagogue, Minute Book G, 1824–32, entry for 31 October 1830, AUS; Hambro Synagogue, Minute Book, Committee, 1794–1809, entry for 22 November 1807, and Minute Book, Committee, 1824–33, entries for 26 December 1825 and 17 December 1829, AUS; Great Synagogue, Minutes of Committee Meetings, 1815–25, entries for 14 November 1816, 22 January 1821, and 24 May 1821, AUS; *Laws of the Great Synagogue, Duke's Place, London* (London, 1827), pp. 63–64.

17. Schomberg, *Emunat omen*, p. 102; Duschinsky, *Rabbinate of the Great Synagogue*, p. 14; An English Israelite, pseud., *A Letter to the Parisian Sanhedrin*, pp. 35–36.

18. Louis L. Loewe, ed., *Diaries of Sir Moses and Lady Montefiore*, 2 vols. (London. 1890), 1:3; London *Jewish Chronicle*, 17 May 1907; *The Voice of*

Jacob, 3 and 17 February 1843; *The Annual Register of the Year 1825* (London, 1826), p. 65.

19. *GM,* vol. 81, pt. 1 (1811), p. 621; Cecil Roth, "The Lesser Synagogues of the Eighteenth Century," *MJHSE* 3 (1937):1–7; *OB* 17 (1774):364–66; New Synagogue, Minute Book F, 1820–24, entry for 17 February 1822, AUS; Cecil Roth, *The Rise of Provincial Jewry* (London, 1950), pp. 21, 60, 105.

The MS rules of Hevrat Margoa la-Nefesh, Society for Administering Pecuniary Comforts, from 1797/98 forbade members from joining other benefit societies, but permitted them to join Hevrat Maariv biZmanah. FS 1/408B, PRO.

20. B. A. Fersht, "Chebrah Rodphea Sholom—Notes upon the First Jewish Friendly Society in England," *MJHSE* 2 (1935):94; MS rules of Path of Rectitude Benefit Society, filed at the Guildhall, 27 October 1817, FS 1/417, PRO; *Rules of a Friendly Society called the United Israelites* (London, 1835), FS 1/486A, PRO; MS rules of the Guardians of Faith, undated [probably 1832], FS 1/443, PRO.

21. H. J. Zimmels, "Pesakim ve-teshuvot me-bet dino shel R. Shelomoh b. R. Zvi ha-nikra Rabbi Solomon Hirschell" [Minutes from the Religious Court of Rabbi Solomon Hirschell], in *Essays Presented to Chief Rabbi Israel Brodie on the Occasion of his Seventieth Birthday,* ed. H. J. Zimmels, J. Rabbinowitz, and I. Finestein, 2 vols. (London, 1967), 2:225–26, 232–33.

22. Duschinsky, *Rabbinate of the Great Synagogue,* p. 15; Lyon, *On Wearing Beards,* pp. 11–12; *Olam hadash,* p. 2.

23. *An Appeal to the Elders of the Spanish and Portuguese Jews* (London, n.d.), p. 16. The copy of this pamphlet at Jews' College, London, has inscribed on the title page the following: "sermon by Jacob Mocatta, grandfather of F. D. Mocatta, about 1800." The copy at the Jewish Theological Seminary, New York, which was owned by Israel Solomons, has the date 1796 in pencil on the title page.

24. Hambro Synagogue, Minute Book, General Meetings, 1811–33, entry for 24 March 1833, AUS; Duschinsky, *Rabbinate of the Great Synagogue,* p. 17; Minutes of the Mahamad, 9 October 1818–21 September 1824, MS 111, entry for 21 January 1821, ASPS; Henry John Marks, *Narrative of H. J. Marks, Formerly a Jew, Now a Follower of the Lord Jesus Christ* (London, 1838), pp. 89–90; Hyamson, *Sephardim of England,* pp. 130–33; *GM,* vol. 65, pt. 1 (1795), pp. 98–99.

25. James Picciotto, *Sketches of Anglo-Jewish History,* ed. Israel Finestein (London, 1956), pp. 294–95; Hyamson, *Sephardim of England,* pp. 209–11; Isaac Espinasse, *Reports of Cases Argued and Ruled at Nisi Prius in the Courts of King's Bench and Common Pleas,* 6 vols. (London, 1793–1807) 1:285–86; Minutes of the Mahamad, 9 October 1818–21 September 1824, MS 111, entry for 1 June 1824, ASPS. There is substantial evidence that King was involved in a variety of shady moneymaking schemes. See J. J. Tobias, *Prince of Fences: The Life and Crimes of Ikey Solomons* (London, 1974), pp. 44–47.

26. *OB* 44 (1802):22–23; *OB* 41 (1799):13–16; *OB* 24 (1783):117.

27. Norman Cohen, "Non-Religious Factors in the Emergence of the Chief Rabbinate," *TJHSE* 21 (1962–67):309; Duschinsky, *Rabbinate of the Great Synagogue,* pp. 21–22, 94, 122.

28. Arthur Barnett, "Solomon Bennett, 1761–1838, Artist, Hebraist, and Controversialist," *TJHSE* 17 (1951–52):106; Solomon Bennett, *The Present Reign of the Synagogue of Duke's Place Displayed* (London, 1818), pp. 64–65; John Haggard, *Reports of Cases in the Consistory Court of London, Containing the Judgments of Sir William Scott,* 2 vols. (London, 1822), 1: 216–61, 324–36.

29. Roth, *The Great Synagogue,* p. 68; Great Synagogue, Minutes of Vestry Meetings, 1825–51, entry for 19 January 1826, AUS; Hambro Synagogue, Minute Book, 1794–1809, entry for 1 April 1801, AUS; Bennett, *Reign of Duke's Place,* pp. 19, 64–66.

30. Zimmels, "Pesakim ve-teshuvot me-bet dino shel R. Shelomoh b. R. Zvi," passim; Hambro Synagogue, Minute Book, 1794–1809, entry for 20 November 1805, AUS; Great Synagogue, Minutes of Vestry Meetings, 1825–51, entries for 22 May 1826, 8 January 1827, and 17 February 1827, AUS; Great Synagogue, Minutes, 1825–41, entry for 22 March 1829, AUS.

31. Arthur Barnett, *The Western Synagogue through Two Centuries, 1761–1961* (London, 1961), p. 108; Mahamad, Minute Book, 1 October 1824–12 September 1833, MS 112, entry for 14 August 1825, ASPS; Great Synagogue, Minutes, 1815–25, entries for 4 July and 4 August 1825, AUS.

32. Richard D. Barnett, "The Correspondence of the Mahamad of the Spanish and Portuguese Congregation of London during the Seventeenth and Eighteenth Centuries," *TJHSE* 20 (1959–61):9; Mahamad, Minute Book, 1 October 1824–12 September 1833, MS 112, entries for 21 October 1824 and 16 June 1825, ASPS; Elders' Papers, 1816–20, MS 290, documents regarding the conversion of Sarah Inness, April 1816, ASPS.

33. Thomas Witherby, *A Vindication of the Jews, by way of Reply to the Letter Addressed by Perseverans to the English Israelite* (London, 1809), p. 6.

34. *A Letter Addressed to the Overseers of the Portugueze Jewish Synagogue, in Bevismarks, London, upon their Extraordinary Conduct in the Dispute Between Mr. Ximenes and Mr. Joshua Lara* (London, 1772), pp. 45–46; Hambro Synagogue, Minute Book, Committee, 1809–24, entry for 25 March 1817, AUS; Picciotto, *Sketches of Anglo-Jewish History,* p. 289.

35. Hyman B. Grinstein, "The American Synagogue and Laxity of Religious Observance, 1750–1850" (M.A. thesis, Columbia University, 1935), pp. 5–7, 42.

36. Duschinsky, *Rabbinate of the Great Synagogue,* p. 15; *Olam hadash,* p. 5.

37. *An Appeal to the Elders of the Spanish and Portuguese Jews,* p. 10; LSPCJ, *Obligations of Christians,* p. 8.

38. Robert Southey, *Selections from the Letters of Robert Southey,* ed. J. W.

Warter, 4 vols. (London, 1856), 4:177. Southey's linking of Voltaire and Mendelssohn, as incongruous as it may seem to us today, was common at the time. For a discussion of whether Mendelssohn was a deist, see Moshe Pelli, "The Impact of Deism on the Hebrew Literature of the Enlightenment in Germany," *Journal of Jewish Studies* 24 (1973):135–40.

39. Marks, *Narrative*, p. 15; Tobias Goodman, *Emunat Yisrael: The Faith of Israel* (London, 1834).

40. *A Peep into the Synagogue,* pp. 32–33; *OB* 52 (1810):144–46.

41. [Isaac D'Israeli], *The Genius of Judaism* (London, 1833), pp. 77–78, 91, 159, 260–63; idem, "A Biographical Sketch of the Jewish Socrates," *The Monthly Magazine*, vol. 6, pt. 2 (1798), p. 36; idem, *Vaurien*, 2:244–45.

42. D'Israeli, *Vaurien*, 2:247; idem, *Genius of Judaism*, pp. 265–66.

43. *Letter to the Parisian Sanhedrin*, pp. 2–3, 15; Levi Alexander, *The Axe Laid to the Root, or Ignorance and Superstition Evident in the Character of the Rev. S. Hirschell* (London, 1808), p. 18; Duschinsky, *Rabbinate of the Great Synagogue*, p. 116.

44. Alexander, *Axe Laid to the Root*, p. 24; idem, *Memoirs of Benjamin Goldsmid*, p. 24; Solomon Bennett, *Netzah Yisrael: The Constancy of Israel* (London, 1812), pp. 224–25; idem, *Reign of Duke's Place*, p. 61.

45. Moses Samuel, *Memoirs of Moses Mendelssohn, the Jewish Philosopher*, 2nd ed. (London, 1827), pp. 110, 113.

46. Samuel, *Mendelssohn*, pp. 2, 18; Shalom ben Jacob Cohen, *Shorshei Emunah: Elements of Faith for the Use of Jewish Youth*, trans. Joshua Van Oven (London, 1815), p. 43; Joshua Van Oven, *Manual of Judaism* (London, 1835), p. ix and passim.

47. Hyman Hurwitz, *Hebrew Tales, Selected and Translated from the Writings of the Ancient Hebrew Sages: To Which Is Prefixed an Essay on the Uninspired Literature of the Hebrews* (London, 1826), pp. 16–21, 34–37.

48. Hurwitz, *Hebrew Tales*, pp. 48–50; Samuel Taylor Coleridge to the Rev. H. F. Cary, 31 December 1820, *Collected Letters of Samuel Taylor Coleridge*, ed. Earl Leslie Griggs, 6 vols. (Oxford, 1966–71) 5:132.

49. For a perceptive appreciation of Hurwitz's achievements, see Siegfried Stein, *The Beginnings of Hebrew Studies at University College* (London, 1952).

50. Roth, *History of the Great Synagogue*, p. 82; Rubens, *Anglo-Jewish Portraits*, p. 91; *A Peep into the Synagogue*, pp. 8–16.

51. Great Synagogue, Minutes, Committee Meetings, 1815–25, entries for 4 May 1820 and 22 June 1820, AUS.

52. Great Synagogue, Minutes, Committee Meetings, 1815–25, entries for 2 June 1823, 16 October 1823, 20 October 1823, 27 January 1824, 9 February 1825, and 28 February 1825, AUS; printed report of the Goldsmid committee on training *hazanim*, Lucien Wolf papers, Mocatta Library, University College, London; Great Synagogue, Minutes of Vestry Meetings, 1825–51, entry for 9 March 1826, AUS; Great Synagogue, Minute Book, Committees, 1811–29, entries for 24 November 1823, 8 December 1823, 5 January 1824, 5 January 1825, and 28 February 1826, AUS.

53. New Synagogue, Minute Book F, 1820–24, undated entry sometime prior to Purim 1824, AUS; Hambro Synagogue, Minute Book, Committee, 1824–33, entry for 7 March 1827, AUS; New Synagogue, Minute Book G, 1824–32, entry for 20 July 1825, AUS; Great Synagogue, Minutes, 1815–25, entries for 28 July, 31 August, and 11 September 1825, AUS; Hambro Synagogue, Minute Book, Committee, 1824–33, entry for 1 November 1830, AUS; Hambro Synagogue, Minute Book, General Meetings, 1811–33, entry for 12 December 1831, AUS.

54. Elders' Minute Book, 5 November 1826–29 June 1837, MS 92, entries for 14 December 1828, 26 April 1829, 17 May 1829, 21 November 1830, and 5 December 1830, ASPS; Minutes of Committees, 1 February 1829–8 July 1845, MS 31, Committee for the Promotion and Improvement of Religious Worship, ASPS; *Appeal to the Elders of the Spanish and Portuguese Jews,* p. 21.

55. LSPCJ, *Obligations,* pp. 6–7; *The World,* 22 August 1827. The response of Joseph Ballard from Boston, Massachusetts, who visited the Great Synagogue one Sabbath in 1815, was typical: "The service was chanted in Hebrew, the congregation joining in at times in 'din most horrible.' I came away disgusted with the little reverence they seemed to pay to that Being who pronounced them His chosen people!" Joseph Ballard, *England in 1815* (Boston and New York, 1913) pp. 128–29.

56. Loewe, *Diaries of Sir Moses and Lady Montefiore,* 1:82–83.

CHAPTER 5

1. Roth, *The Great Synagogue,* pp. 7–8; R. D. Barnett, "The Correspondence of the Mahamad," *TJHSE* 20 (1959–61):3–4.

2. Diamond, "Problems of the London Sephardi Community," pp. 40, 60; V. D. Lipman, "Sephardi and other Jewish Immigrants in England in the Eighteenth Century," in *Migration and Settlement: Proceedings of the Anglo-American Jewish Historical Conference . . . July 1970* (London, 1971), p. 44. Richard Barnett has recently suggested that A. S. Diamond's estimate of the number of refugees from Spain and Portugal in the period 1720–35 has to be revised upward quite substantially, possibly to something like 3,000 persons. Barnett came to this conclusion through a reexamination of the Bevis Marks marriage registers, which record the remarriages, according to Jewish rites, of refugees who had been married in the Church in Spain and Portugal, and which also indicate the Iberian origins of previously unmarried persons by omitting the names of their fathers, who were ostensible Christians there. For more details, see Richard D. Barnett, "Dr. Samuel Nunes Ribeiro and the Settlement of Georgia," in *Migration and Settlement,* pp. 79–80.

3. Barnett, "Dr. Samuel Nunes Ribeiro," pp. 81–87; Hyamson, *The Sephardim of England,* pp. 156–59. Hyamson erroneously describes the first Jewish settlers as "forty poor Ashkenazi families."

4. Lipman, "Sephardi Immigrants," pp. 42–44. A transcription of the entire register appears as app. A to Dr. Lipman's article.

5. Lipman, "Sephardi Immigrants," p. 44; Henry Mayhew, *London Labour and the London Poor*, 3 vols. (London, 1851), 1:507–8. There were a few North African and Gibraltarian Jews in London before the 1770s. For example, Abraham Benjamin, an itinerant merchant, arrived in London from Gibraltar in April 1743. He was unable to speak English and required a translator when he appeared at the Old Bailey, soon after his arrival, on the charge of stealing four moidores (of which he was acquitted). *OB* 4, pt. 2 (1743):159–60. Many of the Gibraltarian Jews, like Mayhew's informant, were themselves originally from Morocco. Messo Shannon, for example, a butcher who had a shop in Petticoat Lane in 1797, had been born in Barbary and then moved to Gibraltar before coming to London. He said, in 1797, that he had been a butcher for fifty years and that he had been in London for the past twenty years. *OB* 39 (1797):225–31.

6. Lipman, "Sephardi Immigrants," p. 41; *An Appeal to the Elders of the Spanish and Portuguese Jews*, p. 6.

7. D'Blossiers Tovey, *Anglia-Judaica, or, The History and Antiquities of the Jews in England* (Oxford, 1738), p. 302; Richard D. Barnett, "The Travels of Moses Cassuto," in *Remember the Days*, p. 103; Hanway, *Review of the Proposed Naturalization*, p. 67; Philo-Patriae, *Considerations*, p. 17; Patrick Colquhoun, *A Treatise on the Police of the Metropolis*, 5th ed. (London, 1797), p. 120; Frederick Augustus Wendeborn, *A View of England Towards the Close of the Eighteenth Century*, 2 vols. (London, 1791), 2:469; Francis Henry Goldsmid, *Remarks on the Civil Disabilities of British Jews* (London, 1830), pp. 69–70.

Interestingly, two estimates of the Jewish population of England made just before 1830 were not too far off Goldsmid's more carefully arrived at figure. In 1827, the Liverpool *maskil* Moses Samuel put the number of Jews living in Great Britain at 22,000; in 1829, Apsley Pellatt put the number at 25,000. (Goldsmid's figure was for London Jewry alone.) Moses Samuel, *An Address from an Israelite to the Missionary Preachers* (Liverpool, 1827), p. 4; Apsley Pellatt, *Brief Memoir*, p. iv. A letter from Moses E. Levy that appeared in *The World*, 12 December 1827, put the Jewish population of London at 3,000 families. Assuming five persons per family, that would make about 15,000 Jews living in London.

8. Lipman, "Sephardi Immigrants," p. 38.

9. For the statistics on Jewish criminal activity, see the Appendix. John Fielding to the Earl of Suffolk, 16 November 1771, SP 37/8, PRO; Colquhoun, *Police of the Metropolis*, p. 41; *The Parliamentary Reporter*, 17 (1802): 63–64.

10. Hambro Synagogue, Copy Book of Letters Despatched, 1808–14, minutes of "treaty" meeting, 16 January 1812, AUS; Hambro Synagogue, Minute Book, Committee, 1809–24, entry for 16 June 1814, AUS; Hambro Synagogue, Minute Book, General Meetings, 1811–33,

entry for 20 October 1814, AUS; Hambro Synagogue, Copy Book of Letters Despatched, 1822–38, 10 March 1824, AUS.

11. Lipman, "Sephardi Immigrants," p. 39; *OB* 23 (1783):743–47; report of Jewish Auxiliary Committee, 19 October 1807, LMS; LSPCJ, certificates accompanying applications for places in the Society's schools, Dep CMJ c.114/2, Bodleian Library, Oxford; *The Jewish Repository* 3 (1815):74–75, 383–84; Westminster Sessions Papers, register of aliens, June–July 1798, parish of St. Martin's-in-the-Fields, WR/A/98, Greater London Record Office.

12. *OB* 4 (1743):159–60; *OB* 5 (1744):29–31; Middlesex Sessions Papers, MJ/SP 1748 Oct/125, Greater London Record Office; *OB* 15 (1771):142; *OB* 27 (1787):263–64, 739–44; Shulvass, *From East to West*, p. 63; Cecil Roth, "The Lesser Synagogues of the Eighteenth Century," *MJHSE* 3 (1937):5–6.

13. Shulvass, *From East to West*, p. 109; John Fielding to the Earl of Suffolk, 16 November 1771, SP 37/8, PRO; *A Peep into the Synagogue* (London, [late 1700s], p. 23. On the *Betteljuden*, also see Shulvass, *From East to West*, pp. 13–14, 67–70, 98–104, 108–10; Menahem Friedman, "Michtavei ha-melitsah la-kavtsanim—'katavim': le-baayat ha-navadim be-Germanyah ba-meah ha-shmoneh-esrei" [Letters of Recommendation for Jewish Mendicants—a Comment upon the Problem of Jewish Vagrancy in 18th Century Germany], *Michael: On the History of the Jews in the Diaspora* 2 (1973):34–51; Shohet, *Im hilufei tekufot*, pp. 27–28, 153–58; Rudolf Glanz, *Geschichte des Niederen Jüdischen Volkes in Deutschland* (New York, 1968).

14. Lipman, "Sephardi Immigrants," p. 40; *The Jewish Repository* 3 (1815):74–75.

15. Statement of Abraham Phillips, 20 February 1809, LMS.

16. Notes on Abraham Moses Lande, 2 April 1806, LMS; W. Clegg, *The History and Conversion of Samuel Harris* (Bradford, 1833), pp. 8–23.

17. M. Dorothy George, *London Life in the Eighteenth Century*, (Harmondsworth, Middlesex, 1965), p. 133; *OB* 5 (1745):50–52; *GM* 21 (1751):424; *OB* 18 (1777):280–84; *OB* 33 (1793):1196–1201.

18. [Charles Cochrane], *Journal of a Tour Made by Senor Juan de Vega, the Spanish Minstrel of 1828–29, through Great Britain and Ireland*, 2 vols. (London, 1830), 2:78; *OB* 54 (1812):123; *GM* 80, pt. 1 (1810):557.

19. Clegg, *History of Samuel Harris*, pp. 23, 37; Mayhew, *London Labour*, 1:384; Israel Solomon, MS history of the Jews in Cornwall, 1885, in the Lucien Wolf papers, BA 29, Provincial Jewries, Mocatta Library, University College, London.

20. *OB* 23 (1783):743–47.

21. Mayhew, *London Labour*, 1:330, 382, 494–96; 2:130.

22. *A Peep into the Synagogue*, pp. 26–27; Southey, *Letters from England*, 3:151–52.

23. Richard Phillips, *Modern London, Being the History of the British Metropolis* (London, 1804), p. 90; Benjamin Silliman, *A Journal of Travels in England, Holland, and Scotland*, 3rd ed., 3 vols. (New Haven, 1820), 1:

270–71; Mayhew, *London Labour*, 2:121; Colquhoun, *Police of the Metropolis*, p. vii. Some old-clothes men offered the servants glassware, earthenware, and china in exchange for the old clothes of the master and mistress of the house. James Peller Malcolm, *Anecdotes of the Manners and Customs of London during the Eighteenth Century* (London, 1808), p. 137.

24. Samuel Taylor Coleridge, *Table Talk*, 14 August 1833, quoted in Rosenberg, *From Shylock to Svengali*, p. 55; *GM*, vol. 100, pt. 1 (1830): 135. In the various series of engravings of London street traders ("The Cries of London"), which were published in the late eighteenth and early nineteenth centuries, the Jewish old-clothes man appears fully bearded, wearing a long black caftan, tied with a sash around his waist, and a broad-brimmed hat. In some versions, four or five hats, obviously his morning's purchases, are piled on top of his own. Many of these engravings have been reproduced by Alfred Rubens in his various studies on Jewish portraits and caricatures. See his previously cited "Portrait of Anglo-Jewry" and *Anglo-Jewish Portraits*. Also see his *Jewish Iconography* (London, 1954) and his *History of Jewish Costume* (London, 1967).

25. Silliman, *A Journal of Travels*, 1:270–71; Phillips, *Modern London*, p. 90; William Austin, *Letters from London Written during the Years 1802 & 1803* (Boston, 1804), p. 67; John Badcock, *A Living Picture of London for 1828* (London, 1828), pp. 110–11; Charles Dickens, "Meditations in Monmouth Street," in *Sketches by Boz* (London, 1866), p. 68 (first published in 1836).

A clipping from an 1830 newspaper (its title missing, unfortunately) in the Colyer-Fergusson MSS at the Jewish Museum, London, tells of a running battle that year between a Christian bookseller named Chubb, who lived in Holywell Street, and the Jewish clothes dealers there. Chubb felt that the practice of Jews dragging persons into their shops to purchase old clothes had driven away his customers. In retaliation, he stuck up the following placard: "Who are the most impudent people in the world? The Jews. Who ask a pound for an article and take five shillings? The Jews. Who pull people into their shops, whether they want to buy or not? The Jews. Who, instead of keeping dogs, have *barkers* outside their door? The Jews. Who are the most ignorant? The Jews." The Jewish shopkeepers then brought a complaint against Chubb at Bow Street. One of them apparently also hurled some mud at Mrs. Chubb.

26. Roth, "The Jew Peddler," p. 132; idem, *Provincial Jewry*, passim; Bill Williams, *The Making of Manchester Jewry, 1740–1875* (Manchester, 1976), pp. 1–16.

27. Southey, *Journal of a Tour*, 2:152; *OB* 66 (1824):77–78; *The London Gazette*, no. 7995, 7–10 March 1740 [i.e., 1741]; *OB* 19 (1779):17; Mayhew, *London Labour*, 1:382; E. P. Thompson, "Time, Work Discipline and Industrial Capitalism," *Past & Present*, no. 38 (1967):70.

28. Williams, *Manchester Jewry*, pp. 68, 115; Gerald Rufus Isaacs, *Rufus Isaacs: First Marquess of Reading* (New York, 1940), p. 5.

29. Mayhew, *London Labour*, 2:130; V. D. Lipman, *Social History of the Jews in England, 1850–1950* (London, 1954), p. 27.

30. *OB* 8 (1755):177–79; *OB* 8 (1756):167; *OB* 55 (1813):69–74.

31. Memoir of Joseph Samuel Frey to the Jewish Committee of the London Missionary Society, 19 October 1807, LMS; An English Israelite, *A Letter to the Parisian Sanhedrin*, p. 33; Camden Pelham, pseud. [Halblot Knight Browne], *The Chronicles of Crime, or, The New Newgate Calendar*, 2 vols. (London, 1891), 2:235; *The Universal Songster, or, Museum of Mirth*, 3 vols. (London, 1834), 1:194, 340; Frey, *Narrative*, pp. 208–9.

32. Daniel Mendoza, *The Memoirs of the Life of Daniel Mendoza*, ed. Paul Magriel (London, 1951), pp. 14–16.

33. Joshua Van Oven, *Letters on the Present State of the Jewish Poor in the Metropolis* (London, 1802), p. 12; Middlesex Sessions Papers, MJ/SP September 1771 and MJ/SP 1798 DEC/71, Greater London Record Office.

34. Levy Alexander, *Answer to Mr. Joshua Van Oven's Letters on the Present State of the Jewish Poor in London* (London, 1802), pp. 24–26; Middlesex Sessions Papers, MJ/SP September 1771, Greater London Record Office; *OB* 36 (1795):293–94.

35. Philo-Judaeis, *A Letter to Abraham Goldsmid, Esq., Containing Strictures on Mr. Joshua Van Oven's Letters on the Present State of the Jewish Poor* (London, 1802), p. 12; Alexander, *Answer*, p. 37.

CHAPTER 6

1. *OB* 35 (1974):735–36; *OB* 66 (1824):85, 451–52.

2. For the sources of all the statistics on Jewish crime that appear in this chapter, see the appendix.

3. *OB* 4 (1743):267. There are no comprehensive accounts of urban criminal life in Georgian England. Dorothy George's *London Life in the Eighteenth Century* contains much valuable information on the subject. *Albion's Fatal Tree: Crime and Society in Eighteenth-Century England,* (New York, 1975), with essays by E. P. Thompson, Douglas Hay, and others, focuses more on crime in the countryside than in the city and more on crimes with a social or political component than on the activities of professional criminals, such as shoplifting, pickpocketing, burglary, and robbery. Two recent essays by J. M. Beattie treat in a much more direct manner the kinds of urban criminality with which we are concerned in this chapter: "The Pattern of Crime in England, 1660–1800," *Past & Present,* no. 62 (February 1974):47–95, and "The Criminality of Women in Eighteenth Century England," *Journal of Social History* 8 (1975):80–116. J. J. Tobias's *Urban Crime in Victorian England,* (New York, 1972) and his *Prince of Fences: The Life and Crimes of Ikey Solomons* (London, 1974) cover the 1820s and 1830s. The latter work is particularly helpful in untangling the confused network of criminal courts in London at this period. On this subject, see also Anthony Babington, *A House in Bow Street: Crime and the Magistracy, London, 1740–1881* (London, 1969).

4. J. E., Gent., pseud., *Some Considerations on the Naturalization of the Jews*

(London, 1753), p. 12. The *Westminster Journal,* 9 July 1753, also charged the Jews with being receivers of stolen goods, as did the *Evening Post,* 10 July 1753.

5. *OB* 5 (1744):10–11; *OB* 15 (1770):55–56.

6. *OB* 14 (1769):389; *The Universal Songster,* 2:429.

7. J. E., *Some Considerations,* p. 12; Andrew Knapp and William Baldwin, *The New Newgate Calendar,* 2nd ed., 5 vols. (London, 1826), 2:263; Henry Fielding, "An Enquiry into the Causes of the late Increase of Robbers," in *The Works of Henry Fielding,* 10 vols. (London, 1806), 10:412 (first published in 1751).

8. William Cole MSS, British Museum, quoted in R. Leslie-Melville, *The Life and Work of Sir John Fielding* (London, 1934), pp. 260–61; *OB* 12 (1765):333; Roth, *Great Synagogue,* pp. 157–59.

9. *OB* 13 (1767):187; *OB* 14 (1769):148; *Journals of the House of Commons* 32 (1770):879; *The Annual Register for the Year 1770* 13 (1771):90.

10. This account of the Chelsea murder case is based on the following sources: State Papers 37/8, PRO; *GM* 41 (1771):518, 521, 566; *OB* 16 (1772):34–47; Knapp and Baldwin, *The New Newgate Calendar,* 3:282; Leslie-Melville, *Sir John Fielding,* pp. 261–64; Elkan N. Adler, *London,* Jewish Communities Series of the Jewish Publication Society (Philadelphia, 1930), pp. 151–57; William Jackson, *The New and Complete Newgate Calendar,* 8 vols. (London, 1800–12), 5:21; newspaper clippings in the Elkan Adler papers, The Jewish Theological Seminary, New York.

11. Jackson, *New and Complete Newgate Calendar,* 5:23; Horace Walpole, *The Yale Edition of Horace Walpole's Correspondence,* ed. W. S. Lewis, vol. 32, *Horace Walpole's Correspondence with the Countess of Upper Ossory,* pt. 1, ed. W.S. Lewis, A. Dayle Wallace, and Edwine M. Martz (New Haven, 1965), pp. 67–68; Francis Place MSS, British Museum, quoted in George, *London Life,* p. 137; William Cobbett, "To Big O," *Cobbett's Weekly Political Register* 69 (1830):732.

12. Adler, *London,* pp. 151–52; *GM* 41 (1771):566; State Papers 37/8, PRO; letter of Anthony Toddsey, Postmaster General, London, to James Clements, Harwich, 9 September 1774, and G.P.O. advertisement, 10 October 1774, copies in the Lucien Wolf papers, Mocatta Library, University College, London.

As a consequence of the pressure applied by the synagogal authorities, there appears to have been a short-term drop in the intensity of criminal activity; at the very least, it became more difficult for thieves to dispose of their loot to Jewish receivers. Lyon Bacharach testified at the Old Bailey in December 1771, immediately after the trial of the Chelsea murder gang: "The Jews are so sharp now we don't know who to trust." Bacharach had tried to dispose of 120 men's and boys' hats he had stolen to David Levi, who kept a shoe and hat "warehouse." (This was probably the same David Levi who engaged in an extended theological dispute with Joseph Priestley in the late 1780s.) Levi went to Naphtali Hart Myers, one of the *parnasim* of the Great Synagogue, who then informed Sir John Fielding. They devised a trap for Bacharach and caught him and his partner, Isaac Asher, with the stolen goods. *OB* 16 (1772):49–51.

13. Alexander Alexander, *A Key to Part of the Hebrew Liturgy* (London, 1775), p. 51; *Morning Post,* 6 December 1775; Richard King, *The Frauds of London Detected* (London, n.d. [ca. 1780]), pp. 111–14.

14. *Morning Chronicle,* 23 May and 26 June 1817; *Parliamentary Papers* (Commons), "Report from the Select Committee on the Bankrupt Laws," 1817, 5:81–82; 1818, 6:64 65.

15. George Parker, *A View of Society in High and Low Life,* 2 vols. (London, 1781), 2:28–34; *Trial of Kinnear, Levy, and Woolf;* Williams, *Manchester Jewry,* p. 33. See also *The London Spy* (London, 1823), pp. 16–17, for another description of swindling.

16. *Parliamentary Papers* (Commons), "Report from the Committee on the Petitions of Watchmakers of Coventry," 1817, 6: 16, 28, 31–32; Kidd, "London and All its Dangers," p. 13; *OB* 68 (1826):673; Williams, *Manchester Jewry,* p. 33; *Universal Songster,* 1:262.

17. Colquhoun, *Police of the Metropolis,* p. 44; idem, *A Treatise on the Commerce and Police of the River Thames* (London, 1800), pp. 196–97; W. A. Miles, *Poverty, Mendicity, and Crime,* ed. H. Brandon (London, 1839), pp. 102, 135–38, 151. For the life of the most notorious Jewish fence of the 1820s, see the above-cited work by J. J. Tobias on Ikey Solomons. It was not only Christians who believed that the principal receivers in London were Jews. A "worthy and sensible Jew gentleman" told Sir William Blizard in the early 1780s that "there was hardly a robbery to any considerable amount in which many of these persons ['the lower order of Jews'] were not, either directly or remotely, concerned." William Blizard, *Desultory Reflections on Police, with an Essay on Preventing Crimes and Amending Criminals* (London, 1785), pp. 43–44.

18. *The Times,* 30 July 1795; [John Feltham], *The Picture of London for 1813,* 14th ed. (London, 1813), p. 60. Earlier editions contain the same warning.

19. Williams, *Manchester Jewry,* p. 7; Colquhoun, *Police of the Metropolis,* pp. 113–14. Colquhoun stated that the Jews confined themselves principally to coining and circulating bad copper and that he knew of hardly an instance of Jews having anything to do with counterfeiting silver coins. This may have been true in the 1790s, but it was not so in later years. For example, in September 1819, Wolf Levy, age 24, was sentenced to one year in prison for selling bad shillings; in December 1819, Moses Lyons, age 19, was jailed for the same offense, as was Levy Hyams, age 27, in January 1824. Colquhoun, *Police of the Metropolis,* pp. 119–20; *OB* 61 (1819):422–23: *OB* 62 (1820):77, *OB* 66 (1824):125.

20. *OB* 15 (1771):479–80; *OB* 44 (1802):153–58; *OB* 56 (1814):117–18, 126; Tobias, *Prince of Fences,* pp. 4–5.

21. Frey, *Narrative,* pp. 209–16.

22. *OB* 8 (1756):135–37; *OB* 9 (1757):360–63.

23. Jacob Rader Marcus, "Shed a Tear for a Transport: The Sad Fate of Feibel, the Son of Joseph Jacob of Jever," in *Raphael Mahler Jubilee Volume: Studies in Jewish History Presented to Professor Raphael Mahler on his*

Seventy-Fifth Birthday, ed. Shmuel Yeivin (Merhavia, Israel, 1974), pp. 53–61.

24. *OB* 56 (1814):360–61; *OB* 58 (1816):169–71; *OB* 67 (1825):150–51; *Parliamentary Papers* (Commons), "Minutes of Evidence taken before the Committee on the State of the Police of the Metropolis," 1816, 5:100. For a band of Jewish criminals operating in northern France and Belgium at the end of the eighteenth century, see Richard Cobb, *Paris and its Provinces, 1792–1802* (London, 1975), ch. 5, sec. 1 ("Dinah Jacob and the *Bande Juive*"); for Jewish criminal bands in Germany, see Glanz, *Geschichte des Niederen Jüdischen Volkes in Deutschland,* chs. 7, 10–13.

25. *The London Guide and Stranger's Safeguard against the Cheats, Swindlers, and Pickpockets that abound within the Bills of Mortality* (London, 1818), pp. 72–73; Madeline House and Graham Storey, eds., *The Letters of Charles Dickens,* 3 vols. to date (Oxford, 1965–), 1:45; William Thackeray, *Vanity Fair,* chs. 52, 53.

26. John W. Derry, *Charles James Fox* (London, 1972), p. 50; Walpole, vol. 28, *Horace Walpole's Correspondence with William Mason,* ed. W. S. Lewis, Grover Cronin, Jr., and Charles H. Bennett (New Haven, 1955), pp. 92–93, 392; idem, vol. 31, *Horace Walpole's Correspondence with Hannah More,* ed. W. S. Lewis, Robert A. Smith, and Charles H. Bennett (New Haven, 1961), p. 378.

27. King, *Modern London Spy,* p. 49; Colquhoun, *Police of the Metropolis,* pp. 159–60.

28. Cole MSS, British Museum, copy in the Lucien Wolf papers, Mocatta Library, University College, London; *London Magazine* 43 (1774):300; *The Commercial Habits of the Jews,* p. 58.

29. *The Times,* 28 June 1827; *The Universal Songster,* 2:61; *GM* 79 (1809):1077.

30. *London Chronicle,* 27 and 29 November 1810; Westminster Sessions Papers, 9 January 1810, Greater London Record Office; *Morning Chronicle,* 30 May 1809; Ed Robson to the Earl of Liverpool, 29 May 1804, HO 42/99, PRO. I am indebted to Navah Haber-Scheim for bringing several of these examples to my attention.

31. James Boaden, *Memoirs of the Life of John Philip Kemble,* 2 vols. (London, 1825), 2:334; Thomas Dibdin, *The Reminiscences of Thomas Dibdin,* 2 vols. (London, 1827), 1:339–46; *Monthly Mirror* 14 (1802): 404–5; *Universal Magazine* 3 (1802):455–56; *The Times,* 20 December 1802; *Morning Chronicle,* 20 December 1802.

32. *OB* 24 (1784):1230–40. This is the only reference I have come across that describes this mode of celebrating Simhat Torah. The testimony of several witnesses makes it clear that this had been going on for a number of years previously. Whether it came to an end with the death of Moses Lazarus in 1784 is unknown. For the custom of exploding gunpowder on Simhat Torah, see Herman Pollack, *Jewish Folkways in Germanic Lands, 1648–1806* (Cambridge, Mass., 1971) pp. 174–77.

33. Anonymous newspaper clipping, 1811, "Various," CF.

34. For this account of Jewish prizefighters, I have drawn on the

following works: Pierce Egan, *Boxiana*, 5 vols. (London, 1812–29); Frank R. Dowling, *Fistiana, or, The Oracle of the Ring* (London, 1841); Henry Downes Miles, *Pugilistica: The History of British Boxing*, 3 vols. (Edinburgh, 1906); Rubens, "Portrait of Anglo-Jewry"; Mendoza, *Memoirs*. A good introduction to the topic in general is John Ford, *Prizefighting: The Age of Regency Boximania* (Newton Abbot, Devon, 1971). For the background to the development of prizefighting as a fashionable sport, see J. C. Reid, *Bucks and Bruisers: Pierce Egan and Regency England* (London, 1971). On the attempt of reformers to suppress boxing and other popular pastimes, see Robert W. Malcolmson, *Popular Recreations in English Society, 1700–1850* (Cambridge, 1973). The comments of Francis Place are quoted in George, *London Life*, pp. 137–38.

35. Magriel, *Daniel Mendoza*, pp. 4–5; Henry Lemoine, *Modern Manhood, or, The Art and Practice of Boxing* (1788), p. 85, quoted in Rubens, "Portrait of Anglo-Jewry," p. 21; Rubens, *Anglo-Jewish Portraits*, p. 78; Egan, *Boxiana*, 1:322; 2:476; 4:521–33; Ford, *Prizefighting*, p. 76; *The Annals of Sporting and Fancy Gazette* 3 (1823):339.

36. Knapp and Baldwin, *New Newgate Calendar*, 2:219; E. M. Forster, *Marianne Thornton: A Domestic Biography, 1797–1887* (New York, 1956), p. 52; Miles, *Pugilistica*, 1:486, 2:353.

37. *Morning Chronicle*, 19 September–21 October 1809; *Observer*, 15 October, 17 December 1809; Roth, *Great Synagogue*, pp. 208–11. The Old Price riots were commemorated in a verse history by Thomas Tegg. *The Rise, Progress, and Termination of the O.P. War, in Poetic Epistles* (London, 1810). The frontispiece is a fold-out cartoon by George Cruikshank of a scene from the pit of the Covent Garden Theatre. A group of scruffy-looking toughs with vicious faces are beating three members of the audience senseless. One victim is on his knees, blood streaming from his face, surrounded by eight or nine men, two of whom are removing a watch and billfold from his pocket.

38. George Borrow, *Lavengro* (London, 1904), pp. 166–67; *Cobbett's Weekly Political Register* 69 (1830):734; *The Annals of Sporting and Fancy Gazette* 6 (1824):364.

39. *OB* 12 (1764):153–55, 180–81; *OB* 16 (1773):147–48; *OB* 41 (1798):13–16; Minute Book, Mahamad, 1 October 1824–12 September 1833, MS 112, entry for 17 October 1827, ASPS; letter to the Mahamad from Mary Denney, 20 May 1829, MS 295 (43), ASPS.

40. Minutes of the Mahamad, 9 October 1818–21 September 1824, MS 111, entries for 23 May and 5 August 1822, ASPS; *OB* 67 (1825): 151–56; New Synagogue, Minute Book F, 1820–24, entry for 21 April 1823, AUS.

41. Great Synagogue, Minute Book, 1825–41, entry for 27 March 1826, AUS.

CHAPTER 7

1. Van Oven, *Letters,* pp. 3–6.

2. *Sketch of a Speech Delivered by the President at the Second General Meeting of the Subscribers to the New Spanish and Portuguese Jews Charity School on July 1, 1821* (London, 1821), p. 10.

3. Hyman Hurwitz, *Elements of the Hebrew Language* (London, 1807), pp. ii, vi–vii; John Mills, *The British Jews* (London, 1853), pp. 292–93.

4. *Rules Framed for the Management of the Orphan Charity School, Known by the Name of H. K. Talmud Torah, Belonging to the German Jews* (London, 1788), pp. 10–11, 18–19; Minute Book, Hevra Kadisha de-Talmud Torah, entries for 21 October 1792, 27 January 1803, 8 January 1812.

5. *Rules of the Talmud Torah,* pp. 10–12, 19; Minute Book, Hevra Kadisha de-Talmud Torah, entries for 8 January 1795, 24 December 1795, 7 June 1797, 16 August 1801, 28 July 1806, 22 July 1807.

6. Minute Book, Hevra Kadisha de-Talmud Torah, entries for 8 August 1793, 19 December 1803; Alexander, *Memoirs of Benjamin Goldsmid,* pp. 114–15; printed list of original contributors to the Jews' Hospital, JH.

7. Van Oven, *Letters,* passim; Picciotto, *Sketches of Anglo-Jewish History,* pp. 250–51; *The Annual Register for the Year 1821* (London, 1822), p. 7. Further evidence that London Jews entered parish workhouses can be found in the synagogue burial registers now in the Office of the Chief Rabbi. These registers include deceased Jews who were living in the workhouse at the time of death. I am grateful to Mr. Charles Tucker of London for providing me with this information.

8. Joshua Van Oven to Patrick Colquhoun, 24 March 1801, in Roth, *Anglo-Jewish Letters,* pp. 217–19.

9. Picciotto, *Sketches of Anglo-Jewish History,* pp. 251–52.

10. Hambro Synagogue, Minute Book, 1794–1809, entry for 10 February 1802, AUS; Charles H. L. Emanuel, *A Century and a Half of Jewish History: Extracted from the Minute Books of the London Committee of Deputies of the British Jews* (London, 1910), pp. 10–12.

11. Philo-Judaeis, *Letter to Abraham Goldsmid,* pp. 12–14, 25, 28; Alexander, *Answer to Joshua Van Oven,* pp. 24, 41–42.

12. *The Parliamentary Register* 17 (1802):63–64; Board of Deputies of British Jews, Minute Book 1, November 1760–April 1828, entries for 14 February and 2 March 1802, Woburn House, London.

13. *Rules of the Talmud Torah,* p. 1; *Rules and Regulations for the Management of the Jews' Hospital, Mile End, called Neveh Tsedek* (London, 1808), pp. xv, 16, 19, 21–22.

14. Jews' Hospital, Governors' Reports of Visits, 1811–63, entry for 2 June 1814; General Committee, Minute Book, 1822–27, entry for 28 May 1823, JH.

15. Jews' Hospital, Lady Visitors' Book, 1811–61, entry for 28 March 1813; Governors' Reports of Visits, 1811–63, entry for 23 March 1817, JH.

16. Jews' Hospital, General Committee, Minute Book, 1822–27, entries for 28 November, 9 July, and 21 July 1823, JH.

17. *Rules of the Jews' Hospital,* p. 26; Jews' Hospital, General Committee, Minute Book, 1819–22, entry for 22 November 1820; Lady Visitors' Book, 1811–61, entries for July and 1 September 1812, JH.

18. A Daughter of Israel, pseud., *The Jewish Preceptress, or, Elementary Lessons Written Chiefly for the Use of the Female Children Educated at the Jews' Hospital* (London, 1818), pp. ix, 52–53, 58–59. The author's preface is dated 1812, as are the forwards by Isaac Lyon Goldsmid and I. I. Bing, but I know of no edition that was printed before 1818.

19. Alexander, *Memoirs of Benjamin Goldsmid,* p. 115; Anthony Highmore, *Philanthropia Metropolitana: A View of the Charitable Institutions Established in and near London, Chiefly during the Last Twelve Years* (London, 1822), p. 277; E. W. Brayley, J. N. Brewer, and J. Nightingale, *A Topographical and Historical Description of London and Middlesex,* 5 vols. (London, 1810–16), 3:121; Henry Faudel, *A Brief Investigation into the System of the Jews' Hospital* (London, 1844), pp. 10–11; *Rules of the Jews' Hospital,* pp. 11, 19.

20. Thomas Witherby, *A Vindication of the Jews, by Way of Reply to the Letter Addressed by Perseverans to the English Israelite* (London, 1809), pp. 101–4; Norris, *Origins,* p. 11; R. H. Martin, "The Pan Evangelical Impulse in Britain, 1795–1830, With Special Reference to Four London Societies" (D. Phil. diss., Oxford University, 1974), p. 325; London Missionary Society, memoir from Frey to the Jewish Committee, 19 October 1807, and letter from the officers of the Great Synagogue to Joseph Hardcastle, 8 January 1807, LMS.

21. Scult, "Conversion of the Jews and Emancipation," p. 203; *Parliamentary Papers,* vol. 4 (1816), "Report of Select Committee on the Education of the Lower Orders of the Metropolis," pp. 37, 97, 268.

22. Minute Book, Hevra Kadisha de-Talmud Torah, entries for 13 May 1811, 8 January 1812, 23 January 1812, 25 May 1812, 8 June 1812, 30 June 1812, 20 August 1812; Salmond S. Levin, "The Origins of the Jews' Free School," *TJHSE* 19 (1955–59):111; Jews' Free School, Minute Book, 28 May 1818–23 June 1831, entries for 21 December 1818, 24 June 1822, 13 November 1822, 1 August 1823, LBJRE.

23. Levin, "Jews' Free School," p. 111; Highmore, *Philanthropia Metropolitana,* p. 271.

24. *The Second Annual Report of the Philo-Judaean Society,* pp. 22, 26; *Hebrew Observor,* 18 March 1853, quoted in Mills, *The British Jews,* pp. 320–21; Jews' Free School, Minute Book, 28 May 1818–23 June 1831, entries for 24 March 1828, 28 July 1828, 21 October 1828, LBJRE; Great Synagogue, Minutes, 1825–41, entry for 22 June 1829, AUS; Abraham de Sola, *Biography of David Aaron de Sola* (Philadelphia, 1863/64), pp. 15–16; letter from the Committee of Hevrat Or Torah to the Mahamad, 17 September 1829, MS 295 (50), ASPS; Minute Book, Mahamad, 1 October 1824–12 September 1833, MS 112, entry for 17 September 1829; ASPS.

25. Katz, *Out of the Ghetto*, p. 126; Mordecai Eliav, *Ha-hinukh ha-Yehudi be-Germanyah biymei ha-haskalah ve-ha-emantzipatziyah* [Jewish Education in Germany during the Period of Enlightenment and Emancipation] (Jerusalem, 1960), ch. 3 ("Batei ha-sefer ha-rishonim be-hitpathutam" [The Development of the First Schools]).

26. David Owen, *English Philanthropy, 1660–1960* (Cambridge, Mass., 1964), p. 27. On the reformation of the manners of the poor, see also Maurice J. Quinlan, *Victorian Prelude: A History of English Manners, 1700–1830* (1941; reprint ed., Hamden, Conn., 1965).

CHAPTER 8

1. Much of the conceptual framework that underlies my discussion of Anglo-Jewish integration has been derived from Milton Gordon, *Assimilation in American Life: The Role of Race, Religion, and National Origins* (New York, 1971). In particular, I have relied on the careful categories that Gordon has constructed to describe the various kinds of mixing that can occur between a minority group and a host people. See especially ch. 2, "The Subsociety and the Subculture."

2. Walpole, 32:207, 28:447; idem, vol. 33, *Horace Walpole's Correspondence with the Countess of Upper Ossory*, pt. 2, ed. W. S. Lewis and A. Dayle Wallace (New Haven, 1965), pp. 182–83; D'Israeli, *The Genius of Judaism*, p. 249.

3. *The Proceedings at large in the Arches Court of Canterbury between Mr. Jacob Mendes da Costa and Mrs. Catharine da Costa Villa Real* (London, 1734); Gamaliel ben Pedahzur, pseud. [Abraham Mears], *The Book of Religion, Ceremonies, and Prayers of the Jews, as Practiced in their Synagogues and Families* (London, 1738), pp. v, 44.

4. Picciotto, *Sketches of Anglo-Jewish History*, p. 90; Walpole, vol. 2, *Horace Walpole's Correspondence with the Rev. William Cole*, ed. W. S. Lewis and A. Dayle Wallace (New Haven, 1937), p. 373; Thomas Pitt to Mr. Hardinge, 3 June 1789, quoted in Nichols, *Illustrations of Literary History*, 6:113; Hershkowitz and Meyer, *Letters of the Franks Family*, p. xxiii.

5. John Coakley Lettsom to Rev. J. Plumptre, 15 May 1810, in *Memoirs of the Life and Writings of the late John Coakley Lettsom*, ed. Thomas Joseph Pettigrew, 3 vols. (London, 1817), 2:153; Alexander, *Memoirs of Benjamin Goldsmid*, p. 111; Paul H. Emden, "The Brothers Goldsmid and the Financing of the Napoleonic Wars," *TJHSE* 14 (1935–39):232–33; *The Commercial Habits of the Jews*, pp. 15–17.

6. Alexander, *Memoirs of Benjamin Goldsmid*, p. 101; Bermant, *The Cousinhood*, p. 22; *The Monthly Repository* 3 (1808):278; John Francis, *Chronicles and Characters of the Stock Exchange* (Boston, 1850), p. 60.

7. Alexander, *The Memoirs of Benjamin Goldsmid*, p. 51; *The Universal Magazine* 9 (January–June 1808):453; *The Times*, 29 September 1810.

8. *The Commercial Habits of the Jews*, p. 53; *The Monthly Repository* 3

(1808):279; *The Universal Magazine* 9 (January–June 1808):454; Bermant, *The Cousinhood,* p. 20.

9. Walpole, 28:447; Westmacott, *The English Spy,* 2:256.

10. *Town and Country Magazine,* April 1786, clipping in CF.

11. Ogden, *Isaac D'Israeli,* pp. 6–8.

12. Picciotto, *Sketches of Anglo-Jewish History,* pp. 187–88.

13. Ogden, *Isaac D'Israeli,* p. 91; Robert Blake, *Disraeli,* (New York, 1968), pp. 10–11; Hyamson, *Sephardim,* pp. 202–3; Samuel, "Dr. Meyer Schomberg's Attack," passim.

14. *GM,* n.s., 11 July–Dec. (1861):441–45; Lewis Edwards, "A Remarkable Family: The Palgraves," in Shaftesley, *Remember the Days,* pp. 304–8.

15. Goodman, *Montefiore,* pp. 30–31; Sraffa, *Works of Ricardo,* 10:31, 34–36; Maria Edgeworth, *Letters from England, 1813–1844,* ed. Christina Calvin (Oxford, 1971), p. 266; *The Voice of Jacob,* 29 November and 6 December 1844; Marcus N. Adler, *Memoir of the late Benjamin Gompertz* (London, 1865), p. 3; *GM,* vol. 80, pt. 1 (1810):514–16. In an earlier letter to *The Gentleman's Magazine,* dated 20 March 1809, Lemoine noted that English Jews were far behind their brethren on the Continent in education and literary accomplishments. Idem, pp. 15–18.

16. *DNB,* s.v., "Braham, John," and "Barnett, John"; Roth, *Provincial Jewry,* p. 30.

17. Hyamson, *Sephardim,* pp. 105–6, 109–10; Martin Folkes to Emanuel Mendes da Costa, 9 August 1747 and 28 August 1747, in Nichols, *Illustrations of Literary History,* 4:636–37.

18. *GM,* vol. 82, pt. 1 (1812):673; *DNB,* s.v., "Lemoine, Henry"; Bennett, *Reign of Duke's Place,* pp. 5–6; Coleridge, *Letters,* 5:xxxvii; *DNB,* s.v., "Gompertz, Benjamin."

19. Thomas Birch to Emanuel Mendes da Costa, 18 January 1763, in Nichols, *Illustrations of Literary History,* 4:540; Emden, *Jews of Britain,* pp. 168–69; *GM,* vol. 80, pt. 1 (1810):514–16; Henry Lemoine, *The Eccentric Magazine, or Lives and Portraits of Remarkable Characters,* 2 vols. (London, 1812–13), 1:215–16; Bermant, *The Cousinhood,* pp. 61–62.

20. [William Granger], "Authentic Memoirs of Mrs. Levy," *The New Wonderful Museum and Extraordinary Magazine,* 1 (1803):400–1; Moses Franks, Teddington, to David Franks, Philadelphia, 8 May 1775, Tench Coxe MSS, Reel 41, Box 1, Historical Society of Pennsylvania, Philadelphia.

21. Myer J. Landa, "Kitty Villareal, the Da Costas, and Samson Gideon," *TJHSE* 13 (1932–35):277–79; Sutherland, "Samson Gideon," p. 87; Mocatta, *Appeal to the Elders of the Spanish and Portuguese Jews,* p. 18.

22. *OB* 2 (1735):29; *OB* 80; 8 (1755):214–15; *OB* 15 (1770):322–25; *OB* 41 (1799):511–12; *OB* 59 (1816):42–48.

23. *OB* 15 (1770):322–25; *OB* 30 (1790):444–46; *OB* 54 (1812):171–72; *OB* 55 (1813):511–13.

24. Mahamad, Minutes, 1 October 1824–September 1833, MS 112, entries for 21 October 1824 and 16 June 1825, ASPS.

25. Jacob Katz, *Jews and Freemasons in Europe, 1723–1939,* trans. Leonard Oschry (Cambridge, Mass., 1970), pp. 12–18; Henry M. Krusin, *History of the Lodge of Tranquility* (London, 1937), p. 5; John M. Shaftesley, *The Lodge of Israel No. 205, 1793–1968* (London, 1968), pp. 11–16; idem, "Jews in Regular English Freemasonry, 1717–1860," *TJHSE* 25 (1973–75):150–69; idem, interview, London, 1 July 1975; Sessions Papers: Freemasons Returns, 1799–1848, MS 219F, City of London Record Office; Freemasons Returns, MR/SF, Boxes 1–3, 1799–1802, Greater London Record Office.

Bill Williams notes that in Manchester, Freemasons' lodges were among "the few social institutions which welcomed [Jews] on equal terms. . . . Freemasonry was perhaps the only organised body of public opinion in Manchester which favoured the integration of foreigners (including Jews) into local society and sought to influence public attitudes towards them." *Manchester Jewry,* p. 25.

CHAPTER 9

1. By-stander, *A True State of the Case,* p. 10; Board of Deputies of British Jews, Minute Book I, November 1760–April 1828, entry for April 1783, Archives of the Board of Deputies, Woburn House, London; Picciotto, *Sketches of Anglo-Jewish History,* p. 187; Moses Gaster, *History of the Ancient Synagogue of the Spanish and Portuguese Jews* (London, 1901), p. 88.

2. David Levi, *Letters to Nathaniel Brassey Halhead, M.P.* (London, 1795), p. 4; L. Cohen, *Torat Emet: Sacred Truths Addressed to the Children of Israel Residing in the British Empire* (Exeter, [ca. 1807]), pp. 21–24, 28; D'Israeli, "On the late Installation of a Grand Sanhedrim," p. 35.

3. Clarke, *History of Ipswich,* p. 319; Alfred Rubens, "Portrait of Anglo-Jewry, 1656–1836," *TJHSE* 19 (1955–59):44; Williams, *Manchester Jewry,* p. 16; W. A. Pitt to Henry Dundas, 1 June 1798, Home Office papers, 50/43, PRO, copy in Lucien Wolf papers, Mocatta Library, University College, London.

4. Solomon N. Carvalho, memoir of the Rev. Emanuel Nunes Carvalho, 13 June 1875, *The Lyons Collection,* vol. 2, *Publications of the American Jewish Historical Society* 27 (1920):463; Rubens, "Portrait of Anglo-Jewry," p. 36.

5. Marks, *Narrative,* p. 18.

6. Mayhew, *London Labour and the London Poor,* 2:141; Israel Finestein, "Anglo-Jewish Opinion during the Struggle for Emancipation (1828–1858)," *TJHSE* 20 (1959–61):127–28, 133; *The Mirror of Parliament* 2 (1830):1423; William Albert, *The Turnpike Road System in England, 1663–1840* (Cambridge, 1972), p. 86.

7. Moses Levy, quoted in A True Israelite, pseud., *A Few Remarks on a Letter which Appeared in The World Magazine of the month of June 1828 Disclaiming a Certain Petition to Parliament Concerning the Jews* (London, 1828), unpaginated; *The World,* 2 July and 6 August 1828; Harvey Meiro-

vich, "Ashkenazic Reactions to the Conversionists, 1800–1850," unpublished MS; Stein, *Hebrew Studies at University College,* pp. 6–7; Finestein, "Anglo-Jewish Opinion," pp. 127–28.

8. Alexis de Tocqueville, *The Ancien Regime and the French Revolution,* trans. Stuart Gilbert, (n.p., 1966), p. 196; Finestein, "Anglo-Jewish Opinion," p. 115.

9. Quoted in Alexander Altmann, *Moses Mendelssohn* (Philadelphia, 1973), p. 221.

10. Lionel D. Barnett, *El Libro de los Acuerdos: The Records and Accompts of the Spanish and Portuguese Synagogue of London from 1663 to 1681* (Oxford, 1931), p. 11; R. D. Barnett, "The Correspondence of the Mahamad," p. 9; Minutes of Committees, 1 February 1829–8 July 1845, Committee for the Promotion and Improvement of Religious Worship, entries for 9 and 23 February 1829, ASPS.

11. David Levi, *Letters to Dr. Priestley in Answer to Those He Addressed to the Jews* (London, 1787), pp. 8, 10; Witherby, *Vindication of the Jews,* pp. 3–4; *GM,* vol. 81, pt. 1 (1811):617; *Report of the Late Public Meeting,* pp. 3–4.

12. *The Times,* 9 March 1827; *The World,* 26 September 1827, 14 November 1827, 2 January 1828, 20 February 1828, 6 August 1828, 27 August 1828; Jews' Free School, Minute Book, 28 May 1818–23 June 1831, entry for 31 December 1829, LBJRE.

13. H.R.H. The Duke of Kent to Isaac Lyon Goldsmid, 27 April 1813 and 16 December 1814, Goldsmid MSS, University College, London; *The Jewish Repository* 1 (1813):195–96.

14. David Hughson, pseud. [William Owen Pughe], *London: An Accurate History and Description of the British Metropolis and its Neighbourhood,* 6 vols. (London, 1805–9), 6:383; Mr. Helmore to the Jewish Committee, 17 July 1809, LMS; LSPCJ, *Third Annual Report,* pp. 89, 96, quoted in Meirovich, "Ashkenazic Reactions."

15. *Reasons for Preventing the Growth of Judaism,* Preface, unpaginated; *The Jewish Repository* 1 (1813):158; LSPCJ, Minute Book, September 1810–February 1815, Dep CMJ c.6, entry for 24 March 1812, Bodleian Library, Oxford.

16. *The Times,* 22 February 1819; Thomas Starkie, *Reports of Cases Determined at Nisi Prius in the Courts of King's Bench and Common Pleas,* 3 vols. (London, 1817–23), 2:458–59.

17. Robert Southey recalled a similar incident when the farce *The Jew Boy* was presented: the Jews "assembled in great numbers and actually damned the piece." To Southey, this demonstration was "sufficient to prove that the liberty which they enjoy is unbounded. It is not merely the open exercise of their religion which is permitted them, they are even suffered to write and publish against Christianity." *Letters from England,* 3:145.

Index